CONCRETE UTOPIANISM

Concrete Utopianism

THE POLITICS OF TEMPORALITY AND SOLIDARITY

Gary Wilder

FORDHAM UNIVERSITY PRESS   NEW YORK   2022

Visit us online at www.fordhampress.com.

Library of Congress Cataloging-in-Publication Data available online at https://catalog.loc.gov.

Printed in the United States of America

24 23 22   5 4 3 2 1

First edition

for Isabel

Contents

III. Anticipating Futures

Preface

The chapters of this book were drafted between 2012 and 2019. They convey my engagement with questions related to temporality and solidarity during the conjuncture framed by late Obama and early Trump, stretching from the global financial crisis to the regional war in Syria. Notable reference points include worldwide anti-austerity and Occupy protests, the Arab Spring, and the Mediterranean refugee crisis. The backdrop included the historic uncoupling of capitalism and liberal democracy, the decline of U.S. hegemony, the consolidation of security states, a global drift toward authoritarian populism, and the acceleration of environmental catastrophe.

In the spring of 2019 I revised these pieces extensively in order to weave them into a more integrated book, which I submitted to my editor, Tom Lay. In September 2020, I learned that Fordham Press would publish it after another round of substantial revision and reduction, following suggestions in the readers' reports. By this time, of course, the Covid-19 pandemic was well underway. It soon became clear that this was the most worldwide event I have ever experienced, or even imagined, whose implications would unfold for decades to come.

This multiplex crisis unfolded along the fault lines of the existing neoliberal order. In the United States, a for-profit medical model and a hollowed-out national state were unable to provide the protective equipment, testing, or treatment that the situation demanded. The absence of adequate labor protections or a robust social safety net meant that some could shelter in place, work at home, and provide conditions for remote schooling while many were forced to risk their lives and sacrifice their children's education in order to make ends meet. As the economy ground to a near halt, enormous funds were gifted to corporations while meager relief was offered to masses of citizens facing unemployment and eviction. As always in this country, those who suffered the most, medically and financially, were Black, brown, and immigrant communities.

Political centrists tended to blame this compound catastrophe on the Trump administration's abhorrent handling of the situation. Its actions were indeed guided by a cynical political calculus that catered to cronies while abandoning—sacrificing—masses of people on the basis of ideology, employment status, race, culture, nationality, and geography. But the underlying conditions that fueled this unevenly distributed social disaster were jointly produced by the Democratic and Republican political parties equally, if differently beholden to the rule of capital, through decades of neoliberal policies (e.g., economic deregulation, privatizing the commons, allowing corporate profits to eviscerate popular democracy, securitizing everyday life, directing state violence at racialized and undocumented populations). In the lead-up to and during the aftermath of the November 2020 presidential election, Trump's authoritarian populist regime revealed even more blatantly its essential white supremacist and neofascist core. It formed a reactionary bloc that included the Republican Party and its elected representatives in state and federal governments, along with significant sections of the justice department, the armed forces, and local police departments across the country. It was fed and sustained by a powerful (social) media machine.

Ultimately, this bloc was unable to overturn the popular election and topple what was left of this already anemic democracy. The specter of actual fascism provided a scapegoat and alibi for liberals, as it has so many times before. Trump's undisguised contempt for constitutional legality, embrace of plutocracy, and explicitly violent racism allowed establishment Democrats to identify themselves with democracy and social justice. They now scramble to restore the status quo ante without committing to the systemic transformation that could possibly place this society, let alone its most precarious and stigmatized members, on a genuinely just, democratic, and sustainable footing. Such transformation can only be propelled by mass popular mobilization on multiple fronts and translocal scales.

This U.S. crisis is only one node and moment of a worldwide situation. The emergence of a zoonotic pandemic that has afflicted every human population on this earth cannot be separated from the accelerated urbanization, runaway consumption, and environmental destruction propelled by global capitalism and uneven development. So, too, has there emerged an international axis of authoritarian, plutocratic, militarized, xenophobic, and violently nationalist regimes (and intersecting ruling classes) across the world. The asymmetrical harm enabled or intensified by Covid-19 within the United States is echoed by structural inequalities within other heterogeneous nations across the world and mirrored between more and less powerful states, regions, and continents. A new global division is emerging between wealthy countries whose populations will have received Covid-19 vaccinations and the rest who will have not. We inhabit a world-historical conjuncture in which various right-wing forces (whatever the blend of capitalism, statism, and communitarianism) are triumphant. But this hegemony is contradictory and volatile.

In May 2020, mass protests spread across the United States following the brutal murder of George Floyd, an unarmed African American who was handcuffed and facedown on the sidewalk while Minneapolis police officer Derek Chauvin infamously kneeled on his neck for nine and a half minutes. During this time fellow officers looked on and Floyd cried out that he could not breathe. Municipal police, National Guard units, and heavily armed federal agents responded to these spontaneous, decentralized protests—which unfolded under the rubric of Black Lives Matter (BLM)—in a consistently and spectacularly brutal fashion. These efforts to challenge the anti–Black American order, led by the BLM movement, crystallized into the largest nationwide progressive uprising in more than sixty years. That the state would respond with militarized violence to any assertion of Black collective power, as we saw in Ferguson, Missouri, in 2016, under Obama, is to be expected. More surprising now, however, were scenes of an enduring popular insurgency. Mass protests called forth a Black-led multiracial multitude demanding immediate accountability and historical reckoning. Confederate monuments were toppled throughout the South. Militants in Seattle seized and burned a police station. Those in Portland held their ground in nightly battles with the cops through the end of 2020. In New York, an Occupy City Hall encampment was established to demand that the city council cut the police budget. It lasted a month before Mayor De Blasio sent the police to destroy it.

The BLM uprising occurred at the height of the pandemic as millions of Americans were losing their jobs, health insurance, and homes. It has converged with promises of ever more austere punitive measures to come. State and city budgets have been devastated by the cost of the pandemic and decline of tax revenues. Public and private powers are already instrumentalizing this crisis to further neoliberal agendas. Huge numbers of municipal workers across the country are threatened with layoffs. A recently activated cohort of public school teachers refuses to sacrifice itself on the altar of back-to-business normalcy. Self-organized mutual aid networks have sprung up in every type of community around the country. Just a few years ago, it would have seemed impossible that "defunding the police" and "socialism" could ever be integral to the national political debate. In short, the current crisis offers a historic opportunity for a mass popular coalition of racialized, poor, precarious working people, along with other alienated and disenfranchised citizens, to come together in a movement for societal transformation and popular democracy.

Historical experience suggests that this will have been a missed opportunity—that state, capital, and common sense will manage once again to neutralize dissent, restore existing power arrangements, and reproduce long-standing inequalities. But there is no way to know how things might unfold or how significant this incandescent moment may turn out to be for future alignments, mobilizations, and visions. At the very least, our experience of this charged moment reminds us that the temporal continuum can be interrupted and history derailed. Economies can be halted and everyday life turned inside out. In the United States, trillions of dollars can be conjured for whatever purpose imaginable. Although the neoliberal net continues to tighten around life chances and future prospects, this world-historic chapter of the human story has not yet concluded. It is our responsibility to place pressure on this moment, to nudge our now in an emancipatory direction.

I decided not to attempt to rework this book so as to relate my argument directly to this tangle of ongoing events. After some deliberation, my sense was that such an attempt would compromise the analytic integrity of the book I had already written. It either does or does not hang together on the terms in which it was composed. Any attempt to integrate these recent events would likely lead to a premature and superficial take on what is now unfolding. This choice risks shifting the book from an engagement with the contemporary to an artifact of the recent past. But I would suggest that these developments do not undermine my case for concrete utopianism and critical internationalism. On the contrary, the current situation confirms the inadequacy of Left realism, presentism, and culturalism—not to mention a metaphysical pessimism—for this political moment. It only strengthens my conviction that Left thinking today must, in conjunction with movements, work to envision new kinds of planetary politics that may anticipate a world we wish to see.

Brooklyn, N.Y., May 2021

Convert the imperialist war into civil war.

—V. I. LENIN

I am on very bad terms with space. So what.
. . . I am on very bad terms with Time. So what?

—AIMÉ CÉSAIRE

We go into the open circle of our relayed aesthetics, our unflagging politics. We leave the matrix abyss . . . for this other one in which we wander without becoming lost.

—ÉDOUARD GLISSANT

Introduction

The Opposite of Pessimism Is Not Optimism

Mankind has obviously reached the end of something. The crisis is absolute. Bourgeois civilization is falling apart and, even while it collapses, devotes its main energies to the preparation of future holocausts. . . . Thought has abdicated. The world is rudderless. . . . Yet never was thought of a fundamental character so necessary to mankind. . . . Never were such universal questions asked by the whole of the civilized world. Never have such inadequate answers been given. . . . Either the revolution succeeds in encompassing the whole of the world or the whole of the world collapses into counterrevolution and barbarism.

—C. L. R. JAMES

The chronicles of revolutions all show how persistent small changes, and altogether unexpected consolidations, added up to enough weight, over time and space, to cause a break with the old order. Certainly, the political forces that hold governmental power in the United States of the early twenty-first century figured this out and persisted for decades until they won. With persistence, practices and theories circulate, enabling people to see problems and their solutions differently—which then creates the possibility of further, sometimes innovative, action.

—RUTH WILSON GILMORE

We inhabit a paradoxical political present. It has never been more urgent to invent new forms of translocal solidarity oriented toward another possible world. Yet it has never been more difficult to do so. This impasse is certainly

1

related to the triumph of neoliberalism's worldwide assault on Left thinking and politics. Prospects for even imagining, let alone realizing, anti-imperial and anticapitalist futures have been continuously crushed worldwide. Growing numbers of erstwhile militants and subsequent intellectuals became disillusioned about the prospect of systemic change. Our bleak times have led a growing number of critics to treat the given as unsurpassable. This is an understandable, if regrettable, symptom of our world-historical predicament. But it amounts to accepting the real as rational. If the current crisis is to provoke Hegelian revenants, let them be dialectical rather than teleological. It is one thing to recognize that the historical conditions that might once have allowed for a certain kind of systemic change have shifted. It is another to contend that such change is now impossible, that even thinking in such terms is anachronistic, misguided, or dangerous. This categorical pessimism perversely mirrors neoliberalism's end-of-history triumphalism precisely when our times call for new practices of concrete utopianism in the service of new forms of Left internationalism.[1]

This book unfolds from the simple proposition that there is only one world, and it is defined by uneven relations of inextricable entanglement. Emancipatory alternatives require planetary politics because the nexus of current and imminent crises poses a planetary predicament. The urgent need to envision other possible worlds raises questions about historical transformation. Political projects presuppose certain understandings of time and history. It follows that if our now requires new political thinking, such thinking should also reconsider conventional notions of historical temporality.

Accordingly, I suggest that Left thinking should attend more directly than it has in recent decades to translocal solidarity and heterodox temporality. Doing so invites us to *unthink* many of the spatial and temporal provincialisms that continue to suffuse so much of our political common sense. Assumptions about the supposed unity of territory, culture, and consciousness or the self-evident differences between past, present, and future subtend the conventional human sciences and the liberal norms that they presuppose and reproduce. Such assumptions are also often embedded within influential currents of critical theory. Specifically, I critique what I call Left culturalism, presentism, and realism.

Left culturalism entails quasi-ontological claims about incommensurable lifeworlds and categorical claims about epistemological differences. It often dismisses solidarity politics and internationalist projects as intrinsically Western, elite, or liberal—as alibis for hierarchy and pathways to imperialism. *Left presentism,* which may assume the more extreme form of Left melancholy, entails quasi-metaphysical claims about the eclipse of futurity and an ever-extending present. It often dismisses visionary projects for structural change as outmoded and misguided, as fated to end in failure, disappointment, dogmatism, or authoritarianism. Both of these tendencies fuel and are nourished by a kind of *Left realism* that, however unintentionally, regards existing arrangements as the horizon of the possible.

These intersecting orientations maintain a skeptical stance toward the prospect of societal transformation and planetary politics. They reproduce provincial assumptions about political geography, temporality, and identity. By treating places, periods, and subjects as self-identical, they obstruct our capacity to forge transversal political alignments in the service of other possible worlds. They mistake political imagination for naïve optimism and utopianism for idealism. Negative critique is treated as an end in itself. Pessimism is conflated with radicalism. Fatalism wins the day.

One does not have to be a scholar or an activist to recognize that we are living in dark and likely catastrophic times. Massive destructive forces are converging—runaway productivism, permanent war, authoritarianism, and climate change among them. These are compounded by systemic financial instability, social polarization, and mass displacement worldwide. Such displacements, in both the North and the Global South, are playing out in territorial, socioeconomic, and cultural domains. They are both real and perceived. A growing proportion of the world's population is living through *unhomely* times. The traumatic conditions and peculiar experience of unhomeliness are crosscut by *untimely* counterparts—processes and practices of repetition, nonsynchronism, and haunting. Available lines of egress seem always already to be barred. Pathways forward loop back to blocked starting points. Political hope is shadowed and mocked by such epochal uncanniness. Neoliberal capitalism, statism, imperialism, techno-science, and mass mediation have created conditions for an unprecedented global crisis (or a series of cascading, intersecting, and ongoing crises) that is undermining humanity's ability to reproduce itself. These developments will certainly compel processes of large-scale restructuring whose outcome and human cost are unimaginable. But the ground upon which to hope that such restructuring will be emancipatory— that worldwide economic, political, or environmental disaster can be avoided, let alone justice or equality constructed—is nowhere apparent. It is difficult to believe that anyone—except the most blinkered, parasitic, or nihilistic among us—can feel optimistic about the future.

And yet . . .

The recent tendency among critical thinkers to frame political differences in terms of pessimism vs. optimism is at best beside the point, and at worst politically disabling. The task of critical analysis is to delineate the challenges that must be confronted and the possible pathways that could help emancipatory forces overcome the existing order so as to promote human flourishing on a planetary scale. It is a different and, I would argue, secondary matter whether we are optimistic that such pathways will be found, that necessary steps will be taken, that success is likely. To state the obvious: Positive outcomes are never guaranteed, yet history continues to unfold and political horizons remain open. Certainly, liberal optimism is implicated in the present impasse. But a race-to-the-bottom among melancholic pessimists will just as certainly foreclose the grounded imaginative and visionary practical efforts without which there can be no prospect of moving beyond it.

In current political discourse, the concepts "pessimism" and "optimism" tend to express one-sided conceptions of realism and idealism. I would argue that to simply weigh in on one or the other, or to critique one from the standpoint of the other, is to uncritically reproduce the barren terms of this dubious opposition.

Let us begin by recalling some of the many Left thinkers who sought to displace the opposition between (idealist) optimism and (realist) pessimism. They wrote in an earlier moment of revolutionary defeat and despair that followed a series of political setbacks: working-class nationalism displaced worker internationalism during World War I; the promise of the Russian Revolution failed to spread to the capitalist West or colonized South; the systemic economic crisis of the 1930s led not to the overcoming of racial capitalism but to fascism in Europe and Latin America, heightened white supremacy in the United States, and a retrenchment of colonial imperialism throughout large parts of Africa, Asia, the Caribbean, and the Pacific. These intersecting catastrophes provided fertile ground for political pessimism, Left melancholy, and provincial entrenchment.

Georg Lukács began to conceptualize alienation and reification in just this context of revolutionary failure. But despite his painful experience and dark view of capitalist society, Lukács rejected the one-dimensional pessimism of his mentors, Max Weber and Georg Simmel. Whereas their romantic antimodernism was subjective, idealist, and resigned, his romantic anticapitalism was collective, utopian, and revolutionary. He replaced an existential conception of alienation as the tragic price of modernity with a sociohistorical understanding of alienation that could be overcome with the abolition of capitalism. Lukács insisted that pessimism "perpetuates the present state of affairs and represents it as the uttermost limit of human development just as much as does 'optimism.' In this respect . . . Hegel and Schopenhauer are on a par with each other."[2]

Lukàcs wrote most of *History and Class Consciousness* (1923) while in political exile in Vienna, following the collapse of the short-lived Hungarian Soviet Republic. He describes this city at that time as "an international transit point" for the "international revolutionary movement."[3] While there, he was in "continuous contact" with fellow Leftist émigrés from Hungary, Poland, and the Balkans as well as with German, French, Italian, and Dutch Communists.[4] During this time, he began to read Lenin in order to develop a more pragmatic understanding of strategy and tactics in a given historical situation. Lukács thereby hoped to reconcile his revolutionary romanticism with the "realistic decisions" that, as a participant in the organized Communist movement and Hungarian government, he would have to make. The result would be a radical political orientation that was at once realist and utopian.[5]

During this same period, the Peruvian Marxist José Carlos Mariátegui was in political exile in Europe. The self-taught journalist from a poor mixed-race family spent his life as a party and trade union organizer. In 1929 he created the Socialist Party of Peru and the General Confederation of Peruvian Workers, which then became the Peruvian Communist Party. In 1919 Mariátegui had been deported from Peru by the dictatorship as a political radical and spent four years living in France and Italy. While there, he encountered a network of international socialists and closely followed debates within the Left and among philosophers and avant-garde artists.[6]

In 1925 Mariátegui responded to accusations that he was a political pessimist. On the one hand, he explains, "the optimism we reject is the easy and lazy Panglossian optimism of those who think we live in the best of all possible worlds."[7] But on the other, he criticizes "the exclusively negative pessimist" who is "limited to gestures of helplessness and hopelessness. . . . That person is nihilistic and melancholy, waiting for the final disappointment. . . . [T]his type belongs to a strange hierarchy of disenchanted intellectuals who are also a product of a period in decline or of a people in collapse."[8] In contrast to both an "absolutely sterile" negativism and a blithe belief in the rightness of the existing order, Mariátegui wrote, "We do not believe that the world should be fatal and eternally as it is. We believe that it can and should be better."[9] To this end, he emphasized the link between revolutionary action and the kind political imagination practiced by figures like Simón Bolívar:

> The liberators were great because they were, above all, imaginative. They were insurgents against the limited reality, the imperfect reality, of their time. . . . Bolívar had futuristic dreams. He imagined a confederation of Indo-Spanish states. . . . *The value of the liberators consists in seeing a potential reality, a higher reality, an imaginary reality.*[10]

Mariátegui recognized that "imagination has its limits."[11] He noted that if it is to serve political action, it must be rooted in a concrete conjuncture. For "the only utopias that are valid are those that could be called realistic. Those utopias are born out of the same entrails as reality. . . . One could say that *people do not foresee or imagine more than that which is already germinating,* maturing in the dark entrails of history."[12] Accordingly, Mariátegui invited socialists to focus less on the reductive distinction between revolutionaries and reformists than on what he regarded as the more significant difference between those on the Left who embrace the imagination and those who do not.[13] Like Lukács, Mariátegui elaborated a concrete utopianism: a politics grounded in specific conditions and guided by the imperative for strategic action even as such action depended on the imaginative capacity to recognize within given arrangements the possibility of a higher reality that may already be germinating.

A similar sensibility animated the work of W. E. B. Du Bois, one of Mariátegui's New World contemporaries. In 1926 Du Bois made a visit to the Soviet Union that decisively influenced the leftward shift in his political thinking. This visit followed an earlier trip to Liberia and a political tour of Europe, which he had not seen since he was a student studying philosophy, sociology, and history in Berlin in the early 1890s (the very intellectual and political milieu that had shaped Lukàcs's romantic anticapitalist thinking about modern history, society, and culture).[14]

Du Bois's political reorientation began after World War I as he came to believe that anti-Black racism in America was deeply rooted in unconscious habits, attitudes, and investments. He also recognized that anti-Black racism was fueled by and, in turn, reproduced economic inequality. This meant that racial and capitalist domination could not be separated from one another. These challenges were compounded by the fact that, as Du Bois began to emphasize, American racism was reinforced by an *international* color bar that had been institutionalized by imperialism and global capitalism. For these reasons, Du Bois concluded that the legal campaign for civil rights through court cases, to which he had devoted himself, could never effectively overcome racial domination. This meant that the Black freedom struggle would have to simultaneously be a struggle to overcome capitalist domination. He also conceded that it would take much longer and that its prospects for success were much smaller than he or his NAACP colleagues had previously imagined.[15]

In his view, this predicament became even more catastrophic in the 1930s when, following the Great Depression, the very economic and existential survival of the Black community was at stake. On the one hand, Du Bois was convinced that racial emancipation could never be possible under capitalist arrangements. If it were to have any chance of succeeding, the Black freedom struggle would have to align with the broader American labor movement. On the other hand, he saw clearly that labor unions, Socialist and Communist parties, and white working-class communities were intensely and deliberately racist; they practiced racial exclusion, perpetrated anti-Black violence, and refused to recognize Black workers and activists as potential comrades.

Du Bois's grim assessment of the predicament facing Black Americans, as well as his growing commitment to anticapitalism, anti-imperialism, and internationalism, was already evident in the essays collected in *Darkwater* (1920). He further elaborated this radical orientation in and through *Black Reconstruction* (1935). This study traces how white supremacy in the 1870s crushed the prospect of genuine Black emancipation and opened a pathway for triumphant capitalism in and beyond America. By demonstrating how the abolition of slavery led directly to legal segregation and how the appearance of Black freedom grounded an even more insidious form of racial domination that was sustained by social groups who placed anti-Blackness above their own economic interests and political prospects, *Black Reconstruction* traces a historical genealogy of the Jim Crow order into which Du Bois was born. This masterwork remains one of the most powerful and persuasive accounts of how the U.S. nation-state is grounded in white supremacy and structurally dependent on racial capitalism. It should also be read as refracting the dire conjuncture in which it was written. During these years, Du Bois argued that Black Americans were more devastated than other groups by the Great Depression. He regularly criticized the way New Deal efforts to alleviate social misery through large-scale agricultural and public works projects consistently excluded Black farmers and workers.

What, then, should we make of the fact that so much of Du Bois's interwar writing is, nevertheless, propelled by utopian vision? *Darkwater* opens with a "Credo" proclaiming "that all men, Black and brown and white, are brothers, varying through time and opportunity, in form and gift and feature, but differing in no essential particular, and alike in soul and the possibility of infinite development."[16] It closes with a lyrical "Hymn to the Peoples" that prophesies "the union of the World!" and calls on the "Human God . . . To make Humanity divine!"[17] This vision of planetary reconciliation depended on an equally utopian belief in the capacity of the "darker nations" to take the lead in overcoming the "human hatred" perpetrated by the "white world" through colonialism, capitalism, and interstate war.[18] "A belief in humanity is a belief in colored men. If the uplift of mankind must be done by men, then the destinies of this world will rest ultimately in the hands of the darker nations."[19]

Likewise, *Black Reconstruction* excavates the past prospect of a new kind of "abolition democracy," an incipient multiracial and cross-class coalition enabled by Reconstruction that might have pointed toward an American worker's republic that was no longer based on white supremacy, the sanctity of private property, and the dictatorship of capital. Recall, too, that during the bleak 1930s, while he was reflecting on this foreclosed potentiality of Reconstruction, Du Bois elaborated a vision for racial emancipation through autonomous Black economic cooperatives that could enact real freedom grounded in economic mutualism and socialist democracy. He argued that the example of these self-managing collectives, combined with progressive Black leadership, could point toward a new *cooperative commonwealth* through which social relations and subjectivity would be revolutionized on national and international scales. American democracy could be reconstructed, colonial capitalism and imperialism overcome, the international color bar abolished, and humanity (composed of myriad groups with particular gifts) allowed to flourish.[20]

How should we reconcile Du Bois's lucid assessment of the unpromising interwar political situation with such extravagantly hopeful visions and programs? To ask whether Du Bois was pessimistic or optimistic misses the mark. He was remarkably clear-sighted about how difficult it would be for Black Americans, the darker nations, or an international working class to form the kind of alliances and build the kind of movement that his vision required. There is little evidence that Du Bois was optimistic that any of this could be achieved in the foreseeable future. But he elaborated as clearly as he could what he regarded as a possible pathway to substantive racial emancipation. To declare, as he did, that "Life and Hope and Death!" depended on it is not to believe that it was likely to occur.[21] But neither would he have conceded that such an outcome was impossible. Beyond pessimism or optimism, Du Bois simply lays out the real stakes of a situation that could only be rectified in a radical political fashion. To wit, his famous warning at the end of *Black Reconstruction*: "This the American Black man knows: his fight here is a fight to the finish. Either he dies or wins. . . . He will enter modern civilization here in America as a Black man on terms of perfect and unlimited equality with any white man, or he will enter not at all."[22]

Like the other interwar Left internationalists mentioned earlier, Du Bois, through his work, invites us to distinguish between analyses which contend that something *should* happen, that it *can* happen, and that it *will* happen. In their different ways, Lukács, Mariátegui, and Du Bois rejected the existing world *and* sought to identify within it the potential for an alternative set of arrangements that may already be germinating. They were concrete utopians whose political orientations pointed beyond empiricist realism and abstract idealism, categorical pessimism and ungrounded optimism. Their legacy may help us to overcome the ways that political thinking today about our dismal world-historical situation tends to reproduce rather than explode its fundaments.

By identifying pessimism with radicalism, political realists seek to disparage utopian imagination as naïve about or complicit with dominant power relations. We need to challenge the ways that realism can wield the shibboleth of optimism to circumscribe political horizons. The correct insight that new thinking cannot in itself change the world should not be used as an alibi for renouncing the imperative to imagine otherwise.

In contrast, I argue that the opposite of political pessimism is not optimism. It is *concrete utopianism*. By *utopian*, I mean thought and action oriented toward that which appears to be, or is purported to be, impossible when such impossibility is only a function of existing arrangements. *Concrete* utopianism is not merely fanciful, phantasmatic, or speculative. It seeks to identify possibilities for alternative arrangements that may already dwell within, or be emerging from, the nonidentical order that actually exists. Such utopianism also seeks to identify concrete interventions that point beyond the logic and framework of the existing order. Consider the ways that prison and police abolition, reparations for slavery, collective debt cancellation, or a prohibition against fossil fuels are real possibilities that cannot be accommodated by the present system, whose realization would crack existing norms. They are at once possible and impossible. They presuppose a world that does not yet exist even as they may help to propel into existence just such a world. Following Henri Lefebvre, we may understand concrete utopianism as a politics of the "possible-impossible."[23]

In the *Communist Manifesto*, Marx and Engels famously attacked "the fantastic pictures of future society" proposed by utopian socialists at a moment when "the economic situation . . . does not as yet offer to them the material conditions for the emancipation of the proletariat."[24] Throughout his work Marx attended to the way novel possibilities may emerge dialectically from within a contradictory social formation. Yet, just as famously, after analyzing the failures of 1848, he declared that social revolutionaries must henceforth draw their poetry from the future. In one sense, this is an impossible task. How could social actors express political desire in terms that do not yet exist, in relation to a social grammar that could only emerge from within another world that cannot yet be fathomed? But, according to Marx, this is precisely what the Paris Commune was able to do, however briefly. Insofar as Marx calls for both immanent critique and political imagination, we may regard him as a concrete utopian thinker.

Philosopher Ernst Bloch indeed credits Marxism and socialism for their concrete utopianism. He identifies Marxism as a "philosophy of the future" that seeks to recognize "what is approaching" by attending to that which is already "fermenting in the process of the real itself."[25] Bloch defines a "concrete utopia" as one which is "historically mediated, but which pours forth history."[26] It is "transcendent without transcendence."[27] This, for Bloch, requires a Marxian understanding of reality as an ongoing, incomplete, and only partially conditioned historical process. He calls this an "anticipatory" utopia that maintains "the point of contact between dream and life."[28] He thus distinguishes "concrete utopia" from the "abstract utopian dreaminess" of bourgeois Romanticism.[29] We might call this a kind of grounded clairvoyance attuned to what Bloch calls "the Not-Yet-Conscious" and the "Not-Yet-Become."[30]

In sum, *concrete utopianism demands both a capacity to identify transformative possibilities that may already exist but are not yet recognized and a capacity to imagine that which is currently unimaginable.* Each of these operations enables the other. Neither can be realized through abstract thought alone. They require experimental practices that nourish radical imaginaries *and* experimental thinking that nourishes radical practices. These are conjunctural operations that refuse simply to apply orthodox formulations or preexisting blueprints (what Marx called "ready-made utopias") to a given situation.[31]

This dual imperative *to recognize that which is inapparent but real and to conjure that which is unimaginable but possible* requires that we free ourselves from the constraints of political realism and realist epistemology. Concrete utopianism requires ways of seeing and knowing that do not mistake immediate appearances with the really real. It requires canny attention to the uncanny and untimely dimensions of social life. This means seeing the familiar in the strange and the strange in the familiar, the past in the present and the future in the past. Conversely, concrete utopianism seeks to *render* everyday life subversively uncanny and untimely. It makes the familiar strange and the strange familiar. It makes pasts present and it anticipates, or conjures, futures now.

Concrete utopianism also recognizes that transformative potentialities may be bound up with supposedly past modes of thinking, forms of life, and political experiments whose anachronistic traces remain discernable, even vital, in a nonidentical now. In this regard, concrete utopianism may be radically romantic. Such romanticism should not be confused with a simple idealization of, let alone a naïve desire to return to, some mythic past in order to evade or escape from the pressing demands of the political present. Rather, it should be understood in terms of the kind of "revolutionary romanticism" identified by Henri Lefebvre and Michael Löwy (as I discuss in Chapters 6 and 8).

Understood in these terms, there is nothing intrinsically optimistic or even hopeful about the concrete utopian and revolutionary romantic orientation of this book.

Liberal and Left critics often deploy the labels "utopian" and "romantic" as conversation-stopping epithets. In contrast, this book calls on critical thinkers to recognize, envision, and pursue the possible-impossible. We can do so partly by examining how a wide range of social actors in concrete situations have attempted to do so—whether in everyday life, political experiments, or imaginative thinking. Rather than simply view history through either a pessimistic or optimistic lens, we need dialectical optics through which to recognize transformative possibilities that may already be persisting, fermenting, and germinating within existing arrangements. Such optics, as I will discuss in Chapter 1, may help us to deprovincialize commonsense assumptions about *here, now,* and *us*.

In the Marxian tradition these nonrealist ways of seeing and knowing are cause and consequence of *immanent critique*. In the Black critical tradition they are cause and consequence of what Aimé Césaire called *poetic knowledge*. Throughout this book, I critique Left culturalism, presentism, and realism from the standpoint of heterodox Marxism and Black Atlantic criticism. Said more constructively, I engage the possible-impossible through dialogue with currents of these traditions that refuse the literalism of realist epistemology and the conservatism of political realism. These currents of criticism reject facile oppositions between optimism and pessimism, idealism and realism, the actual and the inapparent, and the possible and the impossible. Both traditions developed radical critiques of systemic domination, but neither regarded negative critique as sufficient. Each challenged provincial assumptions about political space, time, and subjectivity; they envisioned forms of nonliberal universalism that could be both a means and aim of creating other possible worlds. In different ways, each placed translocal solidarity and heterodox temporality at the center of their efforts. I treat their legacies—their attempts to conjugate thought and world, politics and aesthetics, singularity and solidarity—as sources of still vital potentiality that may help us to grasp and transcend current political predicaments.[32]

A concrete utopian orientation helps us to unthink supposedly self-evident boundaries between here and there, now and then, us and them. It illuminates how seemingly stable entities may differ from themselves and how seemingly disparate entities may be intrinsically related to one another. Such ways of seeing and knowing otherwise may help us to forge the transversal alignments across seemingly self-evident differences that are demanded by solidarity practices, internationalist projects, and planetary politics.

My thinking about the possibility of crosscutting alignments is informed by the early Bolshevik call to "convert the imperialist war into a civil war."[33] V. I. Lenin and Grigory Zinoviev elaborated this slogan in a 1915 pamphlet outlining the Russian Social Democratic Labor Party's position on the Great War. In it, they denounced the "reactionary character of this war, and the shameless lies told by the bourgeoisie of all countries in covering up their predatory aims with 'national' ideology" in order to foster "on the basis of an objectively revolutionary situation, revolutionary moods among the masses."[34] Their aim was to persuade European masses that supporting the nationalist war would undermine what should be their more consequential stake in international class struggle. We don't have to devolve into class essentialism to appreciate what I take to be Lenin's point: Axes of political division are neither pregiven nor immediately apparent. For him this meant that working peoples' political interests aligned more directly with their counterparts in other countries, with whom they should stand in solidarity, than with their own national governments or ruling classes, who were their common enemy. Today, we may take Lenin's insight as an invitation to question seemingly self-evident territorial, cultural, or racial divisions, to attend to how supposedly incommensurable differences may obstruct potential *political* alignments in the service of antiauthoritarian, anticapitalist, and anti-imperial futures. Lenin's call reminds us that apparent conflicts between peoples may be refigured across invidious boundaries as a more emancipatory struggle between the powerful and the powerless.

This book is neither a collection of distinct essays nor a systematic argument. The whole emerged in the process of writing the parts. I did not start with "concrete utopianism"; I arrived there. Many of the chapters can be read on their own. But there is a directional flow to their order and they are best read in sequence. Each is organized around close readings of texts. The works I critique are almost always written by thinkers whom I hold in high regard and whose work has informed or provoked my own. Throughout, my voice as critic is at least matched by my voice as enthusiast regarding modes of thinking that I believe should be embraced and developed for the pathways they open.

Part I calls on critical thinkers to refigure Left politics. Chapter 1 questions the realist epistemology that continues to underlie so much conventional and critical political thinking. Against such realism, I argue that we need dialectical optics through which to overcome provincial, punctual, and identitarian notions of *here*, *now*, and *us*. I elaborate a concrete utopian orientation through which to pursue a politics of the possible-impossible. Chapters 2, 3, and 4 discuss respectively the limitations of, and suggest ways of thinking beyond, Left culturalism, presentism, and realism. In them, I draw on Marxian and Black critical traditions to suggest alternative ways of thinking internationalism, translational solidarity, and utopian futurity. Through these discussions, I criticize certain assumptions about historical temporality and suggest that we attend more directly to untimely and nonsynchronous objects, processes, and practices. I elaborate these temporal issues more directly in Part II. Between these parts is an Intermezzo. It includes one chapter on solidarity as both means and end of transformative politics, and another on anticipation as a concrete utopian practice of calling for and calling forth other possible worlds. These pieces were the initial germs of the project.

Part II focuses on the ways that we need to unthink history if we are to refigure politics. In Chapter 7, I argue that we need to treat time as a real abstraction, a social fact and historical force that is both subjective and objective. Focusing on the dialectical relation between social formations and temporal frameworks, I discuss the nonsynchronous and untimely, or temporally nonidentical, character of social life under modern capitalism. I continue this discussion in Chapter 8 by exploring the Marxian dialectic of past and future, an alternative to Michel Foucault's genealogical critique, which may leverage the transformative potentiality of untimeliness. The following two chapters examine similar issues through the work of Black critical thinkers. In Chapter 9, I explore the power and limitations of Afro-Pessimist ontology and Derridean hauntology for explaining instances of processes of historical persistence, repetition, and return. I contrast these approaches to the more historically specific and politically open orientation to the same phenomena offered by Ralph Ellison by way of Octavia Butler, Stuart Hall, and Hortense Spillers. In Chapter 10, I analyze Édouard Glissant's conceptions of nonhistory, tormented chronology, a painful notion of time, and a prophetic vision of the past. These attempt to recognize both the harmful and potentially subversive character of untimeliness in postslavery societies. The book concludes with a chapter on a planetary politics of world and worlds. It reprises many of the threads of the preceding sections by discussing contemporary concrete utopian thinking and movements oriented toward a possible-impossible world we wish to see.

PART I
Refiguring Politics

1

The Possible-Impossible

Dialectical Optics and Uncanny Refractions (Here, Now, Us)

The only philosophy which can be responsibly practiced in the face of
despair is the attempt to contemplate all things as they would present
themselves from the standpoint of redemption. . . . Perspectives must
be fashioned that displace and estrange the world, reveal it to be, with
its rifts and crevices, as indigent and distorted as it will appear one day
in the messianic light. . . . It is the simplest of all things . . . because
consummate negativity, once squarely faced, delineates the mirror
of its opposite. But it is also the utterly impossible thing, because it
presupposes a standpoint removed, even though by a hair's breadth,
from the scope of existence, whereas we well know that any possible
knowledge must not only first be wrested from what is, if it shall hold
good, but is also marked, for this very reason by the same distortion . . .
which it seeks to escape.

—THEODOR ADORNO

Let everything start moving! The impossible does not differ from the
possible in the way that the abstract differs from the concrete, and vice
versa. . . . The impossible can be perceived only via the possible, and
the possible can be appreciated only via the impossible.

—HENRI LEFEBVRE

The dialectic cannot be imposed on facts, it must be derived from the
facts.

—LEON TROTSKY

In order to place translocal solidarity and heterodox temporality at the center of our political thinking we need to overcome inherited assumptions about here and there, now and then, and us and them. A realist attachment to punctual time, territorial space, and self-identical political subjectivity continues to inform a great deal of both conventional and critical thinking. By conflating immediate appearances with reality, reality with truth, and the given truth with what is possible, such attachments circumscribe political debate and impoverish political imagination. In other words, there is an underlying relation between realist epistemology and the kind of political realism that equates pessimism with radicalism and mistakes utopianism for idealism.

If we are to unthink commonsense assumptions about *here*, *now*, and *us* in order to glimpse transformative possibilities that may already dwell within existing arrangements, we must cultivate nonrealist ways of seeing and knowing. In this chapter, I suggest that Sigmund Freud's notion of uncanniness, Walter Benjamin's notion of awakening, and Aimé Césaire's notion of poetic knowledge offer us precious resources from which to create dialectical optics for envisioning the possible-impossible. On the one hand, such optics allow us to recognize the uncanny character of conventional assumptions about time, place, and identity. On the other hand, they enable us to render conventional assumptions and arrangements subversively uncanny.

The Possible-Impossible

Karl Marx figures the very knot of political, historical, and epistemological problems at stake here when, in the *Eighteenth Brumaire* (1852), he famously declares:

> The social revolution of the nineteenth century cannot draw its
> poetry from the past, but only from the future. . . . Earlier revolutions
> required world-historical recollections in order to drug themselves
> concerning their own content. In order to arrive at its content, the
> revolution of the nineteenth century must let the dead bury their dead.
> There the phrase went beyond the content; here the content goes
> beyond the phrase.[1]

Real revolutionary change, Marx tells us, cannot rely upon or unfold within the parameters of existing concepts and consciousness. Meaningful transformation requires new social realities (content) that exceed the existing conceptual terms and frames (phrase) within which people understand and act. Marx warns against any belief in ready-made solutions, historical predictions, or blueprints for revolutionary change. Yet he also underscores the imperative to act here and now. How can revolutionary social actors ground their language, vision, and subjectivity in a future lexicon that would need to be rooted in an utterly different social formation that does not yet exist? How can they struggle for that which they cannot even name? For they themselves would have to invent the terms of this unthinkable and unknowable order—by drawing their poetry from a future that could not yet be grasped.

Indeed, Marx suggests that the 1848 Revolution in France failed partly because its protagonists drew their poetry from the past. They mimicked their eighteenth-century predecessors for whom the phrase (freedom declarations) exceeded the content (ongoing social domination). They misunderstood that certain political situations may call for one type of untimely practice (reenacting the past in order to propel revolutionary action) and others call for a different type (anticipating by acting as if supposedly impossible futures were already at hand).

With the Paris Commune, Marx witnessed a dazzling attempt by revolutionaries to realize, however briefly, something like the "social republic" that had been envisioned but obstructed in 1848.[2] In his 1871 address to the International Workingmen's Association (IWA) on what he called "the civil war in France," Marx noted that the Communards attempted "to set free the elements of a new society with which old collapsing bourgeois society itself is pregnant."[3] But the outcome of this process was neither mechanical nor predetermined. Marx emphasized this popular uprising's improvisational and experimental character: "The working class did not expect miracles from the Commune. They have no ready-made utopias to introduce. . . . They know that in order to work out their own emancipation, . . . they will have to pass through long struggles, through a series of historic processes, transforming circumstances and men."[4]

Marx praised these revolutionaries for recognizing that under the Second Empire "full-grown bourgeois society had finally transformed [the state] into a means for the enslavement of labor by capital."[5] This meant that "the working class could not simply lay hold of the ready-made state machinery, and wield it for its own purposes."[6] The task was not to seize the state but to abolish it. Marx praises the Communards for "discovering" a new "political form . . . under which to work out the economical emancipation of labor."[7] The social power that had been expropriated from the people and reified in an alien and oppressive state would be reclaimed and restored through this "thoroughly expansive political form" in which "public functions ceased to be private property . . . of the Central Government."[8] The former central state would be superseded by a federation of local self-managing communes based on the "self-government of the producers."[9]

By improvising practices through which this new political form could emerge, the Commune's content exceeded its phrase. Its poetry—language, concepts, consciousness, vision—was seized from a future that it was inventing.[10] Marveling that the Commune attempted to transform land and capital, which had formerly been "the means of enslaving and exploiting labor" into "instruments of free and associated labor," Marx declared, "This is communism, 'impossible' communism!"[11] Rather than ask whether Marx was right or wrong about the Commune as a viable form of communism, let us dwell on his attention to how a concrete attempt to ground political action on a future form of life that was still in the process of being invented overturned conventional assumptions about present and future, possibility and impossibility, realism and utopianism. Marx seems to suggest that from the perspective of a contradictory capitalism—a source of unviable social immiseration, class polarization, and militant mobilization that could not be reconciled with republican precepts—these incipient communists were clear-eyed realists and the bourgeois republicans were naïve utopians. He is reminding the first International that, through this evanescent political experiment, the supposedly impossible actually occurred. Marx thus declared, "Whatever [the Commune's] immediate results will be, a new point of departure of world-historic importance has been gained."[12]

The scandalous threat of this actually existing impossibility was immediately recognized by the reactionary regimes composing the existing inter-state order. Marx notes, "The old world writhed in convulsions of rage at the sight of the Red Flag, the symbol of the Republic of Labor, floating over the Hotel de Ville."[13] Before this unthinkable specter, "Europe seemed, for a moment, to doubt whether its recent sensational performances of state and war had any reality . . . or whether they were the dreams of a long bygone past."[14] Neighboring states felt rightly threatened. For the Communards recognized that real revolutionary transformation—the struggle against capitalist social relations and the bourgeois state, the emancipation of labor and the creation of a new political form, popular self-government by autonomous producers—had to be international. The struggle to emancipate labor would require international solidarity, and a new order would be composed of international federations of self-governing communes that would compose a "universal republic."[15]

In the course of his analysis, Marx explains that capitalist accumulation and class domination were dependent on the national state and that bourgeois states attempted to veil class inequalities through discourses of national unity. Likewise, interstate wars displaced attention from the ongoing class (or civil) war within each of these capitalist states; they obscured the shared social predicament and obstructed the potential relations of solidarity that could link working people across national boundaries. Moreover, Marx recognized that the tyranny of capital was supranational and the concert of European states were waging an international campaign against labor movements and socialist projects.

This is the perspective from which we can understand Marx's use of the term "civil war" to describe the historical drama of the Paris Commune. On one level, this rhetoric emphasizes that the stakes of national class conflict were as great as in any international war: "There can neither be peace nor truce possible between the working men of France and the appropriators of their produce . . . the battle must break out again and again in ever growing dimensions."[16] On another level, it conveys how the interstate war between France and Prussia expressed and obscured a more fundamental international struggle between labor and capital. Marx explains, "National war . . . is now proved to be a mere governmental humbug intended to defer the struggle of classes. . . . Class rule is no longer able to disguise itself in a national uniform; the national governments are one as against the proletariat!"[17] Given "the international character of class rule" and "the cosmopolitan conspiracy of capital" against organized labor, revolutionary workers would have to respond on the same scale. Marx thus extols the IWA for establishing an "international bond between the most advanced working men in the various countries of the civilized world."[18] Likewise he celebrates the Paris Commune for being a beacon of international anticapitalism, "the glorious harbinger of a new society" worldwide.[19] This struggle would require revolutionary actors to un-think their supposedly self-evident identification as national subjects. Indeed, Marx's account suggests that the substantive emancipation anticipated by the possible-impossible Commune exploded conventional assumptions about political subjectivity (by overcoming provincial national self-understanding), temporality (by drawing poetry from a future that must be invented), and territoriality (through worker internationalism as means and aim of struggle).

Marx's lyrical prose about the civil war in France often employed images of enslavement and insurrection. He writes, for example, "The civilization and justice of bourgeois order comes out in its lurid light whenever the slaves and drudges of that order rise against their masters" and are then met with "undisguised savagery and lawless revenge."[20] Marx also paid close attention to the U.S. Civil War.[21] Yet he does not discuss the fact that just as the drama of Paris Commune commenced, another great experiment in proletarian democracy and socialist solidarity—another actually existing impossibility—was already unfolding in the postbellum American South.

Du Bois's indispensable account of this experiment illuminates how we can regard Reconstruction as an example of a possible-impossibility. First, he famously argued that the mass of enslaved Blacks effectively emancipated themselves through a "general strike" whereby they withdrew their labor from Southern plantations and volunteered their services to Union armies.[22] As importantly, he demonstrates how a potentially revolutionary Freedmen's Bureau was established because the U.S. government and Northern industrialists had a shared stake in breaking the economic, social, and political power of the Southern plantocracy. This was an unprecedented executive agency with the power to expropriate and redistribute land, create new schools for formerly enslaved peoples, and organize an independent judicial system in the South. This historical situation, as Du Bois demonstrates, might have allowed emancipated rural Blacks to enter into an alliance with poor Southern whites and Northern "abolition democrats" in order to leverage the Bureau to establish a new "dictatorship of labor."[23] Du Bois thus outlines how a territorial civil war between capitalists (equally but differently racist Northern industrialists and Southern planters) could have been translated into a social civil war between a multiracial popular bloc and a reactionary power bloc.[24]

Of course, Black Reconstruction also recounts how this possible-impossibility was never realized. Poor whites who could not overcome entrenched racism aligned with Southern planters against free Blacks. This did not prevent Northern interests from destroying the plantocracy, restructuring the American economy, and imposing a new dictatorship of capital on America and the world. It did, however, shut down the Freedmen's Bureau and foreclose the possibility for a new kind of multiracial democratic socialism. A world-historic opportunity to radically reconstruct American democracy on a non-racist and socialist foundation was squandered. Instead, the U.S. government restored (white) national unity by allowing declining planters and immiserated whites to establish an apartheid social order which evolved into the Jim Crow system of social violence and legal segregation. The emancipation of enslaved peoples thus created the conditions for a new form of racial domination and phase of racial capitalism in and beyond America. In Du Bois's words,

> God wept . . . the world wept and is still weeping and blind with tears and blood. For there began to arise in America in 1876 a new capitalism and a new enslavement of labor. . . . The immense profit from this new exploitation and world-wide commerce enabled a guild of millionaires . . . to make more thorough the dictatorship of capital over the state and over the popular vote, not only in Europe and America but in Asia and Africa.[25]

Du Bois relates that the United States was then becoming the dominant capitalist state and that European imperialism maintained a global color bar that presupposed and reproduced capitalist accumulation. This meant that the failure of this "great human experiment," the triumph of a new "dictatorship of capital" in America, would harm Black, colonized, and working peoples worldwide.[26]

Dialectical Optics

If we are to envision, let alone realize, the possible-impossible we need to transcend realist epistemologies and embrace dialectical optics through which to unthink self-identical conceptions of *here, now,* and *us.*[27] We may read Freud, Benjamin, and Césaire as elaborating explicitly what Marx and Du Bois enacted implicitly: nonrealist orientations for seeing and knowing otherwise. Considering them together, I suggest, may help us to cultivate subversive optics through which to anticipate the possible-impossible. Such optics may be cause and consequence of the concrete utopianism with which this book is concerned.

Uncanniness

In his landmark 1919 essay, Sigmund Freud seeks to understand the peculiar kind of unsettling fear commonly associated with "uncanny" phenomena and experience. He famously traces how the meanings of the words *Heimlich* and *Unheimlich*, apparent opposites, came to be almost indistinguishable. The comfortable and comforting familiarity of *home* was associated with that which was personal, interior, out of public view. But the private, and therefore veiled, character of home life was also associated with that which is confined to the personal and private domain precisely because it is secret, even shameful; it is that which is concealed because it should not be publicly revealed. As Freud explains, both what is most familiar and what is most strange could therefore be referred to as *Heimlich*. In other words, much of what was named *Heimlich* in fact referred to what was considered *Unheimlich*: that which is strangely frightening, threatening, and unsettling when, or rather because, it was exposed to public view.

Freud's examples of the uncanny, drawn from fiction and real life, relate to objects and experiences that dissolve presumed ontologies and collapse conventional taxonomies. These include bodies that are no longer whole, persons who do not function in a normal manner, beings who are not properly alive: dead, disabled, or malformed bodies, severed body parts, the mad, the epileptic, spirits, ghosts. Animated by unseen forces, such figures violate supposedly settled borders between life and death, spirit and matter, subject and object,

and will and action. Likewise, Freud emphasizes strange experiences of dou-
bling (distorted mirror reflections, encounters with terrifying counterparts)
and repetition (the "unintended recurrence of the same situation," or when,
"having lost one's way . . . every attempt to find the marked or familiar path
may bring one back again and again to one and the same spot"[28]).

Note that for Freud, uncanniness is not produced by the mere idea of such
boundary-blurring phenomena, for these do not provoke the same kind of unsettling fear when they appear in folktales or stories. Uncanny dread only appears when such figures (seem to) cross the boundary from "poetic reality" to
"the world of common reality" such that "the distinction between imagination
and reality is effaced."[29] When the supposed boundary between poetic imagination and material reality is breached, subjects are propelled into something
like a (strangely familiar) waking dream (whose strange familiarity is terrifying). By threatening our sense of reality, uncanny phenomena and situations
also undermine our capacity to apprehend and explain the world. They seem
only to be explainable in terms that are (or accept the) irrational, impossible,
fantastic, magical, or supernatural. By challenging modern adults' sense of
reality, Freud reasons, uncanny experiences compel them to employ primitive
or childlike modes of magical thinking in which they themselves (supposedly)
do not believe. In so doing, their (realist) sense of reality is further unsettled.
Uncanniness begets uncanniness.

With the uncanny, that which we supposedly know most intimately can
suddenly reveal itself as utterly strange. As importantly, uncanny phenomena and experiences are so unnerving precisely because their *strangeness is
familiar.* The shocking surprise is so shocking because it is not surprising
enough. That which, at first, strikes us as utterly unhomely is somehow already
known: "that class of the frightening which leads back to what is . . . long
familiar."[30] Freud explains, "This uncanny is in reality nothing new or alien,
but something which is familiar and old—established in the mind and which
has become alienated from it only through the process of repression."[31] It is
"something repressed which *recurs.*"[32]

I would like to underscore the relational character of the uncanny for
Freud. It refers to a kind of *encounter* with uncanniness that produces an
experience of the uncanny. The frightening and unsettling return of the repressed is activated by worldly encounters. Freud explains how subjects who
believe they are encountering something uncanny *themselves* coproduce the
uncanniness that so unnerves them. An uncanny object does not mechanically cause terror in an anxious subject. Rather, something that is already
subjective and internal is projected onto and reified as something objective
and external. If the uncanny is "something which ought to have remained
hidden but has come to light," this is a matter of failed *self-concealment.*[33]

The uncanny as a relational concept is bound up with practices of disavowal, misrecognition, and transposition.

We may not be persuaded by Freud's attempt to relate uncanniness to unresolved infantile complexes. His primitivist and culturally evolutionist speculations are groundless and indefensible. But his singular reflections on the dynamics of strange familiarity open promising paths for critical thinking. His uncanniness blurs boundaries between material and immaterial, visible and invisible, reality and representation. Subject and object, self and other, past and present become porous. Differences between rational explanation and magical thinking, fact and fantasy, waking and dreaming lose significance.

By revealing the familiar as strange and the strange as familiar, the uncanny invites us to recognize the nonidentical character of reality. It illuminates how, despite appearances, a given self, place, or now may be internally differentiated and dispersed. Conversely, uncanniness illuminates how what may appear to be *other* subjects, *separate* places, and *different* times are already integral elements of a group, a territory, or an era. In a really uncanny world, facts are shot through with effaced histories, obscured connections, and disavowed identities.

Freud's account begs further questions about optics and politics. It alerts us to the uncanny aspect of social and psychic life. But how might we learn to see and know in an uncanny way? What mode of thinking might correspond to the strange familiarity, the dreamlike shock of the known but repressed suddenly come to light? Would it require imaginative and poetic ways of apprehending and illuminating social life that Freud does not provide?

Another set of questions concerns the subversive potential of uncanniness. Can the uncanny be transposed strategically into social registers through which to challenge norms and imagine alternatives? Can political actors productively render the seemingly settled world uncanny for those who have internalized such norms and who mistake the actual for what is possible? What are the political implications of displacing, exploding, reworking the boundaries between reality and imagination, dreaming and waking? What relationship might there be between the uncanny shock of dreadful recognition that renders actors unhomely and the concrete utopian task of anticipating the possible-impossible? I would suggest that the implicit political potentiality of Freud's uncanny may be coaxed forth through Benjamin's "awakening" and Césaire's "poetic knowledge."

Awakening

Walter Benjamin's writings are threaded through with traces and echoes of Freudian theory. He took seriously the way psychoanalytic insights — regarding the porous boundaries between consciousness and the unconscious, the rational and the dreamlike, reality and fantasy, the familiar and the strange, the past and the present—confounded realist notions of time, space, causality, and identity. His concern to extend the sociopolitical implications of these phenomena is especially evident in his reflections on *awakening*. For Benjamin, awakening cuts across the very opposition between being awake and being asleep, thereby blurring the distinction between reality and dreams. His awakening is not simply an indeterminate state, but an elevated orientation that allows those who are awakened to see and know otherwise.

Noting that À *la recherche du temps perdu* "begins with an evocation of the space of someone waking up," Benjamin praises Proust for "staking an entire life on life's supremely dialectical point of rupture: awakening."[34] He describes Proust as "racked with homesickness, homesick for . . . a world in which the true surrealist face of existence breaks through."[35] Benjamin identifies Proust's existential unhomeliness as the source of his literary images which, by crystallizing involuntary memories, offer a "bridge to the dream."[36] For Benjamin, Proust does not simply counterpose dream to reality. Rather, he accesses a dreamworld forged from real memories in order to recognize the dreamlike character of the real world in which the seemingly different may be fundamentally linked and the seemingly identical may be other than itself. As Benjamin explains, "remembering means to penetrate . . . to the universe of intertwining" where "*correspondences* rule."[37] He credits Proust for being able to "reveal them in our lived life" through "the work of *la mémoire involontaire*. . . . When that which has been is reflected in the dewy fresh 'instant,' a painful shock of rejuvenation pulls it together. . . . Proust's method is actualization, not reflection.[38] This is a crucial distinction. If memory reflects (on) the past, remembrance *actualizes what has been*. It does not abandon real life for a dreamworld; it illuminates the former through the latter. Proust's "homesickness" expressed an alienation that refused to accept the real as rational. His "remembrance" cultivated a poetic orientation to the world that disclosed deeper insights into the way things actually are. His involuntary memory, a form of waking dream, reveals reality's truly surreal character. But could this work of illumination be conjugated with practices of transformation?

Surrealism, which sought to overcome the distinction between sleeping and waking by way of (collective) dreams that might have revolutionary effects, helped Benjamin rework Proust's remembrance into a political conception of "awakening." The same year that his Proust essay appeared, Benjamin praised the Surrealist ethos: "Life seemed worth living only where the threshold between waking and sleeping was worn away."[39] These radical poets propelled Proust's "actualizations" into everyday public life. Noting that "the city of Paris itself" was their most "dreamed-about" object, Benjamin relates how, for the Surrealists, new optics entailed alternative practices: "Only revolt completely exposes [Paris's] Surrealist face. . . . And no face is surrealistic to the same degree as the true face of a city."[40] For Benjamin, such interventions demonstrated "how much an excursion into poetry clarifies things."[41] He called this kind of clarification a "profane illumination."[42]

Benjamin compares the effects of "profane illuminations" to those produced by opium, religion, and love.[43] But he warned that to celebrate "the anarchic" for its own sake was a pernicious form of romanticism rooted in an "undialectical conception of the nature of intoxication."[44] His Surrealists did not merely revel in intoxication and transgression as ends in themselves. Nor did they reject the world by fleeing into art. Rather, the Surrealist strategy of "loosening of the self by intoxication" provided "precisely the fruitful living experience that allowed these people to step outside the charmed space of intoxication."[45] Benjamin thus describes the Surrealists as practicing a "dialectics of intoxication" which sought "to win the energies of intoxication for the revolution."[46] Likewise, he warns against forms of critique that place "fanatical stress on the mysterious side of the mysterious."[47] In contrast, he understood Surrealism as a "poetic politics" whose aim was to "penetrate the mystery only to the degree that we recognize it in the everyday world, by virtue of a dialectical optic that perceives the everyday as impenetrable, the impenetrable as everyday."[48] *Surrealism's profane illuminations interrupted everyday reality from the standpoint of intoxication in order to better grasp, transform, and elevate everyday reality.*

Benjamin believed that it might be possible to channel this movement's "revolutionary tension" into a "collective innervation" or "revolutionary discharge" such that "reality [has] transcended itself to the extent demanded by the *Communist Manifesto*."[49] He thereby identified a concrete historical possibility within Surrealism's seemingly anarchic and romantic calls to win the energies of intoxication for the revolution. Just as Benjamin reminded readers that Proust's practice of "remembrance" was more subversive than the great novelist's class position and literary focus might suggest, he demonstrates that Surrealism's "profane illuminations" and "poetic politics" exceeded the ironic and nihilistic limitations of *l'art pour l'art*.[50] These conceptions could be reworked into a poetic-political concept of (revolutionary) "awakening." As he noted in the *Arcades*, "Whereas [Surrealist poet Louis Aragon] persists within the realm of dream, here the concern is to find the constellation of awakening . . . the awakening of a not-yet conscious knowledge of what has been."[51]

Benjamin's awakening transcends the false alternative between a crude realism that insists on appearances and clings to the given, on the one hand,

and a naïve romanticism that seeks refuge in dreams in order to escape reality, on the other. Awakening compels realists into the dreamworld and propels romantics into the real world. This is not a matter of returning from a phantasmic dream to the clear light of rational reality. Nor is it a matter of embracing a dogmatic truth or theological revelation. It is about awakening to the surreal face of the real world through a dialectical optic that perceives the everyday as impenetrable and the impenetrable as everyday.

As Benjamin's quote about Aragon suggests, awakening may also produce *temporal* illuminations which alert us to the persistence, within a nonidentical now, of what has been. In this way, we are awakened to the unrealized dreams of the past as a vital legacy. The task of the critic is both to illuminate the uncanny-untimely character of the world and to render the world uncanny-untimely. The aim is not merely to raise consciousness or to grasp the world in a more adequate manner, but to do so in order to think beyond the existing order and anticipate other possible worlds. Awakening is dialectical in two senses: 1) it renders the strange familiar and the familiar strange; 2) it opens a way of seeing that grounds a way of acting and a way of acting that grounds a way of seeing.

Awakening as dialectical optic is bound up with a poetic politics that, through profane illumination, identifies unrealized potentialities within the actually existing. This theoretical-political orientation also describes Benjamin's method. He developed immanent critiques of Proust and Surrealism (as he did elsewhere of Marx, Baudelaire, Freud, and others); he identified aspects of their work that point beyond their existing limitations. Likewise, in his social and historical analyses, Benjamin developed immanent critiques that identified potentialities within the given that pointed beyond its actually existing form. He explains that "by a displacement of the angle of vision . . . a positive element emerges anew in [every negation] . . . something different from that previously signified."[52] This dialectical optic—a displaced angle of view—is at once poetic, philosophical, and political.

Adorno notes that Benjamin's philosophical "incommensurability lies in the inordinate ability to give himself over to his object" such that it "becomes as foreign as an everyday, familiar thing, under a microscope."[53] This "technique of enlargement brings the rigid into motion and the dynamic to rest."[54] Adorno explains that by pressing so close to the object, such thinking hopes "to penetrate down to the veins of gold which no classificatory procedure can reach" and thereby "establishes the relation to potential praxis which later guided Benjamin's thinking."[55] Awakening indexes just this practice of making the familiar strange by looking deeper than immediate appearances in order to reach the obscured "veins of gold" that might nourish subversive political practice. Could such a poetic politics be practiced collectively and on a so-cietal scale? Aimé Césaire may help us to engage this question productively.

Poetic Knowledge

Like Benjamin, Césaire spent most of the 1930s as an expatriate intellectual in Paris who recognized an affinity between Surrealism and the imperative to link alternative ways of seeing and knowing to subversive politics. Césaire's essay "Poetry and Knowledge" offers an entry point into the kind of dialectical optic that fueled his art, thought, and politics.

Césaire organizes the essay—a piece first presented as a lecture at the Congrès International de Philosophie in Port-au-Prince Haiti in 1944—around a contrast between the poetic image and rational judgment.[56] He conjures the "fulfilling knowledge" that humans once "discovered in fear and rapture," in a state of "trembling and wonderment. Strangeness and intimacy . . . emotion and imagination" before "the throbbing newness of the world."[57] This primordial capacity, he contends, was gradually superseded by an "impoverished" scientific knowledge, "poor and half starved," that "enumerates, measures, classifies, and kills."[58] Professing his preference for the "richness" of ancient poetic images to the "poverty" of modern logical concepts, Césaire announces: "All that was gained through reasoning was lost for poetry."[59] His point is not that poetry became impoverished, but that a poetic relationship to the world was lost, forgotten, foreclosed. Indeed, he insists that this ancient form of knowing *has* persisted in "the nocturnal forces of poetry."[60] The critical and political task is to recover such forces in order to redeploy them in life so as to overcome modern forms of alienation and domination. Accordingly, throughout his thinking and acting, Césaire struggled to identify, *within* African, Antillean, and European traditions and ways of life, persisting resources through which a poetic relationship to being, knowing, making, and relating could be forged anew.

Rather than simply oppose poetry to reason, Césaire displaces the opposition by identifying "poetic knowledge" and "poetic truth" as *alternative forms of reason*. These may lead to more elevated ways of knowing which could cut across the rationalist binaries that impoverish both subject and object. He thus announces that poetic knowledge "resolved . . . the antinomy of one and the other [and] . . . of Self and World."[61] It superseded "the law of identity, the law of non-contradiction, the logical principle of the excluded middle."[62] If this orientation undermines logical or scientific distinctions between true and false, it does not reject truth as such. On the contrary, "poetry is always on the road to truth."[63] But this is an elevated truth that does not mistake appearances for reality. Rather than reduce the world to concepts, it relates (to) the world through images. "The image is forever surpassing that which is perceived because the dialectic of the image transcends antinomies. . . . When the sun of image reaches its zenith, everything becomes possible again. . . . Accursed complexes dissolve, it's the instant of emergence."[64]

This operation referred neither to an avant-gardist flight into aesthetics, a Romantic experience of personal apotheosis, nor a Dionysian celebration of transgression as such. Its aim was worldly and political: to identify the way in which the given may be more or other than it appeared to be so that the real but inapparent possibilities that dwell within or are indexed by it could be pursued. In Césaire's poetic image, everything becomes possible. If poetic knowledge opens a pathway to "the most authentic vision of the world," this is not a matter of epistemological adequacy.[65] *It is a vision of the world as it could possibly be, based on what it actually is.*

If Césaire invokes "poetic violence . . . poetic aggressivity, . . . [and] poetic instability," he regards these as forces of creative destruction, not principles of pure negativity. He thus declares: "In this climate of flame and fury that is the climate of poetry, money has no currency, courts pass no judgment, judges do not convict, juries do not acquit. . . . Police functions are strangulated. Conventions wear out."[66] Poetic knowledge does not simply refuse or negate the profane world; it offers a prophetic vision of a different world organized around alternative forms of exchange, law, and democracy.[67] We might say that Césaire is reflecting on the challenge of how a politics might draw its poetry from the future (by recognizing the transformative potentiality fermenting and germinating in the present). Poetic knowledge reveals how past and future, heritage and destiny may be contemporaneous with one another, even as it also produces such contemporaneity. In the poetic image, everything becomes possible *again*. It identifies the real but obscured "veins of gold" that might fuel a radical politics of the possible-impossible.

Césaire identified "the ground of poetic knowledge" as "an astonishing mobilization of all human and cosmic forces" in which "all lived experience. All the possibility . . . all the pasts, all the futures . . . Everything is summoned. Everything awaits."[68] Similarly the speaker in "Fragments of a Poem" invokes the "second beginning of everything" that may be fashioned out of the "sacred whirling primordial streaming" because the "whole possible [is] at hand." They declaim, "My ear to the ground, I heard Tomorrow pass."[69] This prophetic understanding of the poet as seer is underscored by an epigraph from Rimbaud: "It is necessary to be a visionary [voyant], to make oneself clairvoyant [voyant]."[70]

The past political actors that Césaire engaged and emulated were themselves untimely visionaries endowed with poetic knowledge. He held that the abolitionist Victor Schoelcher had a "lucid view of the conditions for true liberty" whose 1848 interventions and insights spoke directly to the conditions of 1948. In a similar spirit, he identified Toussaint Louverture as "the Precursor" whose 1801 constitution projected an unprecedented political possibility that was 150 years ahead of his time. Regarding contemporaries, he observed, "[Patrice] Lumumba is a revolutionary insofar as he is a visionary. Because, in reality, what does he have before his eyes? A miserable country. . . . The grandeur of Lumumba was to sweep aside all of these realities and to see an extraordinary Congo that is still only in his mind, but which will become a reality tomorrow. And Lumumba is great, through this, because there is always a beyond [au-delà] for him."[71]

Poetic knowledge was an aesthetic, critical, and political operation that attempted to awaken unrealized possibilities sedimented within existing forms and actual arrangements. It regarded given objects as self-surpassing images whose potentiality was neither self-evident nor static. Insofar as it seeks to glimpse the possible within the actual, poetic knowledge has an elective affinity with immanent critique. Both may be recognized in what I have elsewhere called Césaire's subversive practice of "radical literalism."[72] In a 1978 interview, he was taken to task for expressing himself in French, which his interlocutor presumed to be at odds with his authentic cultural self. Against the presumption that Césaire was thereby reproducing his own alienation, he declared: "I am not a prisoner of the French language! . . . I always wanted to *inflect* French. . . . I am re-creating a language that is not French. Whether or not French people recognize themselves in it is their problem."[73] Rather than turn away from French, he inhabited it in order to turn it inside out, rendering it uncanny for its white native speakers as something that was at once known and new, familiar and foreign, French and not. Through this practice of "inflection," white "native" speakers no longer felt at home with or in this language.

Precisely this kind of optic and strategy guided Césaire's untimely vision of decolonization as an opportunity to transcend both colonialism *and* unitary national states in the service of what we might call a possible-impossible politics of the excluded middle. Through departmentalization in 1946, Césaire demanded that the French state accommodate itself institutionally to the cosmopolitan reality that imperialism itself had created but disavowed. By 1956, when it became clear that departmentalization had become an obstacle to rather than a vehicle for Antillean emancipation, Césaire joined his

Senegalese friend and parliamentary ally, Léopold Sédar Senghor, in a constitutional struggle to transform the imperial republic into a transcontinental democratic and socialist federation. It would be composed of self-managing peoples participating on an equal footing, with the wealth of the whole being equitably distributed. Césaire believed that such an arrangement would not only mark the end of colonial domination. It could mark the advent of a new world order and renovated humanity that has recovered its poetic relationship to knowledge and life, that has reconciled human, natural, and supernatural realms, and that has re-conjugated the relation between painful histories and possible futures.

Césaire's untimely vision of nonnational decolonization was a concrete utopian project refracted through poetic knowledge. He recognized how the heterogeneous conditions of imperialism had created the conditions of possibility for this unprecedented federal form. His untimely vision was grounded in a canny understanding of the real dilemmas that anticolonialism, in that conjuncture, had to confront and the opportunities it could seize. It was also propelled by the "dialectic of past and future" (which I discuss in Chapter 8). Césaire addressed predecessors as contemporaries and reactivated (i.e., awakened) potentialities within supposedly outmoded projects. His thinking about departmentalization was refracted through Schoelcher's postabolitionist politics, and his thinking about multinational federation was refracted through Toussaint's efforts to create a new form of federal autonomy. These legacies helped Césaire not only to envision a seemingly impossible future, but to act as if it was already at hand.

I am not suggesting that we treat "uncanniness," "awakening," and "poetic knowledge" as saying or doing the same thing. Nor am I suggesting that there is some kind of linear development running through these conceptions. Rather I am gathering them into a constellation through which to challenge realist assumptions about supposedly self-evident boundaries between visible and invisible, the apparent and the real, the real and imagined, what has been and now. These thinkers offer us legacies out of which to fashion dialectical optics that can awaken us from the pernicious dreams of homogeneous identity, punctual temporality, and provincial territoriality. Such optics would be dialectical in several ways. They would recognize and render the familiar strange and the strange familiar. They would cultivate a circular relationship between nonrealist ways of seeing-knowing and subversive action. They would identify potentiality within the given that points beyond existing forms. They would explode false oppositions between possibility and impossibility, realism and utopianism, is and ought.

Uncanny Refractions

Dialectical optics enable what Adorno calls "the interpretive eye which sees more in a phenomenon than it is—and solely because of what it is."[74] He elaborates, "The means employed in negative dialectics for the penetration of its hardened objects is possibility—the possibility of which their reality has cheated the objects and which is nonetheless visible in each one."[75] We may understand concrete utopianism in terms of this dialectical (and poetic) capacity to recognize the uncanny character of everyday life, on the one hand, and the true insights crystallized in uncanny dreams, art, experiences, on the other. Such profane illuminations may awaken us to the nonidentical character of the seemingly stable as well as to already existing relations that link the supposedly disparate. This poetic knowledge may fuel a politics of the possible-impossible. Dialectical optics may help us to tack between the kind of insight that identifies ideological refractions of the world and the kind that refracts everyday life in productively uncanny ways.

The Oxford English Dictionary reminds us that the term "refraction" is polysemic. Most commonly it refers, as it did for sixteenth-century astronomers and seventeenth-century physicists who developed it, to the way light rays are diverted as they move through a medium, such as the atmosphere, water, or a prism. Such refraction distorts our view of both the light and that which it illuminates. Refraction refers both to this general process and to the specific distorting action of the medium. It indexes the medium, the process of mediation, and the distorted image. For nineteenth-century ophthalmologists, often referred to as "refractionists," the term also referred to the use of lenses to correct the refractive distortions caused by failing eyesight. They were specialists in re-refraction who enabled people to see the world as it actually is. These various meanings of refraction circle around the idea of getting things right, of recognizing and correcting distorted views, misleading images, and failing vision.[76] A parallel set of meanings, also dating from the sixteenth century, understand refraction as "the action of breaking open or breaking up." Beyond the play of distortion and correction, refraction can refer to an interruptive, even destructive, force or practice. It can bend the seemingly immutable in alternate directions.

The historically sedimented meanings of refraction underscore the real ways that seeing and knowing may effect concrete changes in the actual world. Critical optics have the power to illuminate inapparent processes of distortion, to create conditions of possibility for seeing-knowing the world, and to transform any given view of the world (whether by bending it in a new direction or restoring a distorted direction).[77]

The chapters that follow may be read as invitations to recognize and produce uncanny refractions: *to identify the familiar in the strange and the strange in the familiar so as to explode reified conceptions of* here-now-us *in the service of a concrete utopian politics of the possible-impossible.*[78] From one angle, the task is to recognize the normalizing social processes through which the familiar is made (to appear) strange and the strange familiar. From another, the task is to render the familiar strange and the strange familiar. In these ways, the critic can identify how supposedly familiar entities are nonidentical, and how they differ from themselves, in order to activate and actualize intrinsic potentialities within the object that may exceed the object. Simultaneously, the critic can identify how seemingly disparate phenomena—the apparently foreign, different, other, separate, incommensurable—may already be intrinsically related, indissociably intertwined. Both kinds of uncanny refractions, mediated by dialectical optics, may help to open heretofore unimaginable, unforeseen, and seemingly impossible relations, reciprocities, responsibilities, and solidarities. Following this perspective, we may regard critical thinkers as visionary refractionists in the service of a poetic politics that can remember-awaken and recognize-render the possible-impossible.

2
Concrete Utopianism and Critical Internationalism
Refusing Left Realism

Above all he fears being duped, so his actions and relations are characterized by a fundamental mistrust. . . . This boy—or this girl—is a realist. . . . He (or she) is . . . unwilling to commit himself beyond the present moment . . . he is more than capable of facing up to things (immediate, given things), distinguishing between what he will find possible and impossible. . . . He looks at the things around him, and the people. They are what they are, no more, no less. . . . He thinks that anyone who wants to change the world must be slightly unhinged. . . . [He tends] to believe that "ideals" fool people and are deliberately used to fool people, that ideals are a hypocritical front for unscrupulous manipulation. . . . He thinks rebellion is stupid, but that does not stop him from deeply despising society as it is.

—HENRI LEFEBVRE

Critical theory . . . confronts history with a possibility which is always concretely visible within it . . . mankind was not betrayed by the untimely attempts of the revolutionaries but by the timely attempts of realists.

—MAX HORKHEIMER

Like philosophy, [critical theory] opposes making reality into a criterion in the manner of complacent positivism. But unlike philosophy, it always derives its goals only from present tendencies of the social process. Therefore, it has no fear of the utopian that the new order is denounced as being. When truth cannot be realized within

the established social order, it always appears to the latter as mere
utopia.

— HERBERT MARCUSE

In the previous chapter, I argued for a poetic politics of the possible-impossible.
This would require dialectical optics that might enable us to transcend realist
epistemology. The latter's tendency to posit provincial notions of space, punctual notions of time, and homogeneous notions of identity obstructs concrete
utopian visions of societal transformation in which translocal and cross-group
solidarity would be both a means and an end of struggle. In this chapter,
I underscore how realist epistemology and political realism reinforce each
other. Specifically, I discuss how political realism cannot adequately grasp
the kind of anti-imperial internationalism that animated projects as different as Senghor and Césaire's postnational federalism and Samir Amin's Fifth
International. At the center of this discussion is a critical reading of Partha
Chatterjee's recent writing about internationalism and cosmopolitanism.

I do not employ "political realism" in the conventional sense to figure
politics as the intentional pursuit of interests through the use of power whose
aim is greater power. This usage counterposes realism to an idealism that
understands politics as the exercise or pursuit of ethical values and abstract
principles. Rather, I use political realism to describe a presentist reduction of
politics to the practical engagement with concrete concerns, immediate goals,
and the given order.[1] This orientation tends to conflate idealism and utopianism such that the latter signals unrealistic aspirations, unattainable ideals, or
impossible hopes that can only exist in the imagination rather than in the real
world. Such an understanding of utopian idealism connotes naïve optimism
or delusion. Rather, I oppose political realism to concrete utopianism. The
latter seeks to relate real conditions to desirable futures that appear to be impossible from the standpoint of the existing order. Concrete utopianism seeks
to identify possibilities for radically different arrangements that may already
dwell within or be emerging from an actually existing situation. It is at once
grounded in the present and is future-oriented. It entails anticipatory practices
that are mediated by political imagination. This kind of orientation has nourished internationalist projects through the modern period.

Actually Existing Internationalism

In October 1945 the United Nations began its official existence when the five
permanent members of the new Security Council and a majority of other
signatories ratified the Charter.[2] In January 1946, the first session of the UN

General Assembly convened in New York and established the general outlines of the new postwar order. It also responded to more immediate challenges including the question of decolonization. The General Assembly created the Trusteeship Council to oversee the administration of colonized, or "non-self-governing," peoples in accordance with the Charter which had pledged to promote their "well-being" and "to develop self-government" for them "according to the particular circumstances of each territory . . . and their varying stages of advancement."[3]

Over the next ten years, a growing number of colonized peoples in Asia, Africa, and the Middle East obtained political independence. For most anti-colonial movements (whether moderate or revolutionary, liberal or socialist) throughout the world, the national state became the unquestioned framework through which self-determination would be secured. Notably, this preference for a national form of decolonization was shared by the existing world powers. When France and Britain, for example, recognized that they could no longer remain imperial states, they negotiated bilateral agreements with moderate nationalist allies to create spheres of neocolonial influence. The United States pursued a similar strategy toward new Third World nations. It cultivated blocs of non-communist allies, exploitable resources, and potential consumers within a system of "free trade" among nominally sovereign national states.[4]

These powerful international actors were equally invested in a UN world order committed to a stable interstate system.[5] It was to be organized around the already existing principles of territorial integrity, national independence, and state sovereignty. It would be policed and protected through a directorate of great powers (the Security Council) and administered through a series of international agencies staffed by bureaucratic and technocratic experts. Of course, it would also have the ability to override the national sovereignty of member states when it was determined that they violated their own population's human rights. But this *ad hoc* ability to elevate abstract humanity over state sovereignty did not fundamentally challenge the principles of territoriality, nationality, or sovereignty around which the world order would be organized. On the contrary, this internationalist capacity was meant to protect the interstate system that the United Nations supervised.[6]

Geopolitically and economically, the postwar world would be framed by this structure linking great powers, nominally sovereign states, abstract individuals (now possessing human rights), and international agencies and experts. Despite appearances, nationalism, human rights, international law, and global governance composed a single order, or *nomos*, that presupposed the norm of territorial sovereignty.[7] This *nomos* would create conditions favorable for new types of neocolonial capitalism and legalized imperialism.

Since the end of the Cold War and the intensification of neoliberal globalization, the inability of state sovereignty to create conditions for substantive
freedom and human flourishing and the failures of internationalism to create
conditions for global justice and human solidarity have become evident everywhere. Even if populations manage to empower democratic popular assemblies to promote their social and economic well-being, crucial decisions that
would determine their life chances are made elsewhere — by private economic
actors, unaccountable international agencies, and technocratic experts.

The fictions of national self-determination and universal human rights
are underscored by recent developments within Europe. Consider the European Union's punitive treatment of Greece for trying to resist the authoritarian dictates of global finance through a popular Left government. For many
critics this confirmed the priority that national sovereignty should have over
international association. But we might also read it in terms of the European
Union's disastrous decision to constitute itself as an economic and admin-
istrative confederation of states led by experts and bankers rather than as a
truly democratic federation led by a continental association of self-governing
peoples for whom resources were shared, risks were socialized, and autonomy
was meaningful. Or consider Fortress Europe's criminal response to the flow
of refugees from the Eastern Mediterranean following the civil war in Syria.
This crisis does not simply reveal the moral failure or hypocrisy of the West
and the "international community." It makes clear that the existing global order, organized around and managed by the interlocking actions of nominally
sovereign states, international agencies, and the U.S. imperium, cannot meet
the most basic requirements of global coordination, democratic participation,
self-management, human rights, and social justice.

The bankruptcy of international law has long been revealed by Israel's ongoing occupation of Palestine and, more recently, by Russia's unilateral annexation of Eastern Ukraine. Such violations pale in comparison to the mass
violence, in the name of liberal internationalism, perpetrated by the post–
Cold War U.S. state, which is legitimized through UN-sanctioned doctrines
and policies regarding human rights, humanitarianism, and the "responsibility to protect."

The dangers of cultural and territorial autarchy have recently been demonstrated by massacres of foreign workers in South Africa, the mass deportation
of Haitians in the Dominican Republic, the flight of Rohinga Muslims from
Myanmar, and the internment of Central American children in the United
States. Such dangers were amplified by a Donald Trump administration,
which abandoned liberal internationalism entirely in the name of "America
First." Immediately after assuming office, Trump pursued immigrant round-

ups and Islamophobic travel bans, manufactured a military threat from Iran and antagonized China, expressed sympathy for Russian Crimea and offered tacit approval for Israel's likely annexation of parts of Palestine. His rule further underscored the limitations of international law and the lack of frameworks for long-distance solidarity today. The latter was certainly evident as the world watched the Islamic State's siege of Kobani in northern Syria in 2014–2015.

In recent years, scholars have developed valuable critiques of existing forms of internationalism and corresponding cosmopolitan ideologies.[8] Such criticism is warranted and welcome, especially when directed at pious acolytes of international legal procedure, righteous proponents of humanitarian intervention, patriotic defenders of Western civilization, and the unaccountable technocrats who administer the global order. Much of this work comports with the important critique of European internationalism developed by Carl Schmitt in *Nomos of the Earth* (1950).

Schmitt identifies the system of public international law and its humanist ideology as the legitimizing expression of a European imperium based on the sanctity of property and the force of geopolitics. These, he argues, functioned perversely and paradoxically to legalize extreme violence against non-European populations. But we should also recall that Schmitt regarded Europe's invidious humanist internationalism as inseparable from the *nomos* of sovereign states. Far from establishing a boundary between internationalism and state sovereignty, he demonstrated how each required and enabled the other. Moreover, Schmitt developed this critique to advance a reactionary vision of imperial spheres of influence corresponding to civilizational mandates. It was a brief for politics as permanent war undiluted by legal veils or liberal pieties.

I am not suggesting that critics of actually existing liberal internationalism are all realpolitik opportunists or covert nativists. But I would like to underscore the inadequacy of one-sided critiques that simply challenge internationalism from the standpoint of state sovereignty (or vice versa). Such arguments tend to employ an either/or logic that conflates existing forms of liberal internationalism with internationalism as such. It follows, according to this thinking, that the only radical alternative is a realist acceptance of state sovereignty as a quasi-natural fact and territory-ethnicity-force as the inevitable truth of world politics. Such thinking forecloses discussion of alternative forms of radical internationalism as both means and ends of anti-imperial and anticapitalist struggle. The violence and failures of liberal internationalism suggest that the existing *nomos* of the world is entering a moment of unsustainable crisis. Under such conditions we cannot but think seriously about novel forms of political consociation that might at least be adequate to the plural, translocal, and entangled conditions of our world-historical present. As important, we need to envision political forms that might address the dual imperatives of popular sovereignty (or autonomy) and international solidarity (or interdependence).

Internationalism as Democratic Dilemma

In different ways Immanuel Kant and Hannah Arendt explore how internationalism—some version of planetary politics—is at once a necessary condition of possibility of human freedom and a grave threat to that freedom. Their writings illuminate a democratic dilemma that continues to haunt modern political life.

In his reflections on universal history, cosmopolitan rights, perpetual peace, and world federation Kant certainly makes many dubious and, from our vantage point, outmoded claims that warrant criticism.[9] But preemptive rejections of these writings by current critics often have more to do with how he has been claimed by liberal internationalists than with what he actually wrote. On the one hand, Kant argued that all humans have a right to be free within a self-governing polity. By this he meant full participation in the process through which community members define generally valid laws to which they would voluntarily subject themselves on a basis of equality with all other citizens who would be governed by the same laws. This is a conception of political freedom as self-determination whereby humanity would be composed of separate self-governing polities. Each would be sovereign insofar as it was only accountable to itself; no outside authority could rightfully legislate or rule in its place. In this view, legally governed social relations and democratic self-government worked together to create a state of political freedom and public peace. On the other hand, Kant argued that insofar as there existed no overarching legal or constitutional order regulating relations *among* these separate polities, they lived under a permanent threat of unregulated outside aggression. He reasoned that neither political democracy nor human freedom could be fully realized, even for members of self-governing polities, under such lawless conditions within an agonistic international order.

In short, Kant explained that real freedom required the existence of separate sovereign states *and* that such sovereignty would make real human freedom impossible. Conversely, in his view, only the creation of a global political agency could guarantee freedom for self-governing peoples even as such an agency would, by definition, undermine such freedom. His ambiguous response to this dilemma was to envision a federal world republic or world republican federation. By this he meant neither a world state nor a simple confederation of sovereign states agreeing to follow the rules of interstate behavior (as in commercial or nonaggression pacts). Rather, Kant envisioned a self-governing federation of self-governing peoples on a worldwide scale. Through this ideal, he hoped that humanity would be able to reconcile popular sovereignty with planetary entanglement and cosmopolitan responsibility. He thus attempted to envision a cosmopolitan arrangement in which self-determination would not require state sovereignty, and one in which popular sovereignty would not be violated by an unaccountable world government.

Regardless of how we might now evaluate Kant's underspecified suggestions, we should appreciate that he defined a profound and persistent problem for democratic politics. This dilemma did not disappear when, following the French revolution, the Jacobin model of a unitary national state enjoying total territorial sovereignty within its borders became the normal and desirable form through which peoples sought to protect or pursue self-determination. Nor did it disappear in the nineteenth century, when, as the industrial revolution unfolded and capitalism increasingly transformed social relations throughout Western Europe and its overseas empires, sovereign national states facilitated the growth of distinct national economies (and vice versa).

After the end of World War II, Kant's democratic dilemma reappeared as a concrete problem for global politics. Following Europe's self-implosion, the genocidal mass murder of its Jewish "minority" populations, and the dawn of mass movements for decolonization, intellectuals, activists, and policy makers engaged in public debates about the problem of freedom, asking how best to reconcile the imperatives of democratic self-government, national independence, state sovereignty, international law, and global justice. Hannah Arendt, for example, maintained that peoples' humanity depended on their place and participation in a concrete political community through which (public) action becomes (publicly) meaningful. Thus her celebration of the ancient Greek polis as an ideal form of political association.[10] But she reasoned that since citizenship in the modern West had become dependent on national identity, one's human rights could only be recognized and protected through the framework of a national state.[11] In her view, European history between 1917 and 1945 demonstrated that under existing conditions, the concept of human rights was an empty and dangerous abstraction. But we should recall that this insight was paired with a critique of parochial nationalism as the agency that had degraded democratic politics in the modern period. She demonstrated that in a world order grounded in national xenophobia, race thinking, and imperialism, as growing numbers of people were compelled to reside within the boundaries of national states to which they did not legally or ethnically *belong*, nation-states became incapable of guaranteeing them concrete human rights in the form of real citizenship and political belonging.

Like Kant, Arendt recognized that sovereign states were indispensable for a human self-realization that they also made impossible. She demonstrated how this deep and persistent contradiction was revealed in the catastrophic twentieth century when European nation-states and the international order they comprised were unable to address the political problems that they themselves had created, as embodied by diasporic Jews, national minorities, stateless peoples, and refugees. Likewise, neither national nor international legal orders were capable of adequately conceptualizing, let alone addressing, Nazi genocide as a crime against humanity.[12] She insisted that "the right of every individual to belong to humanity, should be guaranteed by humanity itself," even as she conceded that "for the time being a sphere that is above the nations does not exist."[13] She responded to this dilemma by proposing various forms of multinational federal democracy for European Jews and small states.[14] One does not have to accept Arendt's programmatic solutions to appreciate the problems they were meant to address: Are there frameworks for transnational solidarity and postnational democracy that would not invest already powerful states or a new superstate with quasi-imperial authority over other parts of the world? Is there a way to organize the world order such that the autonomy of vulnerable peoples or nations would be protected while also allowing them to make claims on the international community, whether against local states or great powers?

At the inception of the postwar period, a range of political thinkers in and beyond the West shared Arendt's concern with imagining frameworks for transnational solidarity and postnational democracy that would not invest already powerful states or a new superstate with quasi-imperial authority over other parts of the world. New arrangements would have to respect the autonomy of vulnerable peoples or nations while also allowing them to make claims on the international community, whether against local states or great powers.[15]

A Possible-Impossible Decolonization

Imperial states had long subjugated non-Europeans under the guise of protecting populations, generalizing liberty, and improving humanity. They violated subject peoples' autonomy and territorial integrity on the erroneous grounds that they were not capable of self-government. This at a time when the logic of global politics held that a people could not be recognized as a legitimate political actor without being organized as an independent state. Under such conditions, state sovereignty, national independence, and territorial integrity certainly promised a robust alternative to, and protection against, colonial domination by foreign powers. Any international arrangement that would open the door to new forms of intercontinental paternalism and supranational authority would be rightly suspect.

At the same time, many anticolonial thinkers, especially across the Black Atlantic, wondered whether the sovereign national state was the best form in which to realize substantive self-determination. Given the relations of entanglement and dependence that would continue to subordinate postcolonial societies to international economic domination and strong states, formal political liberty would not adequately protect them from the depredations of uneven development and Great Power geopolitics. They foresaw that the relative poverty of their countries would make impossible the experiments in social democracy or state socialism then being instituted in Western and Eastern Europe. Moreover, they insisted that much of the West's wealth and power had been founded upon the exploitation of enslaved and colonial labor, the expropriation of overseas natural resources, and the relations of intercontinental inequality that imperial capitalism had instituted worldwide.

From this perspective, many engaged in the decolonization struggle believed that these small countries should constitute themselves as larger regional federations. Others believed that there should be non- or supranational mechanisms through which this interdependence could be democratized, reciprocity guaranteed, and colonized peoples provided with an enduring claim on the wealth in which they already had a rightful share. How could the West be compelled to pay its historical debt rather than re-subordinate postcolonial national states through financial debt for development projects? What mechanisms for international economic solidarity, political accountability, and justice could help to repair the harms of imperialism, prevent its reemergence in a different form, and ground substantive decolonization?

Of course, the U.S.–UN system that emerged to govern the postwar global order turned out to resemble the very type of international dictatorship of powerful states against which Albert Camus and W. E. B. Du Bois warned contemporaries. Its primary aim was to ensure order among sovereign national states rather than provide a framework for social justice or democratic accountability on a planetary scale. The UN Charter made provisions for checking state sovereignty, whereby it could punish national states for violating individuals' human rights. But these were usually defined according to a set of Western norms to which the West rarely held itself. Moreover, the subjects of this law were individuals rather than communities. In other words, the United Nations defined conditions under which the international community could interfere in the domestic affairs of a sovereign state. But it never attempted to create an alternative *nomos* of the world that would not be founded upon territorial nationality, state sovereignty, and individual citizenship.

By the mid-1950s most colonized peoples—led variously by peasant mobilizations, radical trade unions, nationalist political parties, and urban intellectuals—pursued decolonization through struggles for national independence and state sovereignty. We should also recall that once the movement for decolonization gained historical momentum, colonial powers, the United States, and the United Nations all concurred that separate national states should be the form through which colonized peoples would be emancipated and around which the postwar international order should be organized.[16]

This is the context in which Léopold Sédar Senghor, from Senegal, and Aimé Césaire, from Martinique, attempted to reconcile the imperatives of self-government, translocal interdependence, and human solidarity. Their analysis of mid-twentieth-century conditions led them to conclude that genuine African and Caribbean self-determination would have to entail abolishing colonialism *and* overcoming the unitary national state. Accordingly, they pursued a constitutional struggle to transform the imperial republic into a translocal federation. Socialist and democratic, transcontinental and nonnational, this new type of polity would include former colonies as freely associated and self-governing members. The aim was neither to join nor to separate from the actually existing French state but to explode it immanently. Their starting point was the entangled histories that bound overseas and metropolitan peoples and prospects to one another. It followed that if decolonization did not also seek to revolutionize metropolitan social relations and reconfigure the very *nomos* of the world, it could never ground substantive emancipation.

I have written at length elsewhere about the logic, politics, and limitations of this "untimely vision."[17] Here I would like only to underscore that however contradictory and imperfect, this was a concrete utopian project that sought to address a set of real dilemmas by anticipating another possible world. These efforts were both rooted in a canny reading of the existing world-historical situation and an attempt to draw political poetry from a future that did not yet exist. Senghor and Césaire proceeded from a belief that imperialism itself, by establishing long-term relations of interdependence between seemingly disparate peoples and places, had created the lived conditions and institutional infrastructure for a new form of transcontinental political association. Just as Marx believed that industrial production had itself opened the door to a postcapitalist form of socialism, they believed that empire itself had created pathways to a postnational form of democracy. In Marxian terms, they recognized empire as federation in alienated form.

As political actors, critical intellectuals, and *engagé* poets, Senghor and Césaire developed a pragmatic and experimental relationship to politics. Rather than make transhistorical claims about intrinsically correct political arrangements, they were open to various possible means to best pursue the desired end of substantive freedom in the world they confronted. At the same time, they practiced a proleptic politics, acting as if seemingly impossible futures were already at hand, precisely by recognizing transformative potentiality within existing arrangements. Their multifaceted interventions illuminate the affinity between immanent critique, political imagination, and poetic knowledge. They envisioned and pursued a possible-impossible decolonization that recognized the underlying uncanniness of imperial France *and* sought to invent a new set of arrangements within which familiar assumptions about here-now-us would be rendered uncanny.

Post–Cold War developments have revealed that there is no necessary relation between state sovereignty and self-determination, let alone between being human and possessing rights. Under such conditions human freedom has again become a public problem for which there is no self-evident institutional solution. However problematic Senghor and Césaire's vision of self-determination without state sovereignty may have been, they sought, through this program, to preempt the very national internationalist world that was in fact established in the postwar period. They rightly feared that such an order would enable powerful territorial states to continue to dominate nominally independent nations for whom genuine economic development, democratic socialism, and international standing would become impossible. Likewise, they recognized that as long as there was an expectation that territory, nationality, and state should align, real democracy in plural societies would be impossible. They refused the false choice between sovereign national states, on the one hand, and either an unaccountable world state or a powerless set of international agencies and ethics, on the other. Their unrealized aim—to ground substantive freedom on a planetary scale by democratizing unavoidable interdependence between former colonies and former metropoles—continues to haunt our world-historical present.

We live in an era when planetary predicaments require planetary politics. The imperative to transcend state sovereignty while protecting popular sovereignty persists. Anti-utopian political realism, subtended by a realist epistemology that reifies inherited conceptions of *here*, *now*, and *us* cannot rise to this challenge. Nor can it help us to grasp the potentiality that may be crystallized within (even failed) internationalist experiments to challenge the structural logic of the given global order. Political realism does not recognize how such concrete utopian efforts could have both recognized *and* refused the world as it actually is. It employs an either/or logic that requires us to decide once and for all whether such internationalist experiments were, or are doomed to be, successes or failures. It forecloses the opportunity to allow such past experiments to illuminate present predicaments. It certainly does not invite us to explore ways to reactivate their unrealized potentiality.

Limitations of Left Realism

A recent essay by Partha Chatterjee, one of our most insightful analysts and forceful critics of colonial politics, illustrates the limitations of this kind of Left realism. Chatterjee usefully reminds us that the dominant currents of twentieth-century internationalism were oriented toward securing national self-determination for all peoples through state sovereignty. These included Soviet-led Communist internationalism and the post-Bandung "internationalism of the nonaligned." Chatterjee contrasts these forms of nationalist internationalism to current forms of liberal internationalism which use a "discourse of human rights to "justify intervention in the sovereign domain of non-Western governments by a global civic community acting on behalf of humanity itself."[18] Chatterjee rightly criticizes the "new forms of imperial power" that are enabled by these invidious types of "international politics" and "cosmopolitan imagining."[19] But he then dismisses cosmopolitan politics as such, denouncing them as the "utopian dream" of "a global intellectual elite located principally in Europe and America."[20] He thus leaves us with a false choice between actually existing liberal cosmopolitanism or sovereign national states.[21] Ultimately, he professes a "realist perspective based on the actual record of history" and declares that "cosmopolitanism as a concept . . . is extremely limited in its historical potential."[22]

On what basis does Chatterjee make such a categorical claim? We might identify three entwined lines of argument. One, as the quotes above indicate, he treats actually existing liberal internationalism as delimiting the horizon of possible cosmopolitan or internationalist projects. He contends that the latter are only the concern of Euro-Americans and inevitably facilitate new imperial relations. The indisputable fact that postwar internationalism and post–Cold War cosmopolitanism have been instrumentalized by Western states and international organizations to reaffirm existing global inequalities leads him to an unqualified defense of national sovereignty as the only legitimate and viable modality of anti-imperialism today.

A second line of argument treats historically contingent achievements as inviolable aims. Chatterjee does not only honor the historic significance of anticolonial freedom struggles for national independence. He claims that "the principal achievement of anti-imperialism in the twentieth century" was "the establishment of a universal civic constitution based on the formal equality of sovereign nation-states" which is institutionally "enshrined principally in the General Assembly of the United Nations."[23] But even if we allow this debatable proposition, we might question Chatterjee's demand that our politics continue to align with these past achievements, however contradictory, calcified, instrumentalized, or anachronistic they may be.

We can agree with Chatterjee that "the equal sovereignty of all member states" enshrined by the UN General Assembly "became the site of the internationalist aspirations of the formerly colonized world."[24] We can recognize the right of national self-determination for colonized peoples as a monumental historical accomplishment. But these should not lead us either to reify postcolonial state sovereignty as a transhistorical political good or denigrate those anticolonial actors who sought to envision nonnational futures. Yet Chatterjee contends that the very attempt to think with Senghor and Césaire about the prospect of federal forms of self-determination within an alternative postnational world "seems to deny not merely the overwhelming structural logic of the new global order as it was unfolding in the period but also . . . the most powerful ideas of collective justice sweeping through the whole world."[25] Isn't there an important difference between denying the reality of a conjuncture and tracing the ways that political struggles sought to reject and overcome that reality? For Chatterjee such concrete utopianism, along with scholarship that attends to it, signals a refusal to see the real world as it actually was (as if actuality proves inevitability).

By sacralizing past achievements, Chatterjee implies that it is naïve or dangerous to act against the general direction in which history has unfolded. This belief feeds a third line of argument. He discounts future-oriented visions of postnational politics on the grounds that their outcomes are uncertain. He recognizes the existence of "global social movements" that "represent a critique of . . . existing institutions of popular sovereignty within the nation-state" and "point to the possibility of a future global order that could possibly transcend one where the nation-state is the normal institutional form of the political."[26] But he criticizes the fact that "the institutional shape of that future" is still quite unclear" and that he himself finds it "hard to describe what that form might be."[27]

He thus discounts these movements on the grounds that they do not offer us a "blueprint" for the world they desire.

The various global social movements I have mentioned often succeed in building broad based coalitions of social forces, cutting across classes and social identities. . . . But they do not . . . present anything like a blueprint for a cosmopolitan global order. The latter can only be found in the writings and saying of a global intellectual elite located principally in Europe and America.[28]

I would suggest that it is an analytic and political mistake to conflate utopian visions of possible worlds with technocratic blueprints of what their specific institutional form should look like. Concrete utopianism is propelled by a dialectic of experimental practices and political imagination, not blueprints that contain prescriptive policies for an unknown future.

Chatterjee also criticizes these Global South solidarity movements on the grounds that they are not likely to succeed and may be instrumentalized by reactionary forces. Anticipating objections to his position, he notes, "It could, of course, be argued that the realist perspective based on the actual record of history is precisely what needs to be overcome and rejected. After all, is it not true that many a great idea that came to exercise a profound impact on history began as a utopian dream?"[29] But in response, he doubles down on his realism: "While that may well be true, the question to ask is: which are the social forces that are likely to drive forward and actualize the utopian idea of cosmopolitanism?"[30] This is certainly a relevant question. We need conjunctural analyses in order to calibrate political strategies to relations of force. A politics that wholly disregards "likelihood" can lead either to premature reconciliation or revolutionary suicide. Both outcomes effectively leave the existing order untouched. But it is quite a leap from treating "likelihood" as an important consideration to fetishizing it as the primary determinant of political vision and strategy. Doing so preemptively concedes the political field to whatever forces are currently more powerful, better organized, or have a more clearly defined program.

These three lines of argument converge in a tacit belief that the given world-historical situation is unsurpassable, that the real is rational. Chatterjee buttresses his statist position by ascribing it, without support, to "popular mobilizations" in Africa and Asia:

> The strongest defense of the historical achievements of popular anticolonial nationalism comes not only from the ruling elites of postcolonial countries, though they may be some of the most cynical advocates. The defense also comes from popular mobilizations that demand from postcolonial nation-states a rapid material improvement in their living standards and livelihood opportunities.[31]

This assertion reinforces the idea that internationalism is somehow intrinsically Western, elite, or liberal. We can agree that existing political communities surely care about defending the historical achievements of anticolonial nationalism. But this neither means that all they *really* want is improved living standards nor that they would be necessarily indifferent to what a world organized around internationalist or cosmopolitan principles might offer. Any number of displaced migrants, refugees, and stateless people would likely have a different view.

But let us concede Chatterjee's assertion that ordinary people in the Global South only want national states to secure their material well-being. Such seemingly realist expectations may actually be unrealistic in a world in which global capitalism and U.S.–UN imperialism render Global South national states—many of whom are only nominally sovereign—incapable of addressing such demands. Under these conditions, a rigid defense of state sovereignty as guarantor of a population's material well-being seems to be the utopian position (in the colloquial sense of the term), while pursuing a new set of arrangements in which self-governing peoples can secure economic security and meaningful autonomy would seem to be a more realistic position.

Chatterjee rightly reminds us that a political generation's hard-won gains are not to be dismissed lightly. Certainly, self-determination and popular sovereignty are precious capacities, indispensable for any attempt to organize a just society and world order. But rather than accept a false choice between self-determination and cosmopolitan internationalism, why not envision ways, under current world-historical conditions, to ground each in the other. The question is not whether to support or reject popular sovereignty as such but to envision arrangements that might now make it possible to realize the kind of meaningful self-management and genuine autonomy that are indexed by self-determination and popular sovereignty. The political challenge of our now is to conjugate self-management and translocal solidarity, autonomy and interdependence, and singularities and relational networks.

Chatterjee neither engages such issues nor suggests that others should. His important critique of liberal internationalism and current discourses of cosmopolitanism could be an entrée to doing so. But he takes such questions off the table. He does not call on Left internationalists to elaborate a fuller vision of a possible cosmopolitan future. He does not ask how the lineaments of that desired future might be glimpsed immanently or emerge dialectically from within existing arrangements. Nor does he exhort Left internationalists to persuade ordinary people that another world order might be worth fighting for. He simply concludes that if outcomes are not guaranteed and a blueprint does not exist, then there is no point to the struggle. *For Left realists, it is always already too late.*[32]

But how can we afford to take off the table cosmopolitan internationalism, postnational democracy, and transnational polities when our world is characterized by imperial wars and occupations, mass displacement and labor diasporas, the criminalization of refugees and migrants, and imminent environmental catastrophe? It has never been more urgent to fashion effective democratic frameworks through which accountability, legality, and justice might be pursued either on scales that exceed the boundaries of any particular political community or within plural polities. How can the good of popular sovereignty be reconciled with the demands of global solidarity or plural democracy? How might we protect a people's right to self-government while recognizing how entwined histories, common futures, and a shared planet implicate seemingly separate peoples in each other's calamities and potentialities? How do we preserve the indisputable benefits of being a full citizen within a democratic political community *and* empower such citizens to make claims on distant actors and agencies whose decisions circumscribe their life chances? Criticism of existing arrangements should be relentless; the dangers of certain alternatives should be specified. But the fact that inventing new internationalist forms will be difficult, risky, and contradictory are reasons *for* taking it seriously as an object of study and aim of praxis. It is precisely because the worldly dilemmas that a cosmopolitan internationalism needs to address are real that mechanical critiques of liberal internationalism from the standpoint of national self-determination are analytically and politically inadequate.

For an Internationalism of Peoples

Chatterjee's state-centric assertions about what people *really* want is belied by the long historical record of radical internationalism among non-Western anti-imperialists and socialists. If space provided, we could follow a line of descent beginning with the internationalist "motley crew" in the early modern period and stretching through Caribbean antislavery insurrections; Haiti's nationalist internationalism; Simón Bolívar's pan–Latin American federalism; Mazzini's Holy Alliance of Peoples; Marx's International Workingmen's Association; the Paris Commune's "universal republic"; anarchist anti-imperial internationalism; the internationalist facet of the Russian Revolution and Bolshevik state; the Soviet-led Communist International, which was increasingly internationalized by African, Asian, and Black American comrades; parallel and intersecting forms of Pan-Africanism (especially in relation to the Italian invasion of Ethiopia); internationalist anticolonial struggles; the Bandung project; Cuban-led Tricontinentalism; further experiments in Afro-Asian cultural solidarity; the Non-Aligned Movement; the World Social Forum; the Zapatista struggle and vision; and the ongoing experiment in Rojava, Syria.[33]

Countless other movements and thinkers could be named. This legacy reminds us that internationalism has never been the exclusive purview of Europeans, liberals, elites, on the one side, nor the Soviet Comintern, on the other.

Such internationalist experiments were pursued against the grain of dominant historical developments and doxa. Their very point was to refuse alignment with the existing *nomos* of the world by forging transversal connections, however ephemeral, tense, or contradictory, across supposedly incommensurable places, peoples, and times. These translocal solidarity practices were always bound up with the provincial forms of statism, territorialism, and domination that they challenged. Rather than choose between self-determination and solidarity, most of these actors struggled to envision forms of internationalism that would not violate the principle of self-managing autonomy. If such experiments were imperfect and short-lived, this was because they were confronting real political dilemmas embedded in concrete historical situations for which there could be no ready-made solutions.

By linking conjunctural analysis and strategic choices to political vision and ultimate aims, they pursued a politics of the possible-impossible. These were not simply idealists who privileged principles over power or fantasy over reality. To insist on a gap between the world as it is given and as it ought to be is not to confuse the latter for the former. These experiments remind us that the opposite of realism is not idealism, but a concrete utopianism that displaces the false dichotomy between realism and idealism.

This is the perspective from which I would like to recall the legacy of Samir Amin. The great Egyptian thinker and activist offers a useful counterpoint to Chatterjee's national statist realism. Amin was a militant anti-imperialist whose conjunctural analyses, political practices, and long-term vision were radically internationalist. This orientation may appear to be an outmoded artifact of a superseded historical epoch. If so, Amin was fiercely anachronistic. Until the end of his life in 2018, he insisted that a new "internationalism of peoples" was the only realistic means of confronting the "worldwide apartheid" created by neoliberal capitalism. Amin underscored that "this stand does not put me among the Third Worldists, as many of my superficial critics concluded, but shows my fundamental stance as a universalist internationalist."[34]

Amin is perhaps best known for his landmark analyses of the relation between accumulation on a world scale, uneven development, and global polarization. This work was informed by decades spent trying to link theory to practice. In 1947 he moved from Egypt to Paris where, through the 1950s, he was an active member of both the French Communist Party and the anti-imperial student movement. During this period, he obtained university degrees in law and politics and wrote a doctoral dissertation in economics on development theory. Rather than pursue a traditional academic career, he served in Egypt's Economic and Development Organization under the Nasser regime (1958 to 1960) and then in Mali's Ministry of Planning under its new socialist president, Modibo Keïta (1960 to 1963). He then accepted a position as professor of political economy at the UN-sponsored Institut Africain de Développement Économique et de Planification (IDEP) in Dakar, of which he later served as director (1970 to 1980).[35]

In his early work, influenced by Maoism and anticipating world-systems theory, Amin demonstrated that "underdevelopment was not a backward phase of development" and that "polarization is not an accident attributable to specific local causes in culture or demography. . . . It is inseparable from actually existing capitalism."[36] It followed that under twentieth-century conditions, colonial countries and Third World nations with weak economies would never be able to pursue the "autocentric" policies that had allowed Europe and the United States to secure their positions at the center of the global capitalist order. On the contrary, they would be compelled to "adjust" their economies to the structural demands of the center and thereby reproduce their subordinate status within the existing global order.

Amin criticized the postwar development ideology that was embraced by Western social democrats, Soviet-oriented Marxists, and Third World nationalists. They all shared what he called a "modernist (hence capitalist and bourgeois) vision" that it was possible to *catch up* to the West economically through accelerated industrialization.[37] Such thinking, for Amin, was crystallized at the 1955 Bandung Conference which assembled newly independent non-Western states. On the one hand, Amin criticizes "the Bandung project" for remaining "trapped in the bourgeois concept of 'closing the historical gap' through participation in the international division of labor."[38] These participants, he contends hoped to improve their positions within the global economic order through national development but did not question the capitalist law of value that was the real source of their persistent underdevelopment.[39] In contrast, Amin believed that these Third World states should "negate" the international division of labor by "delinking" from the dominant system of global capitalism.[40] They might then be able to pursue self-directed, or "autocentric," development strategies oriented toward their own social needs.[41] He argued that economic delinking might enable small powers in peripheral regions to act as "genuine partners" within a "multipolar" world.[42]

On the other hand, Amin praises the "Bandung era" for placing real constraints on the capitalist world system through "strong solidarity among the states of Asia and post-colonial Africa . . . in their political support for the struggles of colonial peoples."[43] He regrets the fact that following the demise of the postwar order, "the South in general no longer has a project of its own."[44] This, at a moment when "the construction of a front among the peoples of the South" is crucial to combat American militarism, to prevent global "apartheid," and to construct "a genuinely multipolar world."[45]

In short, Amin calls for a new "common front of the South" that would both revive the solidarity spirit of the Bandung era and transcend the Bandung project's economic and political limitations. These limitations became even more significant after the end of the Cold War. Amin contends that in the neoliberal era, postcolonial states can no longer purport to be legitimate agents of national development or leaders of an anti-imperialist alliance. His work suggests that old axes of international inequality have shifted in ways that require new anti-imperialist strategies. Given what he calls the "re-compradorization" of the postcolonial periphery combined with new forms of dispossession in the center, it is no longer adequate simply to posit a categorical opposition between the exploiter North and the exploited South. He argues, "All countries in both core and periphery are beset with social contradictions" such that "rulers and ruled do not necessarily have the same perception of internal or external challenges and of the responses that need to be made to them."[46] Amin reminds readers, "The victims of the development of liberal capitalism include the majority in every region of the world. Socialism must be capable of mobilizing this new historical opportunity."[47] Post-Bandung solidarity within and across the Global South could not simply be a function of national unity, shared cultural heritage, or political geography. Nor could this task be ceded to national states. Moreover, a radical internationalism capable of challenging ongoing imperialism and global capitalism could not be confined to the South.

For these reasons, Amin concludes that a straightforward "'remake' of Bandung, uniting peoples behind their governments, is today an illusory prospect. The solidarity that is needed today will have to be built primarily by the peoples themselves."[48] In other words, a revived "common front of the South" would need to be part of a "new internationalism of peoples" understood as a radical political project that cuts across regions and hemispheres.

Amin was never naïvely optimistic that such a project could be easily realized in the post–Cold War period. He recognized that "the unequal development associated with the global spread of capitalism has always presented serious difficulties for the internationalism of peoples."[49] He acknowledges that "the construction of a front among the peoples of the South . . . will be a long and difficult process.[50] He offers no "advance 'recipes' for the shaping of [a] future" that can only be "produced through struggles whose outcome is not known in advance."[51] But, he insists, the undertaking is imperative, for "capitalism is a world system. Its victims can effectively face its challenges only if they are also organized at the global level."[52]

Amin pays special attention to what we might call the difficulties posed by cultural and political diversity. In his view, the task is to overcome harmful divisions without erasing cultural differences or minimizing political ones. He calls this work "organizing convergence while respecting diversity."[53] He thus emphasizes that a new internationalism will require maximum respect for cultural diversity within and across potential solidarity partners. Yet he warns against the forms of "culturalism" employed by ethnic, nationalist, and fundamentalist religious movements that fetishize "inherited diversity."[54] Because such movements, he explains, often criticize Western imperialism without engaging "the logic of internal conflict" within their own societies, "they end up counterposing a 'nation' stripped of contradictions to 'the outside world.'"[55]

They reify cultural unity while eliding internal sociopolitical divisions in ways that often collude, however unwittingly, with the interests of global capital and Western imperialism. The North, he reminds us, essentializes differences, treats other societies as self-identical wholes, and works to keep the peoples of the South divided. Amin notes that "what is called the 'clash of civilizations' is, in reality, a political strategy developed systematically by the collective imperialism of the triad."[56] When "the social movements on the side of the victims adopt" this discourse, he explains, they "contribute to making [the clash] a reality."[57] He thus warns against "reactionary forces" that "exert systematic efforts to legitimize conflicts of cultures . . . supposedly based on invariants transmitted by historical heritage, particularly religious ones."[58] In contrast, "the internationalism of peoples must fight these cultural interpretations" by foregrounding "the modern era's true conflict of cultures" which is "between the values of socialism and the culture of capitalism."[59] Accordingly, he calls for a "humanist alternative to worldwide apartheid" that does not "feed on nostalgic delusions" but seeks "to construct a new, postcapitalist form based on real equality among peoples, communities, states and individuals."[60]

Likewise, Amin praises efforts by the anti-imperial Left to embrace political diversity in the service of internationalist politics. He invites militant movements to welcome the "confrontation between different viewpoints" and counsels against the temptation to "excommunicate . . . unbelievers."[61] This entails the difficult work of collaborating with allies who may emphasize different issues, from the standpoint of other ideological frameworks, grounded in diverse cultural assumptions and value systems, with varying degrees of radicalism. In this way, Amin challenges dogmatic tendencies among orthodox Marxists and sectarian socialists.

At the same time, he seems to be warning emerging forces, such as the altergobalization movement, that their inclusiveness risked devolving into liberal pluralism.[62] Like his World Social Forum comrades, Amin appreciated that the multiplicity of antisystemic forces in the post–Cold War moment was a great boon for the Left. They opened new possibilities for translocal alliances that could garner mass support and pursue struggles on multiple fronts. He also recognized that the dominant order provokes and profits from conflicts among the oppressed. But he had no patience for those in these movements who renounced political judgment and made a virtue of inclusivity as such. When he calls for movements to create broad alliances between revolutionary and center-Left participants, he is not suggesting that all actors and groups should be included in a given coalition regardless of their ideology and aims. On the contrary, he warns against including "reactionary movements," however popular, "that are not working to build a 'different' (for example, a multipolar) world."[63] Amin insisted that Left movements have a responsibility to establish criteria for inclusion and to exercise political judgment about potential allies. Solidarity, he insisted, should only be extended to groups that "support . . . struggles working for social progress," whose economic policies are based on "social objectives" and will be pursued through "democratic methods."[64] Conversely, he argues that a demand "is clearly reactionary, and serves the aims of dominant capital, if it presents itself as [being] 'without a social program' . . . claims not to be 'hostile to globalization' . . . [or that it is] alien to the idea of democracy (on the grounds that [democracy] is 'Western.')"[65]

We may not accept Amin's political metric. But he makes the important point that "it is not possible to dispense with detailed analysis and criteria of judgment that only have meaning in relation to the viewpoint of *a plan for the society that one is attempting to promote.*"[66] Creating a multipolar, democratic, and socialist world requires not only "profound and systematic debate," but "a clear choice of objectives and the organization of appropriate campaigns of action."[67] He warns, "The mere accumulation of demands by victims of the systems, though perfectly legitimate, does not constitute either an alternative (which calls for political coherence) or even a strategy for advance."[68] Amin insists that Left internationalism cannot avoid exercising leadership, creating institutions, or engaging with labor unions and peasant organizations (despite their past limitations). Above all, this canny critic insists that a new internationalism of peoples must be informed by a vision of "the world we wish to see."

Against a new generation of activists who believed that it was possible to "change the world without taking power," Amin called for the "movement to become . . . materialized in a party that could respond to the challenge of our era."[69] A *new internationalism of peoples would require a new International capable of organizing convergence while respecting cultural and political diversity, one that would avoid the pitfalls of culturalism, dogmatism, liberal pluralism, and horizontalism.*

Amin's critical analysis and utopian vision indeed converged in his bold call for a new Fifth International that could "provide an effective framework for the construction of the unity necessary for . . . the struggles undertaken by peoples against capital."[70] Given what he regarded as the historic limitations of the Second and Third Internationals, on the one hand, and Bandung statism on the other, Amin instructs, "The Fifth International should not be an assembly exclusively of political parties, but should gather all peoples' movements of resistance and struggle and guarantee both their voluntary participation in the construction of joint strategies and the independence of their own decision making."[71]

A Fifth International would require and enable a new "front of the peoples of the South" through which "to bring about the convergence of struggles of peasants, women, workers, the unemployed, informal workers, and democratic intellectuals."[72] Such an organization would also require and enable new forms of North-South solidarity. He writes,

> The objective of the Fifth International . . . is to contribute to the
> construction of the internationalism of peoples. Note that the phrase
> refers to all peoples, North and South, just as it refers not only to the
> proletariat but to all working classes and strata that are victims of
> the system, to humanity as a whole, threatened in its survival. This
> internationalism does not preclude strengthening the solidarity of the
> peoples of the three continents (Africa, Asia, Latin America) against
> aggression from the imperialism of the triad. On the contrary, these
> two internationalisms can only complement and reinforce each other.
> The solidarity of the peoples of the North and South cannot be based
> on charity, but on joint action against imperialism.[73]

Most immediately, this Fifth International would contest Western militarism and neoliberal hegemony. Its ultimate aim is to overcome imperial capitalism and create a polycentric world as part of a "long transition to world socialism."[74] This is the perspective from which Amin identifies himself as a "universalist internationalist" and calls for a "humanist alternative to worldwide apartheid."

Certainly, Amin's analysis begs many questions. He is too quick to dismiss all forms of political Islam as reactionary fundamentalism. The standpoint from which to determine whether a movement is "working for social progress" is not self-evident. And of course, the task of "organizing convergence while respecting diversity" is no straightforward matter. (We might usefully understand the latter as a calling for the kind of practices of translation I discuss in the next chapter.)

It would be easy to dismiss Amin's archaic language and expansive hopes, easy to wrinkle brows at his identification with a "humanist" and "universalist" socialism or to roll eyes at his extravagant call for a Fifth International. But our current reluctance to recall traditions of radical universalism and radical humanism—the fact that nonliberal and nonabstract forms of universalism are not legible to so many Left critics today—is a loss. Influential currents of critical theory today have made it difficult for young thinkers to recognize militant anti-imperialists as "universalists" or "humanists." Such terms, if not the very project of socialist internationalism, are too often disqualified as historically superseded or insufficiently attentive to how solidarity politics may reproduce racial and imperial hierarchies. Conversely, recent scholars who *are* enthusiastic about internationalism often look nostalgically to earlier experiments in Afro-Asian solidarity, without asking difficult questions about the bourgeois character of the Bandung project or the statist character of the Tricontinental project.

Samir Amin cuts across these positions. He was a fierce critic of the entwined power of global capitalism and imperialism who critiqued Marxism's unexamined Eurocentrism *and* Third Worldism's uncritical culturalism. Amin's work challenges both those Eurocentric Marxists who do not adequately attend to the imperial polarization propelled by capitalist accumulation and those anti-imperialists who bracket the social polarization produced by capitalism in the West. When he calls on Left critics to recognize the contradictions that exist *within all societies* in order to envision new alliances among popular forces in both the North and the Global South, he implicitly reiterates Lenin's call to transform the imperial war into a civil war.

The center of gravity of Amin's thinking shifted over the years from delinking to multipolartity to a Fifth International. But he continued to identify with a tradition of anti-imperial socialist internationalism. His engagement with a changing present was refracted through unrealized past possibilities. Said differently, he developed immanent critiques of the First International, the Bandung project, and the World Social Forum; he identified aspects of each that pointed beyond their actually existing forms. This allowed him to translate insights from these earlier moments of struggle to the neoliberal conjuncture. Amin looked to the past without insisting on orthodoxy or slipping into melancholy. He regarded earlier iterations of international socialism and anti-imperialist internationalism as resources from which to anticipate—to envision, enact, and pursue—the world we wish to see.

At the same time, Amin's internationalist analyses, political projects, and utopian vision were nourished by decades of practical work as an activist-intellectual located primarily in Dakar. As director of the IDEP, he transformed a school for the technical training of African development economists into an influential center for continent-wide research and debate about global political economy and alterative visions of African development. Hoping to challenge the hegemony of French development orthodoxy and "to break the isolation in which colonialism had encircled Africa," Amin organized two major gatherings of African intellectuals with, first, Latin American dependency theorists (in Dakar 1972) and then Asian (primarily Indian, Indonesian, and Malayan) social scientists (in Tannarive 1974).[75] Amin recalls that the institute became both a hub of intellectual ferment and a site for consultative visits from governments, African regional institutions, and Third World organizations including the nonaligned Group of 77. Amin also used his position as director to create the Conseil pour le développement de la recherche en sciences sociales en Afrique (CODESRIA) and the Third World Forum, both located in Dakar. These were meant to protect and extend the work he initiated at IDEP, which was increasingly threatened by anti-Left U.S. administrators who had some oversight of the program.

Amin envisioned CODESRIA as an African analogue to the anti-imperialist Latin American Council of the Social Sciences (CLASCO) founded in 1967. The Third World Forum would be even more ambitious. With colleagues in Africa, Asia, and Latin America, Amin persuaded Salvador Allende to host a planning meeting in Santiago, Chile, in 1973. The new organization was officially launched at a meeting the following year in Karachi, Pakistan. On the one hand, the Third World Forum was to be an alternative to the World Bank's "Society for International Development," which espoused "the mainstream economics of market liberalism."[76] On the other hand, Amin regarded this network as extending while also correcting some limitations of earlier efforts of the Afro-Asian Peoples Solidarity Organization, created by the Non-Aligned Movement (NAM) in 1958, and the Tricontinental, created by the Cuban state in 1966.

The Third World Forum was first organized around three regional bureaus in Asia, Africa, and Latin America. Amin was responsible for coordinating their relationship with each other. Describing the Forum's initial orientation as "Third World nationalist," he recalls,

> The first aim was to give critical Third World thinkers the means to begin correcting the fundamental imbalance within all international bodies, where the world is always seen from the North. A different perspective had to be opened up, and a pluralist critique developed of 'Eurocentrism' . . . Marxist currents obviously had their place within this, but so did other approaches. The main thing was to avoid imprisonment in any orthodoxy; our ambition was to become . . . a center for critical debate.[77]

A few basic criteria held that participants must be: Third World nationals, interdisciplinary thinkers rather than overly specialized academics or development technocrats, and "critical." The latter meant recognizing, first, that the expanding capitalist world system was not favorable to Third World development and, second, that development had to be popular, serving the needs of whole populations. As its work deepened through subregional branches and focused working groups, so did the Forum's internationalist orientation.

Amin recounts that the group's diverse activities were united by a "methodological choice" to treat "each region of the world as part of an integrated system . . . the principal unit of analysis is ultimately always the world system."[78] Each country was analyzed "within the broader 'Third World,' itself a component of the world system," whose historical evolution was also examined.[79] This entailed close attention to "the emergence of qualitatively new forms of polarization . . . to the new kinds of 'social movement,' and to the evolution of ideological debates (increased salience of cultural and religious dimensions, etc.)."[80] Intellectually, the overarching aim was "to study 'the world as seen from the South,' rather than 'the South in the World'" and thereby "challenge the North's monopoly on theoretical reflection concerning globalization and its uneven impact on its geographical components."[81]

In 1980 Amin left the IDEP to direct the Third World Forum. This became an important matrix and medium for Amin's political vision of how a "pluricentric and democratic world system" was integral to "the long transition to world socialism."[82] The Third World Forum participated in the creation of the broader World Forum for Alternatives forged at a 1997 meeting in Cairo. Two years later, with Amin as chair, this group organized a surprise "anti-Davos" gathering adjacent to the neoliberal World Economic Forum meeting in Switzerland. It included "committed intellectuals and figures from mass movements in the five continents."[83] This event became the basis for a more enduring network of networks, the World Social Forum, which was inaugurated in Porto Alegre, Brazil, in January 2001, with Amin as one of the cofounders. All of these efforts were based on the recognition that "capitalism has built a world system and can really be overcome only at the level of the planet" through "a united front against social and international injustice."[84]

During the aughts, Amin was among those who worked from within the hyper-inclusive World Social Forum to push it further left. This aim is expressed in the Porto Alegre Manifesto (2005) — subtitled, "Twelve Proposals for Another Possible World" — and the Bamako Appeal (2006), which emphasizes the forms of worldwide solidarity and internationalism necessary to realize these aims.[85]

Understanding that many Left critics will dismiss both this vision and hope, Amin notes, "The strongest argument for pessimism about the future is based on the lack of visible subjects capable of undertaking the necessary historical transformation."[86] But he refuses the realist defeatism that draws political conclusions based on immediate appearances: "The optimist that I am will reply that active subjects appear only for relatively brief periods in history, when a favorable combination of circumstances allows the different logics of social existence . . . to converge. . . . At such moments . . . impossible to predict in advance, potential subjects may crystallize into decisive agents of change."[87]

By calling for a common front of the South that may form the basis of a more expansive internationalism of peoples in order to envision the world we wish to see, Amin points beyond the limitations of political realism. He recognizes that post–Cold War developments made the project of socialist internationalism only more imperative. He was not an idealist who privileged principles over power or fantasy over reality. He was a critical political economist who placed a premium on political imagination. He sought to link conjunctural analysis and strategic choices to political vision and ultimate aims. In other words, he called on militants to pursue the possible-impossible. His life work emphasizes that despite the evident difficulties, a concrete utopian internationalism of peoples through which to overcome imperial capitalism and create a polycentric, democratic, and socialist world is the only "realistic" option, given the threat to humanity posed by neoliberal capitalism today. This is the standpoint from which Amin demanded that we *revive and rework* the spirit of Bandung for new times.

In order to hasten alternative futures through solidarity practices and produce solidarity relations by envisioning alternative futures, we need to displace the nexus linking realist epistemology to political realism.[88] But in times of systemic crisis and reaction, such as we now confront globally, the appeal of political realism intensifies among frightened liberals and beleaguered Leftists. Think of how the U.S. Democratic Party warns that unless we support moderate, centrist, and "electable" candidates, the Right will continue to triumph. Similarly, liberal commentators challenged the credibility of radical popular movements such as Occupy Wall Street and Black Lives Matter on the realist grounds that they have no clear policy goals, electoral prospects, or even desire for governmental power. Political realism also informs the Left Brexit position which concludes that, because the European Union serves to reproduce neoliberal conditions and norms, political autarchy is a radical move. A similar realism buttresses those who argue that the Greek debt crisis proved that national state sovereignty is the only effective protection against postnational political experiments, which are necessarily imperial. A different conclusion would be that the European Union was always a technocratic instrument of neoliberal accumulation organized along bureaucratic-statist principles, rather than a real experiment in popular federal democracy. Left realism suffuses the national-statist visions of anti-neoliberal politicians like Jeremy Corbyn of the British Labour Party and Jean-Luc Mélenchon of the French Left Party. Such realism may also be recognized in the fateful choice by Hugo Chavez and Nicolás Maduro in Venezuela to enter into financial partnerships with Western oil companies in the service of a policy of massive resource extraction in order to fund Chavismo social redistribution projects.[89]

Varieties of anti-utopian political realism also run through diverse currents of recent critical theory. In the following chapters, I will explore two of these tendencies, which I call Left culturalism and Left presentism. We have already seen how Chatterjee's realist critique of cosmopolitan internationalism links a culturalist claim that solidarity practices necessarily enable imperial arrangements to a presentist claim that it is dangerous or naïve to envision another possible world. Such thinking erects a disabling boundary between the possible and the impossible.

3
Practicing Translation
Beyond Left Culturalism

Much of what passes for radical and critical thought rests on the
notion that the very aspiration toward translocal solidarity, community,
and interconnection is tainted.

— PAUL GILROY

One way to begin thinking about "organizing convergence while respecting
diversity" is through a practice of translation that makes the familiar strange
and the strange familiar. The task is to do so in ways that emphasize both
the irreducible gap and possible relation between strangeness and familiarity.
This potential affinity between translation practices and solidarity politics is
foreclosed by currents of Left culturalism whose important attention to cultural singularity often leads to a quasi-ontological insistence on categorically
incommensurable forms of life. This tendency to ontologize cultural differ-
exnces is evident in their one-sided critique of translation (or solidarity) as an
instrument of racial or imperial subordination. After outlining this tendency,
I will engage other thinkers who elaborate understandings of translation as
a critical practice oriented toward the creation of differential unities. From
this angle of view, translation could serve as both medium and model for the
solidarity practices that Amin's "internationalism of peoples" would require.

From the Incommensurable to the Untranslatable

The recent discourse of Afro-Pessimism exemplifies the way an insistence on
ontological incommensurability implies a presentist assumption that current
conditions are unsurpassable. Frank Wilderson, the thinker who has elab-

orated this position most forcefully, declares, "The structure of the entire world's semantic field—regardless of cultural or national discrepancies . . . is sutured by anti-Black solidarity. . . . Afro-Pessimism explores the meaning of Blackness . . . as a structural position of noncommunicability in the face of all other positions."[1] He insists on a "profound and irreconcilable difference" not only between Black and non-Black experience, but between anti-Blackness and all other forms of white supremacy.[2] Jared Sexton, another influential advocate who identifies this position as a "theorem of political ontology," writes,

> Afro-Pessimism is thus not against the politics of coalition simply because coalitions tend systematically to render supposed common interests as the concealed particular interests of the most powerful and privileged elements of the alliance. Foremost, Afro-Pessimism seeks, in Wilderson's parlance, "to shit on the inspiration of the personal pronoun *we*" because coalitions require a logic of identity and difference, of collective selves modeled on the construct of the modern individual, an entity whose coherence is purchased at the expense of whatever is cast off by definition. . . . The ever-expansive inclusionary gesture must thus be displaced by another more radical approach: ethics of the real, a politics of the imperative, engaged in its interminably downward movement.[3]

From this perspective, Sexton criticizes "'the hope creed' characteristic of those engaging the politics of everyday life through the assumption of a general consensus disrupted by conflict."[4] In contrast, he identifies Afro-Pessimism with "a certain conjuring of spirit, or attitude, of those still willing to fight for what is right and necessary rather than simply in the immediate interest."[5]

The radical implications of the Afro-Pessimist starting point are evident and welcome. If anti-Blackness is woven into the very fabric of the contemporary social order, Black humanity can only be realized by abolishing that order. But transhistorical claims about anti-Blackness as "the structure of the entire world's semantic field—regardless of cultural or national discrepancies," do not allow for the kind of openings that this aim would require. Moreover, because these Afro-Pessimists do not specify the locus of this anti-Black ontology, it is difficult for readers to understand what overcoming it might entail. Is the aim to abolish actually existing U.S. society? The West? Racial capitalism? Modern forms of consciousness and their underlying epistemologies? Also unclear is what the aim of such a revolutionary struggle would be. What kind of world do they wish to see? Such questions relate directly to their rejection of coalition politics on the basis of "ontological incommunicability." We are left with an unspecified "ethics of the real" as the basis for an antipolitical politics.

Are all solidarity practices necessarily based on a "hope creed" that assumes general consensus? At what cost can any subaltern community preemptively and categorically reject the prospect of an intersectional "we"? If we accept that racism and capitalism are indissociably entwined, and if we recognize the planetary character of racial capitalism, the radical struggle against anti-Blackness demanded by Afro-Pessimism would have to entail solidarity and internationalism.

Afro-Pessimism's ontological orientation is a more explicit and hyperbolic iteration of the culturalism that runs through some recent currents of postcolonial thinking. A first generation of postcolonial critique tended to deconstruct the dubious categorial distinctions upon which colonial ideology and imperial power rested.[6] But a second generation of postcolonial scholarship began to treat abstract universalism as the primary modality of (post)colonial domination and to treat concrete particularity (e.g., local communities, cultures, and consciousness) as the self-evident standpoint from which to challenge it. As a result, such thinking often emphasized, even ontologized, categorial, cultural, or civilizational differences between Western and non-Western peoples. Incommensurability and untranslatability become privileged arms in the fight against Eurocentrism.

Consider Dipesh Chakrabarty's influential argument about the distinction between what he calls "History 1" and "History 2."[7] He identifies the former with abstracting and universalizing forces of Western capitalism and imperialism that seek to eradicate or assimilate any differences they encounter. He identifies History 2 with concrete forms of life (cultural practices, beliefs, categories) that are incommensurable with and inassimilable to the universalizing logics of capitalism and imperialism. Chakrabarty argues that the forces comprising History 1 regularly encounter the phenomena of History 2, which they can never fully grasp, assimilate, or eradicate. He thus posits the existence of essentially different kinds of history that are external to one another even as they encounter and interrupt each other.[8]

At another level, Chakrabarty argues that because the Western human sciences view the world from the standpoint of History 1, they misrecognize or disavow the singularity of the culturally specific phenomena that comprise History 2. By seeking to "translate" such singular objects into supposedly universal categories, these forms of knowledge extend the violent abstracting work of capitalism and imperialism. At the same time, he argues, they obscure (or cannot recognize) the fact that such categories are themselves rooted in provincial European experiences and assumptions.

Chakrabarty's call to "provincialize Europe" and its ways of knowing is an indispensable intervention that has rightly influenced a generation of scholars interested in historicizing supposedly universal categories and experiences. But it also reifies the very dichotomies — universal/particular, abstract/concrete, capitalism/culture, center/periphery — that also need to be historicized as instruments of capitalist and imperial domination. In Chakrabarty's framework, the constitutive entanglements between History 1 (primarily identified with the West) and History 2 (primarily identified with the non-West) are elided. This analysis leads to a one-dimensional view of the universalizing West that is counterposed to self-identical Heideggerian lifeworlds.[9] We are left with something like the ethnological concept of culture that early postcolonial thinking had rejected.

A similar current of culturalism may be identified in Talal Asad's influential writings about Islamic tradition. Asad challenges the secular, liberal, Western discourse that consigns Islamic beliefs, practices, worldviews, and societies to a prerational, unchanging, and dogmatic tradition to which adherents are blindly obedient. He rejects the widespread Western assumption that Islamic tradition is based on the singular truths of sacred texts or a theological dogma decreed by (opportunistic or despotic) religious authorities. In contrast, he treats Islam as a discursive tradition that is characterized by intergenerational conflict, debate, persuasion, and revision. Shifting attention from theology and belief to everyday practice and lived experience, Asad also treats Islam as an embodied tradition; it mediates and is mediated by concrete ways of life (subjectivities, dispositions, sensibilities, conduct, norms, institutions, etc.). He thereby emphasizes that Islamic tradition is no less critical and self-reflexive than secular liberalism purports to be. Conversely, Asad demonstrates that despite its claim to have overcome tradition through reason, secular liberalism is itself an embodied form of life rooted in a concrete tradition.[10]

This incisive critique does not only challenge the self-congratulatory and hypocritical discourses that Western liberals employ, often to justify exclusion or violence, against Islam. It also challenges many of the binaries — modern/traditional, reason/culture, secular/religious — that ground Western forms of knowledge. But Asad's analysis also implies a civilizational divide between Western and Islamic traditions that calls to mind History 1 and History 2. It recognizes that Islam as a form of life is internally contested. But it does not attend to the heterogeneous character — the processes of cultural, religious, and ideological multiplicity and mixture — of societies in which Islam actually exists. It cannot easily accommodate, for example, Islamic Marxists or feminists who may challenge the same forms of conservative piety or political Islam that Western liberals do but on different grounds and for different aims. Asad's account implies (and many of his epigones suggest more directly) that to question certain forms of pious conservatism and culturalism is to endorse liberal secularism. Ultimately, we are left with a categorical distinction between Western and Islamic ways of life as incommensurable and untranslatable.

Such culturalist thinking is even more pronounced in Walter Mignolo's influential writings about decolonial epistemology. His argument builds upon Anibal Quijano's important analysis of the "coloniality of power" in which the interlinked forces of racism, colonialism, and capitalism form the substrate of a worldwide modernity that stands in a mutually reinforcing relationship with Eurocentric forms of knowledge.[11] Quijano challenged orthodox Marxism from a Latin American Marxian perspective. He explained that capitalism there always also contained quasi-feudal arrangements. It produced neither a proletarian majority nor a unified working class. Because Latin American social classes are racially inflected, he explains, national independence never led to a bourgeois democratic society. From this perspective, he challenged any conception of the linear transition from feudalism, through bourgeois capitalism, to socialism. Quijano concludes that a revolutionary "socialization of power" would require overcoming not only the bourgeois state and market, but racism, the "coloniality of labor," and Eurocentric epistemology.

Mignolo takes up Quijano's important project to decolonize knowledge. But he reduces Quijano's revolutionary project to "epistemic disobedience."[12] Mignolo's "decolonial delinking" transposes what Quijano regarded as a crucial epistemic-political struggle *within* an entangled colonial situation into categorical claims about incommensurable difference *between* Western and non-Western epistemologies or civilizations. Mignolo distinguishes his "decolonial thinking" from postcolonial critique.[13] But by "unveiling the regional foundations of universal claims to truth as well as the categories of thought and the logic that sustain all branches of Western knowledge," it seems to align with Chakrabarty's project.[14] Like him and Asad, Mignolo insists that all ways of knowing are bound up with particular ways of living. But he grounds this important insight in a reductive dictum: "I am where I think."[15] In so doing, he elevates into a "basic epistemic principle" the very cultural and territorial ontology that allowed colonial power to racially define and rank peoples and regions.[16] Mignolo rightly challenges a colonizing logic that disavows non-European ways of living and knowing. But he links this claim to a dubious conception of self-identical cultural subjects and civilizational wholes. It is difficult to understand how he can reconcile such categorical thinking with his promising invocations of "puriversality as a universal project," a polycentric "world in which many worlds would coexist," "border thinking," and "inter-cultural . . . or inter-epistemic dialogue."[17]

Mignolo also distinguishes Marxism, which he defines as "the struggle against capitalism," from "the decolonial option," which he defines as a project of "delinking from Westernization."[18] He opposes "Marxism focused on class struggle" from "decolonialism" which focuses "on the racism that justified the exploitation of labor in European colonies."[19] We should recall that Quijano did not reduce Marxism to a critique of capitalism focused exclusively on class struggle. Nor did he gloss his focus on the coloniality of modern knowledge and power as a one-sided call to delink from Westernization. Rather, like Mariátegui, he sought to compel Marxism beyond mechanical materialism to attend to the racism, imperialism, and Eurocentric forms of knowledge that anchor modern forms of capitalist domination.

Not surprisingly, Mignolo's culturalism leads him to indigenous epistemologies as the locus for decolonial delinking. His civilizational ontology requires him to identify an outside of coloniality as a standpoint of critique. Like Chakrabarty and Asad, he reduces the modern to the West, the West to white, and the white West to an all-encompassing liberalism. This operation leaves us with a monocultural West and a one-dimensional modernity that can only be criticized from the standpoint of categorical cultural difference.[20]

I am not suggesting that the West should be defended. My point is that such approaches elide internal heterogeneity and contradictions. They disregard processes of historical, sociocultural, and epistemological entanglement, mixture, and mutual implication. Their way of figuring globality differs fundamentally from a Marxian understanding of unevenness within a differential and asymmetrical unity (i.e., the capitalist world system). Thinkers like Samir Amin and Anibal Quijano were no less critical of the Eurocentric universalism that underlies liberal and orthodox Marxist understandings of linear, progressive, teleological history. But they recognize what Chakrabarty refers to as History 1 and History 2 as one-sided aspects of a single but nonidentical world-historical process. Their work demonstrates how capitalism is not only able to accommodate supposedly incommensurable differences (i.e., noncapitalist modes of production and forms of life) but also requires and thrives on them.[21] From this perspective it is not possible to maintain a categorical distinction between an abstract, universal, Western history that is propelled by capitalism and concrete, particular, non-Western histories that are simply rooted in embodied forms of life. Nor is it possible to ignore the long-standing traditions of anticolonial internationalism among non-Western radicals, many of whom were heterodox Marxists. Indeed, such political traditions call into question supposedly self-evident boundaries between distinct ways of life as well as what it means to be a "member of a tradition."

This culturalist orientation is evident in these thinkers' one-sided critique of translation as a violent operation whereby incommensurable differences are reduced to a transparent sameness through the mediation of an abstract universal metric that produces a false equivalence.[22] Certainly, any engagement with the politics of translation must recognize these critical insights into translation as an instrument of colonial domination and cultural hegemony. Such work usefully attends to how—in confrontations between stronger or majoritarian and weaker or minoritarian languages, especially under conditions of colonial and racial inequality—translation can reproduce hierarchies. In such situations, the forces of domination seek to know subjugated people (through translation) in order to better dominate them. The latter are compelled directly or indirectly to conform to dominant linguistic and cultural norms. At a deeper epistemological level this work challenges any notion of translation premised on an idea that there can be a seamless transparency across texts, languages, or cultures. Such an approach to translation will lead, at best, to misunderstanding. More dangerously, such practices of translation become integral to power/knowledge regimes that sustain forms of racial and colonial domination.

But what conclusions should we draw from this important critique? Should we reduce dense networks of social relations that often traverse any number of supposed social and cultural boundaries to delimited traditions or forms of life? Should we try to distill what seem to be universal aspects of social life from what is singular and essentially untranslatable in order to erect a categorical boundary between essentially different types of history—one that is abstract and universal and the other that is concrete and particular? Should we pursue a program of "epistemic delinking" in order to erect rigid boundaries between Western and non-Western epistemologies?

I would argue that the tendency to address the problem of translation by making ontological claims about languages, cultures, and lifeworlds is analytically dubious and politically limiting. The critical challenge is to insist on entanglement and attend to impurity while respecting, even producing, singularities. Are there practices of translation that can recognize incommensurables, refuse to posit false equivalences, and renounce the existence of an abstract universal metric while forging mutually illuminating connections across real differences? Should we not attend to how translation may work precisely to identify, not erase, moments of opacity and incommensurability as starting points for solidarity politics that do the same?

We can usefully route such questions through the remarkable and influential *Dictionary of Untranslatables*, a grand collective project edited by the French philologist and philosopher Barbara Cassin. The *Dictionary* seeks to provincialize supposed universals—in this case, philosophical concepts— from the standpoint of *untranslatability*. It, too, provides a critique of what we might call the fallacy of misplaced equivalence. Most immediately, Cassin challenges the cultural hegemony of English as the common language of the European community. More fundamentally, she challenges analytic philosophy's assumption that there are universal concepts that transcend linguistic and historical specificity. In this line of thinking, because language is supposed to be neutral and concepts universal, the latter can be seamlessly translated into any language without semantic damage or philosophical consequences.

Against global English and analytic philosophy, Cassin contends that languages do not simply reflect the given world. Rather, "the perspectives constitute the thing; each language is a vision of the world that catches another world in its net, that performs a world."[23] Likewise, words do not simply refer to transhistorical concepts. "The universality of concepts is absorbed by the singularity of languages."[24] This means that concepts are always embedded in and assume meanings through specific languages, semantic networks, and historical situations.

On these grounds, Cassin's *Dictionary* seeks to "make perceptible another way of doing philosophy, which does not think of the concept without thinking of the word, for there is no concept without a word."[25] Philosophy must attend to the dynamic relationships between concept, word, and world. By examining the meaning of supposedly universal concepts in specific languages, as well as the modifications undergone in their movement across languages, the *Dictionary* productively introduces the problem of translation into the practice of philosophy.

> We have tried to think of philosophy *within* languages [. . .] In order to find the meaning of a word in one language, this book explores the networks to which the word belongs and seeks to understand how a network functions in one language by relating it to the networks of other languages [. . .] from one language to another, neither the words nor the conceptual networks can simply be superimposed. . . . Each entry thus starts from a nexus of untranslatability and proceeds to a comparison of terminological networks.[26]

For Cassin, understanding is not simply a matter of placing meaning in context. It requires us to reconsider context itself by tracing linguistic and semantic "crossings, transfers, and forks in the road . . . turnings, fractures, and carriers."[27] It requires attention both to the multiplicity of languages and to multiplicities *within* any given language.

This interest in dynamic processes of crossings, transfers, and fractures distinguishes Cassin's untranslatable from Chakrabarty's seemingly similar conception of the incommensurable. Cassin explains that the *Dictionary* is opposed *both* to the "logical universalism" of the analytic philosophers that is "indifference to language" and to the kind of "ontological nationalism" promoted by Herder and Heidegger which "essentializ[es] the spirit of language."[28] She writes, "Our work is as far as could be from such a sacralization of the untranslatable, based on the idea of an absolute incommensurability of languages."[29] Cassin underscores, "To speak of *untranslatables* in no way implies that the terms in question, or the expressions, the syntactical or grammatical turns, are not and cannot be translated: The untranslatable is rather what one keeps on (not) translating."[30]

Once again, the question is what we should conclude from Cassin's powerful formulation of translation as *what one keeps on (not) translating*. At one point she declares, "Babel is an opportunity."[31] But she does not develop this promising idea. She is more concerned with how the attempt to translate untranslatables across languages "creates a problem."[32] Her focus, certainly important, is on challenging erroneous assumptions about abstract concepts, neutral language, and transparent equivalence. She wants to interrupt philosophy's misrecognitions and mistaken impositions. The *Dictionary* gives pause to those who assume that translation is not a problem. But, however implicitly, it still regards translation as a problem — an unavoidable obstacle or necessary evil. In contrast, I would like to consider a constellation of thinkers who treat the dangers of translation as a starting point for analysis rather than the aim of critique. They may help us to more directly embrace *Babel as an opportunity*.

Babel as Opportunity

Cassin invokes Gilles Deleuze's conception of deterritorialization to support her understanding of the untranslatable as "what one keeps on (not) translating." But I read this as a Derridean formulation which displaces any easy binary between territorialized and deterritorialized thinking. Recall that for Derrida, the biblical Tower of Babel story figures translation as both necessary and impossible, as something that God, through the imposition of linguistic plurality among humans, both demands and prohibits.[33] Derrida challenges the conventional dream of translation as seamless equivalence "without remnants."[34] On the contrary, his work suggests that every utterance, even within a given language, must both cross and create the gaps that characterize translation. Demonstrating how singular proper names and iterable common nouns always presuppose one another, Derrida deconstructs the supposed opposition between translatability and untranslatability. Arguing that each is always the condition of possibility of the latter, he figures translation as an inescapable aspect of signification that operates within and across languages.[35]

Derrida crystallizes this orientation in seemingly paradoxical declarations such as, "One never writes either in one's own language or in a foreign language" and "I only have one language and it is not mine."[36] These are abstract philosophical formulations that also describe concrete historical situations and lived experience. In *Monolingualism of the Other*, Derrida relates the singularity of his own predicament as an Algerian Jew whose only language is French. He recounts being triply alienated: from his Jewish (linguistic) heritage, his (Arabic or Berber speaking) Maghreb milieu, and metropolitan France (which, despite his being a Francophone, remained utterly foreign to him). In the eyes of the French state he was a colonized "native" whose citizenship was conditional and revocable (as was proven during the Vichy Occupation). This situation, shared by colonized peoples and subaltern groups around the world, provides the ground for what Derrida calls the two-sided "law of translation": "1. We only ever speak one language. 2. We never speak only one language."[37]

Derrida's reflections underscore that this "law," along with the predicament it embodies, is both an oppressive burden and a subversive opportunity. He relates how as a student in Algiers and Paris he was driven to master French, a language that could never fully be his own. Paradoxically, his "hyperbolic taste for the purity of language," which included an attempt to erase any hint of idiomatic foreignness from his own speech and writing, led him to develop a singular style that made his written French subversively uncanny. It was at once utterly correct (familiar) and idiomatically singular (strange).[38] Like Aimé Césaire, he challenged his (post)colonial predicament through a kind of excessive correctness. This strategy opened the path to a critical method through which a given language or text may be recognized as, or rendered, *other than itself*, because *of itself*.[39]

Derrida thus developed a kind of polyglot monolingualism that disordered the already impure identities that existed on both sides of the translational exchange. When Derrida recounts, "I always surrender myself to language," he is referring to just this hyperbolic fidelity that transforms both the translator (i.e., reader or writer) and the original language or text.[40] This type of subversive surrender was bound up with his desire, regarding French, to "appropriate, domesticate, coax [*amadouer*], that is to say, love by setting on fire . . . perhaps destroy, in all events mark, transform, prune, cut, forge."[41] His dream was "not that of harming the language" but "perhaps to make something happen to this language" such that "it loses itself by finding itself, by converting itself to itself."[42] Derrida thus appropriated French in a way that was correct yet could not be appropriated. He translated the untranslatable into something legibly untranslatable (even within French). His hyperbolic surrender

and transformative appropriation may be understood as a practice of translation that rendered both his own discourse and the French language more
idiomatic, less legible, and resistant to easy translation. But it did so through a
kind of excessive fidelity to pure French. This is one perspective from which
to understand Derrida's claim that all languages or texts are simultaneously
translatable and untranslatable, that translation is both necessary and impossible, that every language is, or can be made, foreign to itself.

Derrida's attempt to deconstruct the untenable opposition between translatability and untranslatability is indebted to Walter Benjamin's "Task of the
Translator," which he reads closely in "Des Tours de Babel." Note that "tour"
connotes both a thing (i.e., a tower) and an action (e.g., a walk around the
neighborhood, taking turns, turning a screw, a turn of events). Derrida thus
embraces Benjamin's understanding of translation as an ongoing practice. He
cites Benjamin when he declares that "a text lives only if it lives *on* [*sur-vit*]
and it lives *on* only if it is *at once* translatable *and* untranslatable."[43]

Benjamin maintained that the most sophisticated texts—those which
are singular and idiomatic, whose deepest meanings can never be simply
transferred from one language to another—are the *most* translatable. Challenging the putative superiority of an "original" text, Benjamin declares, "In
translation the original rises into a higher and purer linguistic air."[44] This is
because translation is neither a matter of "communication . . . of information" nor of establishing "likeness to the original."[45] Shifting focus from dead
texts and fixed meanings to living languages and the *practice* of translation,
Benjamin calls on translators to pay more attention to an original's "way of
meaning" than to what is meant.[46] In his view, translation does not aim to
recreate a perfect fit between content and language, which he likens to a fruit
and its skin. Rather, it seeks to index how that fit is established in any given
language.

For Benjamin, the task of the translator is to illuminate the mediated character of all linguistic exchange in a human, which is to say fallen, world characterized by what he calls the "foreignness of languages."[47] The latter refers
not only to the way "natural" languages differ from each other, but to the
differences within any given language that reveal themselves, and must be
translated, across various discursive registers (e.g., ordinary, literary, sacred).
Benjamin argues that the act of translation elevates and transforms the original
text, the original language, and the translator's language. Consider the remarkable citation where he notes the "mistaken premise" of translators who: "want
to turn Hindi, Greek, English into German instead of turning German into
Hindi, Greek, English. . . . The basic error of the translator is that he preserves
the state in which his own language happens to be instead of allowing his

language to be powerfully affected by the foreign tongue."[48] For Benjamin, translation is a (self-)transformative practice that refuses to sacralize original languages, original texts, translations, or languages of translation.

Both Benjamin and Derrida challenge the idea that any signifying practice can exist outside the space of translation. Each understands translation in ways that explode identarian logic by, for example, displacing the linguistic hegemony and deforming the linguistic certainties of "major" languages. As importantly, each figures translation as an ethical relation in which submission (to the other/'s language) and subversion (of the given) are conjoined. Both thinkers also point to a politics of translation. But they do so at a highly abstract level in order to make general claims about language, texts, and meaning. Benjamin, for example, suggests that translation offers glimpses of a seemingly impossible reconciliation or redemption that, apart from the Messianic end of history, only social revolution could bring about.[49] But he does not offer any clues about how such glimpses may be transposed into the kind of revolutionary action he discusses elsewhere. Derrida asserts that translation (or the impossibility of monolingualism) "opens onto a politics, a right, and an ethics."[50] But he never develops his assertions about how the translator's ethical indebtedness points to an internationalist politics founded upon responsibility for and hospitality to the other. Rather, he examines the singular situation of Algerian Jews in order to elaborate what he regards as a universal predicament bound up with signification as such.

Despite these limitations, Benjamin and Derrida alert us to *Babel as an opportunity*. For both, translation is a transformative practice with subversive possibilities whereby the movement of singular meanings across incommensurable semantic fields may render the strange familiar and the familiar strange. They remind us how translation may emphasize rather than elide just such uncanniness. We may usefully put them in dialogue with Global South thinkers who engage explicitly the ethical and political potentiality of translation as a practice that forges relations across singular differences. These thinkers help us to recognize how translation may serve as a medium and model for solidarity, or how the latter is a fundamentally translational affair.

From the Ethics of Translation to the Politics of Relation

The Senegalese philosopher Souleymane Bachir Diagne has spent his career examining the entangled character of African, Islamic, and European thought. Through this work, he develops a translational understanding of philosophy as an ethical practice that affirms singularities, forges productive connections, and attends to novel configurations.

In *The Ink of Scholars*, Diagne criticizes both Eurocentric assumptions about the nonphilosophical character of African knowledge and ethnological, ontological, or autarchic conceptions of African philosophy. He recognizes that Western philosophy has always been bound up with processes of racialization, social exclusion, and colonial subjection. He explains how, in response, many African intellectuals developed a forceful critique of philosophy itself as a Western instrument of domination that is necessarily foreign to Africa. Diagne appreciates this reasoning but argues that, ultimately, it only affirms the kind of racist claims made by Hegel and Heidegger about Greek and German as the only true languages of philosophy. He reminds us that nineteenth-century Europeans themselves invented this idea that philosophy is intrinsically European.

Diagne rejects the linguistic nativism, ethnological relativism, and Nietzschean perspectivism that would divide human thought into irreconcilable and mutually unintelligible blocs. Sociologically, he contends that "an ethnic worldview carried by every element of the group and naturally expressed in its language, gestures, judgments, postures, et cetera, and serving as thought makes little sense."[51] Epistemologically, he contends, "the differentialist posture, which betrays the ethnographer's initial conviction that he is dealing with an *other* way of being . . . does nothing but invent what it is looking for."[52]

But Diagne recognizes that philosophical orientations are embedded within specific African forms of life. He is a critic of ontological culturalism, yet also insists that philosophical insights are bound up with specific languages and historical experiences. He challenges philosophy's racist and Eurocentric heritage without renouncing philosophy as a general, and generally available, truth-seeking practice. He argues, for example, that African reflections on temporality do not simply demonstrate a specifically African conception of time. They illuminate something about time itself. Rather than characterize African thought as either universal or incommensurable, he invites philosophers to treat it "as if it is born under the gaze that gives it life, careful not to pin it like a dead butterfly . . . with the inventory of ethnographic details . . . which can hardly explain its *presence*: its existence outside of its own time."[53] Like Cassin, with whom he has collaborated, he argues that philosophical insights are always rooted, situated, and worldly.[54] But he also insists that their significance may transcend the linguistic cultural contexts within which they were immediately produced. He thus works to deprovincialize African thinking.

Careful not to treat thought like a dead butterfly in a museum vitrine, Diagne regards philosophy as a dynamic and open-ended practice, not a static body of knowledge. He crystallizes his nuanced position in a multivalent call to "philosophize in Africa" [*philosopher en Afrique*].[55] I read this as a declaration that Africans both should philosophize in African languages and should not hesitate to philosophize in non-African languages. Against the idea that Africans should only seek to produce "an other philosophy, which would keep close to each language's way of speaking," Diagne argues that to "philosophize in African languages" is "a means of thinking philosophically in translation and in crossing perspectives."[56] This orientation frees Diagne from becoming preoccupied with origins vs. imitations, or authenticity vs. alienation, which frequently accompany debates about the coloniality of Western thought. The latter often rely on assumptions about linguistic or conceptual purity that disregard entangled histories and polyglot situations. In contrast, Diagne declares that "only translations exist, without a text that could be claimed as the original one, written in a sacred language."[57]

Rather than debate whether a given philosophy can be adequately translated, Diagne develops an understanding of philosophy itself as a practice of unending translation. Citing Cassin, he rejects any notion of translation as a matter of finding "equivalents of the same concept in different languages."[58] In contrast, he invokes Hannah Arendt's image of "the faltering equivocity of the world."[59] Against reductive, appropriative, and ethnocentric types of translation which erase differences, Diagne endorses an understanding of translation as a process or practice of "putting in touch."[60] This is both an epistemological and an ethical operation. In his view, translation enacts a responsibility to the other whose alterity it seeks to honor, not destroy. We might say that he treats translation as a process of self-displacement (that renders the familiar strange).

Diagne beautifully conveys this orientation when, contra the Italian commonplace "traduttore, traditore" (translator, traitor), he writes, "Translation is treason? Certainly, but this betrayal is the only fidelity."[61] I read this to mean, first, that we must countenance the universal philosophical truths expressed in and through African knowledge and, second, that we must recognize the singularity of the history, modes of understanding, and forms of life that accompany, haunt, and cross Africans' use of Western philosophical languages, discourses, frameworks, and genres. For Diagne, neither philosophy nor translation should begin with a will to transparency or a desire to overcome singularities. He treats both philosophy and translation in terms of opening, dialogue, and *métissage* across different traditions.[62] In his account, these are relational practices that mediate between singularity and universality, situated forms of life and transversal connections, without an assumed metalanguage.

Diagne's understanding of translation as an ethical practice of "crossing perspectives" and "putting in touch" may be usefully read alongside Édouard Glissant's world-figuring "poetics of Relation." Both help us to think further about Babel as an opportunity for solidarity practices. Running through Glissant's reflections on Relation is the problem and promise of translation. Glissant challenges the modern imperial dictum that offers colonized peoples wanting to speak their own language an unacceptable choice: "Either you speak a language that is 'universal' . . . and participate in the life of the world; or else you retreat into your particular idiom—quite unfit for sharing—in which case you cut yourself off from the world to wallow alone and sterile in your so-called identity."[63] Conjuring the spirit of his elder interlocutor Aimé Césaire, Glissant rejects this false alternative between "either . . . seclusion within a restrictive particularity or, conversely, dilution within a generalizing universal."[64] Such a logic is unable to recognize, let alone embrace, "relations of multiplicity or contagion" when "mixtures explode into momentary flashes of creation."[65]

Glissant thus rejects the alternative, which so often defines colonial situations, between an abstract universality that purports to open access to the whole world and concrete particularity that would seem to lock actors in provincial lifeworlds. Against a reductively "monolingual" orientation to the world, Glissant insists that "speaking one's language and opening up to the language of the other no longer form the basis for an alternative."[66] Offering a relational and reciprocal understanding of linguistic plurality, he writes, "'I speak to you in your language voice, and it is in my language use that I understand you.' Creating in any given language thus assumes that one be inhabited by the impossible desire for all the languages in the world. Totality calls out to us."[67] He proposes that when a specific "people speaks its language or languages" it makes its more general "relationship to the world concrete and visible for itself and for others."[68] For Glissant, universality is not abstracted into an underlying or overarching sameness. Nor is singularity reduced to a particularism. He figures Relation as an open totality that points beyond the binary of universality vs. particularity.

Glissant thereby attempts to overcome the false opposition between, on the one hand, a world organized around a united humanity with a universal language that elides differences and, on the other, a confusion of local languages that partitions peoples from each other and precludes translocal relations. This is the basis for his alternative view of Babel:

> On the other side of the bitter struggles against domination and for
> the liberation of the imagination, there opens up *a multiply dispersed
> zone in which we are gripped by vertigo.* But this is not the vertigo
> preceding apocalypse and Babel's fall. *It is the shiver of a beginning,*

confronted with extreme possibility. It is possible to build the Tower—in every language.[69]

This call to build a Tower of Babel in every language conveys a vision of multiple universals, each of which is internally heterogeneous. In this view, every place, language, or text crystallizes a world and refracts the world. Far from signaling a fatal incommensurablity, Babel creates an opportunity for worldwide Relation.

Glissant characterizes Relation as an "open totality" wherein "the whole is not the finality of its parts: for multiplicity in totality is total diversity."[70] Closed or self-identical totalities are founded upon a "root identity" that grounds myths of pure origins and continuous lineages.[71] Root identities also authorize the colonial expropriation of other peoples' territory. In contrast, "Relation identity" is based on the "contacts among cultures" that create a "chaotic network."[72] Relation "opposes the totalitarianism of any monolingual intent."[73] It "does not think of land as a territory from which to project toward other territories but as a place where one gives-on-and-with [*donner-avec*] rather than grasps."[74]

Glissant's open totality, a transversal and relational whole, embraces singularities (often produced through mixture) and entails reciprocity. Central to his vision of Relation as a ramifying network of singularities is his concept of opacity, which he distinguishes from a conventional understanding of difference. He recognizes that "the theory of difference is invaluable" insofar as it has enabled struggles against racism and for minority rights.[75] But he warns, "Difference itself can still contrive to reduce things to the Transparent."[76] It does so by seeking to "understand and accept" others in terms of "an ideal scale" that creates grounds for reductive comparisons and judgments: "I understand your difference . . . I relate it to my norm. I admit you to existence, within my system. I create you afresh."[77] In other words, an identitarian right to difference can enable ethnocentric translations. On this basis, Glissant exhorts readers to demand "not merely . . . the right to difference" but "the right to opacity."[78] Opacity cannot simply be assimilated (or translated) into some other's schema. Yet opacity "is not enclosure within an impenetrable autarchy."[79] It is both "subsistence within an irreducible singularity" and "the most perennial guarantee of participation and confluence."[80] This because, "Opacities can coexist and converge, weaving fabrics. To understand these truly one must focus on the texture of the weave and not on the nature of its components."[81] This fabric does not encompass "Humanity," it expresses "the exultant divergence of humanities."[82]

Glissant's vision of irreducible opacities and divergent humanities coexisting, converging, and weaving themselves into larger tapestries transcends the conventional opposition between transparent equivalence (which informs a traditional notion of translation) and incommensurable alterity (which informs culturalist assertions about untranslatability). Relation constitutes a worldwide weave whose innumerable threads remain irreducibly themselves. This open totality both negates and realizes the very idea of totality. Relation names a dynamic network of opaque singularities that is simultaneously one and many.

Glissant grounds this abstract conception of Relation in the specific historical situation created by the Middle Passage, anti-Black slavery, and plantation production. He argues that "the Plantation matrix" established dehumanizing conditions which dialectically fueled what he variously calls detour, diffraction, errantry, creolization, and Relation.[83] In Glissant's account, the New World plantation was a scene of extreme alienation and dispossession. But these, in turn, created fertile conditions for linguistic and cultural proliferation, connection, and creation. The plantation was designed as an "enclosed space . . . defined by boundaries whose crossing was strictly forbidden."[84] It reinforced supposedly self-evident racial taxonomies and social boundaries. Yet the plantation also generated multilingual and creolized networks, nonidentical ways of life and political sensibilities.

We might say that Glissant traces a dialectic of Plantation and Relation through which specifically Caribbean languages and lifeworlds "entered with the force of a tradition that they built themselves, into the relation of cultures."[85] Of course, this was a peculiar "tradition." It called into question traditional assumptions (identical, territorial, and monolingual) about what constitutes a tradition. *Relation names a fundamentally modern Caribbean tradition that is also the tradition of modernity.* Glissant identifies the Plantation, a "monstrously abortive failure, composed of so many solitary instances of sterility" as a source of "multilingualism" where "the meeting of cultures is most clearly and directly observable. . . . Here we are able to discover a few of the formational laws of the cultural *métissage* that concerns us all."[86] Despite being a space of supposed "autarky," it actually became "one of the focal points for the development of present-day modes of Relation. . . . In this outmoded spot, on the margins of every dynamic, the tendencies of our modernity began to be detectable."[87]

This conception of Relation overturns conventional assumptions about place and identity. "Thought of self and thought of other here become obsolete in their duality. Every Other is a citizen and no longer a barbarian.

What is here is open, as much as this there. . . . This-here is the weave, and it weaves no boundaries."[88] Rather than either seize centers or defend peripheries, Relation "makes every periphery into a center . . . it abolishes the very notion of center and periphery."[89] Relation, like translation, is a dialectical optic through which "the landscape of your world is the world's landscape . . . its frontier is open."[90] Each may render the world productively uncanny.

Glissant warns that the reality of Relation exceeds the grasp of the established human sciences. "Within the space apart that [the Plantation] comprised, the always multilingual and frequently multiracial tangle created inextricable knots within the web of filiations, thereby breaking the clear, linear order" of 'Western thought.'"[91] Relation can only be understood through alternative ways of seeing, knowing, and saying—through a form of poetic knowledge or a "poetics of Relation." As Glissant uses it, "poetics" signals an intersecting aesthetic, epistemological, ethical, and political sensibility. "Aesthetics is an art of conceiving, imagining, and acting."[92] He explains that "a poetics cannot guarantee us a concrete means of action. But a poetics, perhaps, does allow us to understand better our action in the world."[93] Such action is never a matter of following fixed rules or "the preconceived transparency of universal models."[94] Rather, "this is an aesthetics of turbulence whose corresponding ethics is not provided in advance."[95] In Glissant's world, ethico-political action is situational, improvisational, and experimental.[96]

The ethics and politics of Relation are transversal and reciprocal. When Glissant invokes "the complicity of relation," he reminds us that the entangled and dynamic histories of Relation implicate peoples in each other's situations and prospects.[97] He often refers to this as a matter of "giving with" [donner-avec].[98] This figure echoes the translational ethos discussed above, nicely captured in Glissant's reflections on "consensual, not imposed, sharing" whereby "each is changed by and changes the other."[99]

For Glissant, Relation opens *the possibility for each one at every moment to be both solidary and solitary.*"[100] It cuts across any clear boundary between autonomy and interdependence, or singularity and solidarity.[101] Honoring "the opacity of the other," Glissant explains, "To feel in solidarity with him or to build with him or to like what he does, it is not necessary for me to grasp him. It is not necessary to try to become the other (or become other) nor to 'make' him in my image."[102] On the one hand, reciprocity does not require understanding and solidarity does not require transparency. On the other, it must be "implemented by me and you to join the dynamics to which we are to contribute . . . in which each is changed by and changes the other."[103] Conjuring the paradoxical potentiality created by the plantation, Glissant writes,

"Thus, we go into the open circle of our relayed aesthetics, our unflagging politics. We leave the matrix abyss and the immeasurable abyss for this other one in which *we wander without becoming lost.*"[104]

We might say that Glissant's reflections on the reciprocally transformative character of Relation convey a *translational* situation, form of life, and ethical orientation. It posits a world in which every people would enjoy the right to opacity and can build its own Tower of Babel. Here, any specific utterance calls forth all the languages of the world. There are neither universal meta-languages nor self-identical native languages. This is a translational world in which anyone may wander without becoming lost.

Diagne and Glissant may be usefully placed in touch with Boaventura de Sousa Santos, who explicitly links translation to Global South solidarity and a new internationalism. This Portuguese social theorist and alterglobalization militant collaborated with Samir Amin in establishing the World Social Forum (WSF) and signed the 2005 Porto Alegre Manifesto. From the standpoint of "epistemologies of the South," Santos argues that there can be no social justice without cognitive justice.[105] The latter requires grasping non-Western forms of knowledge on their own terms. But cognitive justice also requires an ongoing practice of what Santos calls "intercultural translation," which "consists of searching for isomorphic concerns and underlying assumptions among cultures . . . and developing, whenever appropriate, new hybrid forms of cultural understanding and intercommunication."[106] He reminds us that "translation undermines the idea of original pure cultures and stresses the idea of cultural relationality. . . . [C]ultures are monolithic only when seen from the outside or from afar. When looked at from the inside or at close range, they are easily seen to comprise various and often conflicting versions of the same culture."[107] Translation, in other words, illuminates the disjunctures within as much as between cultures, peoples, and social groups.

Santos characterizes "intercultural translation" as a "living process" that unfolds within the "translational contact zones" created by global capitalism and imperialism.[108] These are zones of historically constituted diversity, inequality, and conflict that compel acts of translation. Santos recognizes that in such situations, practices of "mediation, confrontation, and negotiation" may reinforce existing hierarchies.[109] But he also emphasizes that these are "relatively uncodified" zones in which there is no singular truth or meta-language to which translational differences can be referred or disagreements adjudicated.[110] Here, "the work of translation is basically an argumentative work, based on the cosmopolitan emotion of sharing the world with those who do not share our knowledge and experience."[111] For Santos, this is a relational and conflictual space in which *assumptions about cultural premises become arguments over premises that can never be definitively resolved.* Though such spaces are typically organized around structural inequalities, the imperative to translate in the "absence of a general theory" may also provide opportunities "for normative and cultural experimentation and innovation" that could transform actors' understandings and identities.[112] The result may be new kinds of "equality in differences" or "hybrid cultural constellations."[113] Such translation "aims at reciprocity instead of worrying about source cultures and target cultures."[114]

Santos underscores that intercultural translation as a "living process" through which "to cope with diversity and conflict" is "not a gesture of intellectual curiosity or cultural dilettantism. Rather, it is an imperative dictated by the need to broaden political articulation beyond the confines of a given locale or culture."[115] Accordingly, he invokes the "interpolitical translation" that is indispensable for "intermovement politics."[116] Santos thus figures translation as a mode of political articulation in the absence of a "single universal social practice or collective subject to confer meaning and direction to history."[117] Acts of translation can only be conjunctural, experimental, and strategic. Like Amin, Santos calls on militants "to identify, in each concrete historical moment or context, which constellations of practices carry more counterhegemonic potential."[118]

Santos's vision of interpolitical translation in the service of intermovement politics is not based on the Comintern model of a central directorate, orthodox ideology, and party line. It shares more in common with Glissant's vision of Relation as a worldwide network of entangled but irreducible singularities. For Santos, the aim of translational practices and solidarity politics is to create powerful blocs that do *not* need to be organized under a single directorate, whose multiple political orientations do *not* need to be standardized within an identical program. We may understand interpolitical translation as a concrete utopian practice that anticipates new forms of being-together. "The work of translation . . . is a work of epistemological and democratic imagination, aiming to construct new and plural conceptions of social emancipation."[119]

Of course, "there is no guarantee that a better world will follow or that all those who continue to struggle for it will conceive it the same way."[120] Interpolitical translation risks reproducing existing norms and inequalities. But Santos's work suggests that this risk cannot be avoided; such future-oriented wagers must be made. This is because: the earth is shared, modern Western forms of domination have created webs of global interdependence and subordination, there is no being-outside-of such modern spaces, there are no pure cultures, all peoples are mutually implicated, global forms of systemic domination cannot be overcome through local acts of refusal or resistance, and counterhegemonic projects must somehow seek to operate on global scales to address global problems.

Santos's thinking about intercultural translation for intermovement politics was nourished by his engagement in the World Social Forum. He was one of an international group of founding activists, scholars, and writers (including Samir Amin) that were involved from the start with this experiment in solidarity politics.[121] Its first meeting in Porto Alegre Brazil in 2001 gathered representatives from antihegemonic movements throughout the world in order to enact an internationalist sphere of popular opposition to the existing global order.

The WSF was distinctive for the diversity of its participants, the scale of its organization and imagination, and the absence of a centralized leadership structure. Like its alterglobalization counterpart, it was a movement of movements "opposed to neoliberalism and to domination of the world by capital and any form of imperialism, and . . . committed to building a planetary society centered on the human person."[122] Its "Charter of Principles" declares, "Another World Is Possible!"[123] Santos characterizes the WSF as a "radically democratic utopia" whose "openness" distinguishes it from various "conservative utopias" that deny alternatives in the name of singular visions: "The other possible world is a utopian aspiration that comprises several possible worlds. The other possible world may be many things, but never a world with no alternative."[124] He thus describes the WSF as a "realistic utopia" opposed to neoliberalism's "conservative utopia."[125]

The WSF was an imperfect initiative that risked misunderstandings, inequalities, and ineffectiveness.[126] But, once a general theory or single strategy was renounced, it was a remarkable experiment in intercultural and interpolitical translation. When Santos notes that "the alternative to a general theory is the work of translation," he is not making a facile statement about easy reconciliation based on naïve optimism.[127] Santos recognizes that "fragmentation and atomization . . . are the dark side of diversity and multiplicity."[128] But his efforts were guided by the recognition that an alternative global hegemony will only be possible through the "aggregation and articulation" of struggles. Such risky, difficult, and messy work "entails a wide exercise in translation to expand reciprocal intelligibility without destroying the identity of the partners in translation. . . . Through translation work, diversity is celebrated, not as a factor of fragmentation and isolationism, but rather as a condition of sharing and solidarity."[129] We can debate the methods and merits of the World Social Forum. But this historic experiment in critical internationalism warrants our attention. It underscores the close relation that may be forged between translation practices, solidarity politics, and a concrete utopian insistence that another world is possible.

Translating Solidarity

Diagne, Glissant, and Santos share an affinity with Chakrabarty, Asad, and Mignolo. They, too, begin with a critique of Eurocentric knowledge, provincial universals, and fictions of intercultural transparency. They also reject conventional notions of translation that create false equivalences between languages, cultures, or texts, as if meaning were not inextricably bound up with the specific language or lifeworld in which it is expressed. Each of these thinkers recognizes and values the existence of qualitatively singular phenomena that resist conventional translation. Yet, like Benjamin and Derrida, they recognize that there is no outside-translation. They help us to see that every utterance both crosses and creates the gaps that characterize translation. They attend to the way translation inevitably occurs *within* nonidentical languages, communities, and groups.[130] Each challenges ontological notions of language, cultures, or civilizations. When considered together, they offer us a relational view of social life as mediated by acts of translation in which the prospect of experimental connection and unforeseen creation across incommensurable differences is always possible. We might call this a *translational* vision of sociality. It recognizes translation as an unavoidable imperative, an ethical responsibility, and a potentially transformational political practice.

Because there is no *outside* of translation, there can be no choosing for or against translation. Incommensurability and untranslatability compose the very terrain of our thinking and acting. The question is whether this or that mode of translation affirms or disrupts existing assumptions and arrangements. Certainly, we must reject any positivist or imperialist understanding of translation as transparent equivalence. But to only regard translation as an instrument of domination is to miss the transversal practices and aims that have long fueled radical anticolonial, anticapitalist, and internationalist politics.

Recall Lenin translating Marx into Russian, Langston Hughes translating Nicolas Guillen into English, Paulette Nardal translating Claude McKay into French, Ali Shariati translating Frantz Fanon into Persian, and the militants of Socialist Lebanon translating Marx, Lenin, Trotsky, Mao, and Che Guevara into Arabic.[131] Writing about José Rizal, the Filipino anticolonial novelist, Benedict Anderson evokes the polyglot character of late-nineteenth-century radical internationalism.

Filipinos wrote to Austrians in German, to Japanese in English, to
each other in French, or Spanish, or Tagalog, with liberal interventions from the last beautiful international language, Latin. Some of
them knew a bit of Russian, Greek, Italian, Japanese, and Chinese . . .
real communication required the true, hard internationalism of the
polyglot. Filipino leaders were peculiarly adapted to the Babelish
world.[132]

Ralph Ellison, describes a scene in the late 1930s where he, not yet a published writer, and Richard Wright, who was about to publish *Uncle Tom's
Children*, attended a party in New York where they hoped to raise money
for Wright's new literary magazine. Ellison recalls that this was both where
he "first heard the folksinger Leadbelly perform" and where he met André
Malraux, who was there "to make an appeal for the Spanish Loyalists" then
fighting Franco in the Civil War. "I had never dreamed that I would be in
the presence of Malraux, of whose work I became aware on my second day in
Harlem when Langston Hughes suggested that I read *Man's Fate* and *Days
of Wrath*. . . . And it is this fortuitist circumstance which led to my selecting
Malraux as a literary 'ancestor.'"[133]

Recall the meeting in Mexico between C. L. R. James and Trotsky. He
advised the exiled revolutionary on how to translate Fourth International aims
and strategies into a movement to organize African American workers in ways
that would transform Marxism itself.[134] This, according to James, was one of
the lessons he learned from Lenin, whose "life's work was to translate Marxism into Russian terms for the Russian people."[135] Likewise, James insisted
that they could only build a mass party in the United States by reconsidering
Marxist theory in relation to American history and conditions. In his plenum
address to the 1944 Workers' Party national meeting, James declared, "*To
Bolshevize America it is necessary to Americanize Bolshevism*."[136] This would
not be a simple act of domestication. This task would require and produce a
web of transversal translations among James's cohort of U.S. comrades in the
New York section of the Workers' Party.

Translation was at the very center of their friendship, their theorizing, and
their politics. Grace Lee Boggs, a Chinese American militant with a PhD in
philosophy, relates how translation was a source of productive excitement and
explosive insight. She translated Marx's *Economic and Philosophical Manuscripts* from German while Raya Dunayevskaya, the ex-Trotskyist Russian
émigré activist, translated Lenin's notebooks on Hegel from Russian. The
ensuing discussions enabled James to write *Notes on Dialectics* (1948). Such
efforts allowed them, as the Johnson-Forest Tendency, to grasp the specificity

of the American workers' movement in 1947. The point is not that sacred texts gave them the transhistorical truth, but that the practice of translation helped them to develop a conjunctural analysis of their own specific political situation. Thinking across the semantic networks offered by German, Russian, and English, but also the historical experience of the industrial West, the rural East, and the colonized Caribbean, helped them to grasp the form of racial capitalism that they confronted. It also helped them to envision a revolutionary movement propelled by an autonomous party composed of insurgent Black masses. Here we can recognize translation as an instrument of concrete utopian thinking, acting, and being-together. Boggs recalls: "C. L. R., Raya, and I were inseparable . . . Our energy was fantastic. We would spend a morning or afternoon writing, talking, and eating and then go home and write voluminous letters to one another extending or enlarging on what we had discussed, sending these around to other members of our tendency in barely legible carbon copies."[137] The practice of translation allowed these comrades to anticipate the world they wished to see. Recall that they hoped to situate an independent U.S. Black people's party within the framework of a postwar Fourth International that was opposed to both Western and Soviet variants of state capitalism. We should locate Samir Amin's post–Cold War vision of a Fifth International that would pursue a polycentric, socialist, and democratic world in just such a translational tradition.

In the spirit of Lenin's call to turn the imperial war into a civil war, translation helps us to recognize that what appear to be reified differences *between* groups, cultures, or languages can be refigured as ramifying differences *within* them. The thinkers discussed above illuminate the intimate relation between translation practices and solidarity politics. They help us forge a translational orientation that embraces Babel as an opportunity. In so doing, it challenges culturalist assumptions about self-identical wholes, categorical differences, and impassable boundaries. Insofar as we might envision a world organized around translational relations of reciprocity and solidarity—a world in which anyone may wander without becoming lost—this orientation also points beyond the melancholic presentism I discuss next.

4

Of Pessimism and Presentism

Against Left Melancholy

Despair is the final ideology.

—THEODOR ADORNO

The fact that mankind is plumbing the depths of the abyss, and that the earth is in danger of annihilation, does not mean that we should act *as if* nothingness were already swallowing us up. Every time we act *as if* it were, the chances of annihilation increase.

—HENRI LEFEBVRE

from the depths of the furious piling up of appalling dreams
new dawns were
rising

—AIMÉ CÉSAIRE

In a discussion of the difficult relationship between contemplation and action under conditions of capitalist domination, Adorno revisits Marx's famous injunction to change rather than merely interpret the world. Railing against "the happy spirit" in a time of growing misery and impending catastrophe, Adorno, too, criticizes bourgeois idealists who attempt to resolve contradictions in and through thought alone.[1] But he also criticizes instrumental Leftists who denigrate thinking that does not directly inform immediate action. Noting that "the horizon of . . . happiness need by no means be that of a transparent relation to a possible practice to come," he warns against "making impotence a virtue."[2]

Today, too, the fact that systemic change is difficult to envision and unlikely to occur often fuels a political pessimism that makes impotence a virtue. Likewise, a conviction that systemic change may be possible is often mistaken for an optimistic assessment by a happy spirit that such change is likely or even destined to occur, that current problems will resolve themselves.[3] In this chapter, I will trace some of the ways that a well-founded pessimism devolves into an ungrounded presentism. The latter forecloses concrete utopian attempts to anticipate other possible worlds. For presentist thinkers, reasonable doubt about the probability of historical progress authorizes metaphysical assertions about historical temporality.

From Pessimism . . .

Let us begin with an interview by the anthropologist Fadi Bardawil with Talal Asad. In their discussion of what it means to "take a position" within or toward a tradition, Bardawil invites Asad to reflect on political practice. Asad replies,

> I am very pessimistic, as you may know, especially over the last twenty years or so, about the way in which our world is drifting, and I am not at all sure . . . that the world will be able to survive all these crises accumulating now: financial global capitalism, climate change, nuclear weapons as well as nuclear energy . . . crises that threaten absolute disaster. All these crises, I think, are beginning to merge and together they seem less and less capable of solution. Anyway, I am just spelling out my sense of despair about it all.[4]

Asad certainly has good reason to be pessimistic about the way things are going and about the prospects for meaningful change. He rightly criticizes self-important intellectuals and dogmatic activists (especially in the West) who assume they know what the world (especially the Global South) needs and how we should proceed politically.

But Asad is not only responding to the contemporary situation. His current despair expresses deeper reservations about emancipatory political action. He recalls that he was "always on the Left," but also explains, "In my early years, practice seemed wrong for me because I was uncertain about many things, and because as far as the tension between understanding and political action went, I was more on the side of trying to understand."[5] Even more so now, he relates, "The question of practice seems to be beyond my grasp" primarily because "I find the solution impossible to envisage."[6] More generally, he observes, "The grand project of emancipation has a very rocky history, and I am less eager to see people aiming for that. . . . The fact is that we don't know how to deal with this monster that has the world in its grip. I don't see how talk

about freedom is going to help us in this crisis. It may even be that many of
those grand projects of freedom have contributed to creating this megacrisis."[7]
Regarding whether he is "unsatisfied with the Marxist critique of liberal freedom," Asad confirms that he is and relates how he had become "worried" and
"dissatisfied" by the "Enlightenment heritage" that "Marxism and liberalism
had in common."[8]

Asad's skepticism about political practice flows from his view that it is a
fundamental (and in his view, typically modern and especially American)
mistake to assume that "every social problem has to have a solution."[9] He
asks, "Why not think about the implications of a situation where there might
not be a solution—on the contrary, where things can only get worse?"[10] In
relation to the situation in Egypt, for example, he notes, "I am not sure that
rushing forward with big solutions to 'big problems' ('Freedom and Justice!')
is necessarily right when one does not know all the questions that need to be
pondered."[11] What little hope Asad does have about a better future is

> bound up with a desperate hope that I am wrong, that something
> positive will emerge—a hope that is fed not by utopianism but by a
> sense that we are always predicting history and we are nearly always
> wrong . . . about the big things. Things emerge in ways we haven't
> imagined or couldn't imagine because we were at an inappropriate
> point or because we were too close in time.[12]

Asad thus refuses the lure of utopian thinking but hopes that maybe, nevertheless, something positive will emerge.[13] With characteristic honesty, modesty,
and thoughtfulness, he conveys a kind of skepticism, pessimism, and fatalism
that is not uncommon among Left critical thinkers today.

The modern period has indeed been littered with the harms caused by
emancipatory projects across the political spectrum. And the current knot of
intersecting dilemmas and crises certainly seems to mock any of our inherited
frameworks for understanding, let alone addressing, them. But we should be
wary of any supposed choice between understanding and action. We might
also question the liberal logic dwelling within any assumptions about a transparent or sequential relation between clear understanding, correct action,
and certain outcomes. For such thinking, the very existence of political contingency becomes evidence against the possibility of societal transformation.
The unavoidable imperative to act without knowing how things will turn out,
the fact that history does not unfold in a continuous upward arc, becomes an
argument against efforts to envision and pursue another possible world.

Consider literary critic Lauren Berlant's influential analysis of "cruel optimism." Through this concept, she astutely identifies the paradox whereby

contemporary subjects remain resolutely attached to the very social logics, arrangements, and promises that actively prohibit their own individual and collective flourishing. Berlant traces how under neoliberal conditions, fantasies of a good life obstruct not only material well-being but the very experience of belonging, of having a stable place in the world within a community of reciprocity. Consigned to states of ongoing precarity, neoliberal subjects spend most of their time simply surviving, adapting to, and making their way through the "impasse" of an extended present. Yet by continually renewing their attachments to the social world and form of life that disables them, the good life they desire becomes a harmful illusion.[14] Berlant presents this sophisticated argument with great care for how masses of people struggle to manage everydayness in this historical present. She persuasively suggests that systemic precarity requires us to rethink conventional notions of politics, ethics, and sociality. But her account is so deeply focused on the "survival strategies" required for "living in an impasse" that any possible horizon beyond this endlessly extending present drops out of the frame.[15] Although she writes with a moral urgency that is anything but complacent, a current of antipolitical fatalism seeps into her account.

Berlant rightly notes that the conventional practices and institutions associated with citizenship in a neoliberal state are themselves instruments of "cruel optimism." She is skeptical about the very prospect of participating in a disabling public sphere that will thwart peoples' understandable desire for political connection and effectiveness. Yet she recognizes that "to detach from the life-destructive forms of the normative political world" risks "providing tacit permission for that world to reproduce itself as such."[16] Berlant thus identifies a real dilemma whereby both participation in and withdrawal from the political public sphere may work to reproduce the antisocial precarity that harms so many. But this insight leads her to question the very "desire for the political."[17] She proposes that this double-bind could be better negotiated through gestures of "performative silence" and "performative withdrawal," as found in art-activism, that build upon traditions of silent protests, which may point to a new kind of "ambient citizenship."[18] She allows that some may criticize these as "quietist . . . politically depressive aversions to the political."[19] Her response is that such "performances of departure from the circuit of re-seduction and despair that so often absorb genuine energy for social change" may in fact allow actors to detach "from the cruel optimism of a political fetish."[20] "Facing the fact that no *form* of being in the political or politics—including withdrawing from them—will solve the problem of shaping the impasse of the historical present," she contends that "the best one can hope for *realistically* [is] a stubborn collective refusal to give out, wear out, or admit defeat."[21]

We should certainly recognize that a collective refusal to admit defeat is difficult and important. But on what grounds can Berlant assert that no form of politics can lead beyond the impasse of the historical present? According to what metric is a stubborn refusal to give out the best one can hope for *realistically*?

Against any instrumental conception of politics, Berlant proposes experiments in "ambient citizenship" that focus on "the pure mediality of being in the present of the political."[22] The only end is that of being political together: "Attachment to the political would ideally be an attachment to the process of maintaining attachment."[23] In this way, one's "solidarities and commitments are neither to ends nor to imagining the pragmatics of a consensual community, but to embodied processes of making solidarity itself."[24] This stance allows "the anarchist political depressive" to perform "a commitment to repairing *politics*" without needing to be motivated by either "an ends-oriented consensually held good-life fantasy or confirmation of the transformative effectiveness of one's actions."[25] In this way, "the work of citizenship" becomes a "performative belonging to the now in which potentiality is affirmed."[26]

This ethico-political orientation is nicely captured in Berlant's moving interpretation of the painting that is the cover image of *Cruel Optimism*. It depicts a half-blind dog, happily greeting, at whose feet lies a middle-aged woman whose eyes are closed and who covers half her face with a gloved hand. Berlant reads these two figures as "utopian realists" who are "hanging in there . . . having adventures and being in the impasse together, waiting for the other shoe to drop, and also, allowing for some healing and resting, waiting for it not to drop."[27] For Berlant, the image represents both the predicament of neoliberal precarity and the kind of embodied reciprocity that she proposes in response. These two beings "seem to have given each other what they came for: companionship, reciprocity, care, protection."[28] Ultimately, Berlant can only affirm "their undefeated mutual attachment to living on."[29] This, of course is not nothing. Yet the important attempt to honor such experience may preemptively foreclose nonliberal attempts to recognize and realize potentiality.

So much of Berlant's analysis is on point. She warns that any political attempt to redress, let alone abolish, the sources of a social malady may worsen the condition. She questions any attempt to ground politics in normative conceptions of success. She emphasizes that prefigurative means are no less important than the realization of perpetually deferred ends. But such insights do not warrant our reducing politics to a collective refusal to admit defeat, to the mere fact of being (political) together, or to the "solidarity [that] comes from the scavenging for survival."[30] Berlant is so taken by her powerful diagnosis of neoliberal political pathology that she remains mired in the symptoms she has identified.[31] Isn't it possible to envision and pursue more desirable futures without either presupposing an "ends-oriented consensually held good-life fantasy" or needing a priori guarantees that one's actions will be "successful"?[32] Does the absence of conditions today that can ground reciprocity and solidarity somehow mean that we should distrust and avoid all efforts to construct a world organized around reciprocity and solidarity? In this account, the attenuation of politics under neoliberalism leads to an attenuated conception of politics as such.

Ultimately, Berlant sketches a postpolitical world with no prospect of mass movements for societal transformation. The best we can hope for is to keep scavenging for survival in an unsurpassable now. She speculates that "the neoliberal present is a space of transition" that "impose[s] historical consciousness on its subjects as a moment without edges, and recent pasts and near futures blend into a stretched-out time that people move around."[33] This is an important insight about how the neoliberal now may produce an experience of being trapped in the present. But Berlant implies that neoliberalism really *has* transformed reality into "a moment without edges," a time from which history is absent and the prospect of a different future has vanished.

We can discern a similar movement from pessimism to presentism in anthropologist David Scott's *Omens of Adversity*. This powerful account of the 1979–1983 revolution in Grenada examines how a popular insurgency collapsed because of internal conflicts and an external intervention by the United States. Scott's broader aim is to explore "the temporality of the aftermaths of political catastrophe."[34] In so doing, he offers us a temporally self-reflexive history of the political present that grapples with Caribbean specificity in relation to global politics during and after the Cold War.

Scott writes, "On a Caribbean scale, anyway, the Grenada Revolution . . . was world-historical. . . . More important, perhaps, it was *generationally* historic in the sense that, for the generation who made it . . . the revolution was . . . the vindication and culmination of a certain organization of temporal expectation and political longing."[35] Scott traces this particular generation's tragic inability to free itself from a political past characterized by revolutionary failure. Drawing on Freud's distinction between mourning as the productive working through of loss and melancholia as the self-destructive fixation on it, he traces how the generation that directly experienced the collapse of the Grenada revolution became politically paralyzed: "History had betrayed them . . . it had *robbed* them of the progressive future for which they had so long labored . . . it also . . . signified . . . a collapse of the very conditions of a generation's experience of political time in which past-present-future were connected in a chain of progressive succession. . . . It marked the loss of futures."[36] Consequently its members were "stranded" in a "prolonged and stagnant" present experienced as endless repetition.[37] Afflicted by shame and anger, Scott explains, their grief was expressed through ambivalent nostalgia and a desire for revenge.

Scott argues that this revolutionary failure was "a *watershed* event" across the Caribbean and the Global South that had profound political and temporal implications.[38] In his view, the collapse-destruction of the Grenada revolution marked the end of an epoch in which anticolonial movements could possibly (hope to) create meaningful self-determination through popular democratic socialist experiments. He contends, more generally, that "the political-legal aftermaths of the collapse of the Grenada Revolution is . . . inseparable from the larger story of the emergence of a world in which the socialist past can appear in the present only as a criminal one and in which liberal democracy parades as the single . . . direction of a worldwide political order."[39] He thus situates Grenada within a larger epochal shift shaped by "the protracted aftermaths of the collapse of revolutionary futures past and the rehegemonization of *the world* by a cynical imperial and neoliberal agenda."[40]

Importantly, Scott relates this political break to a "profound—perhaps uncanny—sense of temporal *rupture* and collective *disorientation* brought about by the collapse in our time of the socialist revolutionary project, of which . . . the collapse of the Grenada Revolution is a dramatic instance."[41] For Scott, in other words, this specific revolutionary failure was bound up with the more general eclipse of belief in transformative political futures. He observes that "in our liberal and liberalizing time, emancipation has given way to accommodation, and reconciliation has displaced revolution as the language of social and political change where the future has been reduced to a mirror image of the present."[42] But he leaps from this neoliberal situation to a categorical claim about historical temporality as such: "the past is no longer imagined as a time that can be overcome."[43] He characterizes the current world-historical epoch by "the ruin of time and the accompanying loss of futures."[44]

Scott's attempt to think through the internal connections between the Grenada revolution, the end of a certain politico-historical epoch, and a corresponding shift in temporal consciousness is enormously productive. But it is not clear what kind of claim he is making about the relation between political failure in the postcolonial Caribbean and a more global "loss of futures" under neoliberalism.[45] He persuasively demonstrates how, in the aftermath of a specific political catastrophe, Caribbean actors were traumatized by failure, haunted by loss, and stranded in the present. But how do we get from that event to quasi-metaphysical assertions about ruined time and lost futures? Is Scott claiming that in our current epoch, people no longer *believe* in political futures? That past political failures have rendered them unwilling or unable to envision socialist transformations? His argument about trauma points in this direction. Or is he claiming that under current conditions the socialist futures that might have once been objectively available no longer are, that under current world-historical conditions, the present really cannot be overcome? His argument about neoliberal hegemony points in this direction.

Either way, Scott's claim about fundamental temporal rupture seems to depend on a dubious distinction between a dynamic past in which revolutionary socialist futures were imaginable or possible, on the one hand, and the static present in which social actors are or feel tragically stranded, on the other. On what basis should we believe that counterrevolutionary forces were any less formidable during the period of decolonization or that the prospects for interrupting history are any less plausible now than they were then? Haven't modern emancipatory movements always been the longest of long shots? Scott's own argument in this book about the contingency of human action, about the constitutive risk of politics and the radically open future thereby implied, suggests that any political present can be overcome. If this is no longer the case, which is certainly a possibility, then it would need to be demonstrated through an analysis of the current historical situation.

Of course, there are real reasons to suggest that webs of domination may be tighter and more intractable than in the recent past. But without further elaboration, Scott risks reproducing aspects of either the nostalgic projection and melancholic fixation on the past that he identifies with the Grenada aftermath or the neoliberal end-of-history ideology that he rightly criticizes. A tragic sensibility, fatal resignation, and political melancholy subtend his assertions about being stranded in a postrevolutionary present. Scott risks reproducing the subject position of the traumatized Grenadan revolutionaries he analyzes so incisively. At such moments it is as if he implicitly longs for the kind of progressive temporality he so powerfully calls into question.

I read Scott to be using "stranded in the present" to mean that existing conditions cannot, even in imagination, be overcome. But we might also take it to signal that historical contingency, risky action, and uncertain outcomes are the unavoidable terrain on which politics must always be pursued. To mourn this situation is to assume that the absence or loss of progressive temporality— *which never actually existed*—is an exceptional problem that needs to be rectified. Ultimately, Scott seems to offer us an either/or choice between faith in linear temporality (the certainty, as he puts it, that we are going somewhere) and resignation to a perpetual present (the certainty that we are not).

... To Presentism

Despite the questions it begs, *Omens of Adversity* makes a powerful case that grasping the political present requires temporal self-reflexivity. Scott attempts to contextualize the "strange out-of-jointness of time" that has "made itself pervasively conspicuous" in contemporary consciousness.[46] "For moderns," he argues, the continuous "unfolding of *historical* time" made time and history seem "self-evidently convergent."[47] But in recent years, "a deep *rupture* has occurred in this form of experience" such that they "now seem to be diverging from each other . . . time *has suddenly become more discernable, more conspicuous . . . more palpably in question*" as a "philosophical and political *problem*."[48] He observes that in today's world, "remains from the past stick unaccountably to the hinges of the temporality we hitherto relied on to furnish ourselves with the confidence that we are in fact going somewhere. . . . And what we are left with are *aftermaths* in which the present seems stricken with immobility and pain and ruin."[49] For Scott, "this sense of a stalled present," combined with the newly conspicuous character of time as a problem, explains the recent academic fascination with trauma, memory, ruptures, and futurity. Likewise, he interprets political campaigns for truth and reconciliation, forgiveness, and transitional justice as "symptoms of a larger crisis of time and temporal experience."[50] If such a shift in the historico-temporal matrix has occurred, what might account for it? Scott relates this rupture to the end of the era of decolonization, the advent of American-led neoliberal imperialism, and the end of hopes for Third World sovereign and socialist futures. But because Scott leaps between historically specific events and such general claims about an epochal transformation, his analysis is more suggestive than persuasive. Just this kind of leap characterizes a broader discourse of presentism that, as we saw with Berlant, unwittingly affirms neoliberalism's end-of-history triumphalism.

Historian François Hartog examines how a "crisis of time" may create a new "regime of historicity" whereby "the category of the present in its relation to the past and the future" fundamentally shifts.[51] His approach builds on Reinhart Koselleck's claims that the relation between past, present, and future is organized in historically specific ways, that this configuration shapes the ways that history is represented, and that modern historical time developed from a growing disjuncture between spaces of experience and horizons of expectation.[52] Hartog defines a "regime of historicity" in terms of "the modalities of self-consciousness that . . . every society adopts in its constructions of time."[53] He employs "regime of historicity" to "examine our relations to time historically" and "reach a better understanding . . . of moments of crisis of time" which arise "whenever the way in which past, present, and future are articulated no longer seems self-evident."[54]

Hartog distinguishes three regimes of historicity. First, Renaissance humanism searched for enlightenment in the "glorious antique past."[55] Second, a "modern regime of historicity" commenced when, following the French Revolution, "hopeful expectation was turned toward the future as source of enlightenment . . . and time became an agent . . . palpably accelerating."[56] Third, Hartog contends that "today, enlightenment has its source in the present . . . alone. To this extent . . . there is neither past nor future nor historical time."[57] He notes that while it is too soon to say definitively whether the "modern regime of historicity" has ended, "we can certainly talk of a crisis."[58] Accordingly, he detects the emergence of a new regime "in which the distance between the space of experience and the horizon of expectation has been stretched to its limit . . . with the result that the production of historical time seems to be suspended. Perhaps this is what generates today's sense of a permanent, elusive, and almost immobile present. . . . It is as though there were nothing but the present."[59] He explains, "'Presentism' is the name I have given to this moment and to today's experience of time."[60]

Hartog's evidence for this supposed shift from modern futurism to contemporary presentism is drawn primarily from philosophy, historiography, and anecdotal cultural examples. Above all, he points to a growing public concern in 1980s Europe with questions of memory, heritage, commemoration, and identity. He argues that these phenomena "emerged both in response to presentism and as symptoms of it."[61] For Hartog, this gathering crisis of time culminated in the fall of the Soviet Union. "Our relations to time were suddenly and irreversibly shattered and confounded by certain events of the recent past: the fall of the Berlin Wall in 1989, the collapse of the communist ideal as the future of the revolution, and the simultaneous rise of a number of fundamentalist movements. Everywhere the order of time ceased to be self-evident."[62] Hartog argues that 1989 signified "the end of an ideology that has always regarded itself as the vanguard of modernity. History did not come to an end, not even in Francis Fukuyama's sense, but a break appeared in the order of time (first in Europe, then gradually, in many other parts of the world)."[63]

But Hartog never adequately explains in what way, on what scale, or for whom the events associated with 1989 shattered the old order of time. Why did the collapse of the Soviet Union have the power to create a crisis in time in ways that, for example, Nazism or decolonization did not? It is one thing to trace changing philosophical and historiographical orientations to time in the contemporary moment. It is another to elevate a paradigm shift among Northern European scholars into a world-historical temporal rupture. Hartog offers incisive observations about the tendency by social actors in our media age to turn immediate experience into past history. But on this basis, he offers a series of ungrounded assertions about "our dilated present" in an epoch of "disoriented time" in which the "presentist present seeks to be determined by nothing other than itself."[64]

Ultimately, Hartog's "presentism" signals less a new temporal regime than a new *mentalité*, or set of cultural attitudes about past, present, and future. His inquiry is framed by important questions, largely borrowed from Koselleck, about the relation between how time is lived and how history is understood. We might usefully take up his invitation to examine distinct "regimes of historicity." But his method of argument through anecdote does not justify such grand claims about an epochal break in the very order of time worldwide.

Historian Enzo Traverso applies Hartog's argument about 1989 to a longer history of Left melancholy. In contrast to Hartog, who is not directly concerned with emancipatory politics, Traverso attends to the fate of Marxist and socialist imaginaries in what he, too, regards as our presentist present. He argues that the European Left had long been sustained by a "culture of defeat" in which "melancholy and utopia hypnotically attracted each other."[65] By celebrating martyrs and mourning failures, he argues, Marxism and socialism protected and transmitted their revolutionary tradition. As long as such defeats existed within a horizon of utopian expectation, they could function as empowering experiences that nourished Left sociality and solidarity. Traverso traces how, by the late twentieth century, this expectation vanished and the "dialectic of utopian melancholy, refractory to resignation" ceased to work.[66] With the decline of Fordist capitalism, the triumph of neoliberal ideology, and the crisis of mass political parties, he explains, the institutional framework for Left sociality and solidarity eroded. The "culture of defeat" could no longer stoke revolutionary resilience. A new tendency to commemorate innocent victims (of crimes against humanity, for example) displaced the radical remembrance of militant martyrs. Without a "visible 'horizon of expectation,'" Traverso concludes, "the utopias of the past" disappear and we are left with "a world withdrawn into the present."[67]

Like Hartog, Traverso treats 1989 as an epochal turning point. "Once capitalism is naturalized, to think of a different future becomes impossible. . . . The twenty-first century . . . opens in a world without utopias, paralyzed by the historical defeats of communist revolutions."[68] Without the old utopian horizon, the collapse of Soviet Communism could no longer function to strengthen Left resolve and inspire militants. "The defeat suffered by the left in 1989 . . . was a different one: it did not occur after a battle and did not engender any pride."[69] This "irreparable" loss could not "be mourned and sublimated in the living flow of a political movement."[70] It follows that "the year 1989 stresses a break . . . that closes an epoch and opens a new one."[71]

Traverso makes a persuasive claim that Left defeat in an era without a utopian horizon of expectation is qualitatively different from earlier failures. But in what sense does this experience open a new epoch in which the very character of time has shifted? Like Berlant and Scott, Traverso leaps from historical analysis to metaphysical assertion.

> The twenty-first century engendered a new kind of disillusion-
> ment. . . . This historical impasse is the result of a paralyzed dialectic:
> instead of a negation of the negation . . . we observed the reinforce-
> ment and the extension of capitalism through the demolition of its
> enemies. Blochian hope of human becoming—the 'not yet' . . . is
> abandoned in favor of an eternal present.[72]

Traverso's important insight about the changing significance of Left defeat under conditions of waning utopianism gives way to hyperbolic claims about a historical impasse, paralyzed dialectic, and eternal present.

We might question in what way the collapse of Communism really was a defeat for the global Left. Many heterodox Marxists would argue that the end of Soviet state socialism freed the Left from Third International orthodoxies and dogmatic national Communist Parties.[73] The case could be made that ac-tually existing socialism had itself been an obstacle to Left utopianism.[74] From this perspective, the concrete prospects that revolutionary socialism might re-make the global order ended not with the collapse of Soviet Communism, but with the very beginning of the Cold War. The postwar settlements crys-tallized in Fordist capitalism, bureaucratic state socialism, and Third World developmentalism preempted efforts to establish socialist forms of popular democracy. We could just as plausibly characterize the *postwar period* in terms of historical impasse or paralyzed dialectic. Recall that the Zapatista rebellion, the alterglobalization movement, and the Latin America Pink Tide created Left openings *after* 1989. The fact that they were quickly blocked, largely by the post-9/11 Global War on Terror, only attests to the historicity of the post–Cold War era. It certainly does not support overblown assertions regarding 1989 as a "shipwreck" for the "vanquished Left," ushering in a new epoch marked by an eternal present.[75] Sounding like one of Scott's traumatized mili-tants, Traverso recounts, "Such a defeat was so heavy that many of us preferred to escape rather than face it. . . . The melancholy . . . has lasted an entire generation."[76]

Traverso identifies an important dilemma. How might socialism remain viable in an era marked by the end of utopian expectation? He acknowledges that Left disenchantment can reinforce neoliberal hegemony. But like Berlant and Scott, he declares that future-oriented utopianism has been superseded and suggests that its lure should be avoided. His only alternative is to *revive* the old "tradition of left melancholy."[77] He argues that in a world where "a socialist alternative does not exist," any other attitude "inevitably becomes a disenchanted acceptation of market capitalism. . . . In this case melancholy would be the obstinate refusal of any compromise with domination."[78]

In an attempt to relate anti-utopianism to some kind of futurity, Traverso proposes that we "abandon the Freudian model and 'depathologize' melancholy" in ways that might help "the subject to become active again."[79] In his view,

> Left melancholy does not necessarily mean nostalgia for real social-
> ism and other wrecked forms of Stalinism. Rather than a regime or
> an ideology, the lost object can be the struggle for emancipation as a
> historical experience that deserves recollection and attention in spite
> of its fragile, precarious, and ephemeral duration. In this perspective,
> melancholy means memory and awareness of potentialities of the past:
> a fidelity to the emancipatory promises of revolution, not to its conse-
> quences.[80]

He thus contends, "Left-wing melancholy does not mean to abandon the idea of socialism or the hope for a better future; it means to rethink socialism in a time in which its memory is lost, hidden, and forgotten and needs to be re-deemed. This melancholia does not mean lamenting a lost utopia, but rather rethinking a revolutionary project in a nonrevolutionary age."[81]

Traverso's call to rethink revolution for a nonrevolutionary age is on point. So, too, is the effort to work through painful pasts in order to reactivate sub-jects. I fully endorse this effort to retrieve critical potentialities from former emancipatory struggles in order to reactivate radical politics under current conditions (as I discuss in Chapter 8). But at what price do we identify such a practice with melancholy? Since Freud, melancholy signals a pathologi-cal orientation to past loss that is existentially paralyzing and politically dis-abling. We can agree that this is not a politically productive relation to past defeats. But to "depathologize" melancholy would be to negate the concept's analytic purchase. I appreciate the importance of distinguishing the kind of traumatized attachment signaled by Freud's melancholy from other, less self-defeating, ways of working through past experiences and reclaiming their potentialities. But I do not see the value in calling the latter a (better) form of melancholy.[82] Curiously, Traverso invokes Walter Benjamin as a proponent of the kind of Left melancholy that he wants to revive. He writes, "Benjamin did not reject melancholia per se but only as a mood . . . voided of any political content and deprived of its critical potentialities. Against this fatalistic melancholia made of passivity and cynicism, he valorized a different melancholia consisting in a kind of epistemological posture . . . [that] collected the objects and images of a past waiting for redemption."[83]

Benjamin indeed cultivated such a posture of critical remembrance. But he never "valorized a different melancholia."

Against Left Melancholy

In a widely read 1999 essay, political theorist Wendy Brown regrets "the Left's . . . failure to apprehend the character of the age and to develop a political critique and a moral-political vision appropriate to this character."[84] She ascribes this failure to an attitude of "Left melancholy" in which "the revolutionary hack . . . is, finally, attached more to a particular political analysis or ideal—even to the failure of that ideal—than to seizing possibilities for radical change in the present."[85] This "narcissism with regard to one's past political attachments . . . exceeds any contemporary investment in political mobilization, alliance, or transformation."[86] Her conception of "Left melancholy" builds on the insights of Walter Benjamin concerning the German 1920s and Stuart Hall concerning the British 1970s. Both thinkers criticized the traditional Left for failing, in moments of historical crisis, to fulfill its self-appointed role as the leader of a mass movement for societal transformation. In each case, Brown suggests, a rigid attachment to outmoded ideals prevented Left actors from recognizing new conditions and responding adequately to new challenges. She relates this blindness and paralysis to the overwhelming sense of loss following great political defeats.

Brown sought to warn her 1999 interlocutors against the dangers of political melancholy at a moment when the global Left was suffering another round of historic losses. She was especially concerned about the tendency among traditional Leftists to scapegoat identity politics for these losses, even as they remained anachronistically attached to a reductive materialism and belief in historical teleology. The result was an impoverished "Left traditionalism" that "operates without either a deep and radical critique of the status quo or a compelling alternative to the existing order of things . . . a Left that has become more attached to its impossibility than to its potential fruitfulness . . . a Left that is thus caught in a structure of melancholic attachment to a certain strain of its own dead past."[87] In contrast, she calls for "the Left to invigorate [itself] with a radical . . . critical and visionary spirit . . . that embraces the notion of deep and indeed unsettling transformation of society."[88] She asks, in terms that should still reverberate today, "How might we draw creative sustenance from socialist ideals of dignity, equality, and freedom, while recognizing that these ideals were conjured from historical conditions and prospects that are not those of the present?"[89] Here then is a response to Traverso's dilemma that rejects rather than revives melancholic attachments to past defeats and convictions.

In the twenty years since Brown's essay, a certain kind of inversion has occurred. Her piece was part of an important critique of orthodox Marxism and socialist pieties regarding class essentialism and Eurocentric assumptions about the "real" subjects of history. Such certainties made the traditional Left hostile to poststructuralist analyses of subjectivity and cultural identity. Brown linked this hostility to the Left's inability to confront pressing challenges in meaningful ways. But from our current vantage point, we can see that the poststructuralism and culturalism which she defended subsequently renounced that for which she called *reclaiming socialist ideals in the service of societal transformation*. Fredric Jameson's famous quip, "It is easier to imagine the end of the world than to imagine the end of capitalism," captures not only liberal but much critical thinking today.[90]

To appreciate this inversion, it may help to revisit Hall and Benjamin. Although Brown stitches their positions together, each diagnosed a different kind of problem embodied by a different kind of group that required a different kind of response. In 1979, Stuart Hall challenged the inability of traditional Leftists (i.e., social democrats and orthodox Marxists) to adequately understand the rightward turn in British politics and society. More generally, he criticized the Labour Party's postwar stewardship of the social welfare state. It failed to guarantee employment or improve standards of living as promised, yet remained committed to the same statist, bureaucratic, and managerial focus on economic reform that was the source of this failure. Hall links this social democratic impotence to the fact that the nationalist, traditionalist, familialist, and antistatist self-help rhetoric fueling Thatcherism (and British neofascism) appealed to traditional white workers. It did so, he explained, not because they were duped but because it spoke directly to aspects of their worldviews and lived experiences.

From another angle, Hall argues that the British Left's inability to grasp the current crisis was rooted in its economistic certainties about the logic of capital, the movement of history, and the "real" interests of the working class. These assumptions prevented traditional Leftists from attending to the contingent ways that economic, ideological, and political domains articulate with one another in a given conjuncture. Because this old guard mistakenly regarded "British workers" as a self-evident and ready-made constituency, it did not recognize the heterogeneous character of a new working class that included women, postcolonial citizens and migrants, gays and lesbians, feminists, antiracists, and environmentalists. Hall thus called on the British Left to undertake political and ideological work on the terrain of commonsense conceptions and everyday lived experience. They would have to treat subjectivity and culture as real social forces.

Hall did not simply critique socialism and Marxism from the standpoint of cultural difference. Rather, he called for the *renewal* of socialism and Marxism on the bases of these conjunctural developments. He challenged both a "revolutionary pessimism" that renounced the prospect of transcending the present and a "revolutionary optimism" which complacently insisted that the old "class struggle continues" while underestimating the power of the Right-wing turn."[91] Hall shared the traditional aim of mass action for societal transformation. But he reminded his interlocutors that the masses would have to be *won over* to the Left through political and ideological work. For, "there is no guarantee that socialist ideas must and will prevail over other ideas."[92]

As it turned out, the new Right-wing formation that Hall diagnosed triumphed on a global scale. It was successful partly because, unlike the Left, it had undertaken the political and ideological work necessary to form effective historic blocs through which to realize a (reactionary) program for societal transformation. Following the consolidation of Thatcherism-Reaganism, many critical theorists (attentive, as Brown mentioned, to poststructuralist insights about language, discourse, subjectivity, culture, and identity) came to share Hall's critique of traditional Left economism. But they did not follow Hall's Gramscian call to engage in "political class struggle" and "ideological class struggle."[93] Rather, they tended to reject Marxism as such, along with attendant commitments to mass struggle, revolutionary overcoming, and visions of a postcapitalist world. In this respect, they had an affinity with an earlier generation of cultural critics whose "Left-wing melancholy" Benjamin so forcefully condemned.

Whereas Hall challenged the calcified Left, Benjamin targeted the nihilistic avant-garde. His 1931 essay "Left-Wing Melancholy" uses a review of the poet Erich Kästner to eviscerate the "Left-radical intelligentsia" associated with German Activism, Expressionism, and New Objectivity aesthetic movements.[94] Benjamin challenges the bad faith of this "intellectual elite" for pretending to attack the bourgeoisie to which it in fact belonged and whose values it ultimately shared.[95] These avant-garde poets, Benjamin argues, address themselves exclusively to that "stratum whose only aim was success":

despite appearances, [Kästner's] lyricism protects above all the status interests of the middle stratum—agents, journalists, heads of departments. The hatred it proclaims meanwhile toward the petty bourgeoisie has itself an all-too-intimate petty-bourgeois flavor. On the other hand, it noticeably abandons any striking power against the big bourgeoisie, and betrays its yearning for patronage.[96]

Benjamin contends that "Kästner's poems are for people in the higher income bracket, those mournful melancholy dummies who trample anything and anyone in their path."[97]

For Benjamin these poets performed a "mimicry of the proletariat" that poorly disguised their bourgeois dispositions.[98] They may have been "dissatisfied," but their "heaviness of heart derives from routine . . . And nothing is more routine than . . . irony" which is meant only to stir up "private opinion."[99] Their poetry strikes "the notes according to which poor rich folk play the blues; they correspond to the mournfulness of the satiated man who can no longer devote all his money to his stomach."[100] Benjamin dismisses their poems as "provocations" by representatives of "the decayed bourgeoisie" that merely express "bourgeois dissolution" and have "little to do with the labor movement."[101] This "Left-wing intelligentsia" proclaimed its radicalism while abdicating actual politics by retreating into intellectual games, postures, and feelings. They created political cliques rather than parties. They transposed "revolutionary reflexes . . . into objects of distraction, of amusement, which can be supplied for consumption."[102] They betrayed "a grotesque underestimation of the opponent."[103] Shifting "political struggle from a compulsory decision into an object of pleasure," these Left melancholics embrace attitudes of "know-all irony," "nihilism," "complacency and fatalism."[104] "In short," Benjamin observes, "this left-wing radicalism is precisely the attitude to which there is no longer, in general, any corresponding political action."[105] Rather than regret this absence or loss, such art "makes a great display of its poverty and turns the yawning emptiness into a celebration."[106] Its only aim "is to enjoy itself in a negativistic quiet."[107] Benjamin remarks, "the rumbling in [Kästner's] lines certainly has more to do with flatulence than subversion. Constipation and melancholy have always gone together."[108]

Benjamin regarded this trivialization and abdication of politics as especially grave at a historical moment when the stakes of struggle were so high. "Never have such comfortable arrangements been made in such an uncomfortable situation."[109] He notes that whereas "the truly political poetry of the past decades has for the most part hurried on ahead as a harbinger," the new "radical" poets only embody and express a "tortured stupidity" which embodies the "latest of two millennia of metamorphoses of melancholy."[110] Rather than mourn political failures, this variant of "Left-wing melancholy" celebrates absence, emptiness, and negativity in an ironic performance of mourning. It elevates melancholy into a radical style or posture that cultivates a nihilistic attitude toward the political situation while disregarding actually existing struggles against it. Simultaneously denouncing and reconciling itself with existing arrangements, it is complacent about the present and fatalistic about the future. Benjamin is unequivocal: Left-wing melancholy is deplorable and irredeemable.[111] He regarded naïve romanticism, uncritical progressivism, and fatalistic nihilism to be equally implicated in the political complacency that hastened the coming catastrophe.

It is easy to misread Benjamin as a backward-looking pessimist. He famously figured history as "one single catastrophe, which keeps piling wreckage upon wreckage."[112] But he did not valorize catastrophe as such. Rather, he hoped to derail the self-perpetuating process of social and ideological reproduction that characterizes bourgeois society. Revolution, he argued, was "an attempt by the passengers on [the locomotive of world-history] — namely, the human race — to activate the emergency brake."[113] Note that Benjamin defines "catastrophe" as a "basic historical concept" that means "to have missed the opportunity."[114] He was committed to seizing the opportunity to harness the energy of world-history for a socialist *future*. While there was no guarantee that such a future would ever arrive, he believed that thought should be oriented toward that possibility. On the one hand, "Being a dialectician means having the wind of history in one's sails. The sails are the concepts."[115] On the other hand, because "every epoch has . . . a side turned toward dreams," the critical task is "to pass through and carry out *what has been* in remembering the dream! Therefore: remembering and awakening are most intimately related. Awakening is namely the dialectical, Copernican turn of remembrance."[116] As we saw above, Benjamin calls on us to *awaken from* the illusory dream of the present so that we can *awaken to*, in order to carry out, unrealized dreams of the past. This position points beyond liberal progressivism *and* melancholic fatalism, both of which affirm the capitalist status quo. Rather than prioritize the past over the present, Benjamin, to use Adorno's terms, worked to set "the rigid in motion and the dynamic to rest."[117] (We can understand this as a temporal analogue of making the familiar strange and the strange familiar.)

Any attempt to link Benjamin to melancholy further crumbles when we recall that he praised Proust for having sacrificed all for an "elegiac idea of happiness," noting that the "heart-stopping explosive will to happiness which pervades Proust's writings" was "seldom comprehended by his readers."[118] Benjamin could be referring to his own future readers when he writes, "In many places Proust himself made it easy for them to view his oeuvre, too, from the time-tested, comfortable perspective of resignation . . . The idea that happiness could have a share in beauty would be too much of a good thing, something that their *ressentiment* would never get over."[119]

What Future?

I would not equate today's presentists with Benjamin's pseudosubversives. But their antipolitical disposition shares an affinity with the "Left-wing melancholy" that he diagnoses. Of course, as Hall instructed, different conditions require new strategies. There is no question of returning to ready-made Marxist or socialist solutions. Traverso rightly identifies a post–Cold War dilemma: How to envision alternative futures in a world without utopias? Wendy Brown invoked just this challenge in 1999: "We are without a sense of an international, and often even a local, left community . . . we are without a rich moral-political vision to guide and sustain political work."[120] Likewise, referring to a resurgent Latin American Left in the early 2000s, anthropologist Fernando Coronil wrote,

> On the one hand, there is a proliferation of political activities inspired by socialist or communitarian ideals aiming at fundamentally changing society. On the other, there is pervasive uncertainty with respect to the specific form of the ideal future. While there is an intense desire to change the nation, it is not clear *what* to desire.[121]

In *Undoing the Demos*, Wendy Brown has returned to this persisting dilemma. She praises recent antiausterity protests in the United States, Europe, and Turkey as attempts to reconstitute "the people as a living political body" and "reclaim the *political* voice hushed" by neoliberal capitalism.[122] "But," she asks, "a voice on behalf of what future?"[123] Brown here reiterates her earlier diagnosis: "we know what is wrong with this world, but cannot articulate a road out or a viable global alternative."[124]

How should we now respond to this persisting and pressing dilemma? Critics like Asad, Berlant, Scott, Hartog, and Traverso might suggest that the absence of a compelling alternative vision confirms that we are indeed trapped within an unsurpassable present in which Marxism, socialism, and utopianism are hopelessly, even dangerously, outmoded. But in the spirit of Benjamin, Hall, and Brown I would suggest that this absence of vision is as much an effect as it the cause of a retreat into melancholic presentism. Brown warns the Left against surrendering to "a tide of general despair, this abandoned belief in human capacities to gestate and guide a decent sustainable order."[125]

Traverso offers us a rich account of the empowering ways that socialist militants once memorialized political defeat in sustaining ways. But this practice of working through past loss by linking painful memories, utopian expectations, and renewed commitment to action is the opposite of melancholy. Traverso rightly underscores the disappearance of a social infrastructure that once sustained and was sustained by Left utopianism. But why should this lead Left thinkers now into the contradictory task of inventing "good" forms of melancholy? Why not renew a commitment to concrete utopian practices through which to invent new sources of sociality and solidarity that they might sustain and by which they might be sustained? Only then could Benjamin's critical remembrance be politically effective.

A large number of Left thinkers and actors today experience the present as an impasse. We inhabit a moment when relations of force favor Right-wing projects worldwide. Interlinked systemic crises somehow function to *strengthen* the dominion of capital, racism, and the state. Traditional Marxist and socialist concepts, analyses, and strategies fail us. Prospects for large-scale emancipatory transformation are grim. In these dark times, the Left has good reason to be pessimistic. It would be pathological *not* to struggle with political depression. But I am concerned with how political pessimism can devolve into a melancholic presentism that, however unwittingly, regards the real as rational and the given as unsurpassable.

Left presentism reifies provincial and self-identical notions of "now" in ways that are as politically limiting as the provincial and self-identical notions of "here" and "us" employed by Left culturalism. Categorical claims about cultural incommensurability and temporal unsurpassability often function to reaffirm one another. They foreclose the orientation to the possible-impossible that Marx figured by calling on militants to draw their revolutionary poetry from the future or that Benjamin figured as awakening.

Intermezzo

5
Solidarity

One can give nothing whatever without giving oneself—that is to say, risking oneself.

—JAMES BALDWIN

Politics does not reflect majorities, it constructs them.

—STUART HALL

A Contradictory Concept

The concept of "solidarity" developed simultaneously with the bourgeois social order whose individualist logic it opposed. From the French *solidaire*, it has long signaled the solid bloc of resistance, the forms of association and unity that developed among modernity's dispossessed. Peter Linebaugh and Marcus Rediker use the term to describe the forms of autonomous self-organization and coordinated resistance that developed between the sixteenth and nineteenth centuries, among sailors, slaves, pirates, dockworkers, peasants, religious radicals, and radical republicans across the Atlantic world.[1] Likewise, Thomas C. Holt uses solidarity to analyze forms of slave resistance and postemancipation revolts in colonial Jamaica.[2] Historians E. P. Thompson and William Sewell use the idiom of solidarity to trace how, following the French and industrial revolutions, European craftsman and skilled workers mobilized existing forms of collective identification and corporate organization to resist processes of expropriation and proletarianization through mutual aid societies, workers' associations, and strikes.[3] In Europe these resistant solidarity practices slowly crystallized into a political project to reconstitute society on a nonliberal foundation. The term *solidarité* began to circulate in the milieu of early-nineteenth-century French labor militancy and republican socialism.

The popular current of the 1848 Revolution in France fought to create a social republic that would assume responsibility for citizens' welfare through instituting social rights founded on these same principles of mutuality, reciprocity, cooperation, and collectivity. Pierre-Joseph Proudhon, the self-taught printer and revolutionary socialist who participated directly in this revolution, explicitly used the concept of solidarity to describe his mutualist program for "socialist democracy" through the self-organization of workers into producers' cooperatives and the creation of a democratic system of banking and credit.[4] "Equality in exchange," he argued, would serve as "the basis of the equality of labor, of real solidarity."[5] Likewise, a Bank of the People would "[organize] workers' mutual solidarity" in the service of a democratic socialist republic based on nonexploitive relations of exchange.[6] Proudhon believed that cooperative labor and democratic credit would allow the "democratic and social creed" to triumph on ever larger scales: from workers' associations to collective ownership of small farms and firms to large-scale property and industry to massive ventures such as mines, canals, and railways.[7] These would be "handed over to democratically organized workers' associations" that would serve as "the pioneering core of [a] vast federation of companies and societies woven into the common cloth of the democratic and social Republic."[8] Proudhon remarked that in such an "antigovernmental" society, "the center is everywhere, the circumference nowhere."[9] Accordingly, he believed that these cooperative practices would create "real solidarity among the nations."[10] He thus viewed mutualism and internationalism as two sides of the same coin; solidarity would guide relations within and across social formations.

Marx's thinking was also inflected by the 1848 Revolution. Despite deep disagreement with Proudhon, he, too, regarded social solidarity as both a means and end of anticapitalist struggle. Between the 1840s and 1870s, Marx critiqued industrial capitalism, liberal democracy, and the bourgeois state from the standpoint of "association," a concept that reverberated with solidarity. In one register, Marx used "association" to describe the forms of sociality, organization, and unity practiced by workers in everyday life, in the workplace, and through labor struggles. *The Communist Manifesto* describes how "the advance of industry . . . replaces the isolation of the laborers, due to competition, by the revolutionary combination, due to association."[11] Accordingly, workers "club together in order to keep up the rate of wages; they found permanent associations in order to make provision . . . for these occasional revolts."[12] Through this "ever-expanding union of the workers" local class conflicts would coalesce into a common political struggle.[13]

Marx treats association as both a method of labor militancy and its aim; it would allow workers to enjoy the kind of cooperative sociality that competitive capitalism had obstructed. In his 1844 manuscripts he writes, "When communist *workmen* gather together, their immediate aim is instruction, propaganda, etc. But at the same time they acquire a new need — the need for society — and what appears as a means has become an end."[14] He notes, "In the gatherings of French socialist workers . . . [s]moking, eating and drinking, etc. are no longer means of creating links between people. Company, association, conversation, which in its turn has society as its goal, is enough for them. The brotherhood of man is not a hollow phrase, it is a reality."[15]

These forms and practices of worker association became one model for Marx's vision of a disalienated society. Rejecting any understanding of "society" as an abstract entity that exists "over against the individual," he argues that "the individual *is* the *social being*. His vital expression . . . is therefore an expression and confirmation of *social life*."[16] This formulation was reiterated in his sixth thesis on Feuerbach: "The human essence is no abstraction inherent in each single individual. In its reality it is the ensemble of the social relations."[17] Accordingly, Marx praises "activity and consumption that express and confirm themselves directly in *real association* with other men."[18] He characterizes Communism as "activity in direct association with others"[19] and contends that "in a real community . . . individuals obtain their freedom in and through their association."[20] Association thus indexed a form of sociality that would cut across the modern opposition between the individual and society.

The Communist Manifesto envisions a postcapitalist order in which "class distinctions have disappeared, and all production [is] concentrated in the hands of a vast association of the whole nation."[21] As Marx and Engels famously declared, "We shall have an association, in which the free development of each is the condition for the free development of all."[22] Ten years later, in the *Grundrisse*, Marx contrasts capitalism, where individuals produce "for society" a system in which they produce in a "*directly* social" manner as the "offspring of association" in order to "manage" their "common wealth."[23] Likewise, in the first volume of *Capital* (1867), Marx refers to "directly associated labor" and "production by freely associated men" as his standpoint of critique and emancipatory horizon.[24]

In 1871, worldly events intersected with Marx's proleptic social analysis when the Paris Commune attempted to transform land and capital into "mere instruments of free and associated labour."[25] By these means, Marx believed, "united cooperative societies" could "regulate national production upon a common plan" and thereby institute a form of "'possible' communism."[26] Through "the reabsorption of state power by society as its own living forces," he explained, the "popular masses themselves" made the Paris Commune into "the political form of their social emancipation."[27] The Commune seemed to have realized, however fleetingly, Marx's earlier hope and call for "human emancipation:

> Only when real, individual man resumes the abstract citizen into himself and as an individual man has become a *species-being* in his empirical life, his individual work and his individual relationships, only when man has recognized and organized his *forces propres* as *social forces* so that social force is no longer separated from him in the form of *political* force, only then will human emancipation be completed.[28]

Association thus pointed beyond alienating bourgeois oppositions between public and private, state and society, citizen and human.

Marx also identified in the Paris Commune the germ of a revolutionary internationalism that would be cause and consequence of new solidarity practices. Beyond being the "true representative of . . . French society . . . and . . . the truly national government," Marx explained, "as a working men's government, as the bold champion of the emancipation of labor, emphatically international . . . the Commune annexed to France the working people of the world."[29] He praises the Commune for rejecting the nationalist "chauvinism of the bourgeoisie" and argues that "the international cooperation of the working classes" is "the first condition of their emancipation."[30] Marx contends that the revolutionary aim was not only to create an international alliance of struggling workers against bourgeois class rule, but to institute a new epoch of human history where all of "mankind" could be freely associated "through the Communal form of political organization."[31] By linking communal self-management and human emancipation on a planetary scale, "association" was a concrete universal that pointed beyond the false distinction between concrete particularity and abstract universality.

Marx, of course, had long been committed to internationalist solidarity. *The Communist Manifesto*, which famously ended with the call "Working men of all countries, unite!," pledged that "Communists everywhere support every revolutionary movement against the existing social and political order of things . . . they labor everywhere for the union and agreement of the democratic parties of all countries."[32] Recall that Marx and Engels were originally commissioned to write the *Manifesto* at the November 1847 convention of the Communist League, which Engels described as an international "workingmen's association."[33] Almost twenty years later, in September 1864, they helped to form the International Workingmen's Association in the wake of the European-wide counterrevolution.

In his Inaugural Address to this First International, Marx attributes the failures of 1848 to the absence of "solidarity of action between the British and continental working classes."[34] He warned that "disregard of that bond of brother-hood, which ought to exist between workmen of different countries, and incite them to stand firmly by each other in all their struggles for emancipation, will be chastised by . . . their incoherent efforts."[35] For Marx, international labor solidarity was not merely a matter of abstract morality or disinterested em-pathy. He insisted that the failure of one fraction of the working class would ensure the failure of the movement as a whole. Because conditions of domi-nation were interrelated, their common future depended on one another. It followed that the "working classes" had a "duty to master . . . the mysteries of international politics" in order to "counteract" the "diplomatic acts of their respective governments."[36] Marx praised English workers for opposing Atlan-tic slavery and called on European labor movements to defend Poland against Russian imperial conquest. The Provisional Rules of the International held that "the emancipation of labor is neither a local nor a national, but a social problem embracing all the countries in which modern society exists."[37] To this end, the organization pledged that "when immediate practical steps should be needed, as, for instance, in case of international quarrels, the action of the associated societies be simultaneous and uniform."[38] On a more mundane but no less important level, each national association pledged to provide "the fraternal support of the associated workingmen" to any individual member who moved residence from one country to another.[39] In matters of solidarity, overarching principles could not be separated from everyday practices.

Marx's understanding of international solidarity is nicely condensed in his 1870 letter on Irish nationalism to German comrades in the United States. He explains that because England is the world "metropolis of capital," a so-cial revolution there would be indispensable to the emancipation of labor everywhere.[40] Next, he observed that English wealth and power depended largely on the colonization of Ireland—that is, the expropriation of land and dispossession of peasants, cheap raw materials and a surplus population to fuel industrialization at home, and religious and nationalist prejudices to keep the metropolitan working class divided. Finally, he noted that revolution in Ireland could be more easily accomplished than in England. Marx therefore concluded that "the decisive blow against the English ruling classes (and it will be decisive for the workers' movement all over the world) cannot be de-livered *in England* but *only in Ireland*."[41] These are the grounds on which he called on the International to support Irish national liberation. Its "special task" was "to make the English workers realize that *for them* the *national emancipation of Ireland* is not a question of abstract justice or humanitarian sentiment but the *first condition of their own social emancipation*."[42] This last sentence underscores that Marx's revolutionary internationalism was not a bourgeois humanism.

Marx insisted that international solidarity was both a tactical necessity and a good in itself, declaring that "all societies and individuals adhering to [the International], will acknowledge truth, justice, and morality, as the basis of their conduct towards each other, and towards all men, without regard to color, creed, or nationality; They hold it the duty of a man to claim the rights of a man and a citizen, not only for himself, but for every man who does his duty."[43] This was not a form of post-Enlightenment abstract universalism that would homogenize peoples and standardize differences. Marx does not propose the eventual dissolution of specific worker associations or their amalgamation into a central governing body. On the contrary, he explains that "joining the International Association, will preserve their existent organizations intact."[44] He envisions a global federation of self-managing "workingmen's societies" that would be "united in a perpetual bond of fraternal cooperation."[45] For Marx, both local self-management and worldwide internationalism were grounded in solidarity practices. He hoped to conjugate them within a new differential unity. This was a vision of *concrete universalism* rooted in translocal networks of socialist association.

The *belle époque* European order feared precisely the kinds of revolutionary solidarity promoted by Marxism and embodied by the Paris Commune. At roughly the same time, such solidarity was also expressed in the "general strike" of enslaved Blacks during the U.S. Civil War, the 1865 Morant Bay peasant rebellion in Jamaica, the rent strikes and boycotts against landlords and evictions during the Irish Land War (1879–1882), and the coordinated actions of anarchist networks linking Europe, East Asia, and the Caribbean.[46] National states, colonial administrations, ruling classes, industrial oligarchs, and *ancien régime* autocrats were equally opposed to the prospect of a global federation of self-managing and freely associated producers. Their counterrevolutionary fear, along with the new requirements of mass production, mass politics, and colonial rule set in motion the historic compromise among labor, capital, and the state which led first to social democracy and the Second International, and eventually to Fordist capitalism and Keynesian welfarism. Perversely, this attempt to reform liberal capitalism in order to neutralize Marxism and preempt class war was also articulated in the language of solidarity.

Solidarisme, as elaborated by Léon Bourgeois, famously became a state ideology in Third Republic France.[47] At the same time, the new field of academic sociology, dominated by Émile Durkheim and his circle, elevated social solidarity into an object of analysis, a normative ideal, and a reformist desire.[48] Republican politicians and scholars began to question classical liberal assumptions about society by conceptualizing individuals as intrinsically social beings, born into webs of interdependence. In contrast to contract theory, they reconceptualized society as founded upon reciprocity, mutuality, and shared risk.[49] In this story, individuals assumed responsibility for their neighbors, employers for their workers, and the state for the welfare of its citizens. This new discourse of solidarity appropriated—in order to domesticate—workerist, socialist, and Marxist critiques of liberal capitalism. Its aim was to ensure social integration and public order, not to realize social justice and public freedom. Accordingly, it naturalized solidarity as a social fact rather than recognize it as a political practice. The new politics of solidarity may have blurred the categorical distinction between state and society that Marx regarded as a source of alienation. But it also helped to consolidate a more powerful form of capitalism, to further expand the scale and scope of national state power, and to ground new strategies of imperial rule.[50]

Of course, social democrats, liberal sociologists, welfare states, and colonial administrators were never able to fully recuperate radical solidarity struggles and imaginaries. Marcel Mauss's reflections on the contemporary importance of "archaic" forms of exchange associated with "the gift," for example, indicate how the transformative implications of solidarity practices could point beyond even scholars' own reformist intentions.[51] More broadly, the legacy and spirit of solidarity politics were equally present in popular cooperative movements from the 1880s through the mid-twentieth century among workers and peasants in Europe, the United States, Latin America, the Caribbean, West Africa, and South Asia.[52] The solidarity ethos also infused the mutual aid societies, multiracial labor unions, and mass movements for colonial emancipation among colonized workers and students living in European metropoles between the world wars.[53]

A different example of the enduring legacy of solidarity politics is offered by Antonio Gramsci. He participated in the Turin factory occupation and council movement that culminated in the 1920 General Strike. These insurgent interventions depended on effective solidarity relations between urban and rural actors in order to link factories, cities, and the region in a broad movement for workers democracy.[54] In his subsequent analysis of "the Southern question," Gramsci also engaged the challenge and necessity of revolutionary solidarity. Contending that capitalism, rather than cultural backwardness, was the reason for uneven development in twentieth-century Italy, Gramsci argued for a new alliance between northern workers and southern peasants.[55] The point was not to recruit peasants to orthodox Marxism but to have workers assume peasant struggles as their own. Gramsci's later prison reflections on relations of force, political blocs, and socialist hegemony were also engagements with the problem of solidarity.[56]

Gramsci may be usefully related to W. E. B. Du Bois, his American contemporary, who inherited a legacy of solidarity practices from the Black radical tradition which he related to his specific historical situation. During the 1930s Great Depression Du Bois elaborated a program for Black self-management through consumer cooperatives that would serve as both model and catalyst for transforming liberal democracy in the United States into a new "cooperative commonwealth."[57] For Du Bois, solidarity worked in multiple registers. It was a tactic for community survival under conditions of severe deprivation and persecution. It was also part of a long-term strategy of cross-group alliance for a broad movement to transform American society into a multiracial socialist democracy composed of federated cooperatives. Solidarity was also implied by the mutualist principle of sociality that would be practiced within Black cooperative associations and, eventually, the larger society.[58]

Both Gramsci and Du Bois were heterodox Marxists who confronted the challenge of human emancipation in relation to historically specific political situations within unevenly developed and culturally divided societies. Their respective commitments to solidarity struggles and associative politics were inspired, even enabled, by the Russian Revolution. Yet they embraced and extended solidarity traditions in ways that diverged sharply from the authoritarian centralism favored by Soviet state socialism and the Moscow-led Third International. The latter purported to extend the tradition of Marxist internationalism by creating a worldwide network of revolutionary anticapitalist and anti-imperial organizations (whose infrastructure was formed by various national Communist Parties). But given its preoccupation with ideological orthodoxy, its universalist assumptions about history, revolution, and Communism, and its embrace of bureaucratic statism and opposition to democratic self-management, the Third International may be seen as another instance through which the radical legacy of solidarity practices and politics were instrumentalized and domesticated.

Nevertheless, the Third International did facilitate and extend networks of anti-imperial internationalists across Europe, Asia, Africa, the Middle East, Latin America, North America, and the Caribbean.[59] Such transversal connections proved invaluable to struggles for decolonization and often promoted forms of political association and associative politics that transgressed the bureaucratic statism and Cold War geopolitics that sponsored them. The solidarity politics of anticolonial internationalism linked struggles within and across regions and empires. Examples, among others, include the Pan-African mobilization against the Italian invasion of Ethiopia, Frantz Fanon joining the anticolonial revolution in Algeria, C. L. R. James organizing Black revolutionaries in the United States, and Cuban fighters and aid workers joining their comrades in the Congo and Angola. The African American civil rights struggle identified and allied explicitly with anticolonial national liberation movements (and vice versa). The Bandung Conference was organized under the rubric of "Afro-Asian solidarity." The more radical Tricontinental Congress created in Havana in 1966 gave birth to the Organization of Solidarity with the People of Asia, Africa, and Latin America.

A proper history of solidarity politics would link the legacies of the Paris Commune and anticolonial liberation struggles to the events surrounding May 1968 in France. Many of the militant groups that were active during May 1968 were organized around mutualist principles of association. The larger insurrection depended on and promoted unprecedented solidarity practices between students, factory workers, intellectuals, and technocrats; between the capital, provincial cities, and the countryside; and between white and colonized subalterns.[60] Moreover, this insurrection was part of a global wave of antisystemic rebellion that linked Paris to places like Prague, Mexico City, and Dakar.[61] Solidarity politics have been central to both the internal organization and international support networks mobilized by Sandinistas, Zapatistas, and the current anti-Zionist Boycott Divestment and Sanctions (BDS) coalition. Solidarity politics subtended the global antiapartheid struggle and the Central American sanctuary movement; the alterglobalization movement and World Social Forum; and recent antiautocracy, antiausterity, and Occupy movements in the Middle East, Turkey, Europe, and the United States.

In our current conjuncture, however, when solidarity politics have never been more urgent, the concept has again been instrumentalized and domesticated. This is not only by the statist, populist, and popular forms of nationalism, nativism, and racism that are resolutely identitarian and internal looking. Solidarity today has also been co-opted by proponents of liberal internationalism. Western states, international agencies and institutions (like the International Criminal Court), and the forces of "global governance" regularly justify imperial military interventions through solidaristic doctrines of human rights, humanitarianism, Just War, and the Responsibility to Protect.[62] The internet has allowed solidarity to be further diluted, if not depololiticized, through individuals' immediate capacity to express digital likes, hearts, and thumbs-up. International social media displaces, by perversely mimicking, socialist internationalism.

A Critical Political Concept

Like all concepts, solidarity developed in relation to worldly processes from which it emerged and to which it spoke. Historian Reinhardt Koselleck contends that concepts "register" historical experiences, contradictions, and transition.[63] For Mikhail Bakhtin, linguistic artifacts are "heteroglot unities" that condense diverse, competing, and interrelated socio-ideological forces within a given social field and across historical periods.[64] Étienne Balibar suggests that an "essential element of uncertainty" characterizes concepts.[65] Rather than grasping the world as it really is or settling questions, he suggests that a concept "exhibits dilemmas" by pointing to a "conflictual horizon."[66] Solidarity is just such an ambiguous, contradictory, and contested concept. It has been conscripted for and, in turn, soaked up a range of often incompatible political orientations and projects. It continues to reverberate with and mark a conflictual horizon that includes political challenges posed by translocal entanglement, interdependence, and shared risk. It condenses the enduring dilemma raised by the antinomy of popular sovereignty and planetary politics identified by Kant and Arendt (discussed above).

But the concept's contradictory genealogy does not undermine its potential as a critical political concept. "Solidarity" does not only crystallize persistent dilemmas. It illuminates them in ways that may point beyond some of the limiting frameworks and false oppositions that continue to overdetermine political thinking today. The aim of my genealogy is not to criticize the way discourses of solidarity serve to normalize power relations. Rather, it is to suggest that a tradition of radical solidarity politics may be usefully reactivated today. To this end, I would like to distill from my historical sketch a set of provisional propositions about this concept for our times.

We might usefully distinguish three types or aspects of solidarity. First is solidarity as a principle of struggle whereby actors recognize shared or related conditions of domination and coordinate collective responses. Second is solidarity as a principle of sociality whereby actors pursue self-organization in the spirit of interdependent reciprocity, mutual responsibility, shared risks, and common futures. Third, and related, is solidarity as a principle of cosmopolitan or international linkage across collectivities.

Solidarity is never a given. In contrast to how it is understood by Durkheimian sociology and certain currents of orthodox Marxism, solidarity is a political act, not a social fact. It does not flow naturally from primordial social groupings (whether figured as kinship, community, ethnicity, nationality, or class). Nor should it be conflated with the fiction of self-interested individuals entering social compacts to guarantee security and maximize material welfare. Solidarity presupposes and produces social subjects. Social groups are as much the effect of solidarity as its source. The concept points beyond the conventional opposition between natural communities (supposed to precede politics) and transhistorical individuals (supposed to precede society).

Solidarity is a practice, not a sentiment. The different motives that fuel solidarity practices are less important than the political, social, and ethical work that they pursue.

Solidarity requires risk. In contrast to feelings of compassion or acts of charity from a safe distance, solidarity is a standing-with where something is at stake. It means renouncing safety and sharing risk, putting oneself on the line by propelling oneself over the line that is supposed to mark an outside. Relations of solidarity are forged in shared or common struggle.

Solidarity starts from entanglement. The non-indifferent commitment to "stand with" flows from the fact of mutual implication, from actors' recognition that they are already involved in each other's situations, that they share a common world, and their future prospects are somehow bound together. They may be subject to similar conditions of oppression, recognize a common enemy, or be linked through a broader system of intersecting domination. Alternatively, members of socially dominant groups may recognize their own implication in and responsibility for others' domination, whether near or far. In both cases, solidarity starts from the fact that in a common world, forms of domination create relations of mutual responsibility whereby the fate of each depends on all, and all on each.

Radical solidarity politics contrast with the kind of logic that underlies something like the liberal international "Responsibility to Protect" whereby atomized individuals delegate their social power to alien agencies (such as states) that act, often violently, to "protect" suffering individuals, figured as absolute others, in the name of humanity. But solidarity also differs from Emmanuel Levinas's and Jacques Derrida's ideas about infinite responsibility for the absolute other, which situate self and other on different ontological and ethical planes.[67] Solidarity is the response to a call, not the obligation to a face. It figures horizontal relationships among social individuals within and across struggling collectives who are already concretely implicated in each other's history and fate. But it does not assume that privileged majorities and dominated minorities are equally responsible to one another.

Solidarity is a practice of identification that cuts across conventional oppositions between identity and difference. It calls into question categorical divisions between insiders and outsiders, the threatened and the protected, the implicated and the indifferent, those who must take sides and spectators or commentators who can afford to stay off the field. But this does not mean that solidarity presupposes sameness, levels differences, or assimilates heterogeneity into a singular identity or undifferentiated totality. Nor does it expect consensus. It is an uneven, messy, and risky enterprise, ever incomplete, that reveals systemic contradictions, acknowledges power differentials, and generates real conflicts.

Solidarity emerges from and creates differential unities. It is not based on the concrete particular identity of primordial communities that naturally stick together or act in unison. Nor is it based on the abstract universal identity of generic humans who supposedly share a common essence (e.g., reason, will, compassion, pain). Solidarity recognizes the existence of differences that need to be provisionally coordinated. Yet, at every scale, solidarity also calls into question categorical separations by recognizing or creating knots and networks of interdependent singularities. It establishes forms of heterogeneous commonality and concrete universality that displace false oppositions between the abstract universal and the concrete particular, totality and plurality, the shared and the singular. Solidarity refers to mutuality and reciprocity *within and across* heterogeneous formations. It explodes commonsense divisions between us and them, inside and outside, here and there, proximity and distance.

Solidarity practices work to create new subjects for a different kind of social order and to create new social arrangements for a different kind of social subjectivity. It is both a means and an end in itself, an instrument of politics and a political good, an ethical practice and a practical ethics, a strategy that enacts the relations it hopes to institute. It refers to both a historical legacy and a future aspiration. If solidarity indicates a political practice and envisions a set of social arrangements, it also signals a political challenge—the very challenge of politics—to which there can be no definitive solution. In contrast to pragmatic realism and regulative idealism, solidarity is a real practice that has no intrinsic limits.

Solidarity is as much a temporal as a spatial concept. Just as it seeks to connect diverse groups geographically, solidarity may also link different generations across seemingly separate historical epochs. We can think of traditions and legacies as forms of *temporal* solidarity that invite actors to assume responsibility for past and future generations. Recall Kant's claim that humans "cannot be indifferent even to the most remote epoch which may eventually affect our species," and of Benjamin's "secret agreement between past generations and the present one" that endows predecessors with moral claims on existing actors.[68]

Solidarity reworks conventional assumptions about the grounds of political association. It contends that emancipation struggles should create solid blocs and dense networks in order to overcome multiple and intersecting forms of domination. It also suggests that the aim of such struggles is to create a social world and form of life based on principles of reciprocity, mutuality, and collectivity that are prefigured by forms of struggle. In other words, *solidarity anticipates futures; it calls for in order to call forth*. It displaces conventional oppositions between doing and waiting, the actual and the possible, realism and utopianism. Solidarity practices are always *taking place* and *stretching time*. Propelled by the dialectics of distinction and connection, multiplication and unification, its work can never reach a boundary or come to a stop.

Solidarity conveys a vision of democratic sociality in an interdependent world. By emphasizing association *within and across* social groups, the concept simultaneously affirms and calls into question determinate social communities and the boundaries of polities.

The global swerve toward national populism and authoritarian statism compels all those who can to stand with the many precarious communities targeted by forms of violent nationalism, nativism, and white supremacy. Any number of contemporary political situations call for solidarity politics: the war in Syria, the Mediterranean refugee crisis, the policies of Fortress Europe, the occupation of Palestine, violent imperial interventions perpetrated under US-UN auspices, sovereign debt crises among small nations, and global climate change among them.

More generally and fundamentally, the life prospects of most of the world's peoples and populations are increasingly determined by systemic forces and distant deciders beyond the reach of any state's sovereign power. Demographic, economic, geopolitical, and environmental entanglement and interdependence have never been denser. Processes of structural violence are creating impossible situations for greater numbers of people, a growing proportion of whom are permanently displaced. Like translation and internationalism, solidarity politics always risk slipping into paternalism and reproducing hierarchies. But under current global conditions, the need to coordinate struggles, assume responsibility, and share risks across spurious divisions has never been greater. Equally urgent is the imperative to envision and enact postnational democratic social orders based on principles of reciprocity, mutuality, and collective self-management. Only then might we have any chance of overcoming the rule of capital, the sovereignty of reified states, and social hierarchies based on invidious ontological distinctions among humans.

The concept of solidarity refers to both a method of struggle (in concert) and a principle of sociality (in common) for which the struggle is waged. It indexes forms of unity *within and across* social groups and formations. It conjures nonliberal forms of concrete universality and differential unity founded upon interconnected singularities and federated associations.

Solidarity seeks to transform imperial wars into civil wars.

Solidarity *anticipates a world we wish to see.*

6

Anticipation

... and the Blacks go searching in the dust ... for splinters from
which mica is made from which moons are made and the fissile slate
out of which sorcerers make the intimate ferocity of the stars.

— AIMÉ CÉSAIRE

Futurity and Progress

When Adorno famously declared that "the only philosophy which can be responsibly practiced in face of despair is the attempt to contemplate all things
from the standpoint of redemption," he was calling on thinkers to fashion
perspectives that reveal the world to be "as indigent and distorted *as it will
appear* one day in the messianic light."[1] I suggest we expand this formulation
to include the prospect of *acting as if from the standpoint of what will appear
to have been.* Doing so may serve as a starting point for treating "anticipation"
as a political concept in the multivalent sense of preceding and preparing,
expecting and enacting, calling for and calling forth, acting "as if" and inhabiting the future anterior space of "what will have been."

Adorno's formulation reminds us that radical politics requires a standpoint
of critique. It must posit some kind of gap between "is" and "ought," some
position from which to challenge existing arrangements in the name of a better alternative. Any claim about the relation between the actual, the possible,
and the desirable must presuppose or posit some kind of relationship between
the present and the future. Yet particular understandings of futurity cannot be
separated from a given social formation's dominant ways of organizing time.

In the modern West, historian Reinhardt Koselleck describes "the temporalization of history" whereby time assumed a different *quality*, and history
assumed a *temporal* character.[2] Koselleck identifies a contradiction within
this "new time." It figured history as a contingent process shaped by human
action whose outcome would always be unknown and unpredictable. Yet, at
the same time, it understood history as a systemically integrated and progressively unfolding process.

Any attempt by the Left to think the future or contest liberal conceptions
of progress must therefore address *both* sides of this understanding of history
as contingent and directional, underdetermined and meaningful. On the one
hand, such a critique would have to insist that because humans make history,
the given order is not the necessary or only possible set of arrangements. On
the other, it would also emphasize how, in the modern period, social practices
have set in motion a quasi-autonomous process that compels a certain kind
of systemic forward motion and provokes future-oriented activities, which are
sources of alienation, destruction, and domination over which individuals
have no real control. Critical theory and Left politics must therefore challenge
both the liberal idea of history as a process of automatic improvement *and* its
demand that individuals improve themselves in order to perfect society.

Koselleck's account reminds us that this concept of historical progress and
abstract clock-time reinforced one another. Modern society and thought reduced heterogeneous temporal processes to a measurable, linear, unidirectional understanding of history. And diverse historical processes were treated
in terms of a measurable, linear, and additive conception of time. The result
was a conventional understanding of history as proceeding along a continuum, yet within which categorical distinctions exist between "past," present,"
and "future."

Walter Benjamin famously criticized the bourgeois conception of progress
for being founded on a shallow and quantitative understanding of homogeneous empty time. Reformist Social Democrats, he explained, confused progress of knowledge and skills with progress of humankind. They mistakenly
assumed that the latter would follow an automatic course through time and
as history. This erroneous assumption, according to Benjamin, was linked
to academic "historicism," which treated the present as a transition along a
linear continuum. He thus criticized conventional historians for practicing
an additive and positivist method of history whereby a mass of data is assembled simply to fill homogeneous empty time, events are aligned in sequences,
and causal connections are posited between them. In contrast, Benjamin offered his famous image of progress as a storm blowing from paradise, piling

wreckage upon wreckage within an unending catastrophe. He contended that bourgeois progress, reduced to the technocratic mastery of nature, led to the "retrogression of society."[3]

However differently, both Koselleck and Benjamin remind us that a quantitative understanding of time as abstract and measurable subtended the use of quantitative metrics to evaluate progress (whether in terms of knowledge, expertise, technology, power, or accumulation).[4] Once abstract time and historical progress were elevated into a second nature, futurity could function as an instrument of social reproduction, political legitimation, and normative regulation. State power, capital accumulation, and technological innovation came to depend increasingly on knowing and controlling the future, through experts devoted to statistical prediction and rational planning.[5] These sciences of prediction and planning became entwined with invidious forms of expropriation and expansion, governmentality and technocracy, productivism and consumerism, the imperative to accelerate or perish, and growth for growth's sake. Yet a liberal logic of deferral asked actors to sacrifice today for an idealized future that is both certain to come and will never arrive. Under these conditions, a certain form of anticipation facilitated social domination.[6]

Recent critics have rightly examined how liberal assumptions about progressive futures (where improvement is figured as inevitable and incremental) still function to divert political critique and defer transformative action.[7] Others focus on how discourses of anticipation forecast catastrophic futures in ways that blackmail actors to accept preventative measures and defer radical politics.[8] There is no doubt that cruel optimism and benevolent pessimism often instrumentalize anticipation in depoliticizing ways: to prohibit or require certain kinds of citizen action, to legitimize or exempt certain state interventions, and to produce docile and anxious subjects who become trapped in states of what Berlant has nicely phrased "animated suspension."[9] The constant exhortation to self-manage, improve, and promote is accompanied by precarity and exhaustion, uncertainty and anxiety, disorientation and meaninglessness.

But does this mean that all future-oriented thinking or action is intrinsically disabling, normalizing, and depoliticizing? It would be a mistake to reduce futurity *as such* to a liberal progressive ruse. Doing so leads, as I suggested above, into the impasses of Left melancholy and presentism. Along these lines, Lee Edelman rejects "every realization of futurity," any aspiration to forge "some more perfect social order," any action oriented toward future "good."[10] Instead he celebrates *jouissance* as bound up with the death drive and an absolutist negation of social form.[11] From a less nihilistic perspective, Adams, Murphy, and Clarke ask us to refuse anticipation categorically.[12] Any political project oriented toward societal transformation must recognize how existing relations of domination are mediated by the idea and reality of progress.[13] But to abandon good-life imaginaries and future-oriented practices altogether is to erase the crucial space between how things are and how they ought to be.

Some thinkers have attempted to challenge liberal progressivism without abandoning futurity by turning to ungrounded utopianism (which conjures perfect worlds out of whole cloth), blank futurism (which refuses to identify possible alternatives), or Messianic apocalypticism (which fetishizes the sudden event that will unexpectedly arrive to produce an absolute rupture). But these orientations tend to leave present arrangements undisturbed. Gershom Scholem noted "the paradoxical nature" of the Messianic idea in Judaism whereby the wished-for redemption can have no concrete relationship to previous history. As a "transcendence breaking in upon history . . . from an outside source," he explains, Jewish redemption rejects the Enlightenment idea of historical progress. But it also rules out the possibility of immanent developments or history-making practices. Scholem thus suggests that the "price demanded by Messianism" has been "endless powerlessness in Jewish history. . . . There is something grand about living in hope, but at the same time there is something profoundly unreal about it. . . . In Judaism the Messianic idea has compelled a life lived in *deferment*."[14]

Although Benjamin invoked this Messianic tradition, his reflections "On the Concept of History" do not imply powerlessness, pessimism, or deferment. Noting the Jewish tradition's prohibition on "inquiring into the future," he endorsed its focus on "remembrance" as a way to "disenchant the future, which holds sway over those who turn to soothsayers for Enlightenment."[15] But Benjamin was less concerned with renouncing futurity as such than with challenging the homogeneous empty clock-time and the associated continuum that underlie bourgeois conceptions of predictable futures, automatic progress, and historicist history. His revolutionary Messianism challenged the political passivity of German Social Democrats whose faith in automatic human progress, he argued, had opened the door to fascism and diverted the working classes from making their own history here and now.

Benjamin sought to break the spell of bourgeois progress by understanding history in terms of "Now-time, which, as a model of messianic time, comprises the entire history of mankind in a tremendous abbreviation."[16] This was neither a call to adapt to the present nor to wait for a divine irruption. It was a reminder that "every second was the straight gate through which the Messiah might enter."[17] By Messiah, he means *us*, contemporary human actors. When we read this statement alongside his second thesis, it becomes clear that this is a political, and not a strictly theological, claim: "There is a secret agreement between past generations and the present one . . . our coming was expected on earth . . . like every generation that preceded us, we have been endowed with a *weak* messianic power on which the past has a claim."[18] In this formulation, living historical actors are themselves quasi-messianic agents who, at any second, and in the name of past generations, might bring clock-time to a halt, break the historical continuum, and attempt to redeem the world through political revolution. In this way, modern society would be emancipated from an infernal history of ongoing catastrophe enabled by "progressive" processes whereby human actions constituted the quasi-autonomous force that was propelling them blindly into a future over which they had no control.[19] Benjamin suggested that this revolutionary interruption could end the "storm" of progress, free humans from their "servile integration in an uncontrollable apparatus," and perhaps even allow actors "to stay, awaken the dead, and make whole what has been smashed" (as the Angel of History wished to, but could not, do).[20]

Benjamin is not only offering a formal definition of revolution as redemptive rupture. Despite the Jewish injunction not to inquire into the future, he also elaborates substantive images of a "redeemed" postrevolutionary society. In it, there would no longer exist a "positivist" and "corrupted conception of labor" rooted in "the Protestant work ethic" which collapses human progress with "technological development" and is "tantamount to the exploitation of nature."[21] In contrast, Benjamin envisions a new form of "cooperative labor" that would "increase efficiency to such an extent that . . . far from exploiting nature, would help her give birth to the creations that now lie dormant in her womb."[22] Emancipated from alienated labor, "historical progress," and the tyranny of quantitative clock-time, human actors (honoring their responsibility to enslaved ancestors) would make their own worlds within a qualitative now-time.

Benjamin thus offers us an orientation to futurity that breaks with the logic of deferment contained in both liberal progressivism and apocalyptic Messianism. His reflections imply a conception of anticipation as a kind of political disposition whereby radical actors cultivate a state of readiness for any possibility at every possible moment. By offering elements of what a better society might look like, he also anticipates that future in a more substantive way. But Benjamin does not try to account for how these actors might move from their now to a next now. Beyond routing future possibilities through past eras, he does not indicate how subjects might orient their action, recognize what might actually be possible or even desirable, or identify what conditions might facilitate this or that tiger's leap. He beautifully triangulates revolutionary actors, past generations, and radical thinkers, but does not work out the mediations between radical thinking and revolutionary praxis. He directs our attention to "now time" as cause and consequence of a revolutionary interruption, but does not address the dialectics of imaging and acting, naming and discovering, making and seizing.

Adorno, too, sought to overturn the bourgeois conception of progress without paying Scholem's "price of Messianism." In a 1962 essay, Adorno argues that if we are to reclaim a real concept of progress, we need to avoid both "atemporal theology" (which expects redemption from a "transcendental intervention") and "the idolization of history" (as if progress were automatic or human actions necessarily led toward a more perfect world).[23] He explains that the term *progress* promises "an answer to the doubt and the hope that things will finally get better, that people will at last be able to breathe a sigh of relief."[24] Like Benjamin, he insists that "wherever bourgeois society satisfies the concept it cherishes as its own, it knows no progress; wherever it knows progress, it violates its own law."[25] But Adorno does not simply identify this aporia in order to reject progress as such. He recognizes that "too little of what is good has power in the world for progress to be expressed in a predictive judgment about the world."[26] Yet he insists that "there can be no good, not a trace of it without progress."[27]

Rather, Adorno seeks to sublate progress's bourgeois form through a dialectical reversal. "The nexus of deception surrounding progress *reaches beyond itself* . . . the devastation wrought by progress can be made good again, if at all, only by its own forces, never by the restoration of the preceding conditions that were its victims."[28] Accordingly, Adorno seeks real progress precisely in those places where bourgeois "progress" is interrupted and its concept is called into question. He writes, "Progress means: to step out of the magic spell, even out of the spell of progress . . . in that . . . humanity . . . brings to a halt the domination it exacts upon nature. . . . In this way it could be said that progress occurs where it ends."[29] In other words, *we actually pursue that which progress promises by interrupting or undoing that which, under current arrangements, purports to be progress.* Only then do we have a chance to escape the bourgeois inversion that reduces progress to domination and misrecognizes domination as progress.

Despite Adorno's reputation for political pessimism and philosophical abstraction, he opens the possibility of dialectical reversals through a critical practice of "wresting free." He writes, "Every individual trait in the nexus of deception is nonetheless relevant to [progress's] possible end. Good is what wrenches itself free, finds a language, opens its eyes. In its conditions of wresting free, it is interwoven in history that, without being organized unequivocally toward reconciliation, in the course of its movement allows the possibility of redemption to flash up."[30] Adorno points beyond the opposition between gradual reformism and revolutionary rupture with this image of imaginative and practical everyday attempts to find and wrench free bits of good that can be associated with new languages and rewoven into history in ways that glimpse and prepare—*anticipate*—a possible reconciliation. Adorno suggests that such anticipatory glimpses are as important as the transformative practices that they may facilitate. His critique of (the concept of) progress leads to what I have been calling a concrete utopian orientation.

As with progress, Adorno tries to think utopia against "utopia." In a 1964 exchange with Ernst Bloch, he criticizes ideological forms of "cheap" and "false" utopias which present the given world as already reconciled and realized.[31] He acknowledges the value of the Jewish prohibition against picturing the future concretely "insofar as we do not know what the correct thing would be."[32] Yet he also insists that "something terrible happens" when "we are forbidden to cast a picture . . . the commandment against a concrete expression of utopia tends to defame the utopian consciousness and to engulf it."[33] In the West, he explains "people have lost . . . the capability to imagine the totality as something that could be completely different . . . people are sworn to this world as it is-à-vis possibility."[34] Such concessions to the given, he suggests, can only be overcome through the kind of utopian orientation that insists on "the evident possibility of fulfillment" in modern society or that "a life in freedom and happiness would be possible today."[35] He is equally concerned that in the Communist East, "the idea of utopia has actually disappeared completely from the conception of socialism."[36] He explains, "The apparatus, the how, the means of a socialist society have taken precedence over any possible content, for one is not allowed to say anything about the possible content. Thereby the theory of socialism that is decidedly hostile toward utopia now tends really to become a new ideology concerned with the domination of humankind."[37]

In short, Adorno warns that any claim to know the future should be avoided. Yet he also insists that unless some kind of "picture" of what might be possible can "appear within one's grasp, then one basically does not know at all what the actual reason for the totality is, why the entire apparatus has been set in motion."[38] He concludes by agreeing with Bloch that there can be no transformation, no socialism, and no fulfillment without the utopian-transcendent belief that "something's missing."[39] In terms that recall my ealier discussion of the possible-impossible, Adorno invites critics to undertake the tricky practice of *envisioning without defining*. This balancing act between identifying concrete possibilities through utopian imagination without foreclosing possible outcomes through predictive naming is a crucial dimension of what I am calling "anticipation." This orientation to the future breaks with the liberal faith that things will automatically and progressively work themselves out. But it does so in ways that differ fundamentally from either a Derridean waiting without expectation for a sudden rupture or a nihilistic fatalism about and accommodation with the present impasse.

This concrete utopian orientation to futurity resonates with a similar position formulated by Henri Lefebvre, another heterodox Marxist who sought to make sense of late capitalist alienation in the postwar period. In the first volume of his *Critique of Everyday Life* (1947), Lefebvre argues that material progress had created unprecedented possibilities for the good life, but that its benefits were only enjoyed by the few. Real power was stolen from popular communities and placed in the hands of an elite. As everyday life was colonized by capital, the domination of things was transformed into the domination of humans by other humans.[40] Lefebvre describes a perverse and paradoxical situation, which he calls "backwardness," whereby "life is lagging behind what is possible."[41] This is a dialectical rather than an existential claim. His point is that existing arrangements were lagging behind the very different set of prospects that capitalist modernization was actually making possible. At the same time, because capitalism develops unevenly, "traces of 'another life,' a community life" organized around noncapitalist social logics and values, persisted within a heterogeneous modernity.[42] For Lefebvre, this proximity between an alienated everyday life, new possibilities that capitalism produces immanently, and persisting traces of other modes of sociability opens possibilities for dialectical transformation.[43] "In each thing we see more than itself— something else which is there in everyday objects, not an abstract lining but something enfolded within which hitherto we have been unable to see."[44] In cities especially, he suggests, alternative modes of living and new forms of solidarity appear in the theater of everyday life. In factories and working-class neighborhoods especially, "other modes of everyday living, other needs, other requirements are entering into conflict with the modalities of everyday life as imposed by the capitalist structure of society and life" in ways that tend "to re-establish a solidarity, an effective alliance between individuals and groups."[45]

Against optimistic "partisans of Progress," Lefebvre points to "the decline of everyday life since . . . Antiquity." But he also contends that philosophical pessimists mistakenly accept "this life as *the only one possible*" and are unable to recognize the potential "greatness" that may shine through alienated forms.[46] In contrast to both, he insists on "the breadth and magnificence of the *possibilities* which are opening out for man, and which are so really possible . . . (once the *political* obstacles are shattered)."[47] Rather than focus on a false opposition between progress and decline, Lefebvre, like Benjamin, directs our attention to the difference between quantitative and qualitative forms of progress. He dismisses as a "childish error" the tendency to base our image of "the man of the future on what we are now" and "simply [grant] him a greater quantity of mechanical means and appliances."[48] Rather, he insists, "we should acquire a sense of *qualitative* changes, of modifications in the quality of life—and above all of another attitude of the *human being toward himself*."[49] He thus calls on us to envision a future organized around "total life" or a "living totality" in which a "truly human" and "total man" may be realized.[50]

For Lefebvre, the task of recognizing the possible in the actual requires creative acts of political imagination. But he also criticizes idle speculation about fantastic futures. He insists that understandings of alternatives must emerge through concrete practices. He asserts that "man as a total problem," or "the possibility of the *total*" and "truly human man," can only be "posed and resolved on the level of everyday life."[51] Lefebvre argues that by overcoming both the sentimentalism of petit-bourgeois humanism and the tragic irony of nihilism, the "the critique of everyday life . . . [can] clear the way for a *genuine* humanism."[52] The latter would reconcile "everyday life and festival—mass moments and exceptional moments . . . seriousness and play—reality and dreams."[53] For Lefebvre, everyday (urban) life becomes the scene of a concrete utopianism that combines imaginative vision with experimental practices in order to identify and pursue what he calls the "possible-impossible."[54] These everyday practices are simultaneously rooted in the now and future-oriented, political and aesthetic, strategic and playful. They prefigure an "art of living" in which "the human being sees his own life . . . not just as a means . . . but as an end in itself."[55] We might also call such a disposition, in which visionary thinking and experimental acts come together in a type of "play acting" that "explores what is possible," an art of anticipation.[56]

In the late 1950s, Lefebvre further developed this concrete utopian sensibility. Under modern capitalist conditions, he explains, previous modes of envisioning a truly human form of life (whether based on fantasies of natural living or classical antiquity) had either been lost or discredited as fictive or mythical. But new ones had not taken their place. He does not celebrate this development, as a pragmatic realist might. Rather, he is deeply concerned that after World War II the Left no longer had a myth of "the new life" and spoke only in the language of industrial rationalism, technocratic planning, and productivist acceleration.[57]

Lefebvre seeks to identify immanent possibilities within this instrumental rationality. He contends that the contradictions of postwar planning were fueling a resurgence of utopian thinking. "The advanced countries are lagging behind their own possibilities" and are "less able to satisfy those who ought to be happy with it."[58] As a result, "Utopianism lives again. . . . It is exploring the possibilities of praxis. . . . Imagination is adopting or rediscovering a creative power. It is pooling forces with an obscurely rediscovered spontaneity."[59] He explains, "If we are to build a revitalized life . . . we must use utopian method experimentally, looking ahead to what is possible and what is impossible and transforming this hypothetical exploration into applicable programs and practical plans."[60] Lefebvre called this orientation a "philosophy of the possible" which attends to "relations with the real and the here-and-now" in order to discover "the *opening*, by which [we] may enter in a practical way into the 'possible-impossible' dialectic."[61] This is the spirit in which I have been using "concrete utopianism."

Lefebvre's late 1950s call for a "new romanticism" seemed to receive an uncanny answer in what he regarded as "the explosion" of May '68.[62] He suggests that this unforeseen event "broke into" everyday life even as everyday practices constituted its revolutionary potential.[63] For Lefebvre, May '68 was neither purely spontaneous nor the working out of a blueprint for the future. "A theory of the movement has to emerge from the movement itself, for it is the movement that has revealed, unleashed, and liberated theoretical capacities."[64] Lefevbre called May '68 a "concrete utopia."[65] This is because it was an "unthinkable movement" that nevertheless "actually existed"; it allowed and compelled people to "think the unthinkable."[66] It enacted the "anticipated urban society."[67] Referring to this dialectic of political imagination and experimental practice, Lefebvre writes, "The specifically utopian function of cultural contestation will thus supersede itself by fulfilling itself in practice."[68]

Kristin Ross recognized this sensibility in the Paris Commune. "More important than any laws the Communards were able to enact was simply the way in which their daily workings inverted entrenched hierarchies and divisions . . . what matters more than any images conveyed, laws passed, or institutions founded are the capacities set in motion."[69] If social relations are to be radically transformed, Ross suggests, it will be by mobilizing such capacities, not by teaching people how to be citizens of a future society. Massimiliano Tomba recognizes this same spirit in the "insurgent universality" practiced by the more radical and subaltern forces within the French Revolution. "This insurgency not only interrupted the continuum of a specific historical configuration of power, but . . . disclosed and anticipated new political pathways . . . [that] were molten in the red-hot magma of many experiments, abandoned or repressed."[70] He identifies such anticipation in "the virtuous 'skidding off course (*dérapage*)' of the Revolution during which slaves, women, and the poor gained a voice and *acted as if* they were citizens."[71]

Such a politics of anticipation also runs through important currents of the

Black radical tradition. Consider Du Bois's plan during the early 1930s, which I mentioned above, to organize African Americans into self-managing consumer cooperatives. He took as his starting points the refractory character of the color line (which proved to be invulnerable to rational refutation or legal challenges), the mutually reinforcing relation between racism and poverty, the white supremacy of the American labor movement, and the devastating effect of the Great Depression on the Black community. Given this historical condition, Du Bois sought to identify immanent possibilities within alienated forms by turning the fact of segregation into a source of social strength and political education. He argued that if planned and organized, existing networks of Black sociality and exchange could ground a new form of solidarity and autonomy through which to confront capitalism and racism. He believed that self-managing cooperatives organized along mutualist lines could create opportunities for work without exploitation, production without profit, exchange without stratification, and knowledge production without exclusion—in ways that would reinforce bonds of solidarity across different social sectors of the Black community.[72]

Du Bois's multifaceted program was a pragmatic response to an immediate predicament. These consumer cooperatives would create a basis for economic survival under conditions of Jim Crow segregation during the Depression. By doing so without depending on either state aid or legal reform, they were also meant to transform formal liberty into substantive freedom. In his view, these self-managing cooperatives would allow Black actors to develop alternative forms of labor, exchange, and sociality. By cultivating new subjectivities, everyday practices, ethical relations, and spiritual or cultural orientations, they would: prepare themselves for the future order they desired, model a noncapitalist way of life that was somewhat insulated from everyday American racism, and help to hasten that future by enacting it here and now.

With this plan for strategic self-segregation, Du Bois was not calling for Blacks to withdraw from American society. He was recognizing that their involuntary status as a "nation within a nation" offered them an opportunity (and perspective) to lead the nation as a whole (beginning with the white working class) along a different path, beyond the color line, and toward a new socialist democracy. His program was based on the conviction that racial domination could never be overcome under capitalist conditions and that socialism could never be realized until the color line was abolished. In short, this call for economic self-management was a concrete utopian project to radically reconstruct American democracy by abolishing the color line and overcoming capitalist social relations. It *anticipated* self-managing Black communities playing a vanguard role in a process whereby a whole range of cooperative movements among different communities would form, federate, and help to create a new "cooperative commonwealth." This formation might in turn envision, enact, and enable—*anticipate*—a new order of international solidarity among self-managing peoples of color against global imperialism. Du Bois thereby *anticipated* a seemingly impossible future already made plausible by present conditions and glimpsed through the privileged critical insight, the "second sight," that being racialized had afforded him.[73] We may understand this concrete utopian politics of anticipation as integral to the Black critical tradition.

In *The Black Atlantic* (1993), Paul Gilroy describes a "politics of fulfillment" whose "normative content focuses attention on . . . the notion that a future society will be able to realize the social and political promise that present society has left unaccomplished."[74] He distinguishes this from a utopian "politics of transfiguration" that strives "continually to move beyond the grasp of the merely linguistic, textual, and discursive" and "exists on a lower frequency, where it is played, danced, and acted, as well as sung and sung about."[75] Gilroy argues that this "tradition of expression" "refuses to accept that the political is a readily separable domain. Its basic desire is *to conjure up and enact* the new modes of friendship, happiness, and solidarity that are consequent on the overcoming of the racial oppression."[76] Whereas the politics of fulfillment generated a Black "counterdiscourse" through which to make political claims, the politics of transfiguration constituted a "counterculture of modernity" that sought to expand the very domain and meaning of politics itself, partly by linking it to ethics and aesthetics, imaginative practice and cultural performance, and embodied practices and lived memories.[77]

In Gilroy's discussion we can see that the politics of transfiguration is a practice of anticipation that *conjures up and enacts* new ways of being and relating. It

> emphasizes the emergence of qualitatively new desires, social relations, and modes of association within the racial community of interpretation and resistance *and* between that group and its erstwhile oppressors. It points specifically to the formation of a community of needs and solidarity which is magically made audible in the music itself and palpable in the social relations of its cultural utility and reproduction.[78]

Gilroy's "grounded ethics" and "grounded aesthetics" nicely capture what I have been calling concrete utopian practices that anticipate—by envisioning, enacting, and enabling—an alternative good life, another possible world.[79] He contends that "the memory of slavery, actively preserved as a living intellectual resource in their expressive political culture," helped Black communities, "to fight—often through their spirituality—to hold on to the unity of ethics and politics sundered from each other by modernity's insistence that the true, the good, and the beautiful had distinct origins and belong to different domains of knowledge."[80] This path from the broken present to a utopian future by way of living memory, resonates with Benjamin's conceptions of remembrance and awakening.

Gilroy likely has Benjamin and Adorno in mind when he contends that this "alternative body of cultural and political expression . . . *considers the world critically from the point of view of its emancipatory transformation*," from the standpoint of some future "which is capable of satisfying the (redefined) needs of human beings that will emerge once the violence—epistemic and concrete—of racial typology is at an end. Reason is thus reunited with the happiness and freedom of individuals and the reign of justice within the collectivity."[81] Gilroy affirms that his political orientation converges with a Marxian vision, even if it also diverges from currents of Marxism that valorize "self-creation through labor" as the "center-piece of emancipatory hopes."[82] It does not valorize work, which "for the descendants of slaves . . . signifies only servitude, misery, and subordination."[83] Rather, "Artistic expression . . . becomes the means towards both individual self-fashioning and communal liberation. Poiesis and politics begin to coexist in novel forms."[84] Gilroy thus invokes a tradition of concrete utopianism that anticipates a future good life through experimental practices that are at once political, ethical, and aesthetic.

Fred Moten further elaborates this idea that utopian enactment is a central feature of Black aesthetics. He relates Blackness as "the extended movement of a specific upheaval, an ongoing irruption that arranges every line" to an ethics, politics, and aesthetics of "the cut" or "the break."[85] Moten employs these musical terms to index the gap between, as well as the elevated conjunction of: sound and words, music and text, poetry and philosophy, body and mind, being and knowing. It is through this cut, by lingering in a break that is at once existential, epistemological, and temporal, that the radical work and play of "improvisation" unfolds in and through an "ensemble." Referring to "improvisation's time and the time of ensemble's organization," Moten writes of the "attempt . . . to sustain the desire that you anticipate."[86] Here, improvisation is an untimely operation that expresses the "unsayable claims of Black utopian political desire."[87] It does so by performing an "old new language—tragic, hopeful, fallen," that registers "the fantasy of what hadn't happened yet."[88] This performance works "to activate the foresight that is not prophecy but description . . . embodied and silently sounded in the music's knowing echo of shriek and prayer."[89]

Descriptive foresight in an old-new language of what has not yet happened. Moten distinguishes such improvisation from prophecy as prediction. As we can see in a later interview, he seeks to convey a different form of prophecy: "The prophet is the one who tells the brutal truth, who has the capacity to see the absolute brutality of the already-existing and to point it out and to tell that truth, but also to see the other way, *to see what it could be.* That double-sense, that double-capacity: to see what's right in front of you and to see through it to what's ahead of you."[90] This capacity to recognize the possible in the actual reverberates with the ways I have been discussing dialectical optics, immanent critique, poetic knowledge . . . and the politics of anticipation.

Insofar as Moten's improvisation links future-oriented vision and aesthetic performance to worldly action, it reverberates with the way I have been discussing concrete utopianism. Moten characterizes Blackness and critique as a "lingering" in the "shattering tremble of the improvising ensemble's music. . . . Not in the interest of an understanding or adequate representation of the action whose performance would occur in this lingering, but in the interest of an *enactive invocation, a material prayer,* the dissemination of the conditions of possibility of . . . action."[91] Moten invites us to recognize (Black) aesthetic performances as political acts and political performances as aesthetic acts within a relational (i.e., ethical) ensemble. We might understand concrete utopian anticipation to index practices that are bound up with material prayers.

Moten's understanding of improvisation as an anticipatory way of seeing, knowing, and acting across supposed temporal divisions echoes the "visionary" speaker in Césaire's poem who declares, "my ear to the ground, I heard Tomorrow pass."[92] It reverberates with Benjamin's peculiar understanding of prophecy in which "the seer's gaze is kindled by the rapidly receding past" where "he perceives the contours of the future" and with Glissant's "prophetic vision of the past," which I discuss in Chapter 11.[93]

Dialectics of Anticipation

These concrete utopian experiments, thinkers, and traditions share a distinctive orientation to futurity that points beyond both the fiction of liberal progress and the fantasy of apocalyptic rupture. They reject the given order, envision a better world, and act *as if* the impossible were possible. They recognize that new forms cannot simply be planned and implemented, but can only emerge practically and experimentally. We can think of anticipation as a dual political disposition, both a state of readiness for any possibility *and* a will to overcome existing arrangements by acting from the standpoint of a not-yet redeemed world. Anticipation refers to a politico-temporal orientation, not an affective state or an ideological discourse. It is neither about planning nor waiting. It rejects bourgeois progressivism and nihilistic presentism. Through an immanent critique of actual relations, it allows actors to recognize supposedly impossible possibilities. By tacking dialectically between creative imagination and experimental practices, anticipation seeks to balance the dual imperative to insist on an open future and to envision a good life.

We might therefore refer to a *dialectics of anticipation* marked by the dual imperatives to be open to the impossible and to imagine the possible, to envision and enact, to seize the sudden illumination as it appears and to produce it through everyday life. A dialectical concept of anticipation is a *calling for* that is also a *calling forth*, an enacted idea that may bring into being what it desires through the performance itself (even as that very image of future possibility only arises through such performative acts). Anticipatory politics are therefore also aesthetic operations (and vice versa). They are concrete utopian practices that cut across reified distinctions between immanence and transcendence, present and future, actual and possible, instrumental and utopian, imagination and action, strategy and spontaneity, politics and performance. Practices of anticipation signal a readiness to interrupt the continuum and a commitment to live otherwise. They are not only "practices" in the sense of doing, they are forms of practice in the sense of learning, of getting better at—in this case, getting better at being the kind of person, living the kind of life, entering into the types of social relations that will only be really possible, or possibly realized, in a future order.

PART II
Unthinking History

7

Time as a Real Abstraction

Clock-Time, Nonsynchronism, Untimeliness

Practice is not *in* time but *makes* time.

— PIERRE BOURDIEU

In the Introduction, I suggested that political thinking entails implicit or explicit conceptions of time and history. Any attempt to deprovincialize political imagination should therefore include a reconsideration of the relationship between politics, history, and time. This is especially important in an era such as ours when the discipline of history, a specialized form of knowledge, has so monopolized how we understand the dynamic social practices, processes, and events that compose worldly history. In the last chapter of Part I, I questioned ungrounded theoretical claims about the emergence of a new order of time characterized by an ever-extending and unsurpassable present. But insofar as Berlant, Scott, Hartog, and Traverso attempt to identify the temporal implications of sociopolitical transformations, they open pathways that need to be pursued. If we hope to render social life subversively uncanny, if we hope to deprovincialize here-now-us in the service of solidarity politics and societal transformation, we need to unthink conventional history. In this chapter, I contribute to this task by arguing that there is a dialectical relation between social formations and temporal frameworks. Specifically, I analyze time as a social fact and historical force. First, I focus on clock-time as a real abstraction that emerged under historically specific conditions. Next, I pay equal attention to the challenges posed to historical understanding and political imagination by *untimely* concepts, events, processes, and practices.

I. Time as a Real Abstraction

The History of Time

In *Metahistory*, Hayden White famously argued that the kind of stories historians tell, rather than the facts they've discovered, determine the efficacy of historical explanations. At least as important as White's dazzling but debatable insights about the poetics of historical writing and the fictive character of historical knowledge is his more fundamental insight that every work of history presupposes a *theory of history* that entails metahistorical assumptions about actors and agency, events and contexts, connections and causes, processes and transformations, as well as what counts as a plausible historical interpretation.

White argues that before historians can begin to interpret factual data, "in order to figure 'what *really* happened' in the past" they "must first *prefigure* the field . . . as a possible object of knowledge."[1] If, as he contends, this "prefigurative act . . . predetermines the . . . conceptual strategies [historians] will use to explain" the object, such prefiguration would also have to posit specific ideas about time in relation to society and historical change. But apart from brief reflections on the various "time orientations" implied by different ideological approaches to history, White thematizes neither time as an object of historical inquiry nor temporality as a fundamental dimension of "the deep structures of historical imagination" that he examines.[2]

Reinhart Koselleck, White's German contemporary, similarly argued that every historical interpretation requires a prior "theory of possible history," because "a source can never tell us what we ought to say."[3] But in contrast to White, Koselleck instructs historians to attend directly to "the temporalization of history" in the modern West.[4] His remarkable essays from the 1960s and 1970s offer a series of far-reaching, if underspecified, reflections on modern time as historical and modern history as temporal. Together, they compose an integrated, accelerating, and semi-autonomous process that continually produces the unprecedented. In general terms, Koselleck relates the emergence of what he calls "historical time" to Enlightenment philosophy and the French Revolution. But his claims beg a number of questions concerning how converging social, temporal, historical, and conceptual changes actually relate to one another.[5] He often reverts to technological determinism to explain the acceleration of (modern) time that he posits but for which he cannot otherwise account. He insists that there is something distinct about modern time as historical time, but he does not adequately analyze how what he calls "new time" is socially produced and becomes socially constraining.[6]

Whatever their limitations, both White's and Koselleck's work indicate that critical historical understanding must engage the history of time and the time of history.[7] Their interventions invite us to recognize that practices, processes, and events do not only take place in time as a neutral medium. They shape and are shaped by time.

Many scholars have rightly questioned the universality of the abstract, homogeneous, linear, and measurable form of time that has shaped modern life in and beyond the West. One kind of critique particularizes this notion of time and associated notions of progressive history in cultural or civilizational terms. They are figured as deep structural features of Western consciousness that differ from non-Western conceptions of time.[8] This approach usefully challenges Kant's understanding of time as a universal *a priori*.[9] But, usually employing a Durkheimian understanding of social time as a collective representation, it does not account for the historical production of clock-time.[10]

Another kind of critique treats clock-time as an official ideology or discursive formation, whether propagated by states, scientists, or philosophers. This time is understood to serve ruling interests or societal norms by regulating populations who may have very different conceptions of time. The latter are discounted, repressed, or prohibited.[11] This approach risks making modern time fictive in the sense of imagined or made-up, as if the authority of clock-time depended simply on coercion, habituation, or misrecognition. If this were the case, liberation from clock-time would then only be a matter of refusing authority or thinking differently.

Philosopher David Couzens Hoy points out that vitalist and phenomenologists treated clock-time as the objectively real time of the natural universe, as studied by physicists. This they distinguished from the subjective reality of lived time, the concrete and qualitative ways that humans actually experience temporality.[12] Thinkers in this tradition explored how pasts may be perpetually present in an ongoing now as well as how the tempo of time is not fixed and its direction might bend. But their valuable insights depended on a questionable distinction between clock-time as natural and human temporality as social.

These different approaches have done important work denaturalizing abstract homogeneous modern time. But they rely on untenable oppositions (i.e., between Western and non-Western, ideological and authentic, natural and human, objective and subjective, or public and private conceptions of time). They criticize clock-time from lived or ontological standpoints supposed to exist outside of it. They do not account for the sociohistorical process through which clock-time itself became identified with natural, objective, and public time.

To use Marxian language, we need a notion of social time as a real or concrete abstraction: a historically specific product of social practices that assumes a real objective power to shape subjectivity and orient action.[13] This would help us to recognize how social practices produce specific types of time that, in turn, mediate social practices. Said differently, there is a dialectical relation between social formations and temporal frameworks. This means that we need to analyze social life through a temporal optic and to analyze historical time through a social optic. If specific temporal logics, assumptions, and expectations are embedded in all manner of social institutions, ideologies, common sense, everyday practices, and forms of domination, neither historians nor political thinkers can simply treat time as natural and self-evident. We should attend to the social conditions of possibility for certain types of temporal arrangements and the temporal conditions of possibility for certain types of social arrangements.

We may read *Capital* as, among other things, an account of the social production of abstract time as a historical force. In it, Marx demonstrates how, under capitalism, value, labor, and time were mutually constitutive. As people began to produce in order to sell rather than to meet human needs directly, qualitatively different types of labor and goods had to be made commensurable and exchangeable with one another. A commodity's value was measured in terms of the socially necessary labor time required to produce it and was expressed in money as a universal equivalent. A society of generalized commodity exchange required new forms of value, money, labor, *and* time—all of which were abstract, homogeneous, universal, and measurable. Time had to have invariable divisible segments.[14] Marx insisted that there was nothing natural or inevitable about a system in which people worked not in order to create useful things to be consumed, but in order to produce value, to accumulate not as a means but as an end in itself.[15] It follows that there was nothing normal or natural about the type of time that was required and produced by this system.

In *The Protestant Ethic* Max Weber uses the term "economic traditionalism" to describe the fact that most people, for most of human history, worked only as much as was required to satisfy their needs.[16] He argued that "a long and arduous process of education" was needed to create a new economic mentality for which labor became a calling and people worked and made money for the sake of working and making money.[17] This imperative to accumulate without limit required new practices of rational calculation, which Weber saw crystallized in Benjamin Franklin's adage "time is money."[18] The capitalist ethos held that as time could now be wasted, it had to be measured and managed. Social actors became newly preoccupied with timing: with being paid on time, anticipating profit over time in relation to credit and investment, and reckoning interest over time with respect to savings and debt. Weber indicates how capitalism required a new set of associations between human virtue, on the one hand, and work, money, and time, on the other.[19]

This entailed refiguring the relation between the present and the future. New forms of education, training, work, investment, credit, insurance, and inheritance were not only shaped by specific temporal assumptions and logics; they helped to create and normalize a new temporal common sense.

The naturalization of clock-time has been well documented by social and cultural historians.[20] These studies indicate a long-term temporal shift from the fourteenth to nineteenth centuries that was propelled by processes of urbanization, commercialization, and the emergence of wage-labor for industrial production. Modes of measuring time and synchronizing action that developed within monasteries were transposed onto city life. Religious injunctions to pray on time were repurposed as mercantilist imperatives for efficiency and punctuality. A sense of time as belonging to God or to a larger community was displaced by an understanding of time as belonging to individuals charged with improving themselves. New conceptions and experiences of abstract and shared public time, detached from natural rhythms and specific tasks, did not only serve new systems of production and exchange. They infused new forms of selfhood, virtue, and ethics. Bourgeois subjectivity, dispositions, and habits were sustained by specific notions of abstract, universal, and objective time which simultaneously reinforced that habitus.

The standardization of time, the synchronization of social relations, and the temporalization of institutions like inheritance, mortgages, and pensions also depended on modern bureaucratic states and legal systems.[21] More generally, capitalist development was bound up with the late-eighteenth-century Atlantic Revolutions. In their wake, peoples came to understand themselves as nations, nations were presumed to be the basis for legitimate states, and nation-states were regarded as the highest form of social organization and the only legitimate actors on the stage of world history.[22] Insofar as national states were understood as cause and consequence of liberal development, human improvement, and historical progress, they, too, reinforced new notions of linear time and chronological history.[23] Globally, the naturalization of abstract time propelled, and was propelled by, the worldwide spread of money economies, new systems of long-distance trade and credit, and larger processes of imperial expansion.[24] These translocal interdependencies intensified the need to standardize money and time in order to synchronize activities on ever-expanding scales.

Social theorist Moishe Postone describes this process as a long-term shift from *concrete time*, which was embedded in, and reckoned by, specific social activities, to *abstract time*. He explains that once time began to function as an independent and abstract measure of social activities, it assumed an independent and objective power to set norms for social activity.[25] Clock-time began to compel certain kinds of behaviors. This new temporal regime may have served bourgeois interests in cities and factories, as Le Goff and Thompson demonstrated. But it is important to remember that in a situation where social relations were mediated by commodity exchange and in which the valorization process depended on producing at a rate faster than socially necessary labor time, *all* social actors became subject to the dictatorship of abstract time. Geographer David Harvey, describing how under capitalism, space was conquered through innovations in transportation and communication and time was transformed into a "measurable, calculable, and objective magnitude," calls this a "tightening of the chronological net around daily life."[26]

We can see how a particular kind of social formation may require and produce a certain kind of time that mediates social relations and compels social action. Conversely, new temporal techniques, practices, and conceptions have social consequences. Sociologist Norbert Elias contends that as relations of interdependence in growing social units became more complex, a greater need for coordination and synchronization demanded more sophisticated techniques to measure time. As these became more ubiquitous, they increasingly determined social norms that were internalized by self-regulating individuals. Through this process, Elias contends, time itself began to appear to be a natural phenomenon independent of human action. He explains that this appearance was then reinforced by science and philosophy, which treated time as a natural or universal object whose laws could be discovered. He refers to modern time as a "second nature," an "inner voice," and a "social habitus."[27] On this basis, Elias argues that time as such does not exist. There are only practices of time keeping and time measurement that correspond to behaviors that were learned by societies over centuries. Elias therefore calls on scholars to shift from treating time as a natural thing to focusing on *timing* as a social practice that produces the illusion that time is a natural thing.

Of course, abstract clock-time is not simply an illusion. It may have been historically created by human practices. But it was not merely an idea or ideology with which one could simply agree or disagree. In this kind of society, time really was money. To ignore this dictum was to court marginalization, exclusion, or starvation. Marx demonstrates how, in capitalist societies, competition and the associated tendency of the rate of profit to fall creates an objective compulsion to speed up production, reduce the socially necessary labor time required to produce a given commodity, and decrease the turnover time of the Money-Commodity-Surplus Value circuit.[28] Within capitalism, there really is a constant imperative to annihilate space through time.[29]

This process of intensifying spatial integration and temporal acceleration, which Harvey calls "time-space compression," creates a powerful but unstable social system that can only maintain itself by constantly revolutionizing itself.[30] Harvey explains how capitalist formations regularly avert crises of over-accumulation through "spatiotemporal fixes," employing geographic displacement and temporal deferral to absorb surplus capital and labor. Territorial expansion (which provides new resources, labor supplies, and markets) and long-term investments in future-oriented projects (e.g., physical and social infrastructure, including roads, communications, education, research, and social expenditures) provide temporary remedies for a crisis-prone system.[31] Yet these very attempts at stabilization exacerbate the dilemma they were meant to resolve; in order to keep valorizing itself, capital must circulate ever faster in a self-generating spiral without limit. In similar terms, Postone describes the dynamic required of capitalist accumulation as a "dialectic of transformation and reconstitution." He demonstrates how this imperative generates a very real kind of forward motion, which, in turn, gives the appearance that history itself is inherently progressive.[32]

The Time of History

The consolidation of clock-time as a second nature forms the sociohistorical matrix out of which modern Western-time consciousness and corresponding conceptions of history emerged. Koselleck contends that in Europe there was a direct link between the social and political upheavals that "denaturalized" the "historical experience of time" in the eighteenth century and "the emergence of the modern philosophy of history."[33] Philosopher Karl Löwith, Koselleck's teacher, famously wrote about the providential character of new philosophies of history, whereby history was figured as progressive, intrinsically meaningful, and propelled with purpose toward a redemptive end.[34] Koselleck describes how this notion was institutionalized when the early modern state claimed from religious prophecy and church millenarianism a monopoly right to predict the future. It did so, however, without the certainty or security of a *telos*. He thus describes how the "new time" of modernity was increasingly experienced and represented as a singular world-historical process moving toward, or moving humanity toward, an ever-unfolding yet always unknown future. Time and history, increasingly figured as synonymous, were understood, on the one hand, to be directional and progressive, and on the other, to be contingent and human made. This new historical consciousness was reinforced by discoveries in geology, archaeology, and evolutionary biology that overturned the authority of biblical time frames.[35]

These new experiences of historical time stood in a circular relationship with at least three varieties of post-Enlightenment philosophy of history: progressive theories of human perfectibility, social evolution, and universal history; pessimistic and conservative theories of decline; and Romantic invocations of lost Golden Ages. Such novel temporal experiences also influenced the emergence of history as a specialized university profession. Koselleck recounts how, in the modern period, European scholars shifted from recording histories in the plural, presented as chronicles of singular events (*historie*) to representing "history in general," as a unified process that linked past to future in definite and discernable ways (*geschichte*).[36] Philosophy of history and professional history emerged from the same set of temporal conditions. But the latter established itself in direct opposition to the former's metaphysical speculations.

The new discipline of history presented itself as an inductive science based on the collection of empirical facts that should be described in a realistic and objective manner. Historical research purported to examine concrete particulars, uncontaminated by preconceived ideas, in order to reconstruct the past—*what actually happened*—accurately and impartially, for its own sake. Most famously, the pioneering German historian Leopold von Ranke, counterposed modern historical knowledge to idealist philosophy. In contrast to philosophy's a priori reasoning and deductive method, von Ranke championed history as an inductive "empiricism" that could test philosophical speculation against real "conditions of existence."[37] This method was bound up with a certain understanding of sequence and causality. Von Ranke contends that "what precedes determines what follows; there is an inner connection of cause and effect."[38] He argued that the "inner necessity of the sequence" provided the key to "the totality" of a life or a people.[39] In history, he writes, "there exists clearly for us a unity, a progression, a development."[40]

Resisting metaphysical assertions that Providence was leading humanity in a predetermined direction, von Ranke insisted that "our task is merely to keep to the facts."[41] Yet we can see that his propositions about history form a coherent whole that links a method (the inductive study of documents), units of analysis (events, lives, and epochs), subjects of history (individuals, peoples, nations), notions of causality (based on necessary sequences), and macrohistorical effects (developmental unities and totalities). Despite his rejection of speculative philosophical claims about inevitable human progress, von Ranke's empiricist history (where documents disclose intentional agents causing immediate effects that unfold in sequences) presupposes and reaffirms a particular notion of historical temporality (as the directional and sequential medium within which events take place) in which categorical distinctions between past, present, and future are treated as self-evident and unbridgeable. I would suggest that this implicit temporal worldview leads inductive history to continually "discover," through empirical facts, developmental totalities and self-contained epochs that can be aligned in causal sequences.

Ranke's sequential understanding of historical time had political implications. According to White, the first generation of professional historians generally shared a conservative fear of the kind of revolutionary social change and demands for mass democracy that shook European order in the mid–nineteenth century. Ranke indeed contrasted the "prophetic, forward-directed" character of philosophy, which he criticized, to a backward-looking history that "sees the good and beneficent in that which exists."[42] Historical scholarship, he proudly declared, "opposes change which negates the existing."[43] Reacting to this very link between historicist epistemology and political complacency, Walter Benjamin famously challenged the additive method of history that predominated in German universities whereby a mass of data is assembled simply to fill homogeneous empty time. Benjamin argued that such historicism treated the present as a transition within a straight continuum, claiming to tell the sequence of events "like the beads of a rosary." For him these procedures promoted a superficial and linear conception of *material* progress that culminated in a dubious "universal history" that ultimately reaffirmed the status quo.[44]

The point is not simply that professional history functioned as a political ideology to serve ruling-class or state interests (however true this might have been). It is that, despite disciplinary history's empiricist rejection of speculation, it presupposed and promoted an implicit philosophy of history that tended to treat the real as rational and the given as good.[45] This empiricist conflation of the immediately apparent with the truly real entailed specific notions of agency, causality, chronology, linearity, and self-contained periods. These notions grounded historiographic narratives of progress or decline.

Extending White and Benjamin, I am suggesting that there is an underlying relationship between disciplinary history's empiricist methods and its temporal assumptions. But the latter could not be acknowledged by practitioners. Although professional history owed its existence to the new historical time that had transformed plural histories into "history as such," it treated the problem of time as outside the domain of proper historical research. The conventional view within the field of history is that while social life takes place *in time*, time is not itself a social fact or historical force. Generally speaking, historiography is concerned not with time, but with "the past" (typically viewed as a foreign place). Historians have long proclaimed an interest in examining "change over time." But how could this be done without reflecting on the very time produced by social practices and through which social life is lived? It is as if disciplinary history and realist politics subscribe, however unwittingly, to Aristotle's rules for tragic drama based on the three unities of action, time, and place.[46] The new academic field took chronology for granted, understood time as a neutral medium within which events occur, and treated history as a continuum along which peoples, nations, or civilizations moved.[47] Because this movement was supposed to be linear and irreversible, disciplinary history posited a rigid and self-evident boundary between past and present. Any given now, or period, was presumed to be temporally identical with itself. This is the basis for the persistent fear of anachronism that haunts modern historiography and realist politics.

II. Untimeliness

Anachronism

Chronology indexes both the seamless forward movement of homogeneous time and the sequential movement of history by way of singular periods. Viewed either way, anachronism refers to the error, both logical and empirical, of conflating a given past with a given present. Conventional historical and realist thinking treats the boundaries between tenses as self-evident and categorical. Indeed, historiographic and political discourses reinforce one another's temporal common sense. But when we examine the heterogeneous and contradictory character of any present, we can begin to recognize such putative boundaries as porous and relational, arbitrary and ideological. Numerous thinkers offer analytic resources for doing so.

Philosopher R. G. Collingwood, for example, insisted, "History in the . . . current sense of the word is knowledge of the past; and in order to understand its peculiarities and its special problems, we must ask what the past is. This means inquiring into the nature of time."[48] He criticized historians for treating past, present, and future as real tenses that exist in an external relation to one another. He argues that there only exists a multiplex present within which what we think of as the past lives and what we think of as the future germinates. *The past* and *the future*, he contends, are artificially abstracted from this integrated matrix. In a Bergsonian register, Collingwood calls on philosophers and historians to engage time as pure flux, a process of ceaseless change in an enduring now.[49]

Conversely, Marxist critic Siegfried Kracauer contrasts the chronological time of historiography to the "shaped time" of social life whose every domain is organized around different temporal norms.[50] Kracauer explains, "As a configuration of events which belong to series with different time schedules, the period does not arise from the homogeneous flow of time, rather it sets a time of its own—which implies that the way it experiences temporality may not be identical with the temporal experience of chronologically earlier or later periods."[51] Within a given period, "simultaneous events are more often than not asynchronous."[52]

Kracauer's understanding of a given now as a configuration of multiple vectors of social time challenges a chronological understanding of linear historical development. Periods do not simply succeed one another in a smooth sequence. Kracauer does not deny the existence of chronological time. He only warns against conflating it with time or history as such. He underscores "the inextricable dialectics of the flow of time and the temporal sequences negating it."[53] Arguing that history can only be grasped by attending to this dynamic relation between chronological time and "shaped time," he writes, "the traditional conception of historical time requires qualification. . . . *We live in a cataract of times* . . . there are 'pockets' and voids amidst these temporal currents."[54] An adequate understanding of, or political engagement with, any political present means attending to this moving, churning, cascade of multiple temporalities. To do so means that we "must . . . jump from one period to another . . . the transitions . . . are problematic."[55] Kracauer notes that decades may separate causes from their effects in a process through which the original "cause" has long since been forgotten.[56] It follows that the significance of present political action may only be realized in futures that have not yet arrived. From this perspective, anachronism is a social fact, not a cognitive failure.

Philosopher Jacques Rancière takes up just this relationship between nonidentical periods, plural temporalities, and the political possibilities opened by anachronism. He, too, criticizes the analytic implications of the "empirical time" employed by conventional history.[57] Taking chronology for granted, he argues, such history transforms the "before" and "after" of events into a "chain of cause and effect."[58] Time is also "coagulated into epochs, each defined by the law of the immanence of its phenomena."[59] This means that at any given moment, social actors and utterances, actions and events, are supposed "to belong to [their] time through the mode of belief, through the mode of unconditional adhesion."[60] For this reason, the "charge of anachronism is not an allegation that something did not exist at a given date . . . [but] that it *could not have existed* at this date."[61] According to this view, any actor's period or "time . . . must be a pure present, a principle of the co-presence of historical subjects . . . [who] must 'resemble' their time . . . through contemporaneity with 'their' time; beings who carry their time in their bodies, in all their ways of being and making, and who carry it in their soul, under the name of belief."[62] Ranciére argues that truth according to the science of history depends on this "resemblance between a man and his time" and "the impossibility of thinking something other than what his time rendered thinkable."[63]

Most immediately, the historiographic prohibition against anachronism obstructs understanding. Rancière suggests, for example, that the great historian Lucien Febvre's fear of anachronism prevented him from considering the possibility that in a Christian age, Rabelais could have been an unbeliever. Worse, for Rancière, this prohibition leads to conservative understandings of history.[64] He contends that the notion of historical truth founded upon "empirical time" actually disregards the kinds of consciousness and action that actually make history. He insists that "there is history" precisely "to the extent that men do not 'resemble' their times, to the extent that their actions rupture with 'their' times, with the line of temporality that put them in their place by requiring them to 'use' their time doing this or that."[65] He refers to these temporal ruptures as "anachronies": "events, notions, significations that rub against the grain of time [*qui prennent le temps à rebours*], that make meaning circulate in a manner that escapes from any contemporaneity, any identity of time with 'itself.'"[66]

For Ranciére, such ruptures are not only a matter of thinking or acting against the grain of sociohistorical norms, but of "connecting" one "line of temporality to others."[67] He thus defines "an anachrony" as "a word, an event, a meaningful sequence that has escaped from 'its' time and is simultaneously endowed with the capacity to define unprecedented temporal alignments [*des aiguillages temporels inédits*], to assure the leap or the connection from one line of temporality to another."[68] He identifies the "power to 'make' history" with these "switching points [*aiguillages*], these leaps and these connections."[69] Ranciére thus grounds the very "meaning of time" and "condition for acting historically" in the "multiplicity of lines of temporality that are present in any 'one' time."[70]

This image of multiple lines of temporality, like Kracauer's "cataract of times" and Bakhtin's "essential multitemporality" of modern life, reverberates with Koselleck's provocative but underspecified claim that the "new time" of modernity is a unity composed of a "coexisting plurality of times."[71] Koselleck likens this to "the glass front of a washing machine, behind which various bits of the wash appear now and then, but are all contained within the drum."[72] This understanding of temporal plurality is the basis of Koselleck's generative assertions about "the contemporaneity of the noncontemporaneous."[73]

Noncontemporaneity and Nonsynchronism

How might we account socially and historically for such noncontemporaneity and multitemporality? To speak of clock-time as a concrete abstraction with real social power is not to say that it destroyed or displaced all other forms and experiences of time. Even when clock-time became hegemonic in the West, other forms of concrete time persisted. Experiences of qualitative duration continued to underlie various dimensions of lived and embodied experience whether regarding love, sex, intoxication, art, sports, war, precarity, religion, festival, political protest, and forms of convivial sociality.[74] Under modern conditions, individuals and groups are traversed by a dynamic mix of quantitative and qualitative time orientations, practices, and experiences.[75] Modern life is marked precisely by such tensions between time as an abstract measure of behavior and as a concrete effect of experience, between history as a quantitative continuum and time as a "pure duration" and "qualitative or heterogeneous multiplicity," and between the impersonal compulsions of standard public time and idiosyncratic forms of temporal consciousness, imagination, and practice.[76]

Note that alternative forms and experiences of time did not just escape modernity's tightening chronological net, they were also created by it. In Marx's early account of alienation, the product of workers' labor assumes an autonomous power to compel social action. "The externalization of the worker in his product means not only that his labor becomes an object, an *external* existence, but that it exists *outside him*, independently of him and alien to him, and begins to confront him as an autonomous power; that the life which he has bestowed on the object confronts him as hostile and alien."[77] Note the temporal character of this mechanism through which a living past, the crystallization of workers' previous subjective activities, becomes an objective force within a nonidentical present.

In his later elaboration of commodity fetishism and capitalist valorization, Marx further specifies this untimely operation. For value to be produced under capitalism, "living labor must seize on these [products of past labor], awaken them from the dead, change them from merely possible into real and effective use-values."[78] Dead products are thereby "bathed in the fire of labor, appropriated as part of its organism, and infused with vital energy for the performance of functions appropriate . . . to their vocation in the process."[79] But just as living labor animates dead matter, dead labor assumes an untimely power to compel present practices. Marx refers to commodities as "congealed quantities" of abstract human labor power, and "crystals" of a "social substance" that assume a "phantom-like objectivity."[80] Such spectral bits of the past—at once matter and spirit, inert and vital, object and subject—confront social actors as an alien, autonomous, and hostile force.[81] From this perspective, we can read Marx's famous declaration that "the tradition of all dead generations weighs like a nightmare on the brains of the living" as social description rather than poetic hyperbole.[82]

In Marx's analysis, capital accumulation depends on repetition (through endless circulation) *and* forward movement (through greater centralization, concentration, competition, and geographical expansion; revolutions in productivity, faster turnover times, and circulation patterns). This dynamic, Postone's dialectic of transformation and reconstitution, is the basis for a capitalist time characterized simultaneously by eternal recurrence and uncontrolled acceleration. It helps to account for the uncanny experience in capitalist societies of simultaneously hurtling forward on a runaway train and working ever harder and faster just to stay in place.

For Marx, this self-propelling dynamic is both powerful and unstable. He describes how the valorization process requires alternating sequences of buying and selling, producing and consuming, converting money into commodities and commodities back into money in a boundless circuit of accelerating accumulation. Crucially, the circulation of commodities and transformation of money into capital, depends on time lags: between buying and selling (so that the circuit M-C-M□can be completed) or between producing and consuming (necessary for the realization of value). The sociotemporal coordination necessary to manage these time lags can be tenuous. Such sequences could easily and regularly fall out of sync or even grind to a halt, producing systemic failures. In this social system, temporality becomes a literal object of contestation. Crucially, surplus value depends on employees advancing their labor *before* they are paid to work a full day whose fixed duration is defined by the employer. The struggle over the working day was not only a conflict over how much workers should be paid in a day but more fundamentally about transforming the unit "working day" from a naturally fixed to a constructed social category. The tendency of the rate of profit to fall, repeating cycles of overaccumulation and devaluation, creative destruction, and uneven development suggest that that capitalist history does not only repeat and accelerate. It is a contradictory and dislocating process that hurtles, halts, swerves, lurches, and derails.

In short, capitalism both normalizes and denaturalizes clock-time. If the hegemony of abstract homogeneous time is a source of modern alienation, so, too, is the converse experience of time as unstable, fractured, and recursive. Modern time is neither seamlessly woven into an integrated social collectivity nor into the smooth flow of history as progressive forward motion. Under such conditions, abstract homogeneous time is at once a second nature and an elusive norm. Modern life is both crushingly synchronized and unnervingly disjunctive. This temporal duality has been refracted through attempts within modernist art, literature, and philosophy to grasp what Stephen Kern has called "a thickened present."[83]

Capitalist time both universalizes and particularizes. It is simultaneously one and many. Even as capitalist modernization homogenizes social life by integrating an ever-growing number of social activities within a common synchronized frame, it differentiates society into distinct domains such that synchronization becomes a problem. Mikhail Bakhtin contends that the transition from traditional to modern societies destroyed a shared and unified sense of "social everyday time" that was founded upon collective labor and social integration.[84] By contrast, "in the era of developing capitalism . . . there emerged one scale for measuring the events of a *personal* life and another for measuring the events of *history*. . . . Although *in the abstract* time remained unified."[85] With the rise of social classes, Bakhtin recounts, religion, production, consumption, and the different domains of everyday life were further separated from one another as individualized affairs.[86] These increasingly distinct spheres "no longer . . . line up with one another . . . the all-embracing whole has been lost" and "the unified time of collective human life" fractures.[87] Under such conditions, time only "preserves its abstract unity" in "abstract thought" and "systems of chronology."[88] But in the material world, time becomes plural as "the course of individual lives, of groups, and of the sociopolitical whole do not fuse together, they are dispersed, there are gaps, they are measured by different scales of value; each of these series has its own logic of development, its own narratives."[89] This is the basis on which Bakhtin defines modern life in terms of an "essential multitemporality."[90]

Ernst Bloch uses the term "nonsynchronism" to describe the temporal coexistence of groups or communities that first emerged in different historical epochs and continue to operate according to different temporal logics but share a differentiated present.[91] Nonsynchronism helps him attend to sociotemporal contradictions and potentialities within a given social formation. But we may also use it to understand the temporal heterogeneity of the capitalist world-system. As we saw with Samir Amin, capitalism has always been characterized by a process of uneven development.[92] Scholars have demonstrated how seemingly incommensurable modes of production and forms of life, which emerged at different historical moments, were promiscuously combined in ways that both unified and differentiated the world. The global capitalist order, along with each of the distinct social formations that compose it, contains within itself multiple and intersecting temporal regimes, institutions and practices associated with various epochs, each of which may express and produce qualitatively distinct types of time. Insofar as uneven development entails a dialectic of economic progress (for centers) and regress (for peripheries), it confounds assumptions about linear time, progressive history, or the identity between time and history.

This is the spirit in which, as we will see in the next chapter, Marx identified Germany as an "anachronism." This insight into the uneven character of capitalist social formations was extended by Leon Trotsky regarding "the combination of different stages in the historic process" in pre-Revolutionary Russia, Antonio Gramsci regarding "the Southern question" in Italy in the 1920s, Bloch on how the persistence of premodern forms of life in 1930s Germany benefited Nazism, and Henri Lefebvre on the layered character of everyday life in postwar capitalist cities.[93] With such processes in mind, historian Harry Harootunian proposes "a model of the present thick with different practices from other modes of production, mixed temporal regimes declaring their affiliation with different times now passed but still retained with their corresponding political demands."[94]

Objects created under such untimely conditions condense and refract this untimeliness. Bakhtin, for example, demonstrates how languages, discourses, and texts are "heteroglot unities" composed of disparate social, ideological, and temporal elements.[95] He writes,

> at any given moment, languages of various epochs and periods of socio-ideological life cohabit with one another. Even languages of the day exist: one could say that today's and yesterday's socio-ideological and political "day" do not, in a certain sense, share the same language. . . . Thus at any given moment of its historical existence, language is heteroglot from top to bottom: it represents the co-existence of socio-ideological contradictions between the present and the past, between differing epochs of the past, between different socio-ideological groups in the present.[96]

This mechanism of temporal crystallization, which Bakhtin calls "social heteroglossia," operates throughout untimely social formations.[97] It can be usefully compared with Koselleck's insightful, if less political, account of how concepts "register" historical experiences from earlier epochs.[98] Koselleck suggests that they do so in ways that condense the contradictory discourses that "basic concepts" typically mediate.[99]

III. Political Imagination and Temporal Self-Reflexivity

Since the 1890s, vitalist, psychoanalytic, phenomenological, Messianic, and deconstructive currents of social thought have grappled in different ways with the untimely character of modern life. They have generated important and insightful challenges to modern doxa concerning quantitative clock-time, linear chronology, sequential causality, and separate self-identical tenses. But such challenges have usually depended on either metaphysical claims about the "true" nature of time as such or on dubious boundaries between, on the one hand, natural or official time (as abstract and universal) and, on the other, lived time (as concrete and plural). Alternatively, the thinkers I have discussed signal how we might try to develop *sociohistorical* accounts of phenomena associated with anachronism, nonsynchronism, and untimeliness.

It is not enough to simply oppose attempts to treat clock-time as natural or progress as inevitable with equally transhistorical claims about the "real" nature of time as cyclical, durational, repetitive, or spectral. These are two sides of the same metaphysical coin. Each dehistoricizes time in ways that risk depoliticizing the sociotemporal phenomena under consideration. Nor is it adequate to simply criticize clock-time from the standpoint of untimely phenomena as if the latter were intrinsically emancipatory. In their different ways, thinkers like Marx and Freud reveal the alienating and heteronomous implications of being haunted by a persisting past. (In Chapter 9, I will discuss untimely repetition as a form of racial domination.)

I would like to conclude this chapter by underscoring that historical explanation and conjunctural political analysis are intrinsically related to political imagination and the prospects of transformative action. The politics of the possible-impossible require forms of understanding, imagination, and action that are attuned to the *untimely* character of social life. Attention to ways that a historical present is not identical with itself opens the possibility for immanent critique. Recall that Ranciére relates the ability to break and make temporal alignments in a multitemporal now with the very capacity to make history or do politics.[100] Nonsynchronism, mutlitemporality, and anachronism are indissociable from situations of domination and possibilities for emancipation. But neither empiricist history nor realist politics adequately recognize, let alone attend to, such phenomena.

Concrete utopianism requires analysis, imagination, and action that are not constrained by realist assumptions about chronological sequence, self-identical periods, and categorically distinct tenses. It requires a political orientation that does not shackle historical temporality to the logic of abstract clock-time and the tyranny of tenses. In any given historical situation, critical understanding, political imagination, and radical action need to confront the dialectic of social formations and temporal frameworks. This requires attention to time as a real abstraction — to the typical velocities, rhythms, and scales through which lives are lived, to the specific ways that the relation between past, present, and future is figured, and to the temporal dimensions of various social institutions, ideologies, and practices. It requires attention to how certain kinds of social arrangements presuppose and create historically specific kinds of time (and vice versa). It also means attending to the multitemporal and untimely dimensions of social life. Doing so invites a rethinking of realist assumptions about context, agency, causality, consequences (i.e., political "success"), and a naturalized division between tenses that often foreclose a politics of the possible-impossible.[101]

Concrete utopian analysis, imagination, and action attuned to untimeliness also requires us to be temporally self-reflexive about our own historical present. This means following David Scott's invitation to ask when and why the apparent equivalence between time and history is disrupted such that time becomes an explicit object of public debate and terrain of political struggle. Now that the postwar consensus is unraveling, as we ride the wave of another set of world-historical transformations, including the prospect of planetary demise through climate change, it is hardly surprising that, as during the interwar period, time is becoming an object of reflection across the disciplines. Temporal self-reflexivity also has ethical implications. Recognizing the ongoing presence of the past in a nonidentical now raises questions about actors' responsibility to past and future generations.[102] The politics of sovereign debt, reparations for slavery, and climate justice, for example, cannot be thought apart from questions of intergenerational implication. Looking forward, Kant insisted that humans "cannot be indifferent even to the most remote epoch which may eventually affect our species."[103] Looking backward, Benjamin wrote of the "secret agreement between past generations and the present one" that endows predecessors with moral claims on existing actors.[104] Both remind us that *the concrete utopian pursuit of another possible world may entail not only translocal but transtemporal solidarities.*

Benjamin's belief in this moral claim that the past exercises on the present, his injunction that we have a political responsibility to redeem earlier generations through our actions, leads him to call on critics to identify or construct historical constellations between their political now and previous eras. Doing so does not only provide a retrospective flash of historical illumination. As importantly, it discloses new possibilities for transformative action in the now.[105] The task is not simply to understand the past but to "foresee the present" through such critical remembrance.[106] This is the paradox Benjamin seeks to elaborate when he writes, "The seer's gaze is kindled by the rapidly receding past. That is to say, the prophet has turned away from the future: he perceives the contours of the future in the fading light of the past as it sinks before him into the night of times. *This prophetic relation to the future necessarily informs the attitude of the historian* as Marx describes it."[107] (We may compare this formulation to Glissant's "prophetic vision of the past," which I discuss in Chapter 10.) Benjamin's insight about how vital pasts may mediate between a nonsynchronous now and a redeemed world is rooted in a "dialectic of past and future," which is the focus of the next chapter.

8
Dialectic of Past and Future

my ear to the ground, I heard Tomorrow pass

—AIMÉ CÉSAIRE

Bourgeois evil is the post-existence of older things . . . that have been
subdued, but not wholly subdued.

—THEODOR ADORNO

Grayness could not fill us with despair if our minds did not harbor the
concept of different colors, scattered traces of which are not absent
from the negative whole. The traces always come from the past, and
our hopes come from their counterpart, from that which was or is
doomed.

—THEODOR ADORNO

Marxism thus rescued the rational core of utopia and made it
concrete . . . Romanticism does not understand utopia . . . but utopia
that has become concrete understands Romanticism . . . insofar
as archaic and historical material . . . contains a not yet voiced,
undischarged element.

—ERNST BLOCH

In the previous chapter, I discussed the dialectic of social formations and temporal frameworks—how certain kinds of social arrangements presuppose and
produce certain kinds of time (and vice versa). More specifically, I discussed
the contradictory nature of time under capitalism as abstract and concrete,

single and multiple, homogeneous and disjunctive, repetitive and progressive. I suggested that capitalism both endows abstract time with the status of a second nature and *and* draws constant attention to the contingent and plastic character of time. I concluded with the suggestion that such temporal multiplicity, nonsynchronism, and untimeliness may either be a source of alienating domination or create possibilities for immanent critique and emancipatory transformation. The latter, which depends on the ways in which any given now is temporally nonidentical, is the focus of this chapter.

In the following, I discuss the way Marx and Marxian thinkers attended to how the unrealized potentiality of persisting or repeating pasts within an untimely present may open pathways to other possible worlds. I begin by offering an immanent critique of Michel Foucault's genealogical method through which he proposed writing effective histories of the present. This powerful intervention challenged much conventional thinking about history, origins, and progress. But genealogical critique also depended on temporal assumptions that obstructed its ability to recognize the political potential of untimeliness. In contrast, I argue that critical historical understanding and radical political imagination should develop what I would call an untimely history of the present. Said differently, a politics of the possible-impossible should attend to what Michael Löwy has called the "dialectic between the past and the future."[1]

I. History of What Present?

Genealogy as Critical History

At the start of *Discipline and Punish* (1975) Michel Foucault famously wrote: "I would like to write the history of this prison. . . . Why? Simply because I am interested in the past? No, if one means by that writing a history of the past in terms of the present. Yes, if one means writing the history of the present."[2] Foucault thus announced the kind of genealogical analysis that he would pursue for the rest of his career.[3] I would argue that genealogy has become the dominant mode of critical history and theoretical critique in the contemporary Western university.

Foucault elaborated his new method most explicitly in "Nietzsche, Genealogy, and History" (1971). Here he renounces "traditional history" for seeking to uncover origins and discover truths of stable objects which either persist or develop over time. In contrast, genealogy sought to overturn any metaphysical belief in original and transhistorical truth, reason, meaning, identity, or subjectivity. By tracing historically specific lines of descent and processes of emergence, genealogy dissolves the seeming permanence and necessity of the given world. It targeted both the mundane (bodies, senses, sentiments) and the transcendent (soul, reason, truth). Genealogy reveals that society's most noble concepts, cherished certainties, and indispensable institutions are effects of profane accidents and errors, lowly origins and vulgar passions, and violent conflicts and the will to power. Rather than discover the truth of history, genealogy traces the history of truth. Rather than specify a subject of history, it historicizes subjects. Rather than interpret historical meaning, it analyzes the production of meaning as an operation of power.

Insofar as genealogy rejects foundational, teleological, and progressive thinking, it overturns many of the protocols of traditional historiography and idealist philosophies of history. As importantly, genealogy rejects any scholastic interest in scholarly neutrality or knowledge for knowledge's sake. It is an ethical and political practice that recognizes the intrinsic link between knowing the past and intervening in the present. Foucault criticizes the "groveling manner" in which traditional historians purport "to examine things furthest from themselves" at a safe and "promising distance."[4] In contrast, "effective history" rejects scholars' attempts "to erase the elements of their work which reveal their [own] grounding in a particular time and place, their preferences in a controversy."[5] In a 1976 interview with Marxist geographers Foucault emphasized the direct link between genealogical inquiry and immediate engagements:

> [I]f one is interested in doing historical work that has political meaning, utility and effectiveness, then this is possible only if one has some kind of involvement with the struggles taking place in the area in question. . . . My historical work was undertaken only as a function of those conflicts. The problem and the stake there was . . . the possibility of a historical truth which could have a political effect.[6]

Likewise, in a 1981 interview Foucault reminds readers, "The question I [always] start off with is: what are we and what are we today?"[7] An effective history of the present embraces the fact that "its perception is slanted, being a deliberate appraisal, affirmation, or negation; it reaches the lingering and poisonous traces in order to prescribe the best antidote."[8]

Foucault is not simply suggesting that historical knowledge is always partial or limited by a scholar's social location or ideological perspective. He is not only calling on traditional historians to acknowledge that their supposed disinterested scholarship cannot avoid making qualitative judgments. His aim is not more objectivity but deeper self-reflexivity in the service of greater effectivity. Indifference and neutrality are impossible because historians' concepts are themselves part of the history they study. By insisting that any history needs to trace the relation between the will to knowledge and the operation of power, Foucault highlights historians' own ethical and epistemological implication in the particular histories that they engage. He insists that interpretations of the past always are, and should be, guided by a scholar's ethical and political investments in contemporary conflicts. He is not suggesting that we use current standards to morally evaluate past practices. Nor does he want historians to read the past selectively in order to morally affirm present beliefs. On the contrary, effective history renounces the ceaseless moralizing performed by self-proclaimed objective history (which de facto normalizes present arrangements and naturalizes a view of history as progress). Effective history seeks neither to judge the past nor to justify the present but to intervene into the present by disclosing the arbitrary character of existing norms and arrangements, which emerged contingently through interested and violent historical processes. The genealogist's aim is to identify "those things that, at the present time . . . give some more or less vague indications of the fragility of our system of thought, in our way of reflecting, in our practices."[9] Such investigations "show that . . . by changing strategies, taking things differently, finally what appears obvious to us is not all so obvious . . . from the second that it is historically constituted, it can be politically destroyed . . . there are possibilities for action."[10] Genealogy traces histories of fragile givens and emerging actuality in order to disclose possibilities for political action.

In his later writings, Foucault extended to philosophy this genealogical imperative to politicize history. He called on philosophers to trace critical genealogies of accepted concepts and conventional debates, to orient their inquiries toward present conditions, stakes, and struggles. Such genealogical philosophy would be self-reflexive: "It is a matter of showing specifically and in what ways the one who speaks as a thinker, a scientist, and a philosopher is himself a part of this process."[11] Foucault thus identified a new kind of "historical-philosophical practice" that would reflect on "the relationships between power, truth, and the subject."[12]

This effort to conscript philosophy itself into the project of producing effective histories of the present helps explain Foucault's late writings on Kant, whom he credits with asking "What is it in the present that now makes sense for philosophical reflection?"[13] Subversively employing this Kantian ethos against Kant's transcendental analytic, he contends that when the great idealist asked "What is my actuality?" his aim was to specify "the mode of action that [discourse] is capable of exerting within this present."[14] Foucault interpreted this operation as a "genealogical" effort to "separate out from the contingency that has made us what we are, the possibility of no longer being, doing, or thinking what we are, do, or think."[15] Foucault's late writings on "the critical ontology of the present" are one of the few places where he clearly links the practice of critique to the aim of emancipation: "The critique of what we are is at one and the same time the historical analysis of the limits that are imposed on us and an experiment with the possibility of going beyond them."[16] His aim is to identify how "the growth of capabilities" may "be disconnected from the intensification of power relations."[17] In other words, Foucault proposes historical and philosophical inquiries that might help social actors exceed the normative limits imposed in and by a given present. Genealogy thus assumes and confronts questions of historical temporality.

The Temporality of Genealogy

Foucault's writings on effective histories of the present are punctuated by promising openings that might invite us to historicize time. He declares, "Genealogy . . . operates on a field of entangled and confused parchments, on documents that have been scratched over and recopied many times."[18] He contends that his historical and philosophical inquiries are motivated by the possibility of the "permanent reactivation of an attitude."[19] Such statements could imply an understanding of the present as a temporally heterogeneous now that retains past possibilities that could be redeployed to intervene in present struggles. But Foucault does not develop the temporal implications of these formulations. He asserts that genealogy intends to transform "history into a totally different form of time."[20] But he never elaborates this difference. He declares that the genealogist will

> push the masquerade to its limit and prepare the great carnival of time where masks are constantly reappearing. No longer the identification of our faint individuality with the solid identities of the past, but our "unrealization" through the excessive choice of identities. . . . Genealogy is history in the form of a concerted carnival.[21]

As this passage indicates, Foucault is less concerned with problematizing present time than with challenging coercive norms and identitarian social logics. The "great carnival of time" seems to be more about the multiple identities that may traverse a given present than the multiplicity of temporalities that constitute it.

Foucault relates that the genealogical "search for descent . . . disturbs what was previously considered immobile; it fragments what was thought unified; it shows the heterogeneity of what was imagined consistent with itself."[22] But he does not subject time itself to this operation. He challenges conventional claims about the self-identical character of historical subjects or objects. But

he does not question the supposedly self-identical character of a given historical present or epoch. Genealogy traces surprising twists, contingent breaks,
and violent reversals that characterize any line of descent. But precisely insofar as these pathways of descent are *lineal,* genealogy implicitly accepts conventional axioms about (historical) time as unidirectional, irreversible, and
self-identical. Foucault rejects the idea that history might be intrinsically purposeful, teleological, or progressive. But his historical accounts still move relentlessly forward along the tracks of time. He examines neither the processes
of reification that fix past, present, and future as categorically distinct spheres
nor the social interpenetration of tenses. On the contrary, his concern with
smashing notions of unbroken heritage, inherited traditions, historical continuities, progressive transitions, or teleological purposes leads him to insist on
the essential incommensurability of a given historical present with any other
era. His genealogical aim "to restore the conditions for the appearance of a
singularity born out of multiple determining elements" extends to historical
periods and tenses.[23]

Foucault takes pains to protect every singular present from contamination
by misplaced tenses. Rather than explore how seemingly settled boundaries
between past and present may blur, or could be productively blurred, he insists on maintaining rigid distinctions between them. His rightful concern
with identitarian logics that might posit false continuities leads him to insist
that the "duty" of "genealogy" is "not to demonstrate that the past actively
exists in the present, that it continues to secretly animate the present."[24] This
concern led him to share with conventional history a fear of anachronism.[25]

In *The Order of Things,* Foucault did attempt to historicize the emergence
of a certain kind of historicist common sense in nineteenth-century Europe.
He discusses how scholars shifted from knowing natural and social worlds
through the spatial optics of charts and tables to understanding them in terms
of temporal processes of progress, evolution, and development.[26] Likewise,
Discipline and Punish describes how bodies and selves were subjected to the
tyranny of abstract time, which itself was instrumentalized and monetized.[27]
But it is as if Foucault regarded the institutionalization of a historicist episteme
and the normalization of abstract time as complete and accomplished facts
that did not require further analysis. Readers of Foucault are familiar with his
critique of structural history (whether practiced by the *Annales* school or promoted by Althusser and his circle) from the standpoint of contingent events,
historical ruptures, or singular presents. Yet many of the signature concepts
that informed Foucault's history of the present—episteme, discursive formation, disciplinary regime, political rationality—point to logics and structures
that imply temporal self-presence at any given moment. These concepts do
not easily allow for heterodox thinking about historical temporality.

There is nothing intrinsically incompatible between Foucauldian genealogy and a critique of the assumption that the present is temporally homogeneous. But neither Foucault nor his epigones pursued this line of inquiry
directly. In his accounts, historical events typically take place in time as a
neutral medium. He implicitly treated epochs, periods, and present instants
as temporally self-identical. He insisted on historical contingency, rupture,
and singularity in such a way as to exclude consideration of the present as a
nonidentical now that is shaped in ongoing ways by persistent or recurrent
pasts. More fundamentally, he did not subject social time to genealogical
critique. He sought to produce histories of the present without problematizing
"the present."

Foucault, of course, borrowed and adapted the method Nietzsche used in
his genealogy of morals. Nietzsche announced, "We need a *critique* of moral
values, *the value of these values themselves must first be called into question* —
and for that there is needed a knowledge of the conditions and circumstances
in which they grew, under which they evolved and changed."[28] Against accounts focused on seemingly natural processes of progressive and purposeful
historical evolution, Nietzsche argued that "the entire history of a 'thing,' an
organ, a custom can . . . be a continuous sign-chain of ever new interpretations and adaptations whose causes do not even need to be related to one
another but, on the contrary . . . succeed and alternate with one another in
a purely chance fashion."[29] Nietzsche's genealogy thus identified the historically specific will to power — "a succession of more or less profound, more or
less interdependent processes of subduing, plus the resistances they encounter, the attempts at transformation for the purpose of defense and reaction,
and the results of successful counteractions" — that produce and sustain any
given custom or idea.[30] Curiously, *The Genealogy of Morals* (1887) was one of
Nietzsche's few major works that criticized progress without *also* problematizing abstract time and historical chronology. If Foucault had, for example,
treated *The Birth of Tragedy* (1872) as his model, he would have encountered
a different kind of genealogy that did recognize the present as untimely.

Written against the backdrop of the Franco-Prussian war, this early work
was really a story about the *death and rebirth* of tragedy. After establishing
how, in Hellenic Greece, tragic drama had achieved an extraordinary balance between Dionysian and Apollonian sensibilities, Nietzsche traces how
Alexandrian culture propelled the Apollonian to triumph over the Dionysian
in all domains. In this account, a new Socratic orientation to the world, characterized by theoretical abstraction and scientific knowledge, displaced an
essentially aesthetic one, nourished by music and myth. The latter had been
characterized by overflowing life, joy, and suffering.

Nietzsche identifies modernity with this Socratic form of disenchanted life which places "forces of nature . . . in the service of a higher form of egoism. It believes that the world can be corrected through knowledge and that life should be guided by science . . . to confine man within the narrow circle of soluble tasks."[31] Nietzsche understands "the present age" as one of rootless alienation.[32] It is dominated by "abstract man, abstract law, abstract government . . . a culture without any fixed and consecrated place of origin."[33] This form of "secularization, a break with the unconscious metaphysic of its earlier mode of existence," Nietzsche contends, required the destruction of Greek art, especially tragedy.[34] The result is a "great historical hunger" such that "man today, stripped of myth, stands famished among all his pasts and must dig frantically for roots, be it among the most remote antiquities."[35] Nietzsche thus formulates a critique of this spiritually "famished" modernity from the standpoint of largely forgotten Dionysian ways of being human. But he does not merely mourn this lost past. He offers a history of the present that aims at an overcoming. He argues that traces of this ancient "transindividual" orientation to human being capable of accessing the "beating heart of life" may still be glimpsed in certain contemporary music, art, and rituals.[36] He explains, "underneath the hectic movements of our civilization there dwells a marvelous ancient power, which arouses itself mightily only at certain grand moments and then sinks back to dream again of the future."[37]

Nietzsche suggests that his contemporaries are living through just such a "grand moment." In the book's climax, he discusses how recent German music (Wagnerian opera) and philosophy (Kant, Schopenhauer, and presumably Nietzsche himself) herald "the rebirth of tragedy."[38] In his view, this "miraculous union between German philosophy and music" points "to a new mode of existence, whose precise nature we can divine only with the aid of Greek analogies":

> For us, who stand on the watershed between two different modes of existence, the Greek example is still of inestimable value, since it embodies the violent transition to a classical, rationalistic form of suasion; only we are living through the great phases of Hellenism in reverse order and seem at this very moment to be moving backward from the Alexandrian age into an age of tragedy. And we can't help feeling that the dawn of a new tragic age is for the German spirit only a return to itself, a blessed recovery of its true identity.[39]

As we can see, Nietzsche's assertions are refracted through an invidious nationalist metaphysics (i.e., the rejuvenation and purification of a true German spirit that had been corrupted by the influence of foreign French culture). But his reflections on "the reawakening of the Dionysian spirit" and the "imminent rebirth of Greek antiquity" also convey an attempt to recognize and awaken the persistence of past possibilities in an untimely present.[40] Unfortunately, Nietzsche does not try to account for this "marvelous ancient power" that periodically "arouses itself." Like his writings on the *will to power* and *eternal recurrence*, he offers a mythical invocation of a metaphysical force (and vice versa). But his argument does help us to see how genealogy may relate to a critique of linear temporality and chronological history.

The rest of this chapter will focus on efforts within the Marxian tradition to elaborate just such pathways between past potentials that may inhere within an untimely now and the prospect of new modes of existence. We can surmise that Foucault's anti-Marxism precluded him from engaging with this aspect of that tradition. Recall that Foucault opposed genealogy, as a form of "local criticism," to the kind of "totalitarian theories" that pursued "functionalist coherence and formal systematization."[41] His primary targets were semiology, psychoanalysis, and Marxism. He criticized the latter especially for having scientific aspirations, attempting "to think in terms of a totality," and to "enthrone" a "theoretical-political *avant garde*."[42] But by treating time as a social fact and historical force, this denigrated Marxian tradition offers resources for realizing the effective histories of the present for which Foucault called. It sought to identify how, in any given now, *the growth of capabilities could be disconnected from power relations so that social actors* can *go beyond the historical limits imposed in and by the present.*

II. Dialectic of Past and Future

Inversion as Reversion

We may read Marx's *Capital* as a history of the present that is both genealogical and dialectical. Its structural analysis of capital accumulation is grounded in historical accounts of primitive accumulation, the emergence of large-scale industry, and struggles over the working day. It thus elaborates the "long and tormented historical development" of both the material conditions and the social categories—the real abstractions—around which capitalism, political economy, and the critique of political economy are organized (e.g., money, labor, value, capital).[43] Marx suggests that because these historical creations are internally contradictory (nonidentical), they can be overcome. "By maturing the material conditions and the social combination of the processes of production, it matures the contradictions and antagonisms of the capitalist form of that process, and thereby ripens both the elements for forming a new society and the forces tending towards the overthrow of the old one."[44] Marx thus demonstrates genealogically that capitalist arrangements are nonnatural and nonnecessary. He also demonstrates dialectically that: 1) these arrangements are obstacles to human emancipation, 2) society really could be organized differently, and 3) an alternative set of arrangements may emerge from within the contradictory conditions that already exist. The basis on which Marx made these dialectical claims, his standpoint of critique, shifted over time.

In his early work, Marx critiques alienation from the standpoint of man's essential nature as a species-being who produces himself and his world through free conscious activity, even in the absence of "immediate physical need."[45] Under capitalism, however, "estranged labor reduces spontaneous and free activity to a means . . . of . . . physical existence."[46] This kind of labor, grounded in private property, artificially separates, or alienates, workers from nature, from themselves, and from fellow humans—from their own "human essence."[47] In contrast, Marx figures communism as "the complete restoration of man to himself as a social, i.e. human, being."[48] Communism will enable "the reintegration or return of man into himself . . . and the return of man . . . to his *human*, i.e. *social*, existence."[49] Marx does not explain the basis on which he identifies species-being as the real human essence.[50] Nor does he indicate how laborers trapped in an infernal circle of self-estrangement might abolish alienated labor in order to return to their true selves through communism. Said differently, he does not trace the possible mediation between an alienated present and a future characterized by "the complete *emancipation* of all human senses and attributes."[51]

In his later work, Marx remains committed to the project of abolishing capitalism and realizing human emancipation. He does not employ the latter formulation explicitly. But he announces the imperative to overcome "a mode of production in which the worker exists to satisfy the need of the existing values for valorization, as opposed to the inverse situation, in which objective wealth is there to satisfy the worker's own need for development."[52] The aim is essentially the same as it was in his early work: to institute "an association of free men, working with the means of production held in common" whose "total product . . . is a social product" that "stands under their conscious and planned control."[53] But here, Marx's standpoint of critique shifts from humanity's essence as a species-being to past precedents and immanent developments. This allows him to better attend to the mediation between an alienated present and an emancipated future of "freely associated men."[54]

In this later work, Marx traces the possibilities of dialectical transformation. Consider his discussion of "the organized system of machinery in the factory."[55] In a first development, this "most powerful instrument for reducing labor-time suffers from a dialectical inversion and becomes the most unfailing means for turning the whole lifetime of the worker and his family into labor-time at capital's disposal for its own valorization."[56] By reducing workers to "living appendages" of a "lifeless mechanism," this "labor process becomes an instrument of torture" that "confiscates every atom of freedom" since "the machine does not free the worker from the work, but rather deprives the work itself of all content . . . it is not the worker who employs the conditions of his work, but rather the reverse, the conditions of work employ the worker."[57] But then there is a second inversion. This infernal machinery "operates only by means of associated labor, or labor in common" such that the "cooperative character of the labor process is . . . a technical necessity."[58] In other words, this dehumanizing instrument of capitalist valorization requires and produces "a social means of production" that points *beyond* capitalism.[59]

Likewise, Marx examines the contradictory effects of a valorization process that generates competition and crises which, in turn, lead to the concentration and centralization of capital. As a result, there is "growth of the cooperative form of the labor process" on "an ever-increasing scale," or "the transformation of the means of labor into forms in which they can only be used in common . . . combined, socialized labor, the entanglement of all peoples in the net of the world market, and with this, the growth of the international character of the capitalist regime."[60] Eventually, "the monopoly of capital becomes a fetter upon the mode of production which has flourished alongside and under it. The centralization of the means of production and the socialization of labor reach a point at which they become incompatible with their capitalist integument."[61] The dialectics of accumulation thus nourish a noncapitalist mode of production "alongside and under," or immanently within, the existing order.

These examples illustrate Marx's claim that "the development of the contradictions of a given historical form of production is the only historical way in which it can be dissolved and then reconstructed on a new basis."[62] This is a future-oriented account of dialectical developments that may open the possibility for systemic social transformation. Yet Marx develops crucial aspects of this argument through comparison to earlier social formations. Readers often interpret his references to "ancient Asiatic, Classical-antique, and other such modes of production" as evidence of a stagist view of history.[63] But I understand them, at least in Marx's late work, as attempts to identify a standpoint on the basis of which to claim that things really could be otherwise.

In the *Grundrisse*, Marx contrasts the existing system, in which "production appears as the aim of mankind and wealth as the aim of production," to "precapitalist" production based either on ancient systems of communal landownership or medieval systems of small landed property.[64] In societies such as these, "the human being appears as the aim of production."[65] Marx explains, "Individuals relate not as workers but as proprietors—and members of a community, who at the same time work."[66] Likewise in *Capital*, he invokes "the patriarchal rural industry of a peasant family which produces . . . for its own use" through "collective labor" that creates objects of utility rather than commodities.[67] Such past precedents offer Marx another standpoint for envisioning the possible-impossible prospect of a postcapitalist form of "labor in common, i.e., directly associated labor" that would allow "an association of free men, working with the means of production held in common" to produce "objects of utility" for "the members of the association."[68]

Marx certainly does not call for a return to earlier modes of production which "exclude[d] cooperation" as well as "the social control and regulation of the forces of nature, and the free development of the productive forces of society."[69] He notes that such modes were "conditioned by a low stage of development of the productive powers of labor and correspondingly limited relations between men within the process of creating and reproducing their material life."[70] These patriarchal societies were "founded on the immaturity of man as an individual, when he has not yet torn himself from . . . direct relations of domination and servitude."[71] They could not serve as direct models for a postcapitalist society. The aim, rather, would be to reconstitute aspects of supposedly superseded alternatives to private property, but in more elevated forms, on the basis of modern achievements (i.e., the liberation from material need and relations of direct servitude so that human capacities could be further realized).

Marx does not only invoke past arrangements as a standpoint from which to criticize his alienated present. He also demonstrates how under new conditions (and in alienated forms) capitalism reconstitutes aspects of the social labor and social property that characterized the earlier modes of production that capitalism had supposedly "decomposed."[72] Marx was especially interested in the "intermediate situations" between "social, collective property" and "capitalist private property" in which "the peasant owns the land he cultivates, or the artisan owns the tool with which he is an accomplished performer."[73] Here "the private property of the worker in his means of production is the foundation of small-scale industry" which "is a necessary condition for the development of social production and the free individuality of the worker."[74] Marx explains that capitalist private property destroyed this less-alienated form of individual property. Yet the contemporary development of industrial capitalism on ever-larger scales was leading it to (again) "establish individual property on the basis of the achievements of the capitalist era: namely, cooperation and the possession in common of the land and the means of production produced by labor itself."[75] Capitalist accumulation was itself creating conditions for "the transformation of capitalist private property, which in fact already rests on the carrying on of production by society, into social property."[76] In other words, capitalism creates an incipient form of anticapitalist social property that negates, preserves, and elevates aspects of precapitalist individual property.

Marx neither locates human emancipation in past social formations nor projects it to the end of a fixed set of developmental stages through which all societies must pass.[77] On the contrary, his genealogy of primitive accumulation indicates the many points at which a different process of technical development and social organization *might have* led to a different kind of society in which many of the collective aspects of former social arrangements *could have been* placed on stronger foundations and reworked in emancipatory ways. Modern life might therefore have been based on the free development of human capacities without alienation, immiseration, and the despotism of abstract forces.

Rather than either renounce or idealize the precapitalist past, Marx identifies features of earlier social formations that may orient anticapitalist struggle and inform postcapitalist arrangements. Moreover, he traces the way dialectical inversions may produce historical reversions that could open pathways to a different kind of society. Marx thus invites us to conjugate the unrealized potentialities of previous epochs with immanent potentialities developing within, and pointing beyond, existing arrangements. This requires not only a genealogical understanding of the lines of descent through which present conditions came into being but an untimely understanding that past possibilities are not permanently bound to their epochs of emergence. Their traces may remain available as living legacies within a nonidentical now.

Immanent Critique of the Untimely Present

Marx also addressed the subjective pitfalls of untimeliness. In *The Eighteenth Brumaire,* he contrasts the successful French Revolution, in which the vital energies of ancient predecessors were effectively reactivated, to the failed 1848 Revolution, in which Parisian militants "anxiously conjure up the spirits of the past to their service and borrow from them names, battle slogans and costumes in order to present the new scene of world history in this time-honored disguise and this borrowed language."[78] Marx seems to suggest that this masquerade crystallized the political mistiming and misunderstandings that condemned this revolution to failure. In other words, political effectiveness in a given conjuncture might depend on the difference between knowing whether to try to reawaken pasts or to anticipate futures.

We can understand Marx's practice of immanent critique as one strategy for performing the possible-impossible task of grounding political practice in terms that belong to a future that is yet to be created. In his 1844 letter to Arnold Ruge, Marx explained that the aim of criticism is to "develop from the unique forms of existing reality the true reality as its norm and final goal."[79] I read Marx's claim that "reason has always existed, only not always in reasonable form" as referring to this obscured, obstructed, and desirable "true reality."[80] In other words, he calls on critics to identify within an existing capitalist reality that is organized around an oppressive reason, a more emancipatory reason that could ground a true reality in which human capacities and potentialities could be further realized. Likewise, Marx then employs Hegelian dialectics against Hegelian rationalism in order to critique the actually existing rational state. He argues, "The state everywhere presupposes that reason has been realized. But in just this way it everywhere comes into contradiction between its ideal mission [potentiality] and its real preconditions [actual form]."[81] Even this early, Marx suggests that we critique existing arrangements from a perspective, or standpoint, that is internal to them. He grounds the possibility of a different reality in tendencies that are already present within real life but point beyond it to a truer life.

Marx rejected efforts by utopian socialists to critique capitalism from the standpoint of the "crude communism" of an idealized past.[82] He also renounced those progressive socialists engaged in "the designing of the future and the proclamation of ready-made solutions for all times."[83] He explained to Ruge that not having a "clear conception of what the future should be" was an "advantage" for their circle: "We do not attempt dogmatically to prefigure the future, but want to find the new world only through criticism of the old."[84] Marx's alternative to one-sided attempts to either return to the past or predict the future was *to leverage the past in order to draw poetry from the future through* what I would call *an immanent critique of the untimely present*. He did not only trace the way capitalism itself created conditions and tendencies that pointed beyond capitalism. He also sought within existing arrangements unrealized residues of earlier modes of production, forms of life, and political imagination that might point toward a postcapitalist world.

Marx concludes his letter to Ruge with the suggestion that critics can approach the unknowable future by way of past dreams that remain unrealized. Anticipating Benjamin, Marx calls on critics to awaken humanity to its obscured and forgotten dreams without which it will continue to reconcile itself to the existing world. He explains, "It is not a matter of drawing a great dividing line between past and future, but of carrying out the thoughts of the past. . . . Mankind begins no new work, but consciously accomplishes its old work."[85] If Marx here endorses the backward glance, it is not in order to return to the past. Rather, his aim is to recall, in order to realize, past dreams (futures past) that have been foreclosed, denigrated, or forgotten.[86] To appreciate this operation, we can turn to Marx's observations about the temporally nonidentical character of any capitalist present.[87] I have already discussed the dialectic of living labor that animates dead matter and dead labor that shapes social practices. For Marx, the present is shot through with, and haunted by, persisting and repeating pasts. His understanding of social transformation is informed by this attunement to untimeliness.

In the *Grundrisse*, Marx criticizes the metaphysical assertions of classical "economists who smudge over all historical differences and see bourgeois relations in all forms of society."[88] But, against a nominalism that would fetishize such differences, he also argues that "the categories which express" the relations and structure of bourgeois society "allow insights into the structure and the relations of production of all the vanished social formations out of whose ruins and elements it built itself up, *whose partly still unconquered remnants are carried along within it.*"[89] This understanding of unconquered remnants persisting in a nonidentical present should not be confused with a linear understanding of historical succession, whether figured as mechanical (as if each epoch is a billiard ball knocking into and propelling forward the next in line) or evolutionary (as if each epoch is the life-stage of a progressively developing organic entity). In his later writings, Marx explicitly rejects a teleological conception of linear historical development for which "the latest form regards the previous ones as steps leading up to itself."[90] Criticizing one-sided conceptions of either smooth continuity *or* categorical rupture, he contends that "since bourgeois society is . . . a contradictory form of development, relations derived from earlier forms will often be found within it only in an entirely stunted form, or even travestied. For example, communal property."[91]

If capitalist social formations are temporally nonidentical, so, too, are the epochs in which they are situated. In what might seem like an affirmation of linear evolutionary development, Marx warned German workers that they could glimpse the image of their likely future in the miserable conditions that defined England's industrial present. But rather than situate Germany at some knowable point along a predetermined developmental trajectory, Marx traces how Germany was moving along its own distinct trajectory. This was marked by the emergence of a capitalist economy without either bourgeois social relations or liberal democracy. Such uneven development had created a double bind for modern Germany: "We . . . suffer not only from the development of capitalist production, but also from the incompleteness of that development. Alongside of modern evils, a whole series of inherited evils oppress us, arising from the passive survival of antiquated modes of production, with their inevitable train of social and political anachronisms. We suffer not only from the living, but the dead."[92] This functional articulation of advanced and archaic elements, a capitalist economy and semi-feudal social order, was the source of modern and inherited evils. When he declares *"Le mort saisit le vif,"* Marx suggests that supposedly superseded arrangements did not only survive but were integral to and exercised a haunting power over this nonidentical society.[93] Based on this analysis, Marx reminded militant socialists, "Germany can emancipate itself from the *Middle Ages* only if it emancipates itself at the same time from the *partial* victories over the Middle Ages."[94] For Germany, this meant that remnants of feudal social relations *and* the newly consolidated proletarian labor regime would need to be abolished simultaneously. The more general point is that there can be no ready-made revolutionary strategy that could be applied to every society.

Marx's 1867 reflections on how Germany seemed to be out of sync with English socioeconomic development echoed his earlier observations about Germany being out of sync with French sociopolitical developments. In 1843 he commented, "According to the French calendar [Germany has] barely reached 1789, much less the vital center of our present age."[95] But Marx was not only commenting on German backwardness. He puzzled over the contradictory fact that Germany was also Europe's philosophical vanguard. "We Germans have lived our future history in thought . . . our criticism stands at the center of those problems of which the present age says: *That is the question.*"[96] But it could not join "advanced nations" in their *"practical* quarrel with modern political conditions" since the latter "do not yet exist" in Germany.[97] Marx thus notes ironically that Germans emancipated themselves from the *ancien régime* through an intellectual rather than a practical revolution. In other words, Germans "are the *philosophical* contemporaries of the present without being its *historical* contemporaries."[98] He thereby identifies the contemporaneity of the noncontemporaneous.

When Marx refers to "the present German regime" as "an anachronism, a flagrant contradiction of universally accepted axioms," he is not simply suggesting that it was lagging behind on a fixed developmental trajectory.[99] He is underscoring that history is not linear and modernization is not synchronized. This point is nicely crystallized in his claim that "the German *status quo* is the *undisguised consummation of the ancien régime,* and the *ancien régime* is the *hidden defect of the modern state.*"[100] This provocative formulation conveys how a supposedly superseded social order continues to shape the European present. Insofar as this untimely remnant is the "hidden defect of the modern state," Germany as anachronism reveals the more general unevenness of a capitalist modernity composed of "advanced" and "archaic" elements. It follows that "the struggle against the German political present is the struggle against the past of the modern nations, which continue to be harassed [i.e., importuned or haunted] by reminiscences of this past."[101]

Conversely, such untimely remnants, however stunted or travestied, may ground emancipatory possibilities. Marx suggests as much in his famous 1881 exchange with Vera Zasulich on the political status of the Russian commune. Marx relates that the developmental trajectory he traced in *Capital* was "expressly restricted to the countries of Western Europe" where, through primitive accumulation, *"private property* founded on personal labor" had been "supplanted by *capitalist private property*, which rests . . . on wage labor."[102] He insists that this was a contingent rather than a necessary historical development.[103] From this perspective, Marx argues that the agrarian commune, which he identified as having existed in medieval Europe and as persisting in Asia, is notable for two reasons. First, as it supplanted the "archaic community" it was "the first social group of free men not bound together by blood ties." Second, once its members were "emancipated from the strong yet narrow ties of natural kinship," it combined "communal land ownership and social relations" with "restricted forms of individual private property." In Europe "the property element" had gained "the upper hand" over the "collective element." But this should not be taken as a necessary developmental path for all societies. Under different conditions, Marx contends, the collective element could triumph.

On these grounds, he advises Zasulich that it made little sense for Russian socialists to try to transform the already existing commune into a regime of private property that would have to then be abolished to create a new form of communal property. Rather, he suggests that the still vital Russian commune could open a more direct route to a socialist future. "Communal land ownership offers it the natural basis for collective appropriation, and its historical context—the contemporaneity of capitalist production provides it with the ready-made material conditions for large-scale cooperative labor."[104] By "gradually replac[ing] small-plot agriculture with a combined, machine assisted agriculture," a renovated commune *"may therefore incorporate the positive achievements developed by the capitalist system,* without having to pass under its harsh tribute . . . it may become the direct starting point of the economic system toward which modern society is tending. It may open a new chapter that does not begin with its own suicide."[105]

In contrast to the Russian populists, with whom Zasulich's socialist comrades disagreed, Marx does not advocate an uncritical return to the archaic past. He suggests that the agrarian commune could form the basis of a new socialist society precisely because it would preserve earlier aspects of commu-

nal property and collective solidarity while transcending its traditional isolation. Marx thus envisioned a vast network of communes enabled by modern
infrastructure and nourished by new political sensibilities. Russian socialists
could therefore look to their own supposedly archaic countryside rather than
to English factories for a glimpse of the world to come. Marx thus suggested
that a persisting past could mediate the relation between an untimely present
and an alternative future.

This attention to how noncontemporaneous contemporaneity might create
fertile ground for dialectical reversals is evident in Marx's discussion of how
certain societies rooted in earlier periods of material development were capable of producing elevated forms of art whose power continues to ramify
across epochs. As we would expect, Marx relates cultural production to social
conditions. He explains that Greek art was grounded in a mythology that over-
comes and dominates the forces of nature in imagination. But this mythology,
the "view of nature and of social relations" on which it was based, along with
the art it enabled, "vanishes with the advent of real mastery" over natural
forces.[106] "What chance has Vulcan against Roberts & Co., Jupiter against the
lightning-rod and Hermes against the Credit Mobilier?"[107]

But Marx raises an additional issue: "The difficulty lies not in understanding that the Greek arts and epic are bound up with certain forms of social
development. The difficulty is that they still afford us artistic pleasure and that
in a certain respect they count as a norm and as an unattainable model."[108] He
explains that the "eternal charm" of this art is "inextricably bound up . . . with
the fact that the unripe social conditions under which it arose . . . can never
return."[109] By comparison, Marx notes that adults who are not able to return to
childhood do not only "enjoy the child's naïveté," but "strive to reproduce its
truth at a higher stage."[110] Likewise, the enduring power of Greek art is based
on a modern encounter with "the historic childhood of humanity, its most
beautiful unfolding, as a stage never to return."[111]

We might be tempted to read this explanation as endorsing a linear view
of historical development. It certainly challenges any naïvely romantic desire to return to a vanished past. But Marx does not merely reduce Greece's
charming and childlike art to objects of passive contemplation or antiquarian
interest. He recognizes that this art crystallizes another way of life organized
around poetic forms of imagination and sociality. These were annihilated by
modern science, technology, private property, and centralized corporations.[112]
Marx's aim is neither to reproduce this art nor to reconstruct the society that
created it. It is to "reproduce its truth at a higher stage," on the basis of modern conditions and achievements. Epic poetry still conjures the prospect of
a noncapitalist world yet to be created. Engaging with it is neither simply a
bourgeois pretention nor an escapist diversion.

Marx adds a crucial addendum to his reflections: "If this is the case with the relation between different kinds of art within the realm of the arts, it is already less puzzling that it is the case in the relation of the entire realm to the general development of society."[113] To understand what he might mean, we should let Marx's insights about ancient art resonate with his observation that "the old [precapitalist] view, in which the human being appears as the aim of production . . . seems to be very lofty when compared to the modern world, where production appears as the aim of mankind and wealth as the aim of production."[114] The "limited bourgeois form" of society forgot or failed to realize an earlier understanding of wealth as

> the universality of individual needs, capacities, pleasures, productive forces etc., created through universal exchange. . . . The full development of human mastery over the forces of nature. . . . The absolute working out of [humankind's] creative potentialities . . . the development of all human powers as such the end in itself.[115]

Instead, "in bourgeois economics—and in the epoch of production to which it corresponds—this complete working-out of the human content appears as a complete emptying-out, this universal objectification as total alienation, and the tearing down of all limited, one-sided aims as sacrifice of the human end-in-itself to an entirely external end."[116] In comparison to this inverted, distorted, and impoverished conception of wealth, Marx remarks, "the childish world of antiquity appears . . . as loftier."[117] At least it provided "satisfaction from a limited standpoint; while the modern gives no satisfaction."[118]

Marx neither idealizes the past nor purports to predict the future. Rather, he suggests that an immanent critique of the present may disclose potential links between stunted or obstructed pasts and possible futures. This immanent critique is possible because the capitalist present is temporally nonidentical; it carries within itself the "partly still unconquered remnants" of "vanished social formations."

Revolutionary Romanticism

Michael Löwy and Robert Sayre insightfully link Marx's work to a tradition of "revolutionary or utopian romanticism" which "invests" the conventional romantic "nostalgia for a precapitalist past" with "the hope for a radically new future."

> Rejecting both the illusion of pure and simple return to the organic communities of the past and the resigned acceptance of the bourgeois present or its amelioration by means of reforms, revolutionary or utopian romanticism aspires—in a way that may be to a greater or

lesser extent radical, to a greater or lesser extent contradictory—to the abolition of capitalism or to an egalitarian utopia in which certain features or values of earlier societies would reappear.[119]

Löwy and Sayre remind us that Marx forcefully criticized currents of romantic and utopian socialism that did not recognize the dialectical ways that industrial capitalism was itself creating the conditions for a possible socialist society. But they also emphasize that "from the 1860s on, Marx and Engels manifested increasing interest in and sympathy for certain precapitalist social formations. . . . Their fascination with primitive rural communes—from the Greek *gens* . . . to the German *Mark* and the Russian *obschtchina* . . . stem from their conviction that these ancient forms incorporated social qualities that modern civilizations have lost, qualities that prefigured certain aspects of a future communist society."[120] They emphasize Marx's "rejection of a naïve and linear" idea of historical progress "which views bourgeois society as universally superior to earlier social forms."[121] Rather, they contend, he insisted on the "contradictory nature of the progress undeniably brought about by capitalism" and regarded "industrial-capitalist civilization as representing, in certain respects, a step backwards from the human point of view, in relation to communities of the past."[122] In their view, Marx developed "a new critical and revolutionary worldview" that sought "a dialectical *Aufhebung*" between Romantic and modernizing views of the world.[123]

Löwy and Sayre elaborate how this "visionary perspective" or "revolutionary-Romantic idea of the link between past and future" was further elaborated by subsequent Marxists.[124] Rosa Luxemburg and Georg Lukács notably pursued a critical strategy of "confronting capitalist industrial civilization with humanity's communitarian past" in a way that "breaks with linear evolutionism, positivist progressivism, and all the banally modernizing interpretations of Marxism."[125] Elsewhere, Löwy traces Lukács's enduring ambivalence toward the tradition of romantic writers, including Nietzsche, Carlyle, Balzac, and, above all, Dostoyevsky, who rejected their capitalist present from the standpoint of an idealized past. One the one hand, Lukács criticized this current of romantic anticapitalism as a reactionary rejection of Enlightenment and progress that fetishizes the Middle Ages and leads directly to fascism. On the other, he recognized that the romantic critique of modern capitalism as a source of "human degradation" could be leveraged for Left politics.[126] Löwy underscores that, despite this ambivalence, Lukács's own intellectual development proceeded from an idealist, albeit pessimistic, Left-leaning romantic anticapitalism (in the spirit of Simmel and Weber) to a revolutionary anticapitalism that wove together elements of romanticism and Marxism. This latter

position allowed him to appreciate the strategy of many romantic anticapitalist writers who sought to identify *"the golden age of the past which illuminates
the path towards the utopian future."*[127]

Lukács nicely crystallizes his romantic anticapitalist orientation when he
declares, "Communism aims at creating a social order in which everyone is
able to live in a way that in precapitalist eras was possible only for the ruling
classes and which in capitalism is possible for no class."[128] He thus criticizes
his alienated present from the standpoint of precapitalist societies but does not
call for a simple return to the past. He explains that in precapitalist societies,
the ruling classes were able to enjoy culture as a realm of noninstrumen-
tal creative activity nourished by the "free energies" that are liberated once
the "primary necessities" for "the immediate maintenance of life" have been
met.[129] In contrast, Lukács argues, capitalism reduces all culture to the status
of a commodity.

> The most decisive feature of capitalist society, then, is that economic
> life ceased to be a means to social life: it placed itself at the center,
> became an end in itself, the goal of all social activity . . . Everything
> ceases to be valuable for itself or by virtue of its inner (e.g., artistic,
> ethical) value: a thing has value only as a ware bought or sold on the
> market . . . The inhumanity of this relationship is intensified by the
> expansion of machine production . . . to the point that . . . *man serves
> the machine, he adapts to it*; production becomes totally independent
> of the human possibilities and capabilities of the worker.[130]

As importantly for Lukács, capitalism is distinct from "earlier social orders"
insofar as "the exploiting class itself is subjugated to the process of production;
the ruling class is forced to devote its energies to the struggle for profit just
as the proletariat is forced to devote itself to production."[131] In overcoming
the social inequality of feudal society, capitalism also negated the "cultural
privileges" of estate society such that what was once possible for the old ruling
classes was no longer possible for any class.

For Lukács, the aim of communism was not simply to extend currently
existing material benefits to a wider population. It was to democratize and
universalize the less alienated relation to labor and culture that existed in precapitalist societies. Rather than reduce all of social life to the tyranny of production and profit, the task was to liberate all of society *"from the rule of the
economy."*[132] Revolutionary politics should seek to recall, rework, and elevate
this previous form of life. The hope was to reclaim the economy as a means
to liberate cultural energy for all people—allowing value to be reckoned in
noneconomic terms—rather than allow it to remain an alienating end in

itself for the whole society. He thereby traces a dialectic between past and future.

This kind of revolutionary romanticism was further elaborated by the cohort of interwar German Jewish Marxists that included Ernst Bloch and Walter Benjamin. Despite important differences, both were especially attentive to the political potentiality of untimely periods, objects, and practices. Their writings provide indispensable reference points for what it might mean to produce an immanent critique of an untimely present that is attentive to the dialectic of past and future.

Bloch's 1932 reflections on the politics of nonsynchronism are worth considering at length. They were subsequently published in the middle section of *Heritage of Our Times*, his attempt to understand the appeal of Nazism to ordinary Germans and to outline a Left strategy for organizing a mass alternative to it.[133] In this piece, Bloch criticizes traditional Marxists for their failure to attend to the "nonsynchronous contradictions" that fascists had so effectively leveraged.[134]

Like Marx, Bloch identifies contemporary Germany as "the classic land of nonysynchronism, that is, of unsurmounted remnants of older economic being and consciousness."[135] Because of its "unequal rate of development . . . an anachronistic superstructure . . . still prevails—no matter how obsolete and shoddy."[136] Bloch identifies German peasants in the 1930s as "remnants" or "remainders" whose labor was rooted in an earlier mode of production and their consciousness in "traditional" forms of life. He contends that they, along with a growing mass of petty bourgeois little men, were increasingly unable to find a place in "the Today."[137] The Weimar economic crisis did not only subject these groups to greater social misery. Bloch suggests that they were also suffering from a deeper sense of psychic and spiritual alienation. "Distress is in need for food, and, in the middle strata, in need of something higher as well, something which it can no longer find in life nowadays, which indeed, it has long been missing in the barren land. What has been customarily, ultimately 'psychically,' missed likewise contradicts the Now, just as strongly as missing food and not only economically."[138]

Bloch suggests that mass immiseration and alienation led greater numbers of "creatures not satisfied" under current conditions to romanticize a mythic German past.[139] "The ghost of history comes very easily to the desperate peasant, to the bankrupt petty bourgeois; the depression which releases the ghost takes place in a country with a particularly large amount of pre-capitalist material."[140] This tendency helps to account not only for the rise of Weimar anti-Semitism and fascism, but a range of backward-looking reactions, including peasant traditionalism, petty bourgeois nationalism, and antibourgeois romanticism. Greater numbers of Germans who were dissatisfied with "the present disorderly society" turned to "elements of the old society and its relative order."[141] Bloch explains, "House, soil, and people are examples of . . . *objectively* delineated contradictions between the traditional and the capitalist Now, within which they are increasingly being destroyed and not replaced."[142] He specifies that these "traditional" phenomena, which contradict "the capitalist Now," are "elements of the old society which are not yet dead."[143] In response to "the nihilism of bourgeois life, this becoming-a-commodity, becoming alienated from the entire world," Bloch observes that "needs and elements from past ages break through the relativism of the general weariness like magma through a thin crust."[144] These features of an "uncompleted past, which has not yet been 'sublated' by capitalism" provide a standpoint from which to criticize the capitalist present, whether in reactionary or revolutionary ways.[145]

Bloch criticizes German Marxists for having focused too exclusively on what he calls "synchronous contradictions" in the current conjuncture between forces and relations of production that might fuel class struggle led by the industrial proletariat. They ignored the political potential of "nonsynchronous contradictions" such as those between capitalism's attempt to subsume earlier productive relations and their persistence in the present, between more integrated "traditional" and more alienated modern forms of life—that is to say, between long-standing human hopes and their current nonfulfillment. Bloch recognizes that "the forms and contents of the past naturally do not attract the class-conscious worker at all. If so, only at a few revolutionary points, with which he feels an elective affinity."[146] But he also insists that "the relatively more lively and intact nature of earlier human relationships do become clear to him. These relationships were still relatively more immediate than those in capitalism. They carried with them more 'substance,' both in the people among whom they existed and in the environment upon which they worked."[147] Nazis, rather than Marxists, had effectively linked this living memory of less alienated ways of life to current "pent-up anger" in order to propel mass revolt against the present.[148]

Bloch is not calling on militant workers and communists to romanticize that past uncritically. He reminds us that traditional desires for belonging and community were never fulfilled. This because they were always invoked through reference to an even earlier imaginary past in which they had been realized. Bloch explains, they

> were contradictions even in their origin, contradictions to past forms, which never did realize the intended contents of house, soil or people.

> Therefore, they were already . . . quarrels with the past itself . . . so
> that here contradictions even to history, namely, to *uncompleted inten-*
> *tional contents of the past* themselves join the rebellion if the occasion
> arises.[149]

This meant that peoples' "pent-up anger" was directed "not so much against
the meager inheritance of the past as *against a Now in which even the last*
inkling of fulfillment has disappeared."[150] Even if these human needs for an
integrated form of life had not actually been met in precapitalist societies, the
intention to realize them had existed. It is not that a perfect world had been
lost, but that capitalist modernity had foreclosed the conditions of possibility
for creating the kind of fulfilling life that, as Marx said, the world had long
been dreaming of.[151] Even the remembered "inkling" of a different world allowed disaffected actors "to hold up against the present a past as something
which in part is genuinely not dead. It also positively delivers in places a part
of that matter which seeks a life not destroyed by capital."[152]

Echoing Marx's reflections on the Russian commune, Bloch reminds us,
"obviously, the entirety of earlier development is not yet 'sublated' in capitalism and its dialectics. *World history . . . is a house that has more stairways than*
rooms . . . capitalism is not the only house in history that could be dialectically
inherited."[153] Here, Bloch is not only reminding us that any given present can
lead to various possible futures. He is also suggesting that foreclosed possibilities might still be pursued by discovering alternate stairways in a present that
continues to contain traces of "what is actually incomplete in this past."[154]
Bloch recognized that such stairways could just as easily lead to Nazism as
to Communism. If the latter hoped to succeed, Marxists would have to stop
ceding the field of nonsynchronism to the fascists. To win the pent-up anger
of the masses for the revolution, the Left would have to more directly link the
synchronous (political economic) to the nonsynchronous contradictions that
were experienced by nonsynchronous masses. This would mean awakening
dreams and activating residues of less-alienated forms of collective life that
may persist, that have not yet been fully subsumed, in a nonidentical capitalist present.

Bloch's insight was to link romantic anticapitalism to a future-oriented
Marxism. He argued that efforts to reactivate past possibilities would never
lead to societal transformation unless they also addressed synchronous contradictions and embraced revolutionary struggle. Bloch warns, "Even the possible late ripening of what is actually incompleted in this past can never turn
into a new quality of its own accord. . . . That end could be served at best
by an alliance, which liberates the still *possible future* from the *past* only by

putting both in the present."[155] On the one hand, Bloch suggests that capitalism itself produces new arrangements and subjects which, however degrading and disabled, open possibilities for dialectical reversal. "The alienated individual or proletarian, alienated work or commodity fetishism, the emptiness of nothingness—these negativities have something dialectically positive within themselves, to be sure, even the sublime."[156] They "touch—in the deepest sense—the subversively utopian 'of mankind,' a 'life' which never received fulfillment in any age and is hence the final spur to every revolution, indeed, still the brightest space of every ideology."[157] On the other hand, when compared with earlier forms of life, this alienation calls forth certain kinds of dehumanizing absences and losses that might be critically recuperated "as something rebellious missing from within the synchronous contradiction . . . missing from the whole man, from non-alienated labor, from the earthly paradise."[158] These "positivities . . . were recalled very early against capitalism, precisely because they are forms and contents of older matter . . . the middle ages of romanticism . . . a world set up organically and qualitatively out of the empty spaces of the 'problem of the thing in itself.'"[159] The challenge was to produce such negativities and reclaim these positivities in order to emancipate the "impeded future" that capitalism had both made possible and obstructed.[160]

Bloch calls these forms and contents of older matter, "treasures of a not quite completed past."[161] Through such treasures, present actors may conjure "sentimentally or romantically, that wholeness and liveliness from which communism draws genuine material against alienation."[162] He thus called on Marxists to transform the romantic retreat *from* capitalism into a revolutionary struggle *against* capitalism, to transform a reactionary attachment to a mythic past into a revolutionary critique of an "incompleted past."[163] The Left would have to both challenge "abstract romanticism" and "take into its house the subversive and utopian elements, the repressed matter of that which is not yet past."[164] Bloch declares, "It is our task to extend the agitated Now . . . to extrapolate the elements of the nonsynchronous contradiction which are . . . hostile to capitalism, and are homeless in it, and *to refit them to function in a different context*."[165]

Bloch reserved a decisive role in this process for the urban proletariat who, in his view, uniquely "activates purely the future society with which the present one is pregnant."[166] But revolutionary success and "proletarian hegemony" also depended on "managing" an alliance with "immiserated peasants and the immiserated middle class."[167] Their struggle "gains additional *revolutionary force* from the *incomplete* wealth of the past . . . the still subversive and utopian contents in the relations of people to people and nature, which are not past because they were never quite attained."[168] Bloch calls this "incomplete wealth of the past" the "gold-bearing gravel" that was bound up with "previous labor processes and their superstructures."[169] He also identifies these charged remnants as the "genuine nebulae" from which a new "critical totality" might be fashioned.[170] Following Bloch, the political task is neither to return to the past nor to reconstruct it in the present. It is to move dialectically from past to future by way of these incomplete intentions, unfulfilled possibilities, and glimpses of nonalienated ways of being that may persist in a nonsynchronous now.[171]

Benjamin, too, examined how the relation between the oppressive present and emancipatory future may be mediated by a persisting or repeating past within a nonsynchronous now. Whereas Bloch linked the un-subsumed remnants of earlier forms of life to current struggles, Benjamin linked memory flashes of past struggles to the untimely fragments that compose the present. He praises the French Surrealists' capacity to "perceive the revolutionary energies that appear in the 'outmoded'—the first iron constructions, the first factory buildings, the earliest photos, objects that have begun to be extinct, grand pianos, the dresses of five years ago, fashionable restaurants when the vogue has begun to ebb from them."[172] He attests, "No one before these visionaries and augurs perceived how destitution . . . enslaved and enslaving objects—can be suddenly transformed into revolutionary nihilism. . . . They bring the immense forces of 'atmosphere' concealed in these things to the point of explosion."[173]

Benjamin suggests that the very outmodedness of certain commodities ("enslaving objects") allows them to catalyze "profane illuminations."[174] Perhaps their explosive potential is bound up with their status of having lost both their use-value and their exchange value (but have not yet been revalorized as commodified antiques or heritage). The fact that they are no longer enchanted fetishes able magically to stoke desire and valorize value helps to demystify the system of generalized commodity exchange, the alienated social arrangements that are its premise and product, and the historical progress that they are supposed to enable. Conversely, profane illuminations may reenchant these outmoded commodities—by liberating the collective social power that had been alienated by and displaced onto such enslaved and enslaving objects. Benjamin suggests that Surrealist poetic politics disclosed that "the trick by which this world of things is mastered" (i.e., the way to overcome the alienating logic of commodity capitalism) "consists in *substituting a political for a historical view of the past*."[175] This kind of political view of the past invites us to identify, in order to reactivate, the revolutionary energies condensed within seemingly superseded objects, places, movements, forms of thought, or historical epochs.

Benjamin's first book, *The Origin of German Tragic Drama* (1928), anticipated this operation. In this study of the seventeenth-century German Baroque sorrow play, Benjamin distinguished between radically different ways of
knowing the world and creating art. On the one hand, he identified antiquity,
Renaissance, and Classicist traditions with concepts, symbolism, progress, and
secular transcendence. On the other hand, he identified medieval Christianity, the Counter-Reformation Baroque, and some currents of Romanticism
with allegorical images of earthliness, decline, death, and mourning. Benjamin traces how the latter orientation was historically subsumed by the former.
With this shift, the sorrow plays, which were typically misunderstood as failed
forms of Greek tragedy, became largely illegible to modern scholars. But Benjamin's concerns are not merely scholastic. He places this Baroque past in
dialogue with his "decadent" Weimar present as an "analogous" period of decline. (He would later use the language of constellations to describe this kind
of critical conjoining of eras.) In both periods, rational concepts and symbolic
representations gave way to fragmentary images and allegorical depictions.
Benjamin specifically identifies the reappearance of earlier modes of allegorical figuration in twentieth-century German Expressionism.

Benjamin neither suggests that the Baroque past is merely repeating itself
nor that Expressionism is somehow returning to that past.[176] Like Nietzsche in
The Birth of Tragedy, he traces the untimely return of a supposedly foreclosed
way of knowing that could inform present practices. Rather than simply trace
a line of descent, he blasts the Baroque epoch out of the historical continuum
in order to recognize its relation, and to place it in relation, to the contemporary epoch. He constructs an untimely constellation whose aim is not merely
to better understand the past but to intervene in the present. "All the more
powerful, therefore, is the impact which can be made at this very moment by
the expression of related tendencies [between German Expressionism and]
the eccentric artistic medium of the German baroque."[177] Benjamin warned
that "the danger of allowing oneself to plunge from the heights of knowledge
into the profoundest depths of the baroque state of mind, is not a negligible
one."[178] He praises Expressionism's aesthetic extravagance and vehemence,
its revival of a decadent and allegorical mode of knowing, for a present that
needed precisely this. Benjamin's study itself works to reactivate just this kind
of nonconceptual and nonsymbolic knowing by plunging from the heights of
knowledge into the profoundest depths of the Baroque state of mind.

This book may be understood as a charter for Benjamin's subsequent efforts
to substitute a political for a historical view of the past. It already included
motifs that would appear in his later, explicitly Marxian, work: leaps, flashes,
monads, and constellations. This attempt to elaborate a political view of the

past, animates his uncompleted *Arcades* book. It is further distilled in his final reflections on "The Concept of History" (1939). Woven through his famous theses is a conception of now-time which conveys the temporally layered, heterogeneous, and plural character of the nonidentical present.[179] Now-time condenses all that has been and all that may come to be, past possibilities and revolutionary potentialities. It is both the condition of possibility of a historical break and the kind of social time that such a break would enable.

This figure of now-time challenges conceptions of historical linearity, chronology, and progress (whether practiced by historicist historians or stagist Marxists). "What characterizes revolutionary classes at their moment of action is the awareness that they are about to make the continuum of history explode."[180] Benjamin suggests that this explosion may be mediated by critical remembrance when actors in the present are visited or seized by images from and of what has been. For Benjamin, political transformation is fueled less by future-oriented hope than this ability to "appropriate" images (and fragments) of the past as they appear—"flash up"—in an untimely present.[181] The political aim is "to bring about a real state of emergency" that is "nourished by the image of enslaved ancestors rather than by the ideal of liberated grandchildren."[182] The movement between a given now and an alternative future is mediated by a "tiger's leap" into the past.[183] Here we see Benjamin's political view of the past: remembrance entails awakening (to) earlier struggles in order to bring the immense forces concealed in them to the point of explosion. This orientation is nicely captured when Benjamin declares that "every historical moment" offers a "revolutionary chance" whereby the "political situation" provides "the right of entry" to a "distinct chamber of the past" which "up to that point had been closed and locked."[184] Like Bloch, he rejected one-sided attempts either to return to the past (romanticism) or march straight into the future (progressivism). Benjamin noted ironically, "If . . . one resolves to open up [the] romantic dummy, one finds something usable inside."[185] Both thinkers were able to discover something useful within romanticism that pointed beyond romanticism—in order to elaborate the dialectical relation between past and future.

We may usefully read Lukács, Bloch, and Benjamin's revolutionary romanticism in relation to that of Henri Lefebvre who, a generation later, likewise sought to discover critical treasure in the head of the romantic dummy.[186] Like his predecessors, Lefebvre identifies traces of noncapitalist ways of being(-together) in his nonsynchronous now (e.g., in provincial French villages). But he also extends this revolutionary romantic orientation to nineteenth-century romantic aesthetics.

Lefebvre identifies his alienated postwar present as a new iteration of classicism characterized, as it had always been, by (the defense of) dogmatism, moral order, and state power. Like Nietzsche's Apollonian, Lefebvre's classicism privileges philosophy and reason as ways of knowing. Aesthetically, it "relies on an idea of beauty achieved, or an idea of the absolute, or perfection."[187] Against this reactionary classicism Lefebvre conjures an unruly romanticism whose emblematic figure was Stendhal in the 1820s. This dissident orientation celebrated youth, spontaneity, laughter, love, beauty, pleasure, and intoxication against the prevailing rational order and stifling bourgeois norms. "Thus romanticism brought together the most disparate of elements: women, young people, political rebels, exiles, intellectuals who dabbled in deviant experiments (eroticism, alcohol, hashish), half-crazed debauchees, drunks, misfits, successful and abortive geniuses, *arrivistes*, Parisian dandies, and provincial snobs. And so on and so forth."[188] Their antibourgeois sensibility was crystallized in their commitment to artistic creativity.

Lefebvre contends that romantic art, exemplified in poetry and music, cultivated modes of "orgiastic and frenzied" expressivity.[189] Less interested in imitating existing reality than in creating alternative worlds, this art privileged the possible over the real. In terms that recall Marx's call for revolutionaries to draw their poetry from the future, Lefebvre writes, "While others try to control space, poets—and musicians especially—project themselves into the time created by their own words and songs."[190] They do so in part by conjuring the enchanting power of "archaic magic" through which to alienate themselves from their ordinary existence in order to disalienate themselves from "the unbearable realities of nature or society."[191] "Together the romantics wove a magic tapestry of nostalgia, spleen, lust for life, triumphant and febrile absorption in the present, and the cult of *otherness*, the distant, unlimited, impossible *elsewhere*."[192] This aesthetic sensibility nourished an anticlassical "art of living."[193] Lefebvre explains that the romantic aesthetic sought to underscore the gap between the real and the possible through "an attitude which aimed simultaneously to intensify conflicts and to resolve them. . . . This attitude functioned as a mediation between lived experience and the work of art."[194] In this fashion, romantics hoped to create more authentic and integrated ways of life "to prefigure the transition from the possible to the real."[195] Accordingly, they regarded revolution as a means for "the full development of life's potential."[196] Lefebvre emphasizes not only the parallels between nineteenth-century romanticism and utopian socialism, but the worldly intersections between these contemporaneous countercultural movements.

Yet Lefebvre also underscored the limitations of nineteenth-century romanticism as a critique of modern capitalism. "The romantic attempted to live outside bourgeois society, yet within it, at its very heart, in its kernel, like

a maggot in a fruit, as though this society—contradictory, riven with antagonisms . . . were weak, nothing but a pure and simple façade."[197] Ultimately,
for Lefebvre, the old romanticism was a subjective attitude cultivated by individuals who sought to escape vulgar materialism and philistinism through
communion with nature, distant history, or cultural otherness. Eventually and
fatally, romanticism severed "the cosmological from the anthropological [at-
tention to concrete social issues], dissolving their conflictual unity and giving
predominance to the former."[198]

Given these limitations, Lefebvre wanted not to revive the old romanticism
but to supersede or sublate it—to negate and rework it so as to preserve and
reinvent it in an elevated form. Against an alienating postwar classicism, he
called for a *new* romanticism that would reconnect the anthropological and
the cosmological, praxis and imagination, labor and pleasure, and utopian
socialism and romantic utopianism in ways that addressed contemporary conditions. He identified, or prophesied, just such a movement among a new
generation of angry youth that revived a poetic-politics grounded in spontaneity, laughter, intoxication, and experimentation. But they did so concretely
and collectively. He thus praised the Situationists who were reclaiming urban spaces for playful ways of being-together. These and other new romantics
were reviving an experimental or "lived utopianism," a "practical testing of
utopianism," so that groups rather than isolated individuals could forge "disalienated" ways of living authentically.[199] Far from being seduced by nihilism,
"these young people are testing out what may be possible, and what may be
impossible. They are all in search of the *opening*, by which they may enter in
a practical way into the 'possible-impossible' dialectic."[200] They revived utopianism in pursuit of "the transition from the possible to the real."[201]

III. Untimely Politics

Lefebvre insisted that this revolutionary romantic orientation—one that looks
to past possibilities for glimpses of a fuller life beyond an alienating capitalist
modernity—was always a feature of Marxism. He writes, "Marx thought that
one day men will live out their everyday lives practically, rediscovering in
the process something which perhaps had been accomplished by some societies now lost."[202] By connecting praxis to imagination, he suggests, Marx
hoped that what, in bourgeois society, could only be glimpsed in art could
be reclaimed socially and reintegrated in everyday life as a concrete "art of
living."[203]

In similar terms, political theorist Massimiliano Tomba writes, "Showing the persistence of some forms of community that existed at the same time as capitalist production, Marx delineates the possibility of a new regime of combination of historical times. There is something of the future encapsulated in the past that can be freed from the contemporaneity of the archaic."[204] This is the perspective from which he traces how radical actors in the French Revolution, the Paris Commune, and the Russian Revolution reactivated and refunctioned seemingly outmoded institutions like communal government, the imperative mandate, and collective property. The latter, he demonstrates, also oriented nineteenth-century Haitian Revolutionaries and twentieth-century Zapatistas. They all practiced forms of "insurgent universality" through which to create social worlds that were no longer founded on the logics of private property or state power.[205]

Likewise, Kristin Ross challenges the common understanding of the Paris Commune as a forty-four-day failure that concluded on May 28, 1871. Attending to its "afterlives," she extends the event itself to occurrences in the 1880s and expands it to encompass London, Geneva, Lausanne, and New Caledonia.[206] Ross figures what appear to be exterior and subsequent developments as existing *within* the event of the Commune which continued to ramify in time, space, and imagination. Ross traces how Karl Marx, William Morris, and Peter Kropotkin looked to past forms of life (in Russia, Finland, and Iceland) whose communitarian and democratic remnants persisted in the present. Arguing that "being attentive to the energies of the outmoded was one way to think oneself into the future,"[207] she suggests that these figures tried to model the new on actually existing anachronisms.[208] This strategy offers

> a way of allowing other paths taken through historical time, including the time to come, to become visible. The persistence of non-growth-driven cultures in the present builds confidence in the possibility of anachronism by allowing encounters in one's own moment with actually embodied aspects of the past, stranded or land-locked, as it were, but still sporadically perceptible.[209]

Ross explains that this "is not about going backward or reversing time but about opening it up—opening up the web of possibilities" such that "a vision of non-alienated labor and pre-class society" may be "placed next to contemporary times . . . as a way of recruiting past hopes to serve present needs."[210]

This attention to the relationship between unrealized pasts and emancipatory futures has also been a long-standing feature of Black anticolonialism. In *Freedom Time*, I suggest that in their concrete utopian efforts to transform the imperial republic into a transcontinental democratic and socialist federation,

Aimé Césaire and Léopold Senghor conjured unrealized pasts. These were then articulated with emergent possibilities for a postnational polity. Césaire's subsequent visions of departmentalization and what he called cooperative federalism were mediated, respectively, by the still vital legacies of Victor Schoelcher and Toussaint Louverture. I suggest that Césaire implicitly constructed historical constellations between his now and, first, 1848 and the abolition of slavery, and then the 1790s and the Revolution in Saint-Domingue. Césaire addressed predecessors as contemporaries. He insisted on the ongoing actuality of earlier Antillean slave revolts and metropolitan workers' insurrections.

Césaire and Senghor looked to still vital elements within nonidentical Caribbean, African, and European traditions that pointed beyond existing arrangements. They identified residues and resources for more poetic ways of knowing and less alienated ways of being and relating (to self, others, and nature). These had existed in various ways worldwide but were destroyed by European capitalism, imperialism, and instrumental reason. Accordingly, they routed future-oriented visions through unrealized possibilities sedimented within not only African and Antillean communalism, orality, aesthetics, and anti-imperial revolt, but also pre-Socratic Greeks, the early Christian Church, nineteenth-century socialism, and modernist poetry and philosophy.

We can situate this revolutionary romantic orientation toward an untimely now within a broader Black Atlantic critical tradition. I suggested above that Du Bois's engagement with the contradictory history of Reconstruction does not only offer a genealogy of the Jim Crow order that Du Bois inherited. It is also an untimely attempt to work through a series of political predicaments that continued to challenge the Black freedom struggle in the 1930s. While he was writing *Black Reconstruction*, Du Bois elaborated a transformative vision of Black mutualism through social cooperatives. We may understand this concrete utopian project as an untimely attempt to realize, in a new world-historical opening, the possibility for multiracial socialist democracy that had been briefly possible and then tragically foreclosed in the 1870s. Du Bois implicitly constructed a constellation that linked his now in the 1930s to the unrealized potentiality of Reconstruction.

C. L. R. James also constellated Black anti-imperial struggles in his now with the long history of what he called Pan-African revolt.[211] More specifically, he often triangulated his decolonizing present, the Haitian Revolution, and the Russian Revolution. His thinking about each case in which a revolutionary opportunity for human flourishing was foreclosed by the revolution itself was informed by and refracted through the others, whether explicitly or implicitly. Throughout his life, he treated Lenin and Toussaint as untimely interlocutors. James also constellated his Caribbean now, in which his gen-

eration confronted the problem of freedom on the eve of colonial emancipation, with the form of democratic life and poetic politics he associated with
the ancient Greek polis.[212] Likewise, in Carnival celebrations, cricket play,
and whaling work, James glimpsed the possibility of less alienated ways of
being (together) within a form of "universal republic" that he traced back to
Anacharsis Cloots.[213] As we will see in the next two chapters, Octavia Butler,
Ralph Ellison, and Édouard Glissant were also attentive to untimely politics.

In short, Black radical and heterodox Marxist traditions have much to teach
us about the dialectic of past and future. All of these concrete utopians were
attuned to the untimely character of social life. Their analyses, visions, and
actions were informed by the politics of a nonidentical now. Scholarship that
seeks to grasp their projects and practices must follow this lead by unthinking
conventional assumptions about linearity, chronology, period, and tense. The
point of the kind of inquiries pursued by Tomba, Ross, and me is not simply
to understand how historical actors may have recruited past hopes for present needs or attempted to liberate futures condensed within persisting remnants of what has been. These critical operations are meant to intervene into
our now.

With his "history of the present" Foucault, too, sought to substitute a political
for a historical view of the past. But whereas genealogy seeks to denaturalize
given arrangements by tracing the contingent pathways that led from then
to now, the dialectic of past and future seeks to identify within past forms,
elements of which persist in the untimely present, those forces that might
help to interrupt an alienating "progress" or to rupture the seemingly natural
continuum in order to create historical openings through which to create
a new society. It is about identifying possible-impossible futures crystallized
in unrealized pasts. In contrast to Foucauldian genealogy, this approach to
politics and knowledge treats time itself as a social fact and historical force.

These are not scholastic issues. Attention to the nonidentical character of
any now and to the untimely dimensions of social life (anachronism, duration,
repetition, and haunting), whether oppressive or emancipatory, is crucial for
any attempt to link conjunctural analysis, expansive vision, and anticipatory
action. We should recall Bloch's prophetic warning against ceding the field of
nonsynchronism to the forces of reaction.

Finally, I would underscore that just as a concrete utopian politics of the
possible-impossible may operate in the register of revolutionary romanticism,
it can also be proleptic. This means analyzing the present *as if it were distant
history* in order to envision *what will have been* from the point of view of future
actors who may one day try to constellate their now with our present. This

future anterior optic can help us to identify those openings today that may offer glimpses of other possible worlds. It can try to recognize those anticipatory and experimental practices that may herald the advent of another world (but which are already being foreclosed). These will have been decisive crossroads or fatal turning points. Such fragments of our now may then become untimely traces in a prefigured future.

9
It's Still Happening Again
Ontology, Hauntology, and Ellison's Dialectics of Invisibility

That . . . is how the world moves: Not like an arrow, but a boomerang.
(Beware of those who speak of the spiral of history; they are preparing
a boomerang. Keep a steel helmet handy) . . . the end is in the
beginning and lies far ahead.

—RALPH ELLISON

Those who believe in zombies are fools, *he said.* Those who don't are
even bigger fools!

—RENÉ DEPESTRE

To trace the dialectic of past and future means attending to how transformative possibilities may already be germinating within an untimely now. But, as
Bloch warned, untimeliness may just as likely mediate forms of oppression
and fuel forces of reaction. The circular relationship between, on the one
hand, untimely persistence, repetition, and haunting, and on the other, violence, trauma, and systemic domination has been especially devastating in
modern racial formations. Since the inception of the global plantation slave
economy and anti-Black racism, the Atlantic world has been a charged field of
historical anachronism, uncanny repetition, political aftermaths, and haunting returns. This predicament is forcefully illuminated in the fiction of Octavia Butler and the criticism of Christina Sharpe, which I discuss below. I then
examine the importance and limitations of two currently influential ways of
understanding the fact that historical time does not unfold progressively: the
ontological account offered by Afro-Pessimists and the hauntological account
offered by Derrida. Both, I suggest, lead us away from history in politically

disabling ways. The rest of the chapter seeks to develop an approach to understanding haunting repetition that points beyond the impasses of foundation-
alist ontology and deconstructive hauntology. One section focuses on critical
theory and the other on the Prologue to Ralph Ellison's *Invisible Man*. The
latter, I suggest, deploys an optic of awakening to develop a subversive dialectic of visibility and invisibility (and deploys an optic of invisibility to develop
a subversive dialectic of dreaming and waking).

Is It Happening Again?

In *Kindred* (1979), Octavia Butler stages with particular force the uncanny-
untimely experience of a repeating past that cannot be surpassed. The novel's
African American protagonist, Dana, is a twenty-six-year-old writer in Los Angeles. Immediately after she and her white husband Kevin move into a new
house, she finds it impossible to remain in their middle-class present. Literally. At any moment she may be seized by nausea and dizziness. The world
blurs and darkens as she is suddenly propelled back to the nineteenth-century
Maryland slave plantation on the edge of which her ancestors lived as free
Blacks. She neither has control over when this temporal displacement occurs
nor when she might be able to return "home" to the 1970s. Some of her trips
to the past are brief, others last years. Each involuntary return places her in a
different period of her ancestors' past. Even after living through extended periods of time in the past she will discover, after returning to her "normal" life,
that only minutes have passed in that present. Time moves forward in both
periods, but at different rates; past and present are out of sync.

The novel is organized around such involuntary and traumatic back-and-
forth movements between different nows. When in Maryland, Dana is not
simply a spectral witness. She is fully embodied as a precarious Black woman
in a slave society who has no legal status or legible social identity. She must
quickly grasp her predicament and fashion survival strategies. After repeated
visits, she develops a deeper understanding of the racist social order, the lived
experience of slavery, and various ways of negotiating this historical situation.
She also becomes intimately entangled with the lives of those whose world
she comes to share. Among them is a white boy named Rufus whom she first
meets as a fragile son of the plantation owner. An older Rufus assumes his inherited position as planter and master. He enslaves Dana's free Black ancestor
Alice, whom he rapes, repeatedly brutalizes, and forces to be his concubine.
In this way, Dana is one of Rufus's lineal descendants. Dana recognizes that
Rufus himself is permanently harmed and haunted by the contradictions of
this social order. He understands that Dana visits from the future and comes

to depend on her as friend, confidante, and savior. Yet he also subjects her to the brutality suffered by other enslaved plantation laborers when she does not obey him. Finally, Dana stabs Rufus to death when, in an effort to compel her to replace Alice, he tries to rape her.

Kevin first watches, powerless and bewildered, as she disappears into this dangerous and terrifying past. Later in the narrative, he time travels with her and they get separated in the past. Likewise, nineteenth-century Marylanders, with disbelieving eyes, see Dana suddenly appear amongst them or vanish into another world. Without fully understanding what is happening, these associates ask her, "Is it happening again?" Sometimes Dana simply declares, "It's happening again!" Butler thus uses a fantastic device to stage a mundane but horrifying truth: For contemporary U.S. Blacks in a racist society, the boundary between the enslaved past and the precarious present is porous; it can disappear at any moment and provides no protection from ongoing harm. Butler makes literal the untimely reality, the nightmarish repetition that shapes the waking lives of Black people who remain perpetually subject to the racial violence and social death upon which U.S. society was founded.

At first, Dana's white husband, no matter how sympathetic, is unable to grasp this experience or share this insight. After her first episode of involuntary time travel, she struggles to persuade him that, for her, this is something that can suddenly happen at any time, again and again and again.

> "Well . . . It happened once. What if it happens again? . . . Whatever it was, I've had enough of it! It almost killed me!"
>
> "Take it easy," he said. "Whatever happens, it's not going to do you any good to panic yourself again."
>
> I moved uncomfortably, looked around. "I feel like it could happen again—like it could happen anytime. I don't feel secure here."
>
> "You're just scaring yourself."
>
> "No!" I turned to glare at him, and he looked so worried I turned away again. I wondered bitterly whether he was worried about my vanishing again or worried about my sanity. I still didn't think he believed my story."[1]

Note Dana's haunted repetition of "again" to counter Kevin's realist hope that her painful experience will not recur. He cannot accept that racial difference compels them to inhabit distinct spatiotemporal worlds. Her experience and understanding belies his realist belief in stable distinctions between now and then, here and there, us and them. Like other white characters in the novel, he is tempted to understand Dana's reports of time travel as an expression of madness. But the reader comes to understand how mad it is to maintain the

fiction that racial slavery no longer affects contemporary actors. To use Ellison's terms, which I discuss below, he fears that she may have slipped into a
dreamworld while she recognizes that *he* is the sleepwalker.

On one level, *Kindred* is a story of genealogical descent that traces familial
lineage and transgenerational legacies. Dana is awakened to her predecessors,
her violent origins, and the many fragile contingencies that allow her to live
now in (relative) safety and (precarious) freedom. She develops a richer understanding of herself, her people, and her society. Her harrowing temporal
displacements provide her with a dialectical optic which allows her to engage
the past through the prism of the present and the present through the prism
of the past. But *Kindred* is not simply a story of coming to racial consciousness
by way of an inventory of the systemic racist attitudes, institutions, and atroc-
ities that served as the very ground of American society. It is also a profound
mediation on the relation between race, time, and history.[2]

Time travel awakens Dana to the nonidentical character of past and present
as well as to the nonsynchronous relation between them. Her present vantage
allows her to *intervene* into the past in ways that have material consequences.
More than an account of what once happened, *Kindred* recounts the not-yet
past. It enacts the ways that unfinished social business persists. But it also
indexes how what has been is yet to be determined and created. It is a story
of what might have been and what might come to have been. In Glissant's
terms, which I discuss in the next chapter, Butler offers us a *prophetic vision
of the past*.

My hyperbolic formulation "it's still happening again" is not a redundancy.
Through it, I strain to convey a figure of repeating repetition that emphasizes
the hinge between persistence and repetition. The racist harm that Butler
traces is certainly *still happening*. Most dramatically, this is evident in the
unbroken tradition of police violence perpetrated with impunity against Black
people in the United States. "It" is also woven through the mundane fabric of
American social life, politics, and consciousness. But it is also always *happening again*, for example, through a system of mass incarceration that repeats or
reconstitutes under different conditions the societal anti-Blackness of slavery
and Jim Crow.[3] It is *still happening again* in everyday housing, education,
health care, employment, and environmental policies. On all these fronts,
Black people are figured as less than human, outside the protection of law,
subject to a singular set of harms and indignities. Persistence, repetition, and
aftermaths continue to fuel the uncanny-untimely fact of Blackness in the
U.S. racial formation.[4]

Christina Sharpe's *In the Wake* (2016) beautifully captures this painful
dynamic.[5] Her title refers simultaneously to the wake of a (slave) ship, the

mourning ceremony honoring a deceased loved one, and the awakening that signals a raised consciousness. Living "in the wake" signals, simultaneously, the aftermaths of the Middle Passage and slavery, the kind of caring mutuality thereby required, and the state of being "woke" in and to the contemporary U.S. political field.[6] Sharpe leads readers through a devastating itinerary of ongoing, repeating, and returning forms of anti-Black violence, including both punctual events and systemic domination. She also provides an arresting account of her own lived experience of this labyrinth. Throughout, Sharpe traces the many ways that Black individuals and communities do not only manage to survive such relentless harm and loss. To live in the wake, she demonstrates, is to also insist on life, to cultivate vital ways of being (together). Sharpe uses the term "wake work" to signal the many forms of witnessing, negotiating, caring, remembering, living, refusing, contesting, inventing, seeing, knowing, and writing that such aftermaths require or enable. Yet Sharpe's powerful intervention may be more effective as a description than an analysis. It begs a set of questions about how we should understand the persistence, repetition, aftermath, and haunting that she renders so palpably. What is this wake that possesses such transhistorical power? Is "wake" the source or the effect? Afro-Pessimist ontology and Derridean hauntology offer frameworks that may help us to grasp the fact that *it is still happening again*.

It's Still Happening: Afro-Pessimism's Ontology (of the Unchanging Same)

Building on Orlando Patterson's conception of slavery as social death, Afro-Pessimists argue that from its inception, American society has been organized around and remains ever dependent on a conception of Blackness that stands irreconcilably opposed to, and is forever excluded from, the category of humanity.[7] This anti-Black racism, which they distinguish from a more general white supremacy, is the very ground of American political, legal, social, and cultural orders. Any efforts oriented toward amelioration mistakenly assume that some context of possible recognition among humans exists in which conventional political demands could be made or heard. According to this line of thinking, such demands are founded on the mistaken belief that American society, which depends fundamentally on Black social death, could ever allow this situation to change. For doing so would require the United States to annihilate itself. Progressive political attempts to contest anti-Blackness thus become instruments of anti-Blackness.

This is the perspective from which Frank Wilderson argues that anti-Black racism is incommensurable with all other forms of social domination, including not only class exploitation or patriarchal sexism, but also colonial dis-possession or racism against non-Black groups. He contends that these other forms of domination within and beyond the United States operate according to an instrumental desire for profit, land, or power. Such forms of domination can be challenged through mass movements that make political demands. Additionally, he argues that other groups that have been racialized by imperial and settler colonial systems remain connected to some kind of homeland. They can make a case as a people for peoplehood. Because a context exists in which their demands may be legible and some kind of recognition pos-sible, they can pursue conventional political projects. Wilderson argues that no such conditions or possibilities exist for racialized Blacks. Anti-Blackness is not fueled by instrumental needs. It is a more fundamental phenomenon that is the basis of a "libidinal economy" upon which not only American society, but modern life, is founded.[8] Because Black social death is the very condition of humanity as it currently exists, no space exists for a political pro-cess of demands and recognition. The "total and totalizing nature of Black oppression" along with the "impossibility of Black life" condemns any effort of Black political redress to fail.[9]

> There's no such thing as a Black person making a demand in space or in time that would have an auditor out there, because the collective unconscious is not ready to accept that Black people had something that could have been appropriated, which is to say that the collective unconscious is not ready to accept that Blacks are Human.[10]

If non-Black social actors shaped by this collective unconscious were to accept Black political demands, he explains, they would "lose [their] integrity as a human."[11] It follows that any attempt by Blacks to participate in progressive politics will reaffirm the existing order and deepen their own subjugation.[12]

Wilderson's analysis is based on the assertion that "the problem today [for Black people in the United States] is the same as it was in 1855 even though the technologies have changed."[13] His argument that anti-Blackness is incom-mensurable with other forms of domination lead him to conclude that dis-courses about intersectionality obscure the specificity of Black social death. As we saw in Chapter 3, Wilderson is deeply skeptical about the usefulness of coalition politics.

Speaking about white progressives and allies of color he notes:

> What freaks them out about an analysis of anti-Blackness is that this applies to the category of the Human, which means that they have to be destroyed regardless of their performance, or of their morality, and

that they occupy a place of power that is completely unethical, regardless of what they do. And they're not going to do that. Because what
are they trying to do? They're trying to build a better world. What are
we trying to do? We're trying to destroy the world. Two irreconcilable
projects.[14]

In his view, Blacks could never exist as equals with putative coalition partners.
Nor could their political demands be aligned with those of any other group.
Moreover, every one of the possible social groups with which Black activists
could ally have themselves internalized an anti-Black worldview. Even if they
are capable of being reliable allies at a certain stage in a struggle, once they
have achieved their ends, they will eventually turn against their Black allies.

Likewise, Wilderson argues that because neither Marxism, feminism, nor
postcolonialism can adequately grasp the specificity of anti-Blackness, their
utility for the Black freedom struggle is minimal. In a 2014 radio interview
about the mass Black protests against police violence in Ferguson, Missouri,
he explains,

as Saidiya Hartman has said, Black liberation presents us with the
prospect of a kind of liberation that is so totalizing (i.e., that it is
what Fanon says on page 100, quoting Aimé Césaire: "the end of the
world"), that it can't be ratcheted down and put into political language. If I'm right that the problem that Black people are in is not
colonial exploitation and not racism but social death—which is not
to say that Black people don't experience racism and that Black poor
people are not exploited, but that once all that's over, we're still going
to be socially dead—then I think that we actually don't have a political
framework to deal with that, certainly not in Marxism, Feminism, postcolonialism.[15]

In response to those who criticize him for not offering a clear method for
overcoming this predicament, he replies, "at least if we don't have a strategy
and tactics for this end of the world, at least we will not have altered and
corrupted our space of pure analysis to make it articulate with some kind of
political project."[16]

One does not have to share Wilderson's conclusions to appreciate many
aspects of his critique. Certainly the United States is an irreducible racial
formation and form of racial capitalism with a constitutive investment in anti-
Black racism. The latter has a singular logic, intensity, and effect. Again and
again, moments of supposed emancipation have only created conditions for
new forms of Black social death. Anti-Black racism is woven so deeply into the

fabric of American social and psychic relations that it cannot be adequately overcome as long as that fabric retains its integrity. Given these conditions, the most uncompromising political pessimism is warranted. So, too, is the belief that only a revolutionary break could open the possibility for Black people in the United States to be recognized as fully human. New critical frameworks that point beyond the limitations of Marxism, feminism, and postcolonialism may be necessary for grasping and addressing this political situation.

But we can raise serious questions about the Afro-Pessimist critique without slipping into liberal reformist or orthodox Marxist assumptions about seamless affinities across groups or how progressive politics lead automatically to historical progress. Wilderson's categorical assertions about anti-Blackness as the transhistorical, worldwide, and unsurpassable condition of possibility of humanity forecloses any prospect of emancipatory struggle. He does not, and I would suggest cannot, substantiate his absolutist assertions that the very constitution of the world, including every other social group's sense of itself as human, depends irreducibly on Black social death. These assertions lead him to conclude that short of *destroying the world*, no transformation can be envisioned or pursued.

It is one thing to say that we need critical frameworks and political strategies that can grasp systemic persistence and repetition. It is another to say that everything is still the same and any attempt to change conditions is fated to reproduce those conditions. Afro-Pessimism rightly challenges mechanically progressivist conceptions of politics and history. But it does so through transhistorical assertions of stasis, incommensurability, and ontology. It can only account for the persistence and repetition it perceptively recognizes by positing anti-Blackness as the foundational ground of being as such. Its radical critique devolves into an apocalyptic antipolitics. It renounces the given order in ways that fatalistically accommodate itself to that order.

It's Happening Again: Deconstructive Hauntology (of the Changing Same)

In *Specters of Marx* (1993), Jacques Derrida declares that "hauntology" should replace ontology as a framework for understanding society and history.[17] He persuasively challenges the ability of realist epistemologies to recognize that the world is populated with ghosts and revenants. He suggests that any attempt to engage reality, being, or history must take seriously such spectral beings and haunting phenomena. These, for Derrida, usefully call into question supposedly self-evident ontological distinctions between life and death, presence and absence, matter and spirit, the visible and the invisible, the past and the present. They can only, therefore, be apprehended through an alternative "hauntological" epistemology. He dreams of a world where, through hauntology, scholars will learn to "speak to the specter."[18]

Derrida engages these issues through a dialogue with the specters of Marx and Marxism after the end of the Cold War. By this, he means both the specters that haunted Marx and Marxism and the haunting afterlives of Marx and Marxism. Regarding the latter, he is concerned specifically with the spectral legacy of Marxism after 1989. Politically, Derrida challenges liberal and Left commentators who suggested that, with the end of actually existing socialism, Marxism itself has been superseded or become outmoded. In contrast, he regards the collapse of Soviet Communism as a world-historic opportunity to reconsider the legacy of Marxism. In this spirit, he calls for a "New International" to contest the emerging hegemony of neoliberal capitalism. Theoretically, Derrida contends that there would be no deconstruction without Marxism and conveys that he wishes to radicalize Marxism through deconstruction. The latter gesture entails what he regards as a critique of Marx's ontology. Derrida does so by exploring what he regards as Marx's fear of and obsession with specters in his writings. He demonstrates how Marx repeatedly attempts to conjure up and conjure away haunting ghosts.

Derrida suggests that a renovated Marxism whose horizon would not be state socialism but real democracy would have to abandon realist ontology and ground itself in a deconstructive hauntology which recognizes that "time is out of joint."[19] A hauntology that attends to the reality of spectral beings, he suggests, will allow for a new ethics and politics that extend unconditional hospitality (to haunting revenants), commit ourselves to a kind of justice beyond law or right, and maintain a temporal gap that might create the opening necessary for a radically different democracy to come. He usefully emphasizes that the living are responsible and answerable to returning specters. He exhorts us to recognize and honor spectral revenants either because they demand that past debts be repaid or because they are bearers of messianic gifts, instruments of possible liberation, and harbingers of open futures.

But Derrida never attempts to account socially or historically for why time may be out of joint or why haunting specters may actually exist. He simply asserts that the world is populated by specters, that haunting is an indisputable feature of reality which traditional epistemology cannot recognize. Through such metaphysical assertions about the nature of the world as such, hauntology becomes another ontology (a metaphysics of antipresence). Nor does his framework differentiate between emancipatory and oppressive forms of haunting. Something like a hauntological optic does seem to be required if we are to adequately understand the kind of uncanny-untimely predicament staged by Butler and Sharpe. These harmful and horrifying experiences cannot be grasped by realist ontologies that can only recognize living, material, and visible presence. But hauntology does not distinguish between the untimely character of social life in general and the pain of being haunted, the harm inflicted by spectral returns, for historically specific subjects and communities within a racial formation. It certainly does not indicate how speaking to specters may be deployed for antiracist politics or the Black freedom struggle.

Derridean hauntology thus shares with Afro-Pessimist ontology a set of categorical claims about the world as such. The former insists on a changing same and the latter on an unchanging same. Both deny history and, in effect, nullify politics despite their respective claims to the contrary. Each orientation obscures the historically specific, multiply articulated, and ever contested processes and practices through which the kind of haunting repetition that characterizes anti-Black racism over the longue durée operates.

Historical Articulations and Conjunctural Politics

Stuart Hall's still incisive essay "Race, Articulation, and Societies Structured in Dominance" (1980) offers an indispensable starting point for grasping historically specific processes of racialization "at the social, political, and ideological levels."[20] He suggests that thinking about race may benefit from "the two cardinal premises of Marx's 'method'": the "materialist premise — that the analysis of political and ideological structures must be grounded in their material conditions of existence; and the historical premise — that the specific form of these relations cannot be deduced, a priori, from this level, but must be made historically specific."[21] Following Gramsci's example and using Althusser's language, he calls on thinkers to understand a social formation in terms of the "combination or articulations" of economic, political, and ideological elements, or the "structured relations . . . of dominance and subordination," that compose a "complex unity, structured in dominance."[22] The articulations that form this "complex . . . must be shown — since no necessary correspondence or expressive homology can be assumed as given."[23]

Among Hall's great innovations was to elaborate a critical framework for grasping racism based on this conception of articulation across different domains of social life. This approach "requires us to demonstrate — rather than assume, a priori" the "concrete historical 'work' which racism accomplishes under specific historical conditions — as a set of economic, political, and ideological practices, of a distinctive kind, concretely articulated with other practices in a social formation."[24] Because these can never be known in advance, but must be discovered through sociohistorical analysis, Hall warns "against extrapolating a common and universal structure to racism, which remains essentially the same, outside of its specific historical location."[25] Rather, he calls for "a rigorous application of . . . the premise of historical specificity" such that

> Racism is not dealt with as a general feature of human societies, but with historically specific racisms. Beginning with an assumption of difference, of specificity rather than of unitary, transhistorical or universal "structure." This is not to deny that there might well be discovered to be certain common features to all those social systems to which one would wish to attribute the designation "racially structured." But . . . such a general theory of racism is not the most favorable source for theoretical development and investigation. . . . It is only as the different racisms are historically specified—in their difference—that they can be properly understood.[26]

Hall insists on historical specificity because "one cannot explain racism in abstraction from other social relations—even if, alternatively, one cannot explain it by reducing it to those relations."[27] The task is "to show how thoroughly racism is reorganized and rearticulated with the relations of new modes of production."[28]

Hall is immediately concerned with pushing orthodox Marxists to take racism—a phenomenon they often associate with "secondary" political or ideological spheres—seriously as a constitutive feature of social life in capitalist societies. But he is equally concerned with challenging analyses that ontologize or universalize racism as a monocausal first principle. He insists that we grasp racism in relation to social formations as differential unities. He invites us to explore the historically specific ways that racism articulates with economic, ideological, and political arrangements to do particular kinds of work within a given social formation.[29] By attending to how race articulates with various social processes and practices, Hall remains open to the prospect of disarticulations and rearticulations. He promotes structural analyses attuned to the possibility that concrete struggles may leverage conjunctural shifts to overcome specific forms of systemic racism.

This approach is compatible with understanding systemic racism on larger spatial and temporal scales. But Hall's emphasis on conjunctural articulations does not easily explain how such operations may be the source of anti-Blackness across different social formations and successive epochs as the Afro-Pessimist crtitique rightly demands. To this end, Hall's Gramscian orientation may be usefully supplemented by work that examines how, from the start, capitalist accumulation has depended on and produced racialized differences (e.g., through colonial dispossession, Atlantic slavery, formal subsumption, imperial underdevelopment, and labor market segmentation).[30] Scholarship on "racial capitalism" attends directly to how racialization is integral to the reproduction of capitalist social relations and how valorization is integral to the reproduction of racial social relations.[31]

From another angle, both Hall's conjunctural approach and the racial capitalism framework may be supplemented by analyses focused on the racial logics—at once social, symbolic, and psychic—that exist at the deepest structural level of a social formation. In addition to Orlando Patterson's account of slavery as social death, Frantz Fanon's analysis of the lived experience of Blackness and Sylvia Wynter's analysis of the reduction of human to Man offer invaluable resources for such work.[32] But Fanon's phenomenological and Wynter's structuralist emphases still beg questions about historically specific conditions for dialectical reversals and concrete pathways for a possible overcoming. For an approach that navigates the Scylla of deep structure and the Charybdis of historical specificity, we might revisit Hortense Spillers' landmark essay "Mama's Baby, Papa's Maybe" (1987).

Spillers argues that enslaved Blacks were not simply assigned inferior subject positions within American society. They were de-subjectified, cast back into an undifferentiated sphere of being, outside of and excluded from the social-symbolic order within which persons with bodies, however subordinate, existed.[33] For Spillers, bodies are always already inserted into a normative social-symbolic order. Even when oppressed, bodies occupy legible subject positions. But "before the 'body' there is the 'flesh,'" which Spillers calls a "zero degree of social conceptualization."[34] Whereas subjects have bodies, flesh is not yet subjectivated. It has no "hint or suggestion of a dimension of ethics, of relatedness . . . between one human personality and another, between human personality and cultural institutions."[35] Spillers argues that through the Middle Passage, "African persons" were reduced to "an undifferentiated identity . . . these captive persons . . . were . . . *nowhere* at all . . . the captive personality . . . [was] culturally 'unmade.'"[36]

Spillers demonstrates how this "absence *from* a subject position" was integral to the invidious sociolegal operation through which persons were transformed into property (whose very existence subtended the emergent property regime).[37] As undifferentiated flesh, captive bodies were excluded from a legal order that permitted parents to name children. If legal kinship had been permitted to enslaved Blacks, early American "property relations would be undermined, since the offspring would then 'belong' to a mother and a father."[38] Spillers identifies this mechanism as integral to the U.S. social and symbolic order—an "American Grammar" which "begins at the 'beginning.'"[39] Spillers traces how this constitutive logic continued to ground social relations and collective consciousness long after the formal abolition of slavery. "It is as if neither time nor history, nor historiography and its topics, show movement."[40]

Crucial to Spillers' analysis is the fact that this persisting grammar was founded upon specific articulations (between property and kinship, law and race, slavery and gender) that would need to be constantly reproduced. The challenge of doing so, the unavoidable threat of disarticulation, was compounded by contradictory features of the grammar itself. For Spillers, the "ungendering . . . of African persons" was central to both this systemic oppression and the implicit fault lines within it.[41] In this system, where captured bodies are reduced to flesh as property, "one is neither female, nor male, as both subjects are taken into 'account' as *quantities*."[42] This operation produces "the ungendered female—at once a captive body and a threatening figure.[43]

Spillers' account indicates why feminist critiques must be adjusted once racialization is taken into account and why antiracist critiques must be adjusted once gender is taken into account. She recognizes how important it has been for feminist thinking to distinguish sex from gender, to dissociate biological reproduction (or motherhood) from being female. Yet she also reminds feminists that the American Grammar enacted racial "dispossession as the *loss* of gender."[44] Black women could give birth but could not be legal mothers or recognized females. Accordingly, there were powerful existential and political reasons for Black women to *insist* on gender differentiation by claiming motherhood and womanhood, as female subjects. Yet Spillers also warns that it would be self-defeating for Black women to simply demand inclusion in a patriarchal order that reproduces both white supremacy and gender inequality.

The challenge was for Black women to both elevate themselves into gendered subjects and refuse the disabling forms of subjectivation typically imposed on American women. Herein lay the subversive potential of the "ungendered female." This sociosymbolic ambiguity "actually reconfigures . . . certain *representational* potentialities for African-Americans."[45] Spillers contends that the "absence *from* a subject position" meant that, in comparison to their white counterparts, Black women were less constrained by societal gender norms.[46] This room for subversive maneuver is enabled by contradictions within and between the logics of racialization and patriarchy.

Spillers shows how in a document like the Moynihan Report, racism articulates with sexism to identify Black families as pathological insofar as they are matrifocal and Black men as insufficiently masculine insofar as they are not household heads.[47] Yet she also suggests that, in so doing, the American Grammar works against its own premises:

> the dominant culture, in a fatal misunderstanding, assigns a matriarchist value where it does not belong; actually *misnames* the power of

the female regarding the enslaved community. Such naming is false because the female could not, in fact, claim her child, and false, once again, because "motherhood" is not perceived in the prevailing social climate as a legitimate procedure of cultural inheritance.[48]

Following "the provisions of patriarchy," this misnaming is meant "to declare Mother Right, by definition, a negating feature of human community."[49] But such a declaration inadvertently *re-genders* Black women as heads of matriarchal families. It thereby creates what Spillers regards as a productively monstrous figure: the ungendered female matriarch. "The African-American woman, the mother, the daughter, becomes historically the powerful and shadowy evocation of a cultural synthesis long evaporated—the law of the Mother—only and precisely because legal enslavement removed the African-American male" as fathers and patriarchs.[50]

Racist imperatives thus introduce fissures into patriarchy's founding logic that may be leveraged by insurgent actors and critics. Spillers suggests that this misnaming points to "a radically different text for female empowerment."[51] She underscores that this paradoxical figure—the ungendered female as misnamed matriarch, "both mother and mother-dispossessed" is situated

> out of the traditional symbolics of female gender, and it is our task to make a place for this different social subject. In doing so, we are less interested in joining the ranks of gendered femaleness than gaining the *insurgent* ground as female social subject. Actually *claiming* the monstrosity . . . which her culture imposes in blindness.[52]

To *claim the monstrosity* of a different kind of social subject is to point beyond the unacceptable alternative between demanding conventional female subjectivity (a self-defeating attempt to be socially legible and recognized as human) or simply embracing one's degraded status as de-subjectivated and ungendered flesh (which reproduces social death and invites all manner of violent harm).[53]

Spillers' unalloyed portrait of systemic and persistent social death (although she does not use the term) helps to explain its appeal to Afro-Pessimists. She, too, argues that anti-Blackness has structured the American social and symbolic order such that neither time nor history appears to move. But her attention to the way this foundational sociopolitical logic is formed by historically contingent articulations disrupts any ontological account of the unchanging same. Spillers' approach is not, like Hall's, explicitly Marxian. But because she attends to the contradictory imperatives that produce this racial predicament, she is able to develop an immanent critique that points beyond it. By focusing on deep but dynamic structures that repeat across epochs, Spillers neither ontologizes anti-Blackness nor relates it narrowly to conjunctural conditions. She helps us to identify the concrete mechanisms through which historically specific logics and structures stubbornly persist over the life of an otherwise evolving social formation.

But Spillers, like Hall, does not engage directly with the haunting repetitions and returns that, as Butler staged so perspicaciously, overdetermine Black social experience in racial formations. A fuller understanding of what it means to say "it is still happening again" requires engagement with the particular operations of untimeliness in specific social worlds. This means attending not only to how racial structures may reconstitute themselves again and again despite apparent changes, but how they do so in ways that unsettle commonsense notions of time and history.

Avery Gordon offers just such a sociohistorical understanding of haunting as "one way in which abusive systems of power make themselves known and their impacts felt in everyday life, especially when they are supposedly over and done with (slavery, for instance) or when their oppressive nature is denied (as in free labor or national security)."[54] Placing Derridean hauntology in dialogue with Marxism, feminism, and psychoanalysis, Gordon offers a politically attuned understanding of specters. "Haunting is not the same as being exploited, traumatized, or oppressed, although it usually involves these experiences or is produced by them. What's distinctive about haunting is that it is an animated state in which *a repressed or unresolved social violence is making itself known*, sometimes very directly, sometimes obliquely."[55] This unresolved past does not simply persist. It has the power to actively intervene in, by interfering with, the present. "Haunting and the appearance of specters or ghosts is one way . . . we are notified that what's been concealed is very much alive and present, interfering precisely with those always incomplete forms of containment and repression directed towards us."[56] These insufficiently repressed contradictions produce uncanny and untimely effects:

> I use the term *haunting* to describe those singular repetitive instances when home becomes unfamiliar, when your bearings on the world lose direction, when the over and done-with comes alive, when what's been in your blind spot comes into view. Haunting raises specters, and it alters the experience of being in time, the way we separate the past, present, and the future.[57]

Haunting deforms supposedly settled notions of home and world, here and now.

For Gordon, haunting does not only describe an uncanny subjective experience. "A ghost . . . has a real presence and demands its due, your attention."[58]

Haunting indexes an ethico-political relation between returning specters and living actors. "The ghost is alive, so to speak. We are in relation to it and it has designs on us such that we must reckon with it . . . out of a concern for justice."[59] If such specters demand a reckoning with and for past harms, they may also express "a path not taken" or even "a future possibility, a hope."[60] Either way, haunting distills itself into a concrete "something that must be done" here and now.[61] We can see how Gordon echoes but extends Derrida when she notes "haunting is a part of our social world . . . understanding it is essential to grasping the nature of our society *and for changing it.*"[62]

Like Derrida, she underscores that engaging "the ghostly aspects" of social life "requires (or produces) a fundamental change in the way we know and make knowledge."[63] Conventional epistemologies cannot grasp "how that which appears to be not there is often a seething presence, acting on and often meddling with taken-for-granted realities."[64] Accordingly, Gordon hopes to "draw attention to a whole realm of experiences and social practices that can barely be approached without a method attentive to what is elusive, fantastic, contingent, and often barely there."[65] In essays on misogyny in the early psychoanalytic movement, mass disappearance in Latin America during the 1970s dictatorships, and the legacies of racial slavery in American society, she seeks to make contact with these haunting pasts. In contrast to Derrida, she also reworks elements of Marxism, psychoanalysis, feminism, and critical race studies to trace how disavowed violence and unresolved contradictions return to specific social situations, to disorder in order to make demands on the present.[66]

I would like to suggest that in the Prologue to *Invisible Man* (1952), Ralph Ellison elaborates another subversive way of seeing, knowing, and acting which begins with the fact that "it is still happening again." This novel is widely recognized as one of the great accounts of how anti-Black racism is woven inextricably into the very fabric of American society. Ellison's telling of the violent, absurd, and impossible predicaments into which racialized African Americans are perpetually hurled is unsurpassed. But we rarely read this magisterial work as a resource for understanding the untimely and uncanny character of Black lived experience as mediated by haunting repetition. Following Césaire's understanding and practice of poetic knowledge, we should be alert to the unlikely places and forms in which philosophical-political insights may appear.

Ellison's Dialectics of Invisibility, or the Uncanny-Untimely Fact of Blackness

The Prologue to *Invisible Man* is one of the most iconic set pieces in American literature. It is also one among innumerable scenes in which Black writers have figured racialization in terms of uncanny-untimely repetition. In the Prologue, Ellison's unnamed narrator speaks to us *after* the journey of (failed) social encounters and (blocked) self-realization that he will recount in the novel. At this point, following the events described in the book, he lives in a basement squat on a "border area" adjacent to Harlem. Here, he has "been carrying on a fight with Monopolated Light & Power for some time now. I use their service and pay them nothing at all, and they don't know it. Oh, they suspect that power is being drained off, but they don't know where."[67]

It is from this "home—or a hole in the ground, as you will . . . warm and full of light" that this nameless narrator famously announces to readers of the novel,

> I am an invisible man . . . I am a man of substance, of flesh and bone, fiber and liquids—and I might even be said to possess a mind. I am invisible, understand, simply because people refuse to see me. Like the bodiless heads you sometimes see in circus sideshows, it is as though I have been surrounded by mirrors of hard, distorting glass. When they approach me they see only my surroundings, themselves, or figments of their imagination—indeed everything and anything except me. . . . That invisibility to which I refer occurs because of a peculiar disposition of the eyes of those with whom I come into contact. A matter of the construction of their *inner* eyes, those eyes with which they look through their physical eyes upon reality. (3)

In other words, this Black man has been rendered invisible by a particular social optic. Reduced to a socially dead being and racial metonym, he is not legible as an individuated human. He literally cannot be seen. The narrator relates, "You're constantly being bumped into by those of poor vision" (4). He recounts the night a blonde-haired man accidentally bumped into him. In response, this white man insults and curses the narrator who then counterattacks. But while beating him bloody, demanding an apology, and preparing to slit his throat with a knife, the narrator suddenly stops himself. "It occurred to me that the man had not *seen* me, actually; that he, as far as he knew, was in the midst of a walking nightmare! . . . He lay there, moaning on the asphalt; a man almost killed by a phantom" (4–5).

Ellison stages a peculiar form of invisibility where the Black man is in fact

seen, but only as a phantom. Racialized in this way, the Invisible Man begins
to doubt, and is compelled to assert, his own actuality:

> you often doubt if you really exist. You wonder whether you aren't
> simply a phantom in other people's minds. Say, a figure in a nightmare
> which the sleeper tries with all his strength to destroy. It's when you
> feel like this that, out of resentment, you begin to bump people back.
> And let me confess, you feel that way most of the time. You ache with
> the need to convince yourself that you do exist in the real world, that
> you're a part of all the sound and anguish, and you strike out with your
> fists, you curse and you swear to make them recognize you. And alas,
> it's seldom successful. (4)

Insofar as the Black person in this situation is both a "phantom in other people's minds" and "a man of substance, of flesh and bone, fiber and liquids," he
is a visible phantom, neither fully human nor wholly spectral, an impossible
being consigned to an impossible situation. The Invisible Man is an uncanny
figure, strangely familiar to both himself and others. For white people, this visible phantom seems to blur ontological boundaries—between real and imaginary, phenomenal and spectrality, waking and dreaming, visible and invisible.
He becomes an object of fear and target of violence. To paraphrase Spillers,
the Invisible Man claims the monstrosity of this predicament.

The narrator comes to recognize that this racial formation has also created
an impossible situation for itself. Whites are haunted and tormented by their
own racist projections. Following this insight, the Invisible Man's anger turns
into amusement as he contemplates the white man's absurd predicament as a
sleepwalker inhabiting a dreamworld in which he is tormented by phantoms.
"I was amused: Something in this man's thick head had sprung out and beaten
him within an inch of his life. I began to laugh at this crazy discovery. Would
he have awakened at the point of death? Would Death himself have freed
him for wakeful living? . . . Poor fool, poor blind fool, I thought with sincere
compassion, mugged by an invisible man!" (5).

In short, Ellison suggests that whites fear and hate Black men for the absurd condition this society has imposed on them: simultaneously visible and
spectral, existential threat and nonexistent, fatally concrete and fantastically
abstract. Ellison is not suggesting that Blacks and whites inhabit equivalent
dreamworlds or suffer symmetrically within them. Nor does he believe that
because whites are sleepwalkers acting on unconscious impulses and fantasies, they should be absolved of responsibility for their anti-Black violence. He
underscores that whites ultimately control the very real dreamworld to which
they are subject.

> Responsibility rests upon recognition, and recognition is a form of
> agreement. Take the man whom I almost killed: Who was responsible
> for that near murder—I? I don't think so, and I refuse it. I won't buy it.
> You can't give it to me. *He* bumped into *me*, *he* insulted *me*. Shouldn't
> he, for his own personal safety, have recognized my hysteria, my "dan-
> ger potential"? He, let us say, was lost in a dream world. But didn't *he*
> control that dream world—which, alas, is only too real!—and didn't
> *he* rule me out of it? And if he had yelled for a policeman, wouldn't *I*
> have been taken for the offending one? (14)

Whites created and inhabited the violent dreamworld that obscures their capacity to see reality as it is. Conversely, that dreamworld endows Blacks, whom
it consigns to a phantom existence, with acute social vision.

The narrator relates that he is able to "*see* around corners" (130). Invisibility allows him to recognize clearly that this is a hostile world of violent
sleepwalkers ready to annihilate racialized Blacks whom they engage as dangerous phantom beings. Invisibility becomes a canny optic for recognizing
racial uncanniness. The narrator henceforth attempts to avoid the dangerous
game of bumping into or being bumped by haunted whites: "Most of the
time (although I do not choose as I once did to deny the violence of my days
by ignoring it) I am not so overtly violent. I remember that I am invisible and
walk softly so as not to awaken the sleeping ones. Sometimes it is best not to
awaken them; there are few things in the world as dangerous as sleepwalkers"
(5). But to recognize this situation is not to accept it.

Steering clear of these dangerous sleepwalkers does not mean conceding
to them or their distorted view of the world. Rather, after an endless stream of
painful attempts to find a place for himself in American public life (which the
novel will recount), he has stopped desiring or pursuing the kind of visibility
and recognition that he concludes can never be conferred on someone like
him in a racist society. Referring to his former attempts to play by the official
rules (including paying for rent and utilities), he notes, "no more. I gave up all
that, along with my apartment and my old way of life: That way based upon
the fallacious assumption that I, like other men, was visible. Now, aware of my
invisibility, I live rent-free in a building rented strictly to whites, in a section
of a basement that was shut off and forgotten during the nineteenth century"
(5–6). He has liberated himself from the harmful illusion of what Berlant
identifies as cruel optimism.

The narrator thus makes a strategic choice to embrace, rather than deny,
this uncanny invisibility. Doing so provides a vantage point for social critique,
practical knowledge, and subversive struggle. He relates, "It is sometimes

advantageous to be unseen, although it is most often rather wearing on the nerves" (3). He "learned in time that it is possible to carry on a fight against them without their realizing it" (5). If his spectrality provoked terrified and terrifying violence, it also rendered him unseen in ways that he learns to leverage. "Since you never recognize me even when in closest contact with me, and since, no doubt, you'll hardly believe that I exist, it won't matter if you know that I tapped a power line leading into the building and ran it into my hole in the ground" (13). He explains, "When you have lived invisible as long as I have you develop a certain ingenuity. I'll solve the problem. . . . Though invisible, I am in the great American tradition of tinkers. That makes me kin to Ford, Edison, and Franklin. Call me, since I have a theory and a concept, a 'thinker-tinker'" (7).

The Invisible Man thus renounces his earlier efforts to become visible and be recognized. He has awakened to the fact that under existing conditions, he will not be able to awaken whites from their perverse slumber. He therefore retreats to his squat, makes a home of his hole, and ingeniously drains enough power from the system that oppresses him in order to get by and minimize further encounters where he would continue to be molested. But this "thinker-tinker" is not only developing survival strategies so that he can live on. His move underground, to the shadowy margins of the society that will not recognize him, does not imply an accommodation with his status or reconciliation with the existing order. Nor does it signal a nihilistic renunciation of the world through an attempt to escape from society or abandon political action.

Monopolated Light & Power is a metonym for white culture, American society, and Western civilization. The Invisible Man defines his undetected ability to divert its power for his own use as "an act of sabotage" (7). He reminds us that his underground "hole is warm and full of light" (8). Like invisibility, this subterranean vantage offers him a dialectical optic through which to "see the darkness of lightness" (6). This means recognizing the peculiar inversions that characterize modern American society. The supposed "lightness" of the enlightened white world is actually a perpetrator of "darkness." It transforms Blacks into invisible phantoms who are attacked for this spectral invisibility. It employs reason and science for social domination. It asserts historical progress while oppressing social groups in ways that mark human regression. The narrator boasts that his "hold" has "more light than Broadway or the Empire State building" even as he confesses that this is an unfair claim because "those two spots are among the darkest of our whole civilization" (6). Seeing the darkness of lightness also means recognizing how, above ground, sleeping and waking, nighttime and daytime, have been inverted. Whites have consigned Blacks to the status of nightmares while it is the whites who are actually trapped in a dreamworld from which they cannot awaken.

Conversely, embracing invisibility allows the underground narrator to see the lightness in darkness. He enjoys an excess of illumination. By stealing and redirecting white power, he literally lights up his hole underground, which now pulses with energy. More figuratively, his invisible and underground subjectivity—his supposed "darkness"—affords clear insight into racist social relations. "Before . . . I lived in the darkness into which I was chased, but now I see. I've illuminated the Blackness of my invisibility—and vice versa" (13). Stealing power and light from white capitalists—the thinker-tinker's ingenious sabotage—energizes and humanizes him. Phantomlike invisibility, his (self-imposed) darkness, does not only permit him to survive, it vitalizes him; it shocks him awake in ways that are not available to socially powerful white sleepwalkers. He relates, "I myself, after existing some twenty years, did not become alive until I discovered my invisibility. That is why I fight my battle with Monopolated Light & Power. The deeper reason, I mean: It allows me to feel my vital aliveness" (7).

The Invisible Man's retreat from everyday social interactions signals neither passive accommodation nor fatalistic renunciation. It is a subversive act of strategic *hibernation* in the service of a struggle against social death. "Mine is a warm hole. And remember, a bear retires to his hole for the winter . . . then he comes strolling out. . . . I say this to assure you that it is incorrect to assume that, because I'm invisible and live in a hole, I am dead. I am neither dead nor in a state of suspended animation. Call me Jack-the-Bear, for I am in a state of hibernation" (6). There is no ambiguity here: he defines hibernation as "a covert preparation for a more overt action" (13). Far from fleeing the world, he is biding his time in order to recognize when to seize the moment. He compares this political strategy to the weaker of two boxers, the underdog, who willingly takes a beating while waiting for just the right time to strike the winning blow.

> Once I saw a prizefighter boxing a yokel. The fighter was swift and amazingly scientific. His body was one violent flow of rapid rhythmic action. He hit the yokel a hundred times while the yokel held up his arms in stunned surprise. But suddenly the yokel, rolling about in the gale of boxing gloves, struck one blow and knocked science, speed and footwork . . . cold. The smart money hit the canvas. The long shot got the nod. *The yokel simply stepped inside his opponent's sense of time.*
> (8, emphasis added)

The narrator thus relates invisibility not only to critical illumination but to time, or what we might call the politics of timing: an ability to seize the moment by stepping inside, in order to disorder, the opponent's very sense of time. When the long shot gets the nod, the seemingly impossible is realized.

In the Prologue Ellison relates Black invisibility to both uncanniness and untimeliness. Each is a source of domination and possible subversion. Recall that Freud recognized the untimely dimension of uncanniness when he associated the latter with processes of haunting repetition, terrifying experiences where every attempt to move forward or reach a destination only leads back to the point of origin, such that no matter how hard one tries, change or progress is impossible, and one is always confronted with that which was supposedly left behind. This is the optic through which we might read the Invisible Man's claim that the products of civilization (Broadway or the Empire State Building) are in fact spots of darkness and regression. He explains that this "might sound like a hoax or a contradiction, but that (by contradiction, I mean) is how the world moves. Not like an arrow, but a boomerang. (Beware of those who speak of the spiral of history; they are preparing a boomerang. Keep a steel helmet handy.)" (6). Through the boomerang of history, supposed progress works recursively to further entrap Black Americans within a phantomlike invisibility.

Like invisibility, this untimeliness is both a source of terrifying domination and a medium of critical insight and subversive practice. "I know; I have been boomeranged across my head so much that I now can see the darkness of lightness. And I love light" (6). As with the dominant society's *light* and *power*, the boomerang of history can be subversively redirected. The uncanny-untimely fact of Blackness allows these invisible actors to render the world subversively uncanny and untimely. Recall the famous scene where the Invisible Man is transported (out of self and out of time) by Louis Armstrong's "What Did I Do to Be So Black and Blue."

On one level, Ellison figures Armstrong as a refractionist who employs the medium of music to divert the martial aims that the trumpet in Western society has traditionally served. "Louis bends that military instrument into a beam of lyrical sound" (8). Armstrong's playing refracts canonical and ideological trumpet music into a form of enlivening pleasure and subversive poetry. He does so precisely by redirecting invisibility from a symptom of dehumanized darkness to a source of vitalizing enlightenment. On another level, the narrator is able to recognize in Armstrong's playing that which was not apparent even to the musician but is only now legible to someone, like him, who has come to terms with his own invisibility. The narrator muses, "Perhaps I like

Louis Armstrong because he's made poetry out of being invisible. I think it must be because he's unaware that he is invisible. And my own grasp of invisibility aids me to understand his music" (8). From this perspective, the Invisible Man is a second-order refractionist, able to redirect Armstrong's musical poetry of invisibility in uncanny-untimely directions.

The narrator declares, "Invisibility, let me explain, gives one a slightly different sense of time, you're never quite on the beat. Sometimes you're ahead and sometimes behind. Instead of the swift and imperceptible flowing of time, you are aware of its nodes, those points where time stands still or from which it leaps ahead. And you slip into the breaks and look around. That's what you hear vaguely in Louis' music" (8).[68] This untimeliness—being off the beat, out of sync, inside of someone else's time—is both cause and consequence of a canny ingenuity born of painful experience. It derives from the fact of invisibility (as with African Americans generally), unawareness of invisibility (as with Armstrong), and a canny grasp of invisibility (as with the narrator). At work here are the dialectics of being and knowing, playing and listening, offering and receiving. Armstrong's unselfconsciously lived invisibility enables him to make untimely music (to bend the military trumpet in a poetic direction). The narrator's knowing embrace of invisibility enables him to recognize this music as untimely, to hear it in an untimely fashion. In other words, intentional invisibility allows the narrator to play with Armstrong's playing, to fully hear his uncanny-untimely poetry of invisibility.

The narrator declares his "urge to make music of invisibility" (14). His whole body becomes an instrument of sensory perception-apprehension: "When I have music I want to *feel* its vibration, not only with my ear but with my whole body" (8). Ellison stages this alternative way of hearing-seeing-knowing through the whole body when the Invisible Man recounts the night that he smoked a joint in his illuminated hole and listened to Armstrong.

> Once when I asked for a cigarette, some jokers gave me a reefer, which I lighted when I got home and sat listening to my phonograph. . . . So under the spell of the reefer I discovered a new analytic way of listening to music. The unheard sounds came through, and each melodic line existed of itself, stood out clearly from the rest, said its piece, and waited patiently for the other voices to speak. That night I found myself hearing not only in time, but in space, as well. I not only entered the music, but descended, like Dante, into its depths. And *beneath the swiftness of the hot tempo there was a slower tempo and a cave and I entered it and looked around.* (8–9; original emphasis)

Here the Invisible Man literally slips into the break, inhabits another's tempo and time, and looks around. Just as his whole body was an organ of hearing, his ears become organs of seeing. In this state, the Invisible Man is now able to see around *temporal* corners (i.e., across tenses and eras).

Armstrong's music serves as an untimely portal through which the narrator can access multiple pasts whose collective voices continue to speak across spurious epochal divides. The music does not simply evoke the listener's memories. It conjures pasts that are actually sedimented within Louis Armstrong, his music, and the (self-consciously) invisible narrator. We might relate this experience to Ernst Bloch's "nonsynchronous contradiction" and Reinhart Koselleck's "contemporaneity of the noncontemporaneous." The Invisible Man does not only suddenly see the many pasts that formed him and which still dwell within him, he is thrown back into them.

> *And beneath the swiftness of the hot tempo there was a slower tempo and a cave and I entered it and looked around and heard an old woman singing a spiritual as full of Weltschmerz as flamenco, and beneath that lay a still lower level on which I saw a beautiful girl the color of ivory pleading in a voice like my mother's as she stood before a group of slave owners who bid for her naked body, and below that I found a lower level and a more rapid tempo and I heard someone shout: "Brothers and sisters, my text this morning is the 'Blackness of Blackness.'" "And a congregation of voices answered. . . ."* (8, original emphasis)

We have seen that the narrator's darkness — racialization, invisibility, his underground hole-home — becomes the very condition of his illumination, lucidity, and insight. In similar terms, Ellison here plays with the Platonic metaphor of "the cave," which was supposed to have obscured its inhabitants' ability to see the true world clearly.[69] In contrast, Ellison's narrator enters the darkness of the (uncanny-untimely) cave in order to finally see the world as it really is. Its illuminating darkness allows him to access truth and attain (self-)knowledge. The deeper he descends into darkness, the more clearly he can see.

This insight may be contrasted to the experience of white Westerners who claimed to employ reason (and Platonic philosophy) to leave the distorting cave and see the world truthfully. But we have seen that in this racist society, they actually only stalk the daylit world as violent sleepwalkers, chasing and being chased by their own unconscious fears and projections. The white waking world is deformed by a murderous and suicidal dream-logic. Conversely, the cave allows access to a dreamworld that reveals the true character of the real world's dream-logic which is governed by unconscious impulses, haunting specters, concrete phantoms, and the terrifying trap of endless repetition.

Here is the boomerang of history. The Invisible Man travels to and through these persisting pasts. Within the dream of the cave, which reveals the obscured logic of the real world as a racist nightmare, the rational precepts of time, space, and causality that are supposed to govern the phenomenal world no longer obtain. The Invisible Man is simultaneously here and there, now and then, self and other.

Within the dream-cave, the narrator sees and hears the preacher and congregation transform into a woman singer of spirituals. He enters into a spirited dialogue about freedom with her. After being attacked by one of her sons, he flees from her and suddenly finds himself catapulted forward, into his own recent past, where he is pursued by his real-life nemesis, Ras the Destroyer, about whom we will read in the ensuing pages. Commenting on his own disordered narration, he notes, "But that's getting too far ahead of the story, almost to the end, although the end is in the beginning and lies far ahead" (6).

Just as the music's narrator recounts that the scenes he witnesses in the cave were accompanied by the music's "hot tempo" that had allowed him to access these temporal depths, the steady beat and screaming trumpet also call him back to the surface of his now, as if awakened from a dream. "Then somehow I came out of it, ascending hastily from this underworld of sound to hear Louis Armstrong innocently asking, *What did I do to be so Black and blue?*" (12). The Invisible Man recognizes that this is not only a rhetorical question. "At first I was afraid; this familiar music had demanded action, the kind of which I was incapable, and yet had I lingered there beneath the surface I might have attempted to act" (12). As haunting revenant, Armstrong (and his legacy) was making a demand on the present that required action. Like hibernation, intoxicated listening is not about escaping from the world. It is, as Benjamin insisted, about winning the energies of intoxication for the revolution. But the Invisible Man is ambivalent about the prospects of acting in the light, on the surface. His painful experiences have affirmed his invisibility and impossible situation. The danger of bumping into or being bumped by white sleepwalkers compounds his worry about being capable of acting in the way that is demanded.

When the narrator remarks, "Nevertheless, I know now that few really listen to this music" (12), he is signaling that present actors must strive to hear this kind of untimely demand. This point resonates with Benjamin's insight that every now is a "now of recognizability" such that objects may only become fully legible in subsequent epochs.[70] Like Benjamin, Ellison links such untimely apprehension to political action based on an intergenerational responsibility to past struggles. More generally, the Prologue resonates with Benjamin's discussion of the dialectics of remembrance and awakening.

Both suggest that one awakens by entering dreamworlds that allow one to grasp the dreamlike character of the waking world, in order to act here and now.

After resurfacing, the Invisible Man relates:

> I had discovered unrecognized compulsions of my being—even though I could not answer "yes" to their promptings. I haven't smoked a reefer since, however; not because they're illegal, but because to *see* around corners is enough (that is not unusual when you are invisible). But to hear around them is too much; it inhibits action. And despite . . . all that sad, lost period of the [Communist] Brotherhood, I believe in nothing if not action. (13)

If action is mediated by the refractionist's ability to see around corners and to bend time, it may also be obstructed if one slips into a condition where no temporal coordinates exist. The narrator relates that "the drug destroys one's sense of time completely. If that happened, I might forget to dodge some bright morning and some cluck would run me down. . . . Or I might forget to leave my hole when the moment for action presents itself" (13). For "hibernation is a covert preparation for more action" (13). The Invisible Man's trip into these temporal depths parallels and complements his strategic retreat into the basement hole-home. Both vantage points, like invisibility more generally, offer something like a dialectical optic through which to recognize the darkness of lightness and the clarity of darkness. As he declares "I've illuminated the Blackness of invisibility—and vice versa. And so I play the invisible music of my isolation" (13).

In one sense, the involuntary invisibility, the phantomlike existence (i.e., social death) that has been assigned to him by this racist society, absolves the narrator of ethical responsibility toward white sleepwalkers and the violent social order that has placed him in an impossible situation. For "responsibility rests on recognition, and recognition is a form of agreement" (14). Like Afro-Pessimists, the narrator suggests that racialized invisibility negates any shared context within which mutual recognition or ethical responsibility might be possible. He thus declares, "I am one of the most irresponsible beings that ever lives. Irresponsibility is part of my invisibility: any way you face it, it is a denial. But to whom can I be responsible, and why should I be, when you refuse to see me? And wait until I reveal how truly irresponsible I am" (14).

Yet Ellison does not retreat into antipolitical nihilism. Riffing on Kierkegaard, the narrator declares, "All sickness is not unto death, neither is invisibility" (14). He explains that however justified his irresponsibility might be—however just it would have been to kill the white man who, lost in a dreamworld that he himself created and controlled, bumped and insulted him, "this kind of foolishness will cause us tragic trouble" (14). It is not clear whether the narrator here is referring to the white foolishness of maintaining a racist dreamworld or a Black foolishness of violently striking back from such a precarious position. Nor is it clear whether the tragic trouble would befall Blacks impelled to violent action or an American society perversely intoxicated by its racist dreamworld. But given that each community is fatally entangled with the other, we could read him as referring to all of the above. As Ellison's sly narrator comments, "All dreamers and sleepwalkers must pay the price, and even the invisible victim is responsible for the fate of all" (14). He informs us that the story to come will demonstrate how, before awakening to his invisibility, he "shirked that responsibility" and "was a coward" because he was "too snarled in the incompatible notions that buzzed within my brain" (14).

Ultimately, the narrator implores readers to "bear with me." He thereby begs our patience for the long story to come, hoping that we will appreciate how many times he had to be struck in the head by the boomerang of white good intentions, "improving" interventions, and promised progress before recognizing the darkness of lightness and vice versa. He begs our patience for what he retrospectively regards as an extended period of ignorance, cowardice, and irresponsibility. Of course, the narrative recounts all the ways in which—on the surface, in the light of the waking white dreamworld—the Invisible Man bravely and responsibly pursued knowledge and insight. But it is only when he abandons efforts to be recognized (whether as equal to whites or as distinctively Black) and achieve justice (whether through liberalism, Communism, or Black nationalism), and retreats into his hole that he is able to assume real responsibility for the world and act responsibly in it, by acting on different terms with deeper knowledge in ways that might actually make a difference.

From this perspective, *bear with me* is also an invitation to fellow Black readers to follow his lead by embracing invisibility and practicing hibernation—like a bear. *Bear with me* becomes less a plea for understanding than a call to action. *You, too, can/should be a hibernating bear like (or with) me. You, too, can recognize the darkness of lightness by seeing around corners and hearing across epochs, entering and disorganizing the opponent's (very sense of) time, waiting for the right moment to seize the opportunity, strike the blow, and change the world.* From this angle, when he says, "call me Jack-the-Bear," he is offering himself (and his strategy) as an alternative to (that of) Brother Jack, the duplicitous and racist Communist organizer in whom he had misplaced his trust, as we will learn in the story to come.

Invisible Man stages the perils of different strategies for inhabiting, negotiating, abolishing, or transcending this impossible situation. It traces how every attempt to move forward—to gain recognition and improve one's situation—

boomerangs back to trap racialized actors in a system of infernal repetition. But the Prologue and the story also stage the kind of intoxicating possibilities for profane illumination that may be enabled by this voyage into darkness (the darkness of American racism, of being condemned to invisibility, of living an impossible situation). This voyage allows Ellison to develop poetic ways of recognizing and reworking this predicament. The dialectic of invisibility affords acute insights into the nonsynchronous and untimely character of social life, especially as bound up with forms of racial domination. But it also illuminates strategies for dialectical reversal as we see in the Prologue, which we learn is the end of the story. The Prologue suggests that Ellison will do to and for readers what Armstrong's music did to and for the narrator. The latter describes his "compulsion to put invisibility down in Black and white" as "an urge to make music of invisibility" (14). Like the song "What did I Do to Be so Black and Blue," the novel may also serve as an untimely portal for those capable of recognizing what it opens and offers—the refractionist's capacity to bend appearances, see around corners, or slip into the other's time in order recognize a distorted reality whose correction will require seizing the moment in order to create real distortions.

Ellison's insights into the boomerang of history resonate with aspects of the Afro-Pessimist insistence on the unchanging same. But his attention to subversive strategies and dialectical reversals suggest that he is neither cynical about politics nor willing to bracket history. His staging of the uncanny-untimely fact of Blackness resonates with a hauntological attention to phantoms and with time being out of joint. Like Derrida, Ellison displaces conventional boundaries between visibility and invisibility, presence and absence, reality and imagination, and past and present. The Invisible Man's capacity to see around corners and hear across epochs certainly comports with Derrida's call to recognize and speak to specters. But Ellison grounds spectral invisibility and haunting repetition in the U.S. racial formation. In contrast to Derrida, Ellison examines the social process through which certain subjects are *made spectral*—turned into phantoms who unwillingly haunt the present that produced them. These racialized specters are themselves burdened by history, haunted by violent pasts that repeat in present arrangements and are enacted by dangerous white sleepwalkers. Ellison's specters do not simply bear messianic gifts or herald desired futures-to-come. They are trapped in the uncanny-untimely labyrinth. They require a steel helmet to protect themselves from the boomerang of history. They both haunt and are haunted. Their capacity to see and know otherwise has been paid for with violence and suffering. Like Derrida (and Benjamin), Ellison underscores that we who are now living have a responsibility to spectral *revenants*. But whereas this untimely answerability leads Derrida to promote a passive ethics of hospitality, it leads Ellison to envision an active politics of subversion. Derrida makes quasi-ontological claims about spectrality. Ellison stages invisibility as a historical and dialectical phenomenon.

It's Still Happening *Again*

Ellison is only one of many Black artists and thinkers who have explored this uncanny-untimely fact of Blackness. As I suggest above, his reflections on the dialectics of invisibility and the capacity to see around corners should be read in relation to Du Bois's conception of "second sight."[71] Recall that Du Bois figured segregation as a "dark cave in a side of an impending mountain" in which Black subjects, as "entombed souls" can be glimpsed but not heard as the cave is sealed tight: "some thick sheet of invisible but horribly tangible plate glass is between them and the world."[72] Ellison's exploration might also be situated in relation to Fanon's landmark account of the lived experience of Blackness.[73] The Invisible Man's discovery of a different, embodied, way of seeing and knowing resonates with Césaire's of "poetic knowledge." So too does Ellison's choice to convey a series of critical theoretical and social historical insights through literary fiction. As Gordon demonstrates, Toni Morrison developed a sophisticated analytics and poetics of haunting in relation to the socially embedded character of American racism. In the next chapter, we will see Glissant's account of how Antilleans are burdened and endowed with a "painful sense of time."

These different thinkers explore how racialized Blacks are assigned to an uncanny status that confounds familiarity and strangeness, the everyday and the impenetrable, waking and dreaming, reality and fantasy, human and spectral, past and present. They cultivate nonrealist optics through which to reconsider conventional assumptions about here, now, and us. They illuminate the paradoxical operation whereby racialization ontologizes in ways that blur conventional ontological boundaries. They also illuminate how such uncanniness is typically bound up with untimeliness: the nightmare logic of running faster only to fall further behind, where every possible path forward or out leads back to the same entrapped starting point. Every promise of freedom serves to reinforce domination. Any wager turns into a losing bet. No matter how much time passes or how successful struggles seem to have been, racialization, dehumanization, alienation, and domination persist. The uncanny-untimely fact of Blackness is bound up (subjectively and objectively) with endless repetition and haunting returns. Racialized subjects are both condemned to an endless present and prohibited from fully inhabiting any given present.

In other words, this Black critical tradition, as I have suggested through this chapter and will continue to explore in Glissant, demonstrates, and calls on readers to recognize, that "it is still happening again." I use this grammatically skewed formulation, which deliberately blurs tenses, to index the peculiar ways that persistence, repetition, and aftermath entwine or converge. *It is always still happening. It is always happening again. It never ended yet it's starting again.* This formulation signals the peculiar mix of stasis and dynamism, of running on a path that turns out to be situated on an enormous treadmill. *Still happening* suggests a changing-unchanging same. *Again* suggests that this is something strange but familiar, something supposedly ended that has started anew. *It's still happening again* condenses sameness and newness, the never changing and the ever changing (in ways that never change enough). Through the dialectics of invisibility Ellison stages this uncanny-untimely predicament, offers a nonrealist optic through which to grasp it, and traces subversive strategies through which to transcend it.

10

A Prophetic Vision of the Past

Glissant's Poetics of Nonhistory

I am a memory that does not reach the threshold . . .
I reascend to haunt the sinister thickness of things.

—AIMÉ CÉSAIRE

Barbarity
of the dead who circulate through the veins of the earth
and sometimes come to break their heads against the walls of our ears
and the never heard cries of revolt
that move to the rhythm and timbre of music

—AIMÉ CÉSAIRE

In the previous chapter, I analyzed attempts by Black critical thinkers to grapple with what Ellison called the boomerang of history, or the uncanny-untimely ways that every instance of supposed emancipation created conditions for a new form of racial domination for African Americans. Here, I extend this discussion to Édouard Glissant's reflections on this kind of experience in the postplantation Caribbean. Specifically, I analyze how his conceptions of "nonhistory," "tormented chronology," and a "painful sense of time" illuminate such processes of historical persistence and haunting repetition. Through them we may begin to understand his claim about the Antillean capacity for a "prophetic vision of the past." Through this paradoxical formulation, Glissant conveys that the painful Caribbean past of existential, geographic, and historical alienation (which were perverse sources of creative mixture and interdependence) prefigured the oppressive conditions and transformative possibilities of the global future that is now. We may understand this as another way to figure the dialectic of past and future.

In Chapter 3, I discussed Glissant's reflections on how the possibility of a new "poetics of Relation" emerged dialectically from the abyss of the Middle Passage and the Plantation. His image of Relation conjures an ever-ramifying network of opaque singularities that confounds realist boundaries between here and there, us and them. Here I would like to suggest that nonhistory, tormented chronology, a painful sense of time, and a prophetic vision of the past confound realist boundaries between now and then. They explode conventional assumptions about linear chronology, self-identical periods, and discreet tenses. Here, too, Glissant suggests a dialectical reversal whereby a disabling affliction could be transformed into a critical capacity. I would argue that these terms are as central to understanding Glissant's broader critical vision as are his more familiar conceptions of rupture, creolization, detour, wandering, and Relation. Throughout his work, he explores what we might call the "creolization of time"—through *temporal* ruptures, entanglements, detours, wandering—in and beyond the Antilles.

Nonhistory, Painful Time, Tormented Chronology

Glissant introduces these terms in *Le Discours antillais* (1981), a compendium of essays, lectures, aphorisms, and poetic fragments on the cultural, political, and historical situation of the French Antilles in relation to contemporary global processes. The book's multivalent title refers at once to Glissant's critical discourses, French imperial discourses about the Antilles, and commonsense discourses—or forms of Antillean self-understanding—that circulated in these Caribbean islands. Ultimately, Glissant hopes to contribute to a new collective consciousness and political subjectivity—a disalienated discourse—through which Antilleans could act historically to exercise real self-determination.

Glissant's analysis unfolds from his observation that the French Antilles "were destined to be always in an unstable relationship with their own reality . . . since they were paralyzed by being scattered geographically and also by [assimilation,] one of the most pernicious forms of colonization."[1] Middle Passage deportation and dispossession ruptured enslaved Africans' relation to their past and deformed their relation to their New World present. This double alienation was then compounded and obscured by centuries of cultural assimilation. The effect, Glissant argues, has been "painless oblivion . . . terrible and definitive muteness . . . anxious serenity . . . detached stillness . . . [and a] state of trepidation. . . . We are at the outer edge and remain silent."[2]

Studying "Antillean discourse" entails "tracking down every manifestation of the multiple processes . . . that have ultimately woven for a people . . . the *web of nothingness* in which it is ensnared today."[3]

How can the critic see a web of nothingness? What does it mean to hear a terrible muteness, track a silent discourse, or recognize a painless harm? Conventional methods and frameworks for seeing, recording, and knowing the given world would surely miss the mark. Glissant warns, "Caribbean discourse cannot be readily seized."[4] He explains, "The attempt to approach a reality so often hidden from view cannot be organized in terms of a set of clarifications."[5] Rather, the critic should attend to "those stubborn shadows where repetition leads to perpetual concealment, which is our form of resistance."[6] Given that colonial domination has long been mediated by such "clarifying" discourses, a genuinely critical discourse could not be conventionally discursive. Rather than try to seize and clarify opacities, it would recognize and relate them in order to preserve, not expose, practices of concealment. Instead of clarifying—using conventional social scientific explanation to illuminate what appears to be obscure—Glissant proposes "piling up" as "the most suitable technique for exposing a reality that is itself being scattered."[7] We may read his own scattered reflections in this book as just such an attempt to track down and pile up "realities that *keep slipping away*."[8] As we saw in Chapter 3, Glissant identifies poetics as a method of knowing that both illuminates and conceals. In order to grasp Antilleans' "unstable relation to their own reality," Glissant produces what we might call "a poetics of nonhistory."

He introduces the idea of "nonhistory" in a chapter entitled "The Quarrel with History," which he first delivered at the 1976 Carifesta Colloquium in Kingston, Jamaica. It begins with the discussion provoked by the Jamaican poet Edward Baugh on the supposed absence of history in the West Indies. Baugh challenges the imperial discourse, which held that Caribbean peoples were bereft of cultural traditions and lacking historical agency, and that nothing of historical significance occurs in these places. Glissant, too, rejects the idea that Antilleans have no history. Yet he also insists that they cannot have, inhabit, or relate to history in ways that remain available to peoples (including Europeans and Africans) who had not been deported and enslaved. For Antillean people, "the lived circumstances of this daily relation with its surroundings . . . is in a discontinuous relation to its accumulation of experiences (what we would call its culture)."[9] For Glissant, this contradiction deforms and obstructs collective self-understanding. Antilleans are condemned to a "consciousness that it feels is 'vital,' but that it is unable to 'bring to light.'"[10] He characterizes this predicament as one of "nonhistory."

The French Caribbean is the site of a history characterized by ruptures . . . that began with the brutal dislocation, the slave trade. Our
historical consciousness could not be deposited gradually and continuously like sediment . . . as happened with those peoples who have
frequently produced a totalitarian philosophy of history, for instance
European peoples, but came together in the context of a shock,
contradiction, painful negation, and explosive forces. This dislocation
of the continuum, and the inability of the collective consciousness to
absorb it all, characterize what I call a nonhistory.[11]

In one sense, nonhistory refers to the fact that Antilleans are disenfranchised political subjects, not permitted to determine their own life conditions.
"What is an event for us? A fact that is produced elsewhere, without us, yet
nevertheless (and even more so) [pourtant (pour autant)] resounds here and
in us."[12] In this sense, Antilleans share the fate of other people in colonial
and imperial situations where consequential political decisions are made by
distant hegemons. Nonhistory also identifies the specificity of domination
in New World plantation societies whose majority Black populations were
shaped by historical rupture, dislocation, and negation. For Glissant, these
traumatic experiences undermined efforts to forge the kind of collective consciousness that could fuel vital anticolonial movements. He thus contrasts the
Caribbean to Africa where, "the ancestral community of language, religion,
government, traditional values—in brief, a worldview—allowed these peoples, each in its own way, to offer continuous, open resistance."[13]

But Glissant also relates nonhistory to the peculiar predicament of the
French Antilles where imperial subordination exists within a framework of formal political inclusion following centuries of cultural assimilation. He refers
to a "slow and relentless degradation" whose reality is difficult for both insiders
and outsiders to recognize.[14] These objective conditions produce insidious
subjective effects. "For a people that does not express itself, for a people that is
mentally subjugated, there are no events, there is only nonhistory: the absence
of all decision and all growth about its own concerns."[15] Nonhistory refers to
the uncanny effects produced by a form of (often indirect, invisible, or mystified) domination that is never what it seems.

Glissant notes that this placid façade is periodically shattered by a "derisory
violence" that "mocks history."[16] He offers the example of a senseless murder
in Fort-de-France in May 1971. It occurred against the backdrop of public
protests against the French government's suppression of striking agricultural
workers in Guadeloupe. According to a citizen witness, it was a peaceful afternoon and a group of *lycée* students were calmly talking amongst themselves

on the sidewalk of a commercial street. A military truck passed by and, for no apparent reason, a soldier fired at the group, killing one of the young men, before it vanished without a trace. "This truck, like so many others, disappeared, along with its occupants and phlegmatic killer, into the thickness of our abdications and the pale clarity of judicial procedures."[17] Glissant is not only emphasizing the senseless violence and soldier's impunity. He is also suggesting that something about this tragically banal event expresses the (uncanny) singularity of Antillean nonhistory. It "sketches an 'objective' tableau of the [Martinican] situation: full of boutiques, pharmacies, an advanced urban life, it is stalked [traversé] by a phantom murderer that we do not drive away [débusquer]."[18]

Glissant invokes this unsettling scenario to illustrate the absurdity of Antillean nonhistory. "What strikes me most about this murder is its tranquil and derisory quality. As if the situation in the *petites Antilles* 'called for' this type of peaceful snickering and mocking of history."[19] This kind of event both connects the French Antilles to and distinguishes them from the many places worldwide that are plagued by more spectacular "tortures, massacres, genocides."[20] Glissant notes that "we are a cartoonish echo" whose forms of violence are "punctuations of derision."[21] Because this kind of murder is uncommon yet recurrent, meaningless yet symptomatic of Antillean dependency, low-stakes globally yet devastating for the local community, similar to and distinct from the larger-scale organized violence in other parts of the world, there is something parodic and dreamlike about it. It mocks Antilleans who believe they are no longer colonized. It mocks the wider Global South in relation to whose suffering this tragedy is infinitesimal. It mocks History itself, which is supposed to unfold progressively.

Conversely, through such meaningless political violence, History mocks an Antilles that it both isolates from and subjects to the ravages of global politics. *To be mocked by history through this kind of nonevent is the fate of those peoples constituted by and condemned to nonhistory.* The uncanny character of this situation is underscored by the spectral way in which the military truck violently appears and suddenly disappears without a trace, leaving a dead body in its wake like a stone, or kidnapped African, sinking silently to the bottom of the sea without a ripple. This uncanniness extends to social actors who are reduced to baffled spectators caught in an other's dream. In this "derisive" set-piece — banal, demeaning, parodic — History mocks the Antilles and the Antillean situation mocks History.[22]

In Glissant's view, this nonhistorial condition has devastating political consequences. "A people without events, a people cut off from the world, is a people that does not see or think itself: this is our most certain calamity."[23]

He thus bemoans the inability of Antilleans to create a robust collective will through which to act as an effective historical subject. This "calamity" also refers to how nonhistory condemned Antilleans to "a painful notion of time."[24] The idea of time itself as a source of harm certainly refers to the violent historical ruptures of the Middle Passage and slavery. It underscores that Antilleans had a *temporally* unstable relationship with their own reality. They could not synchronize past traditions with present surroundings. But this "painful sense of time" also refers to the peculiar course of historical development *after* the abolition of slavery 1848, when every moment of apparent liberation in the Antilles enabled a new form of domination that was further obscured by assimilation. Emancipation enabled republican colonialism. Third Republic citizenship enabled proletarianization. Departmentalization enabled socioeconomic dependency. Postwar development enabled welfare consumerism. Glissant thus invokes a "tormented chronology" whereby every supposed step toward freedom further eroded the grounds of self-determination.[25] We might think of this as a negative dialectic of liberation and domination (or progress and regress) such that time in the Antilles could not be experienced as linear. Nor could history be experienced as progressive.

Tormented chronology and a painful sense of time convey that Antilleans were out of sync with both metropolitan France (into which they were not fully integrated, despite the promise of departmentalization) and other colonized societies (whose subject status they did not fully share because of departmentalization). More fundamentally, it refers to this uncanny and untimely experience of a people charging forward only to find itself back in a situation that had supposedly been left behind. Nonhistory actually means being *saturated* by history, but in ways that blur boundaries between visible and invisible, presence and absence, movement and stasis, linearity and circularity, past and present. Referring to the "traumatic shock" of slavery and its "reactivation" during the 1848 emancipation, Glissant asks rhetorically: "Would it be ridiculous to consider our lived history as a steadily advancing neurosis" that was expressed in a collective "horror of 'returning to those things of the past?'"[26] We do not have to accept this sweeping generalization that Antilleans have a pathological relation to the past to appreciate Glissant's point that social rupture, cultural alienation, blocked progress, and endlessly reactivated trauma endowed the past with a malignant power that continued to haunt the Antillean present. These processes nourished an experience of historical time as dangerously chaotic and frighteningly uncanny. In a world of nonhistory, *it's always still happening again.*

A "painful sense of time" underscores the nonsynchronous character of the Antillean now. Describing fierce rainstorms, Glissant invokes the "fissures that become visible when the landscape unfolds."[27] This is not only a spatial observation about the natural landscape. It is also an observation that in moments of crisis, *temporal* fissures in the *social* landscape may become visible. Just below the colonized and cultivated surface of the Martinican countryside, Glissant discerns untimely traces of collective suffering and historical struggle. The mountainous North still harbors an insurgent legacy that returns to the visitor. "Today, the flat fields of pineapple cut arid grooves in this aloof and remote world. . . . The strikers of the Lorrain district, coolies and Blacks, all Martinican, were trapped there in 1976: they turned over with their machetes the field of leaves soaked in blood."[28] Likewise, in the hilly center of the country, still marked by old cane fields, Glissant identifies "ruins of factories" which "lurk there as witness to the old order of the plantations. Where the setting sun yawns . . . the ruins of the . . . Château Dubuc . . . where the slaves disembarked . . . and where slave prisons still lie hidden underground."[29] So, too, in the plain, where "the delta has been chewed up by make-believe enterprises, by an air strip," untimely traces of repressed labor unrest haunt the present: "On the walls of a house in Lamentin star-shaped bullet holes still remain from which year we no longer know when three striking cane workers were slaughtered by the police."[30] And in "the South, with its scattering of goats. The agitation of the beaches, forgetful of all who climbed the coconut trees, once trying to reach out to Toussaint Louverture in the land of Haiti. The salt of the sea claimed them."[31]

On one level, Glissant offers an inventory of historical memories that may be read off the landscape. But he also suggests that these spectral predecessors have the capacity to arrest contemporary actors. "We come to a halt, not certain what slows us down at that spot with a strange uneasiness. These beaches are up for grabs. The tourists say they own them. They are the ultimate frontier, visible evidence of our past wanderings and our present distress."[32] Here at the edge of the sea, the primal scene of catastrophic nonhistory and matrix of painful time, the boundaries between past and present, memory and visitation, domination and refusal, stasis and flight become porous. Concluding his imaginative tour of Martinique's temporally layered landscape, Glissant remarks: "History is spread out beneath this surface, from the mountains to the sea, from north to south, from the forest to the beaches. Maroon resistance and denial, entrenchment and endurance, the world beyond and dream. (Our landscape is its own monument: its meaning can only be traced on the underside. It is all history.)"[33]

Note that Glissant does not seek to recover the real but hidden or forgotten history of Martinique. Rather, he insists, "This landscape . . . is not saturated with a single History but effervescent with intermingled histories, spread around, rushing to fuse without destroying or reducing each other."[34] To say that time is painful is not only a claim that Antilleans have been harmed by time. It is also a claim about the peculiar character of time in a place where, at any moment, temporal fissures can become visible and specters may demand recognition or compel reckoning. Conjuring both the legendary scene in May 1802, where the defeated mulatto general Louis Delgrès led his [Black] troops to commit collective suicide rather than be re-enslaved by Napoleon in Guadeloupe, and the July 1953 attack on the Moncada Barracks, led by Fidel Castro, which marked the start of the Cuban Revolution, Glissant writes:

> Today we hear the blast from Matouba, but also the volley of shots fired at Moncada. Our history comes to life with a stunning unexpectedness. The emergence of this common experience broken in time (of this concealed parallel in histories) that shapes the Caribbean at this time surprises us before we have even thought about this parallel. That means also that our history emerges at the edge of what we can tolerate, this emergence must be related immediately to the complicated web of events in our past. The past, to which we were subjected, which has not yet emerged as history for us, is, however, obsessively present.[35]

Through this image, Glissant conveys how the insistent past is itself obsessed with returning to make a claim upon present actors. When he declares that this past "has not yet emerged as history for us," he underscores its nonhistorical character. It has not been officially recognized, but it is unruly and undomesticated. It is not (yet) a source of collective consciousness and is incommensurable with historicist modes of understanding.

Glissant alerts contemporary intellectuals that they have a special responsibility to reckon with these spectral revenants.

> The duty of the writer is to explore this obsession, to show its relevance in a continuous fashion to the immediate present. This exploration is therefore related neither to a schematic chronology nor to a nostalgic lament. It leads to the identification of a painful notion of time and its full projection forward into the future: without the help of those plateaus in time from which the West has benefited, without the help of that collective density that is the primary value of an ancestral cultural heartland. That is what I call *a prophetic vision of the past*.[36]

Nonhistory imposes a painful sense of time that cannot be contained by linear chronology or progressive unfolding. It defies the backward-looking gaze of nostalgic lament. It requires writers to unthink the normative relation between past, present, and future. It tasks them with a duty to identify this painful notion of time and its full projection forward into the future. I read this to mean that critics *must try to grasp how nonhistory has shaped an untimely now whose spectral traces may offer glimpses of what is to come.* These operations and insights compose what Glissant calls a prophetic vision of the past. To appreciate what Glissant might mean by this paradoxical formulation, we should first consider his critique of History and historiography.

The Trap of History

Is Glissant longing for a less tormented chronology or suggesting that nonhistory might require a critique of chronology? Is Antillean nonhistory exceptional or exemplary? Is nonhistory only disabling or might it enable new critical and political possibilities?

Glissant does seem to posit a questionable dichotomy between supposedly normal history (marked by smooth chronology and continuously accumulating historical consciousness) and nonhistory (marked by rupture, dislocation, and blocked consciousness). We might protest that there is no such normal history anywhere. But Glissant rightly emphasizes that Middle Passage displacement, dispossession through slavery, and further alienation through assimilation deformed historical experience and consciousness in singularly harmful ways. He underscores how such historical conditions have impoverished collective consciousness, narrowed political imagination, and blocked historical agency. He also insists that nonhistory allowed Western imperial discourses to continually diminish and disavow the actuality of Antillean historical and global significance.

But I would argue that Glissant does not simply wish for Antillean history to be more "normal." Rather, he uses the Antillean situation to challenge conventional assumptions about history and historiography. He writes, "History is a highly functional fantasy of the West, originating at precisely the time when it alone 'made' the history of the World."[37] But Caribbean multiplicity and mixture belie this fantasy. "History [with a capital "H"] ends where the histories of those peoples once reputed to be without history come together."[38] In the Antilles, there is no organic alignment of place, people, culture, consciousness, and tradition. Nor can assumptions about natural chronology, historical progress, or distinct tenses be maintained. Antillean social life is characterized by heterogenous, nonsynchronous, and recursive dynamics that confound any "concept of linear and hierarchical History."[39]

Glissant both recognizes the harms produced by nonhistory and identifies the critical openings it may create. It produces opacities that cannot be seized and clarified. "History has its dimension of the unexplorable at the edge of which we wander, our eyes wide open."[40] It "allows [Antilleans] to live not only another rhythm, but another notion of time" that requires a different conception of history.[41] "For history is not only absence in us, it is vertigo. This time that was never ours, we must now possess. 'We do not see it stretch into our past and calmly take us into tomorrow, but it explodes in us as a compact mass, pushing through a dimension of emptiness where we must, with difficulty and pain, put it all *back together*.'"[42] Glissant thus implies that this painful sense of time is both a burden and an endowment. It compels Antilleans to recognize that time does not simply pass, it explodes. History does not simply unfold, it has to be made from the exploded fragments. Fragmentation is both destructive and creative. Nonhistory produces a second-order attunement to the non-self-evident relation between time and history. "Today the French Caribbean individual . . . understands that from all this history (even if we lived it like a nonhistory) *another reality* has come about . . . that synthesis is not a process of bastardization . . . but a productive activity through which each element is enriched."[43]

Creolization is the dialectical counterpart of nonhistory; each is the condition of possibility of the other and the medium through which the other unfolds. Glissant's conception of transversality crystallizes this intrinsic relation between creolization and nonhistory. He explains that "diverse histories in the Caribbean" are marked by a "subterranean convergence" that "bring to light an unsuspected . . . dimension of human behavior: transversality."[44] Said differently, "The implosion of Caribbean history (of the converging histories of our peoples) relieves us of the linear, hierarchical vision of a single History that has roared around the edge of the Caribbean. . . . The depths are not only the abyss of neurosis but primarily the site of multiple converging paths."[45] When Glissant cites Edward Brathwaite's poetic claim that "the unity is submarine," he conjures the common and intersecting legacy of extreme violence that constituted Caribbean societies:

> To my mind, this expression can only evoke all those Africans weighed down with ball and chain and thrown overboard whenever a slave ship was pursued by enemy vessels and felt too weak to put up a fight. *They sowed in the depths the seeds of an invisible presence*. And so transversality, and not the universal transcendence of the sublime, has come to light.[46]

Transversality names these "submarine roots . . . floating free, not fixed in one position in some primordial spot, but extending in all directions in our world through its network of branches. We, thereby, live, we have the good fortune of living, this shared process of cultural mutation, this convergence that frees us from uniformity."[47]

The concepts of Relation, creolization, nonhistory, and transversality reverberate with one another in an attempt to grasp the Caribbean past as a nonidentical whole constituted by multiple converging paths. Transversal history illuminates the abyss as a scene of convergence in which each of the entwining paths is enriched. It figures historical temporality as fundamentally creolized. Transversality compels us to think space and time differently. Doing so affords deeper insight into the New World past *and* the global present. For Glissant considers transversality to be a worldwide condition that is disclosed by the Antillean experience. Far from being a people without history, Antilleans experienced characteristic aspects of a modern historicity propelled by global capitalism and imperialism. Glissant thus points beyond the false choice of figuring Antilleans either as a people without history or as normatively historical, just like any other people. The constitutive power of Atlantic slavery undermines both propositions.

Glissant attempts to unthink History by attending directly to the extreme violence that propelled such processes of transversal fragmentation and convergence. But he never suggests that abyssal conditions mechanically determined social life or subjective experience. Rather, Glissant explores how nonhistory opened possibilities that may actually liberate actors from conventional (and politically limiting) conceptions of time and history. He warns, "It would be perilous to envision planetary Relation in terms of a logical succession of conquests. . . . Any generalizing theory of history that underestimates the formidable experiences of the world [les redoutables vécus du monde] and their reversals [or swings, *sautes*] (their possible impasses) can constitute a trap."[48] For Glissant, "the trap of history" is not only a matter of being burdened or constrained by a traumatic, persisting, and repeating history of domination (i.e., being trapped by historical violence). It is also a matter of being trapped by a conception of history (as linear, successive, progressive) that both enabled *and* obscured such domination. *To avoid the trap of (being determined by) history one must evade the trap of (believing in) History.*

In Glissant's telling, Antillean nonhistory is characterized, on the one hand, by violent rupture, dislocation, dispossession, and alienation, and on the other, by ongoing creolization, transversality, and Relation. Both the dehumanizing abyss and the generative relations challenge historiographic assumptions about territorial stability, historical continuity, and parochial identities.

In such a context, history as far as it is a discipline and claims to clarify the reality lived by this people, will suffer from a serious epistemological deficiency: it will not know how to make the link [between surroundings and accumulated experiences] . . . the rigid demands made by the historical approach can constitute, if they are not restrained, a paralyzing handicap.[49]

If "passively assimilated," conventional historiographic "methodologies . . . will simply contribute to worsening the problem."[50] The counterpoint to this is Glissant's cryptic formulation, "Surpassing is projective exploration."[51] I read this to mean that alternative epistemologies might facilitate political overcoming. To think with Glissant is to appreciate how historians might want to take their lead from Antilleans who are not only condemned to but endowed with a painful sense of time. In Glissant's view, this sensibility is both an affliction and an aptitude, a source of blindness and insight, an obstacle that may generate an opportunity. The Antillean abyss that produced this painful sense of time may propel ordinary actors and critical intellectuals to develop new ways of knowing.[52] Nonhistory "makes a creative approach necessary."[53] Forging such an approach would have to be a deliberate undertaking.[54]

Counterpoetics

If rational discourse mediates racial inequality and colonial domination, wouldn't a rational counterdiscourse reproduce the very conditions it seeks to overcome? But if Antilleans abandoned discourse as such, wouldn't they risk rendering themselves illegible, enacting the myth that they are a people without history, conceding the very instrument of critique? Could Antillean discourse be effectively challenged in a nondiscursive idiom? Such a critique would have to perform the paradoxical task of using language, an instrument of clarification, to "welcome opaqueness.[55] Like Aimé Césaire (his mentor), and Jacques Derrida (his contemporary), Glissant notes, "We would have to deconstruct French to make it serve us in all these ways."[56] Likewise, "We will have to structure Creole in order to open it to these new possibilities."[57] In light of this dilemma, Glissant proposes not a counterdiscourse but a "counterpoetics."[58]

Glissant identifies "counterpoetics" in the everyday language used by ordinary Antilleans to express "the instinctive denial that has not yet been structured into a conscious and collective refusal."[59] In such language, "the residue of our troubled consciousness" is "deposited in the structures of speech."[60] He recognizes a counterpoetics in the way Martinicans simultaneously employ and deform—stretch, twist, obscure, invert, defamiliarize—French. They transpose aspects of Creole into French so as to render the language unfamiliar to metropolitan native speakers. They use language as a "strategy for diversion" through "antiphrasis" and "ornate expressions and circumlocutions."[61] Through such practices, they refuse "positive and semantically straightforward" forms of prosaic communication.[62] This "attempt to escape the French language by using variations" signals a subversive "mastery" that can be made "an integral part of a resolute collective act—a political act."[63] Counterpoetics conveys a commitment to creolization that refuses the false choice between proper French and real Creole, each of which can be a source of alienation.[64] By familiarizing the strange and estranging the familiar, this counterpoetics renders language, and the world to which it refers, productively uncanny. The result is "subversion of the original meaning; opposition to an order originating elsewhere; creation of a 'counterorder.'"[65]

Glissant relates these insights about the subversive strategies employed in everyday or vernacular counterpoetics to knowledge production by writers. He notes, "Because the collective memory was too often wiped out, the Caribbean writer must 'dig deep' into this memory, following the latent signs that he has picked up in the everyday world."[66] But this work of recovery and reconstruction cannot proceed along realist lines. "Because the Caribbean notion of time was fixed in the void of an imposed nonhistory, the writer must contribute to reconstituting its *tormented* chronology."[67] Glissant reminds us that conventional historiography contributed to deforming Antillean experience. "A reality that was long concealed from itself and that took shape in some way along with the consciousness that the people had of it, has as much to do with the problematics of investigation as with a historical organization of things."[68] He thus refuses to grant academic historians a monopoly on the production of historical knowledge. "As far as we are concerned, history as a consciousness at work and history as lived experience are therefore not the business of historians exclusively."[69] Counterpoetics names Glissant's attempt to grasp nonhistory in ways that reject the logic of History and refuse an epistemology that seizes and clarifies.

Antillean history is traversed by persisting legacies, repeating traumas, and returning specters that cannot be adequately understood through archival documents, chronological narratives, or neat periodization. An adequate history of this world would have to use a "creative method" of "projective exploration" to produce a "counterpoetics." Creative writing and attention to cultural expression are indispensable for grasping the painful sense of time that is the matrix of Caribbean experience and locus of its historical truth. Accordingly, Glissant suggests that literary fiction may be more able than historiography to recognize and represent the untimely and uncanny processes that really shaped Caribbean society. But he does not simply propose substituting historical inquiry with fiction writing or literary criticism.[70] He rejects the boundaries that typically separate these genres of knowing. Each in combination with the other may contribute to new ways of understanding (the relation between the present and) the past. A poetics of history (i.e., a counterpoetics of nonhistory) requires new genres of writing that explode supposed boundaries between history, philosophy, criticism, and poetics. (*Le Discours antillais* is just such a work.)

This is the perspective from which Glissant calls for "a new relationship between history and literature."[71] Rather than criticize one from the standpoint of the other, he seeks to identify traces of the poetic and mythic thinking that once animated each idiom but have long been purged from both. He wants to invent new forms of knowing and writing that share the "peculiarity (like myth in the past) of obscuring as well as disclosing."[72] But, he warns, such forms would have to avoid traditional mythology's obsession with pure origins and clear lines of descent, its will to recount stories of heroic sacrifice in the service of community reconciliation. Myth's capacity for nonhistorical revelation is canceled by this tendency toward historicist linearity. Only a new synthesis of myth, literature, and history could adequately grasp nonhistory.

For Glissant, modernist fiction and Creole folktales contain traces of this anachronistic capacity "to plunge into the depths of . . . lived experience" in order to disclose *and* obscure it. These genres also retain a mytho-poetic will to both remember and foresee. Yet they avoid myth's concern with foundational origins and linear descent. In reference to William Faulkner, Glissant writes,

> Literature *continues* . . . one of the aspects of myth: its *coiled nature*.
> But the coiled pattern of myth led to a linear line of descent, the fun
> damental order, whereas, for instance, the coiled structure of *Absalom,*
> *Absalom!* is linked to an impossible quest. Linearity gets lost. The
> longed-for history and its nonfulfillment are knotted up in an inextri
> cable tangle of relationships, alliances, and progeny, whose principle is
> one of dizzying repetition.[73]

Similarly, he praises Alejo Carpentier and Gabriel García Márquez for staging how a mythic desire for origins actually condemns actors to self-negating circularity and repetition. For Glissant, this Atlantic modernist sensibility resonates with Antilleans' creole consciousness and untimely experience. "It is a case of perversion of the original line of descent . . . here man has lost his way and simply turns in circles. How could he fix himself in the center of things while his legitimacy seems uncertain? A community can so doubt itself, get lost in the swirl of time."[74] As in the forests claimed by maroons, "There is no clear path, no *way forward*, in this density. You turn in obscure circles. . . . The formulation of history's yearned-for ideal, so tied up with its difficulty, introduces us to the dilemma of peoples today still oppressed by dominant cultures."[75] Glissant suggests that Caribbean folktales, in which "no chronology can emerge," also stage such untimely experiences.[76] Because "the tale . . . deals only with stories that cannot be generalized," it functions "to combat the sometimes paralyzing force of a yearning for history."[77] These stories "save us from the belief that History is the first and most basic dimension of human experience, a belief inherited from the West or imposed by it. . . . The Caribbean tale . . . is anti-History."[78]

In short, Glissant seeks to identify, reactivate, and invent a counterpoetics that would transcend generic distinctions between history, literature, and myth in order to better grasp Antillean nonhistory, painful time, and tormented chronology. His novels and plays do just such analytic and political work. It is no accident that it was in these literary writings, rather than in his critical or philosophical essays, that he introduced and elaborated his conception of a prophetic vision of the past.

Poetics of Nonhistory I: Epic Entanglement

Glissant's 1964 novel *The Fourth Century* exemplifies the "creative approach" to nonhistory that he later calls for in *Le Discours antillais*. It is set in Martinique between 1940 and 1945, on the eve of departmentalization, when the colony would be legally integrated into the French nation-state. It tells the epic story of two Black families beginning in 1788, when their respective African ancestors and lineage founders endured the Middle Passage together. The story unfolds from the depiction of a brutal fight between these two men on the deck of the slave ship after its arrival in Martinique. We learn that the man who would found the Béluse family had betrayed the man who would found the Longoué family to slave traders before he, too, was captured and deported to the Antilles.[79] The man who would become Longoué is prevented from killing the man who would become Béluse, and they are each sold to a different white planter (La Roche and Senglis). During Longoué's first night of captivity, Louise, a young girl who is enslaved on La Roche's plantation, unties him. Longoué flees to the mountains but returns the next day to liberate Louise, who is being tortured for this offense. She joins him and they found a maroon community in the hills.

In contrast, Béluse ("good use") lives his life as an enslaved worker on the

Senglis plantation on the plains, near town, which is bound up with market life.[80] The novel begins when one of his descendants, Mathieu Béluse,
visits the elder Papa Longoué, a distant relative and the last descendant of
that first maroon ancestor, who is still living in the hills. Over the course
of many days Mathieu interviews Papa Longoué about the tragic history of
their long-entangled families. Through this painful and tortuous tale, alternatively related by Papa Longoué, Mathieu, and the narrator, Glissant traces
Martinican nonhistory from the period of plantation slavery in the 1780s to
departmentalization by way of slave revolts and abolition in 1848. The novel
treats departmentalization as initiating a period of mass forgetting—characterized by cultural assimilation, economic rationalization, and political complacency—that closes this epoch of intergenerational conflict and drama. The
novel thus unfolds as a practice of remembrance coproduced by Mathieu,
Papa Longoué, the narrator, and the author. It works to save the distant African past and more recent Martinican history from being forgotten, elided, and
obscured. But this is not a realist narrative with a legible chronology whose
aim is recovery or reconstruction.

The Fourth Century stages a series of tragic encounters between these opposed but entangled Martinican families, worldviews, and forms of life. It
proceeds through a series of social knots that the listener must behold and
confront, rather than a linear narrative that the reader need only follow. Initially, Mathieu tries to engage Papa Longoué from the perspective of a modern rational investigator (i.e., historian) who wants to determine the facts in
order to construct a chronology. But this elder distant relative does not allow
such information to be extracted from him in this fashion. He is not only an
heir to maroon autonomy and a transgenerational repository of lived history.
Like the Longoué men who preceded him, he is also a quimboiseur (healer-
sage-seer) who has inherited and preserved African technical knowledge and
ways of knowing. Through a series of visits, during which the account glides
between past and present and across different narrative voices, Papa Longoué
determines the pace, direction, and form of this epic story. His knowledge
is embodied, bound up with lived experience and everyday practices. It is
also embedded in the natural landscape and material objects. His narrative
does not correspond to the protocols of chronological sequence, individual
intentions, or punctual causality. It emerges slowly and haltingly through a
series of intimate and friction-filled face-to-face encounters between the elder
sage in the hills and the younger French-educated writer from the town. Papa
Longoué shifts from being a native informant to a storyteller, a creator of tales,
just as Mathieu shifts from being an interviewer to a listener.[81]

The Fourth Century does not simply oppose modern, Western, abstract, rational, and discursive knowledge to traditional, African, concrete, magical, and poetic forms of knowledge. On the contrary, it demonstrates that in this creolized Antillean society there are no such clear divisions. The epic tale emerges through the confrontation, negotiation, and collaboration between the distinct ways of being, knowing, and relating embodied in these two men. We accompany Papa Longoué on the circuitous pathways through which these two families are inextricably and often tragically entwined. Ancient resentments and unresolved conflicts, murder and intermarriage, provisional alliances and grudging respect produce all manner of tense intimacies between families whose fates are bound up with one another. The Longoué and Béluse families can neither fully reconcile nor definitively separate from each other. Each is equally entwined with the white planter families that first enslaved their African ancestors. La Roche spends his life obsessed with recapturing Longoué and waging war on the fiercely autonomous maroon community he founded. The enslaved Béluse attempts to endure the plantation life imposed upon him, yet he joins a mass slave revolt. The novel also stages a transgenerational conflict, marked by hatreds, infidelities, and resentments, between the La Roche and Senglis families.

Through this epic tale, Glissant relates Antillean nonhistory. He figures a world organized around supposedly self-evident oppositions—traditional and modern, African and Western, hills and plains, wild country and commercial town, revolutionary refusal and patient endurance, separation and engagement, indigenous and imported, past and present—that relentlessly undo themselves. Each form of life and way of knowing depends upon or contains the other within it. Glissant conjures a social formation that has been thoroughly shaped by centuries of creolization in all spheres of public and private life. This Antillean abyss is scene and source of both dehumanizing violence and collective possibility, utter alienation and emergent subjectivities, nonhistorical stagnation and world-historical dynamism.

Crucial to the novel is the contrast between distinct ways of figuring time, knowing the past, and relating history. The fraught, frustrating, and intimate dialogues between the young and educated Mathieu Béluse and the aged and unlettered Papa Longoué revolve precisely around their differing temporal orientations. The scholar and the seer begin by dueling over what it means to live through time and how one might understand the relation between past and present. Running through the novel are their second-order reflections on temporality and historicity. We may read this work as illuminating the points of tension and intersection between mythic, folkloric, narrative, and historicist modes of telling a story and relating the past.

Mathieu presumes and pursues a family story and collective history that is based on truthful facts that can be organized into a linear chronology. Its intelligibility depends on individual intentions and rational choices, clear causes and discernible effects, self-evident boundaries between what once happened and what now actually exists. In contrast, Papa Longoué takes the very long view. He recognizes persisting pasts within an untimely present. He discerns the vital presence of inapparent traces and spirits within objects and landscapes. He has an enchanted view of the world that is rooted in magic, memory, poetics, and prophecy. This does not mean that Glissant simply figures Mathieu as French, discursive, and historical, and Longoué as African, mythic, and timeless. Neither can be categorically separated from the other. In the novel's 1945 now, Mathieu Béluse has, by then, become the youngest descendant of the entwined Longoué-Béluse families. He is Papa Longoué's literal heir. Each is an artifact of Antillean history and embedded in Antillean social life.

The Fourth Century does not simply rehearse a set of tired dichotomies between reason and magic, truth and myth, history and memory, fact and fiction, recording and imagining, prose and poetry, movement and stasis, linearity and circularity. It explodes them from the standpoint of Antillean nonhistory. The novel conveys another way of recognizing and relating history (as nonhistory), time (as painful), and chronology (as tormented). Papa Longoué helps Mathieu (and us) to see how supposedly long past but never resolved interfamilial conflicts can *carry forward* to shape lives and constrain possibilities. Such conflicts are grounded in deep social contradictions that produce an impossible situation that presents untenable choices to actors: flight or endurance, suicidal confrontation or self-destroying accommodation, illegible ritual or alienating reason, obsessive attachment to outmoded African traditions or obsequious assimilation of alienating French norms. Papa Longoué, as refracted through Mathieu and Glissant, helps us to see how a founding structural contradiction—a social formation founded upon deportation, dispossession, and enslavement—makes linear development or social progress impossible. In this situation, decades pass but fundamental contradictions endure.

Glissant's nonhistory thus helps us to account historically for that which conventional history cannot recognize but which actually shapes Antillean social life: persistent, repeating, haunting pasts that either remain ever-present or can be reactivated in a nonsynchronous now. Throughout the novel, Glissant figures time through the image of wind. Wind from the past, wind that embodies the past and propels that past into a nonidentical present. This is an apt figure for time as a social fact and historical force. Wind is both material and inapparent, forceful and spectral, menacing and comforting, violent and reparative, local and planetary; it is a residue of what has passed and a herald of what is to come. It will be useful to keep this multiplex image of wind in mind when we think with Glissant about "a prophetic vision of the past." This formulation is not explicitly mentioned in the novel. But Papa Longoué, through Mathieu, offers us an actual prophet's vision of the past.

Clues to how we might read *The Fourth Century* as (elaborating the concept of) a prophetic vision of the past may be found in Glissant's reflections on William Faulkner. The latter's writings stirred Glissant's imagination and exercised a profound influence on his fiction. We can plausibly read Glissant's epic novels as, among other things, attempts to rewrite Faulkner in an Antillean register. Glissant recognizes that Faulkner's novels are threaded through with racist thinking. But he implores Black readers, including African Americans, to engage with Faulkner's work because of its singular ability to illuminate a creolized society founded upon illegitimate grounds (i.e., slavery, racial divisions, the transformation of a wild landscape into private property).

Glissant is especially interested in the modernist method Faulkner invents to convey this cursed and haunted social world. He argues that Faulkner's novels unfold from a founding but not immediately evident presupposition, a structural contradiction that is the source of an impossible situation. Glissant calls this "the inextricable."[82] Faulkner's white Southern characters are obsessed with founding legitimate lineages and stable communities. They want to possess property, accumulate wealth, and protect status that can be willed to future generations. But such efforts inevitably lead to failure and catastrophe: mixed bloodlines, broken lineages, and social decline. They either cannot or will not recognize, let alone reckon with, the "inextricable" presupposition that fuels their transgenerational malediction. Glissant reads Faulkner's works as tragic epics that convey the impossibility of legitimate foundations under such contradictory conditions.

Faulkner also ensures that his readers are equally unaware of the illegitimate presupposition that mediates social relations, refracts outcomes, and propels his narratives. His sinuous narratives are organized around what Glissant calls "deferred revelation."[83] He explains that Faulkner's writing "originates from . . . three elements: a hidden truth . . . that regulates the description of the real; a visionary description . . . and the disturbed assurance that the secret of this truth will never be realized."[84] In this manner, "Faulkner invented . . . a language that . . . describes and *at the same time* seeks to say what cannot be said through description yet fully signifies (establishes through disclosed reason) what is described . . . it constantly reminds you that this full disclosure is impossible."[85] This recursive technique—constantly approaching a presupposition that can never be revealed, ever disclosing the impossibility of disclosure—carries "the reader to a vertiginous unknown, which is the most precise manner of approaching what can be known."[86]

In what sounds like a self-description, Glissant identifies in Faulkner a "deferred writing" that is "wandering and dense, swinging and transported, straight to the point and suspended."[87] "What is seen and described infers the underlying and the invisible."[88] Realist methods cannot adequately convey the true character of an (uncanny and untimely) reality. "Because the presupposition of the county will always be percolating beneath the real that is apparent, Faulkner's writing takes on the risk of revelation rather than simply being an exposé, a presentation, an analysis, a description, or a story."[89] Faulkner thus "establishes another dimension, a poetics that is not narrative."[90] This writing "rips open . . . the traditional fabric of narrative."[91] It operates according to a nonrealist understanding of causality and truth.

Glissant explains that Faulkner never mechanically relates "the presupposition of the county's damnation" to "the damnation of particular residents of the county."[92] His writing "dissociates cause and effect, delays revelation, diffracts the perception of the real. . . . Revelation and contamination follow the circuit of uncertain but adamant traces."[93] Operating over great distances and long time spans, Faulkner's causality is anonymous, collective, and circuitous. A hidden but powerful presupposition subtends social relations, refracts social practices, and propels tragic outcomes. Its "truth is distant, inaccessible, deferred. No one person or even a group of people can gain access to it through established facts, reasoning, or deduction . . . it is formed through contamination and interplay of shared suffering."[94] Faulkner's writing thus challenges the notion "nurtured by the Western tradition" that "truth is directly attainable."[95] Instead, it offers "the relentless vertigo of feeling that truth is . . . deferred infinitely."[96] It can only be tracked and glimpsed through untimely traces, "spurts of disclosure, the way water withdraws . . . leaving behind muddy streaks and silt and spores of life from the deep."[97]

Faulkner's wandering narratives enact the tortuous character of social time in the world he conjures. Glissant compares them to a great river, which "tells you at the same time that everything is different and yet nothing has changed":

> a chaos-time when even the idea of a future, of a logic of transformation, of an energy to move farther ahead, seems to have been whirling forever. The river does not follow the rules of linear thought . . . it proceeds not in long loops but in a circularity that seeks and rediscovers itself endlessly. It comes and goes in time, deviating and turning time around in a stationary drift.[98]

In Faulkner's post-bellum South *everything is different, yet nothing changes*, intense activity amounts to *stationary drift*. Social life is propelled by a churning *chaos-time* where forward motion is obstructed. The logic of transformation does not obtain. The very idea of a future is mocked. If Faulkner's damned characters cannot escape this chaos-time, it is neither because they are misled by their own passions or blindness nor because they have been cursed by the gods or providence. They suffer a sociohistorical malediction based on the impossible attempt, in the service of which they sacrifice all, to create a community on the basis of violent expropriation and historical disavowal. Their lives are shaped by processes of persistence, repetition, and haunting that are fueled by a founding contradiction that is neither named nor resolved.

Glissant suggests that such a world could only be understood by a backward-looking seer (or nonrealist writer) capable of recognizing the "inextricable presupposition" at work behind and beneath immediate appearances and individual intentions. Once this unresolved contradiction is identified, it becomes possible to foresee aspects of a repeating and haunted future. Glissant thus calls Faulkner "a prophet of the fundamental defects of our world" whose "writing . . . corresponds, prophetically, to the current disorder that looms in the contemporary sensibility."[99] In other words, Faulkner developed *a prophetic vision of the past.* This capacity to foresee tragic outcomes should not be confused with scientific prediction or theological prophecy. It is a kind of imaginative knowing attuned to powerful but invisible forces that persist within an untimely present such that the knower can envision aspects of what is likely to come. This is just the kind of prophetic vision of the past that *The Fourth Century* offers us.

Glissant argues that Faulkner attempted to transpose the tragic epics of Aeschylus and Shakespeare into a modern register. He contends that in classical tragedy, suffering and sacrifice lead to reconciliation and redemption. But for Faulkner, the original sin of illegitimate foundation meant that there can only be suffering, failure, and catastrophe. Similarly, Glissant argues that traditional epics are based on the model of Genesis. They establish a single origin and stable identity for enduring communities. To do so, they distinguish between insiders and outsiders; they trace clear lineages. In contrast, Faulkner's works "are endless detours, by which a *digenesis* weaves its traces."[100] Glissant's Caribbean resembles Faulkner's American South insofar as it, too, is a "composite culture" in which "there was no Genesis, but a historical fact established over and over again and erased over and over again from public memory: Slavery. The holocaust of the slave trade and the belly of the slave ship . . . confer a much more imperative Genesis, even if the origin proceeds from a point that is hybrid."[101] Glissant explains that "every composite culture originates from [this kind of] digenesis."[102]

Such hybrid origins and impure communities call for a "new form of writing" that could express "another form of truth" and point to a "new type of humanity" by reworking the epic.[103] In contrast to the "excluding epic, of yesterday . . . when human communities conceived of themselves in ethnic and almost genetic terms," digenesis requires a "participatory epic" that would posit an alternative "universal" composed of "all cultures and all humanities."[104] Glissant declares, "the world-community calls forth this other epic, which was prefigured by Faulkner: that of the difficult Relation."[105]

For Glissant, Faulkner prefigured but never realized this participatory epic of Relation. Although he "invents a new epic" that explodes the fantasy of Genesis, Faulkner never adequately embraced the transformative possibilities afforded by the digenesis whose traces he discloses. His characters existed "in opposition to any form of creolization wherein a new epic (one of openness and sharing) could have taken root."[106] This was partly because, in his life, Faulkner shared the impossible situations to which his characters were condemned. He had identified the hidden presupposition that would make any kind of legitimate and continuous family or community impossible. But, Glissant argues, he could never fully abandon the desire for just that community. Like his characters, Faulkner "preferred the torments of withdrawal into self and the damned solitude of a refusal that does not have to speak its name."[107] He withdrew and resigned himself to the "tragedy of the impossible."[108] Faulkner remained melancholically attached to the failure, loss, and decline that he describes.

Faulkner's ability to invent a new epic of Relation was also limited by his entrenched racist assumptions. Glissant notes that, however cursed and tragic, Faulkner's Southern whites are historical actors. Because they live in bad faith, cannot recognize the source of their damnation, and refuse to accept their malediction, they are destined for tragic failure. But they are intentional, passionate, suffering humans who reflect, decide, and act. In contrast, Glissant demonstrates, Faulkner's Black characters are timeless abstractions who represent metaphysical absolutes. They neither act nor change. They can only suffer, bear witness, and endure. Faulkner only presents the tragic drama of (more or less dispossessed) oppressors. His Black characters are tragic victims but not tragic actors. Glissant notes that while Faulkner "traced backward into the past" the lineages of the county's great white families, "he does not, however, go back as far as the trauma of the slave trade, which for Blacks, is the source of everything. It is as though, suffering object of the South's neglect, the Blacks had no need for ancestors."[109] Because Faulkner fails to treat Black characters as historical subjects whose own lineages and presuppositions need to be traced back to their founding trauma, he cannot create the kind of epic that would be adequate to that world or his times.

Glissant credits Faulkner, Albert Camus, and Saint-John Perse for having been able to "sow the seeds of a poetics of becoming."[110] But these seeds would have to be cultivated by other authors.[111] Glissant assumed just this task by conjuring worlds in which Black characters are cursed by history and grapple directly with their impossible situation.[112] They make choices, found lineages, rage against their damnation, and suffer catastrophic outcomes. They are victims of their own blindness, passions, resentments, and dreams. They are the dramatic personae of a New World epic that illuminates Antillean nonhistory.

By going all the way back to the slave trade, Glissant's creole epic identifies a painful notion of time and projects it forward into the future. Through a wandering narrative that confounds realist chronology, causality, and narrative, Glissant helps to account for the untimely persistence, repetition, and haunting that has shaped Antillean social experience. Through his tale of tragically intersecting families, we see that this history can only have been one of inextricable creolization. But because Glissant also explores the transformative possibilities that impure lineages and nonidentical communities might open, he goes further than Faulkner in offering a prophetic vision of the past. He recognizes that the Antillean abyss was also a matrix of transversality charged with potentiality. Digenesis is not only a scene of loss and source of malediction. It also creates the conditions of possibility for a new epic of becoming that is able to glimpse, even anticipate, an emergent world-community—one that envisions "wandering as the site of assembly."[113]

We can see this vision enacted at the end of *The Fourth Century* when Papa Longoué dies in 1945. With this passing, as a new period of alienation through departmentalization commences, the era of tragic entanglement and haunting repetition between these great Martinican families seems to end.[114] The founding conflict between Béluse and Longoué loses its transgenerational force. Through Mathieu, as Papa Longoué's unlikely heir, there emerges the possibility of a new synthesis between the distinct forms of life and ways of knowing that these families embodied.

Initially, the seer's death frustrates Mathieu's plan to return to the old prophet's cabin in the hills "possibly for the last time, so that he and Papa Longoué could provide the indefinable chronicle with something like a conclusion, and at least decide if 'logical sequence' in the end had won out over 'magic.'"[115] Some part of Mathieu still longed for the comfort of conventional and continuous history. He "would have preferred to proceed peacefully following the long, methodical procession of causes followed by effects, logical chronology, history unfurled like well-carded cloth."[116] But by the time Papa Longoué dies, Mathieu's way of seeing and knowing had already been transformed through their extended encounter. Following the elder's tormented chronology, Mathieu recognizes that conventional chronology and causality could not grasp the wandering, repeating, and intersecting dynamics of the (family) histories he set out to understand. The narrator informs us that when he died, Papa Longoué "had succeeded in communicating to a chosen descendant—Mathieu Béluse—the bodiless, faceless worry that was his lot."[117]

The novel ends with Mathieu's untimely recognition of the inextricable presupposition that had haunted Antillean social life across the centuries:

> far away over all the islands and the mown fields and the echoing forests, he saw the tall transparent ship that sailed through the lands. He heard the sound of chains being manipulated, the rhythmic beat of *yesyesyes*, the canes snapping off under the propeller, in the sun . . . this is fever this is a world the world and the word sinks in the voice gets louder the voice burns in the motionless fire and inside his head he is spinning bearing off sweeping away ripening—and it has no end and no beginning.[118]

This inescapable abyss which *has no end* also heralds a new world and a new word, a rising voice that will enable a *ripening*—Mathieu's coming to consciousness but also a possible societal transformation. This transgenerational *yesyesyes* is a haunting echo. Perhaps it is not only the sound of forced assent among enslaved laborers but also their call for heirs like Mathieu to struggle for a different future. The novel's conclusion suggests that Mathieu has awakened to just such a call, to which he responds, *Yesyesyes*. Through this untimely vision, Mathieu continues his dialogue with the now spectral seer. "Exhilarated by this revelation of bygone days like light, like a bolt from the blue. So—in his vision—he kept talking to the old *quimboiseur*. . . . And, 'it makes you dizzy,' he said, 'the speed of falling without breathing . . . instantly into a light so solid that you crash into it. . . .'"[119]

This solid light of revelation separated Mathieu from his "old present" and endowed him with a painful sense of time.[120] "This was the country, so tiny, all loops and turns; possessed (ah, not yet, but grasped) after the long, monotonous journey. The country: reality torn from the past, but also, a past dug up from things that were real. And Mathieu saw Time henceforth bound up with the earth."[121] The narrator quickly adds, "But how many of those around him could sense or access the hidden work that lay behind appearances. How many could know it?"[122] The implication, which begins to dawn on Mathieu, is that individual revelation is not sufficient to the demands of his present. "Could knowledge thrive if it was not shared?"[123] The task is to make the kind of prophetic vision that Mathieu inherited (the capacity to see the past as present) collective. This became possible only after the seer's death, when "the Longoués had run dry" but "were buried in everyone."[124] Fleeing to the hills and living the life of a traditional *quimboiseur* who has withdrawn from the broader society would not be enough. The solid light of revelation would have to inform present practices and future-oriented projects. "What is the past if not the knowledge that braces you in the earth and thrusts you in huge numbers into tomorrow?"[125] After Papa Longoué's death, "other roads were opening up . . . the cabin's shadow no longer drew [Mathieu] upland anymore but on the contrary (by bringing the past back into the feverish present) would from now on, perhaps, lead and help everybody on the surrounding farmlands."[126] The way to a different future would lead *through* but not reproduce the haunting past that Longoué embodied and prophesized.

Glissant offers Mathieu the opportunity and responsibility to realize a new synthesis of Longoué and Béluse. But the novel also suggests that if this synthesis has any chance of being realized, it would depend on the union of the Béluse and Celat families through Mathieu's 1946 marriage to Marie Celat (aka Mycéa). The narrator recounts the moment Mathieu first met Mycéa: "Sensing perhaps that inside her the stubbornness, the powers, the clairvoyance of the Longoués was preserved. But Mathieu did not know, or rather he had forgotten that the Celats were the *Longoués from down there*."[127]

In *Le Discours antillais*, as in most of his work, Glissant associates the start of departmentalization with an era of alienating assimilation, mass forgetting, and political stagnation. But *The Fourth Century* presents this moment as a historical turning point that could have marked a different kind of new beginning in Martinique. Mathieu and Mycéa's union was an attempt to establish a new creole lineage through which to cultivate the seeds of a poetic politics of becoming and a social epic of Relation. Although Mycéa barely appears in this novel, she is an indispensable catalyst for the attempt to politicize Longoué's prophetic vision of the past. Through her influence, Mathieu's earlier distance from ordinary people "was already ceding, . . . to the drunken euphoria of what he himself had called 'light that is so solid,' the revelation. Mycéa encouraged him to begin learning about real life again."[128] She declares, "it is not time that is required . . . it is action."[129] She "knew in one of those intuitions . . . why . . . together, a Béluse and a Celat . . . would go beyond knowledge and finally begin to act."[130] Mycéa understood that action would require recognizing *and* transcending the haunting past that Mathieu was now capable of seeing all around them.

> Because she knew that ahead of them, there in the future, other more concrete and harder tasks awaited, she broke the thread and pushed the dazzling light of the past far behind her, and . . . she fought off the

kind of vertigo that Mathieu had inside him. She sensed that it was both fatal to ignore this vertigo (failing to understand where it came from) and fatal to wallow endlessly in it.[131]

Rather than either ignore or wallow in this haunting past, the task was to identify within it a pathway to another possible future.

Following Papa Longoué's death, the couple inherits (the secret of) the "little barrel." Passed down through generations of Longoué men by their maroon ancestors, this "little barrel" recurs through the novel as a mysterious source of this maroon family's occult power. When Mathieu and Mycéa finally receive and open this enchanted repository, they learn that it contains the skeletal remains of a poisonous snake long turned to dust. This snake is the symbolic expression and material embodiment of the long war between white planters and Black maroons during and after slavery in Martinique. After the first Longoué escaped, La Roche and his associates imported crates of snakes which they let loose in the hills in order to terrorize the maroons. But over time, the white community itself became terrorized by these dangerous snakes. Planters then imported mongooses to hunt the snakes. In other words, although the poisonous snakes were introduced by the ruling order, they become associated with dangerous maroons. In an act of dialectical reversal, the *quimboiseurs* appropriated and fetishized this power; they mystified and turned it against the planter community who came to fear the mysterious "little barrel." Mathieu and Mycéa inherit both the little barrel's occulted secret and its occult power. It is a moment of enchantment-disenchantment that symbolizes, and may nourish, new action through further reversals in the struggle for a disalienated world-community. *The Fourth Century* (1964) should be read in relation to its companion novels, *La Lézarde* (1958), *La Case du commandeur* (1981), and *Mahogany* (1987). Each work, as well as the epic whole, narrates how this prospect of a new cultural synthesis and political beginning was immediately foreclosed with the beginning of departmentalization.[132]

Poetics of Nonhistory II: Untimely Drama

Glissant first employs the phrase "prophetic vision of the past" in the Preface to his 1961 play *Monsieur Toussaint*. He explains that his play about this leader of the Saint-Domingue revolution was informed by his reading of the great works on Toussaint by C. L. R James, Aimé Césaire, and Victor Schoelcher. But he contrasts his dramatic creation to these earlier historical interpretations of Toussaint's political strategy:

the present work is not politically inspired; rather it is linked to what I would call, paradoxically, *a prophetic vision of the past*. For those whose history has been reduced by others to darkness and despair, the recovery of the near or distant past is imperative. To renew acquaintance with one's history, obscured or obliterated by others, is to relish fully the present, for the experience of the present, stripped of its roots in time, yields only hollow delights.[133]

Conversely, Glissant suggests that literary works can also provide existential relief for those Antilleans who "feel that they are laboring under the tyrannical burden of the past."[134] He thus suggests that whether people suffer from the obscured absence of history *or* its crushing presence, they are confronted with "the same basic insecurity of being."[135] The purpose of the play, he explains, is to "diminish" that feeling.[136]

This does not sound like the theorist and novelist I have been discussing. But the play itself belies these claims that the work is a nonpolitical attempt to recover the past in order to reassure present spectators. Even in the Preface, there are clues of the play's critical and experimental ambitions. When Glissant addresses "those whose history has been reduced by others to darkness and despair . . . obscured or obliterated by others," he is making a claim about nonhistory as a source of alienation and domination. With his promise to "recover" and "renew acquaintance" with this past in order to "relish fully the present," he signals his intention to overcome this darkness and despair through a literary-historical engagement with the charged past of the Haitian Revolution. When he characterizes this as "a poetic endeavor," he is reminding readers that this drama is not simply a pretext for engaging in conventional political debate or historical scholarship.[137] Far from marking a retreat from politics, the play attempts to transcend oppositions between politics and aesthetics or history and literature. *Monsieur Toussaint* is a response to and dialogue with Glissant's predecessors, including James, Césaire, Shoelcher, Toussaint, Dessalines, and others. It engages *what has been* poetically, in ways that rip open the fabric of empiricist history and realist politics.

Monsieur Toussaint is set during the last days of Toussaint's life in the French prison where, after being kidnapped and deported, he is incarcerated. Throughout the play, Toussaint engages immediately with his European captors, jailers, and minders. At the same time, he is visited by a steady stream of remembered and conjured interlocutors, living and dead, from Saint-Domingue with whom he enters into spirited dialogue and cutting debate. In the Preface, Glissant underscores "the simultaneity of the two time-frames in which he lives" and "the equivalence of past and present" that is enacted.[138]

He notes, "It may be useful to point out that Toussaint's relations with his deceased companions arise from a tradition, perhaps particular to the Antilles, of casual communication with the dead."[139] Glissant thus gives notice that this tragic drama challenges a set of conventional Western notions about linear time, chronological history, the past as categorically separate from the present, only the visible as really real, and the dead as ontologically inaccessible. Yet, importantly, Glissant locates this practice of communication with the dead in Antillean society rather than in ancestral African traditions of divination. He associates this untimely capacity with the New World history of Atlantic slavery and plantation society; it developed within the abyss of Western modernity. At the very outset Glissant posits a political view of history and a historical view of haunting that presupposes even as it produces *a prophetic vision of the past*.

In both form and content *Monsieur Toussaint* is as much about a painful sense of time as it is a retelling of the Haitian Revolution. The play continually tacks between the present in which Toussaint interacts with his prison minders, a present in which he engages in agonistic dialogue with Caribbean and French specters, his memories of past events, and scenes in which those events are literally restaged. These different nows continually mix with and intrude into one other.

The haunting interlocutors include long departed predecessors including a Voudon priestess, the legendary maroon leader Mackandal, the Black revolutionary general Delgrès, Toussaint's former master, and a rebel leader named Macaïa. They also include living contemporaries who are still participating in the Saint-Domingue revolution. Among these are Suzanne-Simone (Toussaint's wife), Étienne Laveaux (the French governor who supported his rise to power), Jonathas Granville (his mulatto secretary), Jean-Jacques Dessalines and Henri Christophe (generals in his revolutionary army), André Rigaud (his southern rival), a French general, and white planters. From one angle, Black critics challenge Toussaint's loyalty and integrity. From another, his memory is mocked by French specters who praise Toussaint for being exactly what the others accuse him of: egotistical, power hungry, compliant, and a potential collaborator in European attempts to re-subjugate the Antilles. Throughout the play, Toussaint attempts to account for his choices and actions during the revolutionary struggle by responding to and arguing with these revenants.

In the opening act we witness a painful exchange between Toussaint and his spectral wife. She invites him to recall their happy past together. He replies: "I can no longer hear you, I do not know where you dwell now."[140] Her voice and image are supplanted by the other spirits who come to hold him to account. He declaims, "I see the dead. Piled up, burned, drowned . . . I see this choice: on the right, terror, on the left, fate. There are too many dead coming to see me every evening, crying 'Toussaint, Toussaint, what have you built on our graves?' I say to them 'my friends, I want to build freedom.'"[141] Much of the play's dialogue revolves around whether he should have done things differently and whether things could have turned out otherwise.

In one sense, Glissant has Toussaint respond to the interpretations by C. L. R. James (he lost touch with and failed to communicate with the masses) and Aimé Césaire (he sacrificed himself for the revolutionary future).[142] But this Toussaint is more concerned with the judgment of his Antillean prede-cessors than with his reputation among future historians. His radical ances-tors and revolutionary peers criticize him for betraying the people, pursuing his own personal power and glory, creating an authoritarian state, executing Moyse (a loyal Black general who was Toussaint's nephew), reinstituting com-pulsory plantation labor, and collaborating with white planters and European powers. In turn, Toussaint pleads that he was only ever motivated by his love of the people, a commitment to freedom, and the need to protect the revolution under tragically impossible conditions. He insists, as Césaire later argued, that he sacrificed himself so that his field generals could be victorious. As he explains to the spirit of Granville,

> Dessalines . . . needs me. I must recognize his treachery so that his treachery can become fidelity. I must fall again, and he must forget me again, so that my defeat can illuminate his victory . . . just when we put our complete trust in each other, I hide from you my most import-ant strategy. It is because it is my ultimate tactic, Monsieur Secretary. It is so deeply rooted in my heart that I cannot reveal it . . . my country needs me to be absent.[143]

At another point Toussaint compares his choice to sacrifice himself for the greater good to that of Delgrès who had chosen mass-suicide over re-enslavement. "Colonel Delgrès, you think it is a long way from your Matouba to my prison? That I was free to choose another fate? That I was worthy of another death, a powder more glorious than this dust-like snow in which I will perish slowly, wretchedly?"[144]

Glissant places Toussaint in a peculiar relation to these revenants. They question his actions and challenge his legacy, but they do not demand a re-sponse from him. On the contrary, they suggest, perhaps sarcastically, that what is done is done and he will always be remembered as a great leader. They beseech him to stop tormenting himself and surrender to a peaceful death. Even as they convey their belief that he betrayed their earlier freedom struggles, they invite him to join them as ancestral "gods."

MACKANDAL: Look. Here comes the night, we are rising into the
night. Come with us. I have walked into the future to meet you.
Why all these dates, different accounts, reasons? Let them lie sleeping on the side of the road.

TOUSSAINT: At last, at last. I will give you proof my cause is just.
I will say how I will govern. I will be reunited with my wife and
children.

MAMAN DIO: We beg of you. Let your story lie sleeping in the fire
and chaos. Beware of the word that shed light on what was hidden! . . . Come, we can take you with us: Do not tell your story out
loud, O Toussaint, for there are none so deaf as those who will not
hear!

TOUSSAINT: Leave me alone! I am starting my work all over. I will
cross the seas again in the other direction.

MAMAN DIO: But your task of weeding is completed, your field has
been tilled. Warrior Ogoun has gone far away from you—ever since
you began to give commands as governor, and no longer like a
brother among brothers.[145]

Despite these calls for him to stop pleading his case and join the ranks of the
departed, Toussaint refuses to be silent, surrender, die, or even allow himself
to be sanctified before he settles accounts with these judgmental specters. He
understands that if he simply wanted to liberate himself from his anguished
conscience and these tormenting revenants, he could easily steal the keys of
the sleeping guard and attempt to escape which would compel his captors to
kill him. But he declares, "I will not take the keys. No. I do not wish to die
without hearing it all."[146]

Because Toussaint feels answerable to these revenants, he first needs to
hear the case against him and hold himself to account. The specters comply
because their own ability to rest in peace depends on Toussaint letting go and
joining them. Only then would the dead be able to bury the dead. Delgrès,
speaking for the spirits who close in on Toussaint, asks: "Who therefore, O
Toussaint, will lay us in our final resting place?"[147] In a mocking tone, Toussaint replies,

The dead ask for help. . . . After giving life to the living, I must thrust
the dead back into their death! What do you expect from this circle
in which suddenly I am the center? When I galloped on horseback
through explosions and volleys of gunfire, were you there to save me?
When I was in command, when victory was mine, did you enlighten
my mind? . . . Do not take another step forward, do not move away

from your realm, or . . . you will endlessly whirl in the furthest reaches of hell that you should never have left . . .[148]

The living and dead are existentially entangled. Their relation is at once antagonistic and intimate. Each threatens and requires the other.

When Toussaint refuses to die quietly, these haunting specters begin to prosecute their case against his dictatorial rule. As Maman Dio reminds him, "We told you: Take care! . . . Let your people get used to the land, be patient, don't go and put a new yoke around their necks."[149] In response, Toussaint oscillates between guilty defensiveness and righteous defiance. He declares, "The dead are forever courting the living. . . . None has managed to defeat Toussaint—you will not be the first to change this! From the outset, it has always been death or victory for me."[150] But the number of challenging specters multiply, their questions are relentless, and the process is exhausting. "For my companions have not finished with their reproaches. They will have me descend to the bottom of the hill from which there is no return. And I, in all this upheaval you bring me, without knowing yesterday from tomorrow, I press on."[151] It is as if his dialogue with the dead—this confrontation with his conscience, predecessors, and legacy—is no less difficult than either the revolutionary struggle or his current imprisonment.

Woven through these spectral dialogues are Toussaint's immediate exchanges with his actual European captors. He also pleads his case to them (and by association, to Napoleon, the republic, and the French people). But his white prison guards are government functionaries and menial workers. They either have no stake in the issues being debated or simply regard Toussaint, whom they watch raving at unseen interlocutors, as a delusional and dying madman. Resentful of his great reputation and contemptuous of his pride, they also taunt him with racist insults, beseeching him to hurry up and die.

Through the play, Toussaint maintains that he had to make unavoidable pragmatic choices in order to protect the revolution and preserve the freedom of the people. He enforced harsh discipline against his own troops and required freed slaves to labor on plantations. He promulgated a constitution under which he would be Governor for Life. He made necessary compromises with white planters and foreign governments. Without these acts, Toussaint insists, there would have been no food, no army, and no government "to defend the freedom of all."[152] In response, the rebel maroon Macaïa, scoffs, "An army to defend Toussaint's rights."[153] In a similar spirit, Moyse (pace James) accuses Toussaint of allowing political abstractions to lead him to lose touch with the toiling people and become enchanted by his own power:

You say, "the people" with your republican highmindedness; I see
only those who weed, cut, and bundle sugarcane. . . . The Republic
designated us general and governor. Why, why? There was a beguil-
ing mirror in our officer's gold braid, we got lost in it. You say, "the
people," I shout in reply, "the wretched ones."[154]

Toussaint's spectral comrades do not accept his revolutionary pragmatism.
They condemn him for slipping into what would become a familiar postcolonial predicament whereby new elites subject the people in whose name
freedom was fought to the old forms of capitalist and statist domination in the
service of territorial sovereignty and national security. They implicitly contrast his regime of formal freedom (the abolition of slavery, legal equality for
all, and territorial sovereignty) with a more substantive form of popular self-
management and social equality.

Toussaint pleads that he did not only act defensively and pragmatically.
He reminds his inquisitors that he had always pursued a broader vision of
translocal solidarity and universal brotherhood. He declares, "Let us construct
a country, not a walled-in enclave."[155] In other words, while marronage may
have embodied a form of radical autonomy under a regime of plantation slavery, it could not provide an adequate model for the kind of society (or world)
that the Saint-Domingue revolution hoped to create.[156] Toussaint insists on
an expansive vision of political community: "Someday men will know one
another, they will weep for the same sorrows! No one alive has a monopoly on
suffering; martyrs are scattered throughout the earth."[157] In response, Macaïa
accuses him of being manipulated by European whites whose conception of
universal humanity he uncritically accepts: "They plant in your humanity the
tree of their inhumane domination. Give in to their idea of generosity and
they will use it to crush you."[158] But Toussaint holds firm: "I cry out for human
brotherhood. May it soon fill the earth. Lord, pardon me for my wrongdoings,
for I was only fighting for my people."[159] Toussaint thereby maintains that his
vision of human brotherhood may have been utopian, but was not simply a
function of naïveté, hypocrisy, or opportunism.

Dessalines accuses Toussaint of protecting white planters and collaborating
with the French consuls who were planning to re-enslave Saint-Domingue
Blacks. He suggests that Toussaint is blinded by their flattery and cannot recognize their real intention. Insisting that France will never agree to "equality
for everyone," he warns Toussaint not to "be taken in by their words" and believes that Blacks should "only rely on [their] own strength."[160] But Toussaint
maintains his internationalist vision: "An army, a fleet, Dessalines! We will set
free our brothers in Africa. If only the Revolution had triumphed in France!

For Robespierre would have helped us. Think on that. Africa freed and Saint-Domingue free of danger!"[161] Here is a moment of concrete utopianism as Glissant through Toussaint conjures the prospect of an alliance between insurgent slaves and revolutionary republicans that might have led to a different republic, a different Saint-Domingue, and a different postimperial world.

This unrealized possibility is mirrored in the final scenes between Toussaint and his prison guard Manuel, a humble peasant-soldier of Italian descent who wears "a mix of peasant and military clothing, including clogs."[162] Manuel discovers that guarding Toussaint is an easy job. The prisoner refuses to eat, seems to be only concerned with having the opportunity to explain himself to Bonaparte, and spends the nights talking incoherently to himself. Manuel and Captain Langles, his superior and second in command at the Fort de Joux prison, spend much of their time drunk on rum discussing this prisoner and their predicament. Langles is filled with petit bourgeois resentment. He believes he was "born for great deeds" that he was never allowed to accomplish. And here an imprisoned former slave has already made his mark on history and speaks of his relation to Bonaparte. Langles complains about having been overlooked for the expedition to invade Saint-Domingue, which he compares in greatness to Bonaparte's Egyptian campaign. He calls Manuel a "bum," an "idiot" for not understanding the historic importance of these military undertakings. Careful not to contradict his angry, arrogant, and drunk superior, Manuel simply replies: "Excuse me, I am just a poor ignoramus."[163] This performatively self-deprecating statement calls to mind the kind of sly subversions that Glissant often identified among enslaved Blacks negotiating the broader white world. The subaltern Manuel understands that the system will never work in his favor.

Following the lead of his superiors, Manuel begins by derisively calling Toussaint "Domingue" and "Colonel."[164] But Manuel himself is also regularly belittled by Langles. Given that he had served as a soldier in the fight for Bonaparte's imperial republic, Manuel chafes at this disrespect. He remarks sarcastically: "I am a bum. . . . And I am no brain. Been wounded only four times. Not decorated, mind you. Just retirement in this nice little mountain tomb, keeping an eye on this Blackie general."[165] Here the humble prison guard has a flash of insight: He may have something in common with the Black prisoner with whom he is condemned to share the mountain tomb. By the play's final act, Manuel's sense of Toussaint, and perhaps himself, has shifted dramatically. After Bonaparte's envoy comes to strip General Toussaint of his French republican military insignia, Manuel is left alone with Toussaint, to whom he offers words of support. "I don't agree, that's all I have to say. I don't agree. Look, you make me think of the boys where I come from. I must admit they would take to their heels if they saw you, you bet, but they don't know about you."[166] Manuel comes to appreciate that guarding Toussaint has placed him in proximity to a great historical figure. He relates that the simple and suspicious people in the countryside where he grew up would have a difficult time understanding the significance of Toussaint.

When Manuel describes his native land, he and Toussaint discover that their lifeworlds may not be as different as metropolitan functionaries might suspect. Manuel recounts, "Everything is green and yellow at the same time. You shiver when you go out to check the traps. . . . Above the fields you see the mist. . . . On one side the poplars. . . . Look, at the crossing, there was the burial ground. . . . That is where the dead gather. Don't go there at night, Domingue, they come out and laugh behind you! You take off, eyes, shut, running. . . ."[167] Toussaint, now shorn of his military regalia, shocks Manuel by responding with immediate understanding. Without skipping a beat Toussaint adds, "And you climb up to the ridge and see the sea beating against the stand. . . . Your land speaks, your land sings, Manuel. I can hear it in your voice."[168] Toussaint then seamlessly shifts to speaking about his own country: "The cane is young, you lose your perspective, you are drowned in a tempest of branches, you raise your head, the sun is strong on your feet, you see it is midday. . . ."[169] Manuel is overcome: "I am happy. So happy! . . . He's a peasant, a real peasant, that's all I have to say. The words dance in his mouth once the boots have been changed for clogs."[170] At this point, Toussaint seems to lose the thread of their conversation. He speaks to Manuel about the dead on the other side of the wall who are preparing "his resting place."[171] Believing him to be delirious, Manuel replies, "Those people don't exist, Toussaint."[172] But he also promises to chase these spirits away from his new comrade. In turn, Toussaint shares a bit of untimely insight with Manuel: "Protect yourself from the dead, they are trickier than we are!"[173]

Glissant thus stages a moment of improbable solidarity between Toussaint and Manuel, former plantation slave and former European peasant, both nominally French, outsiders who did their best to join the republican struggle against the *ancien régime*. They each have a flash of recognition that the imperial war could be transformed into a civil war. Mirroring the revolutionary internationalist alliance that *might have been* between Toussaint and Robespierre, Antillean and French popular forces missed the opportunity to have joined forces against global capitalism, imperialism, militarism, bureaucracy, and elitism. They might have had the prophetic foresight to transform an apparent antagonism of cultural difference into a substantial struggle against hegemonic power. In other words, Glissant has Toussaint sketch a flickering vision of a worldwide politics of Relation.

Such an opening was foreclosed by converging forces in Paris, the Jura, and Saint-Domingue. Just after this concrete utopian possibility flickers, Toussaint sees Mackandal, the last spirit "left to keep [him] among the living."[174] He finally concedes: "Let me rest, wait a bit, the road is steep. Be patient while I get used to this final leave taking."[175] Langles rejoices at the prospect of Toussaint's imminent death. He mocks a barely conscious Toussaint, reminding him that regardless of the struggle's outcome, future history will condemn him to failure and disrepute:

> Your companions have discredited you and you are fated to vomit in your misfortune. . . . Men will erase you. . . . They will write: the victorious Saint-Domingue expedition. They will publish it in their books, they will write it in their encyclopedias. . . . They have the power to decide what is true and what is false! They will lock you up in a fort more terrible than Joux . . . official silence. Cure, beg, implore, the centuries will close in on you! Thus, you will die a thousand times over. We are masters at this game. They will forget you . . . they will shout to your children: "Toussaint, the loser from Saint-Domingue!" . . . And eventually, they will believe it themselves, that is the best of all.[176]

But Manuel protests (perhaps on behalf of his fellow global subaltern masses): "No one can erase the memory of a man who has been victorious."[177] Toussaint pays no attention. Again, he is more concerned with the judgment of past prophets than the interpretations of future historians.

By this time in the play, Toussaint has relived the entire revolutionary struggle, tried to settle accounts with the absent and the dead, and is ready to leave this world. "Come Mackandal, I await only your death in order to die."[178] As we saw, neither the living nor the dead can find peace without the other. Each requires and regrets the death of the other. Glissant figures Toussaint's death-after-struggle as a repetition of Mackandal's earlier death-after-struggle. In Glissant's drama the two deaths become entwined as a single event. As Toussaint expires, Mackandal conjures the image of a transgenerational spirit of rebellion. He relates how through the scrim of resistant laughter, he envisioned (prophesied) Toussaint's future appearance.

> No, you were not born when they made me climb that pyre at the end of the square. I could see the slaves all lined up. They were laughing, laughing. I had predicted that Mackandal could not die. They were laughing, my General, and you see, I was laughing too. The executioner shouted insults at me, not able to understand. I was gone in the midst of a thunderclap that drowned out my screams. That laughter

was stronger than the flames. And you were not yet born, but I saw you standing there as real as the officer who commanded the drum roll! The flames around you, standing beside me on the platform. Here is your army, the people. See Haiti with its ancient name, which beyond death has tied back together the vines of destiny.[179]

Mackandal's "destiny" may refer both to the independent Haitian state that would one day be realized and to the political predicaments that would haunt it.

Remembering the Future

At stake in Toussaint's untimely dialogues are pressing and vexing political questions. Did the slave uprising honor the maroon legacy of radical refusal and collective autonomy? Did Toussaint's Black republic honor the slave uprising's spirit of popular freedom? Would, could, should Dessalines extend or revise Toussaint's political orientation? Would national independence better realize or further betray the political tradition established by autonomist maroons and populist cultivators? What kind of arrangements could neutralize internal and external threats to revolutionary freedom and collective self-management? What kind of accommodations should be made with global capitalism, imperial geopolitics, the international order? Variants of these questions still had to be confronted in Glissant's postwar now. In 1961, the limits and possibilities of state sovereignty in a world order overdetermined by global capitalism, Western imperialism, and metropolitan cultural hegemony was an immediate concern for Antillean departments, the Haitian nation-state, and the rest of the Third World. Equally pressing were questions about global entanglement and neocolonial dependency, territorial versus popular sovereignty, and conflicts between metropolitan oriented elites and still disenfranchised masses.

One way that *Monsieur Toussaint* stages a prophetic vision of the past is by demonstrating how Haitian history presaged the global future. Another is by illuminating Caribbean (non)history through a poetic and clairvoyant rather than empiricist and realist way of apprehending the past (in relation to the present). In the play, Glissant conjures actual prophets who had envisioned and pursued emancipatory futures for the Antillean people. Insofar as Glissant calls forth their unrealized visions, he offers us yet another prophetic vision of the past. Glissant is less concerned with evaluating Toussaint's record than with exploring how what *might have been* could fuel political imagination and mediate political practice in the present.

Glissant's literary works enact the dialectic between past and future. They explore how a backward-looking clairvoyance may help actors reactivate struggles for possible futures envisioned by past prophets. Vital traces of these struggles and visions (futures past) may be discerned within their nonidentical now. In *Monsieur Toussaint* agonistic dialogue with revenants nourishes an internationalist vision of subaltern solidarity across supposedly incommensurable divisions. Likewise, *The Fourth Century* ends with Mycéa exhorting Mathieu to rediscover reality and undertake meaningful action nourished by Papa Longoué's revelation. Mathieu and Mycéa seek to transform individual revelation into collective consciousness, and tragic entanglements into a subversive synthesis. They will do so by carrying forward unrealized pasts as concrete utopian possibilities.

As a writer, Glissant himself attempts to perform just such an untimely operation. In these works, for example, he revisits world-historical turning points (1803 and 1945) in order to recognize and reckon with pasts that continue to haunt his own alienated present. He does so in the service of a concrete utopian vision of world-community grounded in a poetic politics of Relation. Wandering as the site of assembly! Glissant suggests that this practice, what I would call political anticipation, depends on a dialectic of everyday life and creative imagination: "What the artist expresses, reveals, and argues in his work, the people have not ceased to live in reality. The problem is that this collective life has been constrained by the process of consciousness; *the artist acquires a capacity to reactivate.*"[180]

I suggested that *Le Discours antillais* explores how Antillean nonhistory prefigured the global future, or haunted present, that Glissant actually inhabited. On the one hand, Glissant's now was characterized by mass displacement, dispossession, and alienation. On the other hand, it was characterized by forms of creolization, transversality, and wandering that created untold possibilities for nonidentitarian being and belonging (beyond genetic origins, pure lineages, and fixed borders). Borrowing from Benjamin, we might say that Glissant's now provided the right of entry into a chamber of the abyssal past that presaged the open totality of worldwide Relation. His book traces this tortuous path.

In its final section, "The Caribbean Future," Glissant offers a "poetic litany" that leads from "The lure of the Caribbean (the outer edge of space and time)" through "A people finding expression (the country coming together) / A politicized people (a country that acts)" to the prospect of another world which he figures as a transversal totality unconstrained by existing dogmas:

> and at the end of our rooted wanderings, the unrestrained will to
> propose for this collective action specific paths, woven from our reality
> and not falling out of the blue ideologically; and the no less firm

> resolve to resist being locked into the premeditated . . . dogma of those
> who do not focus on the cross-cultural contact between peoples; the
> ideal being a unified whole, a collective and creative daring, to which
> each one will contribute.[181]

This utopian vision of a new kind of differential unity composed of interweaving singularities is grounded in concrete reality and rooted wanderings. It requires and enables contingent practices (of cross-cultural contact) and creative daring. Most immediately, this is a figure of regional unity: "The notion of *antillanité*, or Caribbeanness, emerges from a reality that we will have to question, but also corresponds to a dream that we must clarify. . . . There is potential in this reality" which must be "grounded in collective affirmation, supported by the activism of the people."[182] In turn, the long-term Caribbean experience may nourish a political orientation that transcends conventional oppositions between local and global, particular and universal, cultural singularity and human solidarity. "When one rediscovers one's landscape, desire for the other country ceases to be a form of alienation."[183]

Glissant suggests that the experience of Antillean nonhistory, at once abyssal and transversal, "points to the future of this cross-cultural process; this is why it struggles to repossess the memory of its fragmented past."[184] Nonhistory may herald a new planetary politics that should not be confused with a generalizing universalism.[185] "This practice of cultural creolization is not part of some vague humanism, which makes it permissible for us to become one with the next person. It establishes a cross-cultural relationship, in an egalitarian and unprecedented way, between histories that we know today in the Caribbean are interrelated."[186] This is a vision of *concrete universality*. "The universe for the restless wanderer does not appear as a world limited by the concrete but as a passion for the universal anchored in the concrete."[187] Glissant insists that the "poetics" informing such "visions of the world" are "inseparable from the growth of a people, from their time for belonging and imagining."[188] They require an understanding of "similarities *that are not to be standardized*."[189]

In a different register, Glissant relates his concrete universal vision of a transversal totality to the internationalist task of "uniting of all those who struggle for independence."[190] He does not endorse a facile reconciliation between the nominally independent Third World and the neocolonial West. Rather, he envisions new forms of South-South solidarity that would abolish global hierarchies and institute a new epoch of real independence in which the ethic of Relation may be pursued on a worldwide scale. This is the perspective from which we should understand his lyrical invocation of "the world, in its exploded oneness" and his call (for Antilleans) "to *risk the Earth*, dare to explore its forbidden or misunderstood impulses. Establish in so doing our own dwelling place. The history of all peoples is the ultimate point of our imaginative unconscious."[191]

Glissant's reflections on Antillean nonhistory attend directly to the boomerang of history—the long legacy of blocked progress, persisting and repeating domination, and uncanny-untimely alienation that have characterized Black Atlantic lifeworlds. But like Ellison, Glissant also attends the social contradictions and temporal fissures that might allow for privileged insight, dialectical reversals, and transcendent possibilities. He refuses the fatalistic Left melancholy that has obstructed so much political imagination in our times.

Let me conclude by specifying the multiple meanings that I see to be condensed in Glissant's conception of a "prophetic vision of the past."

First, it signals the kind of creative, imaginative, and poetic relationship to the past that is required to grasp the uncanny-untimely character of (Antillean non)history. It rejects realist frameworks that cannot recognize immaterial specters, blurred tenses, and haunting repetition.

Second, it identifies systemic predicaments or unresolved structural contradictions that obstruct linear progress. Doing so allows critics to account for and to foresee how, under such conditions, despite intentional actions and historical contingencies, the structural situation will tend to reproduce itself again and again.

Third, it conveys Glissant's attempt to trace how aspects of the Antillean past crystallize, prefigure, and set in motion crucial aspects of the worldwide future.

The racism, imperialism, and capitalism of the Atlantic slave system wrought mass displacement and violent entanglement. They created conditions of creolization, wandering, and transversality. As a result, the Antilles were marked by "nonhistorical" disjunctures between place, people, culture, consciousness, and tradition. These conditions distinguished Black majority New World plantation societies from the rest of the world. But they also already expressed fundamental characteristics of the modern world order whose emergence they played a crucial role in propelling. Glissant's now continued to be a scene of mass displacement, violent entanglements, and ongoing creolization. A prophetic vision of the Caribbean past thus allows us to foresee contemporary forms of dispossession and domination. It reminds us that the future we now inhabit is still-again characterized by nonhistory, tormented chronologies, and a painful sense of time. The nonidentical character of past Antillean now provides prophetic clues for the kinds of disjointed temporality and untimely processes that continue to shape the globalized modern world.

Finally, a prophetic vision of the past identifies within an untimely now the traces and fragments of earlier visions and experiments that may fuel contemporary political praxis. It is a backward-looking clairvoyance that strains to glimpse missed opportunities, unrealized possibilities, and portents of what might have been. This is not only a matter of mourning losses or commemorating victories, but of pursuing the possible world anticipated by past prophets. From this perspective, Glissant prophesizes that, "staggered by the singular wisdom of creolization," the rest of the world may one day recognize the "hesitant clairvoyance" possessed by Antilleans regarding types of possible contact between peoples and cultures.[192]

PART III

Anticipating Futures

11

The World We Wish to See

Life is more than meat.

—W. E. B. DU BOIS

Poetry is not a luxury.

—AUDRE LORDE

I want the sole, the pure treasure
the one that endlessly generates all the others
. . .
I want a more brilliant sun and purer stars
I shake myself into a mobility of images
of neritic memories of suspended
possibles, of larva-tendencies
of obscure becomings

—AIMÉ CÉSAIRE

From Universal History to World Politics

Theodor Adorno maintained that by the mid–twentieth century, the triumph of instrumental rationality and the capitalist law of value had transformed "history into a single unfolding process" that established the "internally divided unity of a global society."[1] He used the term "negative universal history" to characterize this as a unified process with a worldwide character that was not progressive, if we understand progress as improving human welfare or expanding human freedom.[2] Negative universality does not index a smooth,

homogeneous, or linear process. Like Hegel, Adorno recognizes that historical universality is dialectically propelled by concrete particularities (conflict,
violence, and suffering). Contra Hegel, he insists that emancipatory reconciliation—between subject and object, humans and nature, individual and
society, or the course of historical development and human well-being—can
never be realized under modern capitalist conditions.

Adorno thus developed an immanent critique of Hegel whose dialectical
insights grasped something indispensable about capitalist modernity but in a
distorted form. Accordingly, Adorno warns, "Simply to erase universal history
from our thinking about history . . . would be to blind oneself to the course
of history."[3] But he also warns, "We would blind ourselves just as effectively
by doing the opposite . . . subsuming the facts of history into its overall course
(which is what I have shown Hegel to have done) without emphasizing the
non-identical side of history, since to do this confirms the course of history."[4]
Adorno concludes, "The task is both to construct *and* to deny universal."[5] In
other words, Hegel was not wrong to attempt to grasp history in relation to
universality, progress, reason, and freedom. But Adorno, in a Marxian spirit,
argues that modern conditions created a *negative* universality through which
the domination of nature has progressed, technical rationality has increased,
and formal freedom has veiled social subjugation. In contrast to this merely
quantitative progress, real universality, reason, and freedom could only be
possible in a radically different kind of society that did not sacrifice human
welfare to the imperative to produce value and accumulate capital.

This is the perspective from which Adorno reworks Hegel's formulation
about universality as "the identity of identity and nonidentity." Adorno characterizes negative universal history as "nonidentity of the identical and the
nonidentical."[6] This nonidentity is what allows for the possibility that existing
forms of social and natural domination, despite their systemic power, could
be overcome. It follows that a transformative vision or project should, through
immanent critique, attempt to identify an "objective possibility" for societal
transformation that may already dwell within or be emerging from existing
arrangements.[7] This dialectical orientation rejects the liberal view that counsels us to stand back or be patient while universal history can automatically
progress while human quality of life improves. But it also rejects both the critique (whether perspectivist or positivist) of universality as a mere ideological
mystification and the fatalist claim that things will never improve, regardless
of our actions. Adorno posits the objective possibility of a revolutionary rupture. But he pays little attention to the forms of collective action and practical
politics through which to realize such a break. He identifies universal history
as a contradictory unity. But he does not elaborate the concrete forms of (im-

perial) unevenness that characterize the negative universalism of the postwar global capitalism he purported to analyze.

While Adorno was delivering these lectures on negative universal history at the University of Frankfurt, Samir Amin was teaching and conducting research at the Institut Africain de Développement Économique et de Planification in Dakar, Senegal. He accepted this position after spending several years working to support the popular democratic socialist tendencies in Nasser's Egypt and Keïta's Mali in the era of decolonization. As we saw in Chapter 2, Amin's work demonstrated that global capitalism was irreducibly imperial. His structural analyses of polarization, uneven development, and accumulation on a world scale suggest that Left thinking cannot dispense with an understanding of worldwide processes of domination. His insights thus intersect with Adorno's understanding of negative universal history. But in contrast to his German Jewish counterpart, Amin elaborates a concrete utopian vision of a post-capitalist world which he links more directly to a practical program. As we saw, Amin joined a fierce critique of global processes to a bold and compelling call for a new internationalism of peoples—a Fifth International—through which to invent a polycentric, democratic, and socialist "world we wish to see." His program would link concrete situations and conjunctural strategies to political imagination and planetary vision. He conjured a "universalist" and "humanist alternative to worldwide apartheid" that would be grounded in the ongoing work of "organizing convergence while respecting diversity."

When Amin invokes "the world we wish to see," he is not only referring to the fact that global forms of domination require worldwide political responses. Nor is he only demanding that power be more equitably dispersed across the world's groups and regions. He is also making a qualitative claim about the *kind* of world he would like to see. He is anticipating a new *nomos* of the world, organized on an alternative socioeconomic basis that would require and enable a different planetary politics. The latter would be worldwide while nourishing concrete lifeworlds and protecting the autonomy of distinct political communities. Think here of the Zapatistas' declaration, "In the world we want many worlds to fit."[8]

In the phenomenological tradition, "world" signifies a concrete formation: a singular totality and meaningful whole, a social and ethical matrix through which particular ways of being, knowing, making, and relating are inherited and cultivated.[9] This conception of "world" resonates with Chakrabarty's History 2 and Asad's discursive and embodied traditions. Hannah Arendt politicized this phenomenological understanding of world in order to signify common matters of public concern. She revived a notion of the *polis* as a space of public action whose condition of possibility is a shared world of meaningful speech and practice. Irreducibly human, collective, and public, such a political world cannot be reduced to the utilitarian necessity of merely preserving life itself (e.g., biological survival, mastery of nature, material accumulation).

Arendt traces the modern process through which such utilitarian necessity shifted from being the condition of possibility for meaningful social worlds to being an end in itself, the very meaning of society. She regards this as a catastrophic process of "world alienation" propelled by instrumental reason, utilitarian ideology, the mathematization of human relations, and the triumph of vulgar materialism, individualism, and the nation-state. The result, in her view, was the boundless accumulation of capital by firms and of territory by imperial states. This accumulation was cause and consequence of the eclipse of the public, the political, and the domain of action by the private, the social, and the domain of labor.[10] In contrast, she offers an understanding of a shared, plural, and open world that simultaneously "relates and separates" people.[11] It neither presupposes nor produces abstract universality.[12] For Arendt, this kind of diverse common world creates the conditions of possibility of (democratic) politics, which she understands as an acting in concert; not a means to instrumental interests, but as an end in itself. But, as we saw in Chapter 2, Arendt also insists that provincial polities can never adequately ground real democracy or human freedom. She calls for a "sphere above nations" that does not yet exist.

How might a "world we wish to see" accommodate concrete lifeworlds, situated political communities, *and* the worldwide? How might such a world politics recognize a multiplicity of worlds and the internal heterogeneity of every world? These challenges are compounded when we also attend to the kind of translocal "worlds" that traverse singular lifeworlds but do not include all peoples on this planet.[13]

As we saw in his discussion of the "poetics of Relation," Glissant has paid special attention to this challenge of grasping "the world" as a differential unity. In his late writings, he makes a useful distinction between *mondialisation* and *mondialité*. The former refers to processes of capitalist globalization. Insofar as it entails both imposed standardization and the imperative to resemble the West, *mondialisation* extends the old generalizing universalism and forced assimilation of colonial conquest. In contrast, *mondialité*—globality as worldity or worldness—figures the world as plural and multifaceted. Glissant uses this term to refer simultaneously to the worldwide, the qualitative character of any world, the qualitative character of the whole world, and the worldwide character of any particular lifeworld. "In *mondialité* . . . we do not exclusively belong to 'fatherlands,' to 'nations,' and not at all to 'territories,' but henceforth to 'places' [lieux] . . . to geographies woven from materials and visions that we will have forged. And these 'places,' having become inescapable . . . enter into relation with all the places of the world."[14] *Mondalité* signals a "Relational" way "of thinking oneself, of thinking the world, of thinking oneself in the world."[15] It conveys a nonabstract understanding of globality that is firmly grounded in the concrete details of particular places. Conversely, it conveys an understanding of concrete places as inescapably inflected by innumerable other places, which exist through processes of perpetual change and exchange.

Glissant employs poetic-philosophical formulations to conjure this dynamic relation between the *monde* that always already inhabits every *lieu* and the innumerable, interconnected, and interdependent *lieux* upon which any conception of world must rest. This dialectic of *lieu* and *monde* informs several of Glissant's poetic formulations: "I write in the presence of all the languages of the world. They resonate through each other's echoes, obscurities, and silences."[16] "The poem produces its shocks [manifeste ses éclats] in all the languages of the world . . . in all directions . . . it extends the truth of a lived country to another . . . it unfolds from time to time [il roule de temps à temps]."[17] "One's own language and the faraway language interrogate each other (it is a cosmic intimacy)."[18] "A detail is not a fragment, it interpellates the totality."[19] "Live the *lieu*, speak the world . . . to live the world [is to] first feel your place, its fragilities, energies, intuitions, its power to change, to persist."[20]

This relational understanding of the inescapable and vivifying presence or echo of the world in each place and every place in the world is condensed in Glissant's provocative conception of *Tout-monde*: All World, One World, Whole World, Total World. Glissant's all or whole assembles without dissolving. It refers both to every single one and to the composite whole. It signals all the places and the fact that there can be no place that is not already a part of, mediated by, somehow bound to, the All or the whole composed of all the other places. *Tout-monde* emphasizes the internal differentiation, or nonidentity, of any world, including *the* whole world. This image-concept rejects both generalizing universalism (as practiced by dominant Western ways of knowing and figuring the world) and parochial particularism (as deployed in identitarian forms of culturalism, nationalism, and territorialism). Glissant regards these as two sides of the same colonial coin; he seeks to transcend the opposition between generalizing univeralism and parochial culturalism.

Like Amin's internationalism of peoples, Glissant's *Tout-monde* points to a planetary politics that would break the nexus of liberal internationalism and national statism that has underwritten the postwar *nomos* of the world. It would also point beyond the invidious alternative for poor countries, in our post–Cold War now, between nationalist retrenchment and neoliberal global-ization.[21] *Tout-monde* both recognizes the world as it actually is and anticipates the world Glissant wishes to see: a differential unity, open totality, or network of singularities in which wandering is the site of assembly. He is neither an idealist romantic mourning a past paradise nor an abstract utopian speculating idly about a prefect world. As with Relation and transversality, *mondalité* is rooted in Caribbean historical experience. His poetic-politics of *Tout-monde* is a form of revolutionary romanticism and concrete utopianism.

The World We Wish to See

Glissant's reflections on *mondalité* and *Tout-monde* point toward what we might call a New World politics of world and worlds.[22] It is no accident that some of the most creative attempts to envision the world against the grain of dominant scholarly frameworks have emerged from thinkers shaped by and grappling with conditions created by the Atlantic slave system which called for nonnormative conceptions of place, period, and identity. We may thus situate Glissant's orientation in a longer tradition of Black radical humanism.[23] It also has contemporary counterparts throughout the Black Atlantic.[24]

Paul Gilroy, for example, suggests that there is a perverse parallel between the racist "postcolonial melancholia" that grips contemporary Britain and the anti-racist "ethnic absolutism" that "makes the practice of substantive politics impossible . . . there seems to be no workable precedent for adopting a more generous and creative view of how human beings might communicate or act in concert across racial, ethnic, or civilizational divisions."[25] As a result, "much of what passes for radical and critical thought rests on the notion that the very aspiration toward translocal solidarity, community, and interconnection is tainted."[26] This, he believes, is why there are so few "projects capable of . . . a creative conjuring with the possibility of better worlds rather than embattled criticism of this comprehensively disenchanted one."[27] To this end, he suggests that everyday interactions across differences in the postcolonial metropolis are producing a new "demotic cosmopolitanism" that is "distinguished by some notable demands for hospitality, conviviality, tolerance, justice, and mutual care."[28] Such experiences foster "a novel sense of interdependence, simultane-ity, and mutuality in which the strategic and economic choices made by one group on our planet may be connected in a complex manner with the lives, hopes, and choices of others who may be far away."[29] On these bases, Gilroy calls for "the cultivation of cosmopolitan disloyalty" that entails "a new way of being at home in the world through an active hostility toward national solidar-ity, national culture, and their privileging over other, more open affiliations."[30]

Achille Mbembe elaborates a similar critique of what he regards as dominant modes of postcolonial African self-understanding—reductive Marxism, nationalism, and nativism—that tended to fetishize state power and hypostatize identity by racializing geography. The result is a "mad dream of a world without Others."[31] In contrast, he argues that Africa has always been characterized by a "circulation of worlds" rooted in a "history of itinerancy . . . mixing, blending, and superimposing."[32] Mbembe uses the term "Afropolitanism" to name this "cultural, historical, and aesthetic . . . awareness of the interweaving of here and there, the presence of the elsewhere in the here and vice versa."[33] Attention to this interweaving reveals "the impossibility of a world without others" and renders dubious "any project aimed at disentangling Africa from the West."[34] From this perspective, "the world is no longer perceived as a threat. On the contrary, it is imagined as a vast network of affinities."[35]

Like Glissant, Mbembe traces how a long history of violent encounters, rooted in racial slavery, colonial conquest, and postcolonial conflict, nourished this Afropolitan orientation to the world. And like his elder Martinican interlocutor, Mbembe suggests that this dehumanizing past heralded the global future that we now inhabit. The invidious logic of classification and associated practices of segregation, exclusion, and extermination developed by Europeans through the slave trade, on Caribbean plantations, and during African colonialism have now assumed a worldwide character. This is a process, which Mbembe variously calls the "the becoming Black of the world" or "the planetarization of apartheid" whereby the current "unification of the world as part of capitalism's limitless (albeit unequal) expansion . . . goes hand in hand with the reinvention of differences, a re-Balkanization of this same world and its division along a variety of lines of separation and disjunctive inclusions. These lines are at once internal to societies and states, and vertical, insofar as they reveal lines of division pertaining to planetary-scale domination."[36] Every region of the world, he argues, is now affected by this "society of enmity" or "necropolitics," however unevenly.[37]

Like Glissant and Gilroy, Mbembe is attentive to the possibility of dialectical reversals. He contends that these violent processes of global integration also create the conditions for a new planetary ethics and politics that would be based on the fact that "there is only one world" which "belongs to all of us, equally . . . even if our ways of living in it are not the same . . . this is not to deny the brutality and cynicism that still characterize the encounters between peoples and nations. It is simply to remind us of an immediate and unavoidable fact . . . the processes of mixing and interlacing cultures, peoples, and nations are irreversible.[38] Under such conditions, the task is "to foster the emergence of a thinking able to help consolidate a world-scale democratic politics" organized around "a relation of care" that begins with the fact of common vulnerability, unavoidable interdependence, and the need for reciprocity on every scale.[39]

Mbembe suggests that Black historical experience has nourished a long tradition of struggle and thinking oriented toward just such a demand. Ever since the slave trade reduced humans to merchandize, he argues, "the question of the world" has been "our question."[40] Beyond proclaiming difference *and* demanding the full rights of inclusion, he argues, Black freedom struggles have also offered a "message of joy" oriented to "the project of a world that is coming . . . whose destination is universal, a world freed from the burden of race, from resentment, and from the desire for vengeance that all racism calls into being."[41] This task requires a "critical thinking capable of nourishing lateral universalism" and "renewing transversal solidarities . . . that go beyond clan, race, and ethnic affiliations."[42] For "at bottom there is no world or place where we are totally "at home," masters of the premises. What is proper always arises at the same time as what is foreign. The foreign does not always come from elsewhere."[43]

This is the perspective from which Mbembe elaborates an "ethics of the passerby," a figure who does not return but always continues "his journey, going from one place to another . . . always at the periphery of his birthplace, yet not calling himself a 'refugee' or a 'migrant,' and less still a 'citizen' or a 'native.'"[44] Against identitarian ontologies, the "passerby" learns that "one can inhabit a place . . . only by allowing oneself to be inhabited by it," that "Passing from one place to another also means weaving with each [place] a twofold relation of solidarity and detachment."[45] This is a messy process that leads to conflict and misunderstanding; it requires endless translation. The (ethics of the) passerby demands and embodies the kind of subjectivity that would correspond to the kind of world that Mbembe, like Glissant and Gilroy, would like to see.

Mbembe relates this ethico-political "message of joy" to a longer tradition of Black Christianity that linked the struggle for Black emancipation to the prospect of human redemption.[46] This line of thinking reverberates with Cornel West's call for an "Afro-American Revolutionary Christianity" that would weave together the radical aspects of what he calls Black prophetic Christianity and the democratic aspects of progressive Marxism.[47] For West, the prophetic tradition "exemplifies a courage to hope in the face of undeniably desperate circumstances rooted in a love that refuses to lose contact with the humanity of others or one's self."[48] In terms that I would call concrete utopian, he explains, "To prophesy deliverance is not to call for some otherworldly paradise, but rather to generate enough faith, hope, and love to sustain the human possibility for more freedom."[49] West thus emphasizes the revolutionary power of love, rooted in experiences of Black suffering and vitality, to nourish a future-oriented politics through which not only Black emancipation, but a democratic world worthy of humanity might be realized. His attention to the relation between subjectivity and social justice resonates with Audre Lorde's contemporaneous ruminations on the politics of difference and the challenge of solidarity.

Lorde identifies a crucial political dilemma. "Without community there is no liberation. . . . But community must not mean shedding our differences, nor the pathetic pretense that these differences do not exist."[50] She relates that from the moment of their birth, Black women in the United States are targets of a "societal death wish" and are compelled to absorb unimaginable quantities of social hatred, "for our color, for our sex, for our effrontery in daring to presume we had any right to live."[51] In her telling, this experience often makes it difficult for these women to treat themselves and others with kindness. As a result, "connections among Black women are not automatic by virtue of our similarities, and the possibilities of genuine communication between us are not easily achieved."[52] She recognizes that "it would be ridiculous to believe that" forging such connections among individuals who have been subject to this kind of harm "is not lengthy and difficult."[53] But she also warns, "It is suicidal to believe it is not possible."[54] This possibility may draw upon "a tradition of closeness and mutual care and support" among Black women in ways that do not deny fundamental differences within the group.[55] For Lorde, the "interdependence of mutual (nondominant) differences" can generate "true visions" of the future, "new ways of being in the world," and "the courage and sustenance to act where there are no charters."[56]

Lorde embraces the legitimacy and even effectivity of anger as a response to anti-Black racism. But she also notes the political limitations of hatred, which she describes as "a death wish for the hated, not a life wish for anything else."[57] Her wish is to "fashion a world where all our sisters can grow, where our children can love, and where the power of touching and meeting another woman's difference and wonder will eventually transcend the need for destruction."[58] Through a long history of collective suffering, she notes, Black women have learned that "the power to kill is less than the power to create, for it produces an ending rather than the beginning of something new."[59] Lorde thus links an ethics of mutuality and interdependence, through which to cultivate new ways of being in the world, to the capacity to act, under conditions where there are no charters, in order to create a world where all can flourish.

These contemporary Black Atlantic visions of a world we wish to see have (post-)Marxist counterparts with whom they may be placed in productive dialogue. Michael Hardt and Antonio Negri, for example, envision a new "commonwealth" that could arise if the multitude of the poor overcome the empire of property worldwide. They shift the locus of revolutionary possibility from the proletariat to the poor, from identities to singularities, and from "being common" to "making the common."[60] In their account, contemporary capitalist globalization is creating the conditions of possibility of this "multitude"—a new political subject composed of a multiplicity of nonidentical, intersecting, and metamorphosing singularities.[61] This "democracy of the multitude," will require "intersectional analysis" that identifies "potential correspondences" and "translational processes" that create "articulation and parallelism" across different social spheres, political struggles, and geographical regions.[62] Making the common is neither a matter of reducing to the same nor a matter of reifying difference. It entails "a proliferation of differences" that "requires the destruction of all the institutions of the corruption of the common . . . such as the family, the corporation, and the nation."[63] From this perspective, Hardt and Negri describe revolution as a "monstrous, violent, and traumatic" process through which "existing identities will no longer serve as anchors."[64] Attentive to the intrinsic relation between revolutionary politics, new subjectivities, and different possible worlds, they declare, "You have to lose who you are to discover what you can become."[65]

"Making the common" also indexes the world they wish to see. Private property and imperial domination would be abolished so that all people everywhere may produce and enjoy the world's common wealth (material, intellectual, cultural, and spiritual). This would seed the ground for a new type of federal commonwealth that "is not oriented toward state sovereignty, but rather serves to articulate a wide variety of powers and mediate diverse political institutions with different and separate objectives . . . [and] an array of diverse territorial mediations."[66] This formation would "support life against misery" and establish "equality against hierarchy so that "everyone . . . will be able to participate equally in the collective management of society" through "something like a global citizenship" that would provide "to all both the means and the opportunity to participate equally in the government of global society."[67] Insofar as the aim is to minimize human misery, which they define as "the condition of being separated from what one can do, from what one can become," politics would seek to foster joy and happiness grounded in love and laughter.[68] How, they ask, "can we restore or reinvent such political conceptions of happiness, joy, and love for our world?"[69]

We do not have to agree with Hardt and Negri's categorical demand for the "abolition of identity" to accept their argument that making the common requires both forms of solidarity that may generate singularities and types of plastic singularity that may foster solidarities. Their orientation aligns with recent anarchist and autonomist Left thinking that emphasizes experimental and prefigurative practices.[70] It also resonates with contemporary attempts to theorize new forms of radical democracy that refuse the liberal premises of market and state. These include Jacques Rancière's radically egalitarian conception of the "part of no part"; Étienne Balibar's reflections on citizenship without community, transindividuality, and equaliberty; Miguel Abensour's "insurgent democracy"; Wendy Brown's attempt to reclaim the demos; and Sandro Mezzadro and Brett Neilson's "border struggles" over and for the common.[71] All of the above may be placed in fruitful dialogue with otherwise different Marxist attempts to envision forms of anti-capitalist struggle and sociopolitical association adequate to the current world-historical conjuncture. These include recent attempts to reactivate communism and radical internationalism.[72]

A Marxist thinker like David Harvey explicitly rejects horizontalist fantasies about changing the world without taking power and disagrees on fundamental points with Hardt and Negri.[73] Yet his writings about "spaces of hope," "dialectical utopianism," "the right to the city," and a "new urban commons" also recognize the potential power of a mass politics rooted in forms of everyday life that do not treat the proletariat, the party, or the state as first principles.[74] Despite his sober analysis of the aftermath of the 2008 financial crisis, he also notes, "Spaces have been opened up within which something radically different in terms of dominant social relations, ways of life, productive capacities and mental conceptions of the world can flourish."[75] He underscores that "all manner of experiments in social change in different places and at different geographic scales are both likely and potentially illuminating as ways to make (or not make) another world possible."[76]

In his reflections on another "possible communism," Harvey pays special attention to solidarity politics and political imagination. Contra class-essentialism, he writes, "The dream would be a grand alliance of all the deprived and the dispossessed everywhere."[77] He recognizes that an effective political force would need, like recent movements for a new urban commons demonstrate, to be constituted by a multiplicity of groups operating on many fronts with no privileged insight into necessary practices or guaranteed outcome. Recalling Marx and Engel's belief that communists are not simply party members but "all those who work incessantly to produce a different future to that which capitalism portends," Harvey suggests that "disparate political movements" may "begin to merge, transcending barriers of space and time," into a broad anticapitalist "Party of Indignation."[78]

Contra Marxist realism, Harvey notes, "Just because there is no political force [currently] capable of articulating, let alone mounting, such a program . . . is no reason to hold back on outlining alternatives."[79] Accordingly, he suggests that a postcapitalist world would be based on common property, respect of nature, democratic procedures, "labor processes organized by the direct producers, daily life as the free exploration of new kinds of social relations and living arrangements, mental conceptions that focus on self-realization in service to others and technological and organizational innovations oriented to the pursuit of the common good."[80] This is not a universal blueprint for the one true communist society. Harvey's sketch simply flows from his belief that "a global anti-capitalist movement is unlikely to emerge without some animating vision of what is to be done and why."[81] He declares, "Of course this is utopian! But so what! We cannot afford not to be."[82] Insofar as he insists on the dialectical relation, or "spiral" between alternative visions and oppositional movements, and between new mental conceptions and different institutional arrangements, Harvey practices a form of *concrete* utopianism. He invokes a "revolutionary humanism" that seeks to radicalize a tradition focused on "the liberation of human potentialities, capacities, and powers . . . the uninhibited flourishing of individuals . . . 'the opportunity to live a joyful and fulfilled life.'"[83] Neither optimistic nor pessimistic about this future possibility, Harvey simply notes, "There are . . . enough compelling contradictions within capital's domain to foster many grounds for hope."[84]

When read together, these intersecting Black critical and (post-)Marxist visions compose and disclose a future-oriented politics of world and worlds. They are quite different from and often in tension with each other. Certainly, analytic and political differences matter. But I have assembled them into a constellation for several reasons. First, most of this book has questioned recent critical theory from the standpoint of earlier Black thinkers and heterodox Marxists. But it is also important to identify and engage with contemporary heirs to these traditions who continue to embrace translocal solidarity, concrete utopianism, and a commitment to societal transformation and planetary politics. Second, I have constellated these interventions to enact the point I have made in earlier discussions of internationalism, translation, and solidarity: Even significant differences may serve as a starting point for the difficult, imperfect, and risky work of translation—discovering and inventing, through dialogue, possible parallels, correspondences, alignments, intersections, commonalities, and novelties. They should not be the source of disabling sectarian or identitarian roadblocks that would foreclose the constitution of popular forces capable of forging a world we wish to see. I am less interested, here, in evaluating these thinkers' substantive proposals than in underscoring that their otherwise different interventions point beyond the realism, presentism, and culturalism that I called into question above. Third, considering these thinkers together helps us to distill a politics of world and worlds that have the following features:

The given order is contradictory. Existing arrangements, however dire, may create conditions for dialectical reversals and transformative possibilities—new ways of being that might ground new ways of being-together.

These possibilities will only be realized through experimental practices or associations that traverse conventional boundaries between politics, ethics, and aesthetics. A poetic politics recognizes the transformative power of care, love, and joy which must be allowed to flourish in any world we would wish to see.

Vision and creation cannot be separated. Political transformation calls for a dialectic of imagination and action.

Effective political visions and experiments are situated, grounded in specific historical situations, inflected by singular ways of life. Yet they also recognize the nonidentical character of any community, place, or time. They entail practices of self-defamiliarization, dis-identification, and dis-association. They recognize affiliations across supposed differences and alterity within supposed identities in order to create new subjectivities, assay different identifications, and forge transversal alignments. (They work, in various ways to transform imperial wars into civil wars.)

Such a political orientation requires messy, difficult, and risky translations and articulations across various axes of putative difference— that may open possibilities for new alignments around previously obscured axes of political difference. They will be fueled by encounter, mixture, and invention. Through this process, existing singularities will be affirmed while new subjectivities are forged.

We share one world in relation to which there is no definitive outside. For singular worlds to flourish, new planetary arrangements—a different *nomos* of the world—must emerge. Conversely, worldwide justice, equity, and democracy can only be constructed on the ground of a multiplicity of worlds. A global political future worthy of humanity must find ways to conjugate singularity and solidarity, autonomy and interdependence, and self-management and planetary politics.

The pathway between a contradictory present and a desirable future may lead through (persisting, repeating, or haunting) pasts. The unrealized potentiality of still vital legacies, whose traces remain

available, may be recognized, reactivated, and reworked in and for
a given now.

The Black Atlantic experience, the tradition of Black critical reflections on it (which reverberates with parallel Marxian reflections on
social domination and human emancipation), and Black freedom
struggles are beacons for a politics of worlds and world. They offer
invaluable resources, precedents, frameworks, and leadership for
the work of anticipating the world we wish to see.

A Possible-Impossible World to Win

Thus far in this chapter, I have focused on recent thinkers who insist on the
dialectic of vision and action. We can also recognize this concrete utopian
nexus in recent movements that help us to see how targeted interventions
in specific historical situations cannot be separated from expansive visions of
the world we wish to see. Let me begin with the current U.S. prison abolition
movement. Black radical activist scholar Angela Davis notes that in "most
circles prison abolition is simply unthinkable and implausible. Prison abolitionists are dismissed as utopians and idealists whose ideas are at best unrealistic and impracticable, and at worst mystifying and foolish. . . . The prison is
considered so 'natural' that it is extremely hard to imagine life without it."[85]
But Davis suggests that precisely such reasoning, which has sustained mass
incarceration in the United States, is itself based on the mystifying assumption
that prisons actually resolve rather than exacerbate the social problems they
purport to address.[86]

Davis identifies the prison as one element of a larger assemblage of interests and actors—the prison industrial complex—that is itself embedded in a
broader set of economic, political, and ideological arrangements that sustain
the existing order and affects all Americans, however differently. Strategically,
this means that antiprison activism cannot only focus on "the prison system as
an isolated institution but must also be directed at all the social relations that
support the permanence of the prison."[87] Antiprison activism that does not
"address racism, male dominance, homophobia, class bias, and other structures of domination will not, in the final analysis lead to decarceration and
will not advance the goal of abolition."[88] Conversely, as long as this complex
persists, the goals of anti-racist, anti-capitalist, or feminist politics can never be
realized. From this perspective, "the antiprison movement [is] a vital means
of expanding the terrain on which the quest for democracy will unfold."[89]
Given the "relationship between global capitalism and the spread of U.S.-style
prisons throughout the world," this must also be an internationalist project.[90]

In short, prison abolitionism requires solidarity politics in the service of a vision of large-scale societal transformation that requires us to think otherwise. The current system of incarceration "has become so much a part of our lives that it requires a great feat of the imagination to envision life beyond the prison."[91] Activists must undertake the "ideological work" necessary to "create a new conceptual terrain for imagining alternatives to imprisonment."[92] Most immediately, this means challenging the mutually reinforcing relation between the criminalization of Blackness and the dehumanization of prisoners. More fundamentally, it requires us to imagine "an entirely different—and perhaps more egalitarian—system of justice" that is more focused on reparation than retribution.[93] Rather than "looking for prisonlike substitutes for the prison" the task is "to envision a continuum of alternatives to imprisonment—demilitarization of schools, revitalization of education at all levels, a health system that provided free physical and mental care to all, and a justice system based on reparation and reconciliation rather than retribution and vengeance."[94]

Just as we cannot abolish prisons without imagining a fundamentally different system of justice, the prospect of a different kind of justice compels us to imagine a radically different society. Abolitionism is not about closing prisons but about "the creation of new institutions that lay claim to the space now occupied by the prison" that "can eventually start to crowd out the prison" in "our social and psychic landscape."[95] This strategy of "crowding out" would eventually render the prison "obsolete." Such a transformation would require multiple constituencies struggling on various fronts for another possible world in and beyond the United States. Davis writes, "Identity, by itself, has never been an adequate criterion around which communities of struggle could be organized. . . . Communities are always political projects."[96] The task is not simply to unify preexisting racial or ethnic groups in ways that elide internal contradictions but to organize novel associations "around political goals."[97] She recognizes that prison abolition and societal transformation will depend on solidarity experiments that will foster new political subjectivities.

The movement's use of the uncompromising term "abolition" works on several levels. Most immediately, it challenges liberal attempts to reform prisons. Davis warns that such attempts to improve conditions in order to create "better" prisons, reinforces the commonsense idea that there are no alternatives to the prison as a social institution. The call to abolish the prison system also conjures the legacy of the nineteenth-century abolitionist movement. Davis reminds us that slavery was such a normal and natural feature of American society that it was impossible for most of its contemporaries to imagine a world in which it did not exist. Yet from one generation to another, slavery was made obsolete; the supposedly impossible was realized. Davis thus underscores that prison abolition today is no more impossible than the abolition of slavery was then. The rhetoric of abolition also works to situate the current movement within a legacy of earlier "more or less successful" antiracist freedom struggles.[98]

More specifically, "abolition" conjures the unrealized vision of what W. E. B. Du Bois called "abolition-democracy." He used this term to name an incipient coalition of free Blacks, Northern liberals, and Southern laborers for whom the abolition of slavery was, or could have been, tethered to a more expansive vision of a nonracist and anticapitalist democratic society that rejected the rule of "property and privilege."[99] According to this view, "the abolition of slavery . . . could be thoroughly accomplished" only if enslaved Blacks became economically self-sufficient, sufficiently educated, and fully enfranchised citizens. More radically, abolition-democracy questioned what Du Bois called the "American Assumption" that through hard work any laborer could become a successful capitalist. Abolition-democracy thus pointed toward "a dictatorship of labor . . . over capital and industry."[100] This future-oriented vision of real democracy within a transformed society would be grounded in political solidarities that traversed geographical regions, class positions, and racial identities. Du Bois writes, "Here for the first time there was established between the white and Black of this country a contact on terms of essential equality and mutual respect . . . in a thousand schools of the South after the war were brought together the most eager of the emancipated Blacks and that part of the North which believed in democracy."[101] As we saw above, this Reconstruction that *might have been* was foreclosed by a "dictatorship of property" based on a counterrevolutionary coalition of Northern capitalists, Southern planters, and poor whites who refused to recognize their common interest with free Blacks.[102] Prison abolitionism today explicitly conjures and claims this unrealized attempt to leverage the abolition of slavery into substantive freedom for U.S. Blacks and real democracy for the nation.[103]

In short, the prison abolition movement is a concrete utopian project for societal transformation that pursues the possible-impossible.[104] It traces a virtuous circle between a concrete demand, a project to transform society, and the capacity to envision another possible world. The same kind of orientation, whereby a concrete intervention presupposes and propels a (vision of a) radically different social order now characterizes the multiplicity of movements pushing municipal governments to defund police departments across the United States.[105] Like prison abolitionists, defund activists employ what seems like a negative position as the starting point for a constructive project. Their demands are often straightforward: Police forces must stop growing;

public funds sunk into bloated police budgets must be reclaimed for social investment in (racialized) communities that have been abandoned by the neo-liberal state; police must be removed from schools and prohibited from being first responders to situations related to mental health, homelessness, and substance abuse; and police brutality must cease and offending officers must be held politically and ethically accountable. Such demands are often envisioned as preliminary steps to abolishing the police altogether, *crowding them out* through an alternative set of arrangements that would create conditions for real public safety rooted in economic self-sufficiency and community self-determination. Defund activism raises fundamental questions about white supremacy as the very ground of U.S. society, about the racialization of crime and the criminalization of poverty and mental illness, and about social priorities, equity, and justice in this society.

The Black Lives Matter movement exemplifies this holistic approach to political imagination and social transformation. It began as a hashtag when in July 2013 a Florida jury declared George Zimmerman not guilty for the murder of Trayvon Martin. It emerged as an insurrectionary movement following the fatal shooting of Michael Brown in Ferguson, Missouri, in August 2014. In the wake of these and other unpunished killings of African American men and women at the hands of police and civilians, the Movement for Black Lives (M4BL) developed as a collective of Black organizations from across the country seeking to contest the systemic state violence and social neglect of African American communities.[106] This movement does not only identify links between state violence, political economy, and everyday racism. It suggests that in order to really embrace the seemingly straightforward insistence that "Black lives matter" we would need to forge a radically different social formation than the one that currently exists.

The M4BL's 2016 Platform—which was published as both an interactive website and a downloadable document, entitled "A Vision for Black Lives," available in English, Arabic, and Chinese—demonstrates that this is not a provincial, single-issue, identitarian movement.[107] It is organized around six basic demands: End the War on Black People, Reparations, Divest-Invest, Economic Justice, Community Control, and Political Power. Each of these sections is accompanied by a more specific demand, a description of the general problem, and an explanation of proposed solutions. The site offers additional downloadable flyers, posters, and policy briefs on the many specific issues addressed in the document. The program for action is based on a deep understanding that real change will have to be pursued on many fronts—intersecting policy domains, legislative initiatives, education campaigns, and direct action—through a broadly inclusive movement pursuing both short-

and long-term aims. It links concrete policy reforms that would address immediate suffering to an expansive vision of "a fundamentally different world" that does not "place profit over people and make it impossible for many of us to breathe." It is guided at every step by specific information, concrete proposals, and practical steps to be taken. At the same time, it announces itself as a "visionary agenda" formulated by "dreamers and doers . . . to forge a fierce, free and beautiful future together that we can only imagine into reality."

The M4BL agenda focuses on Black community self-determination. Yet it also recognizes that the kind of transformations envisioned cannot be achieved without solidarity politics. "We are a collective that centers and is rooted in Black communities, but we recognize we have a shared struggle with all oppressed people; collective liberation will be a product of all of our work." It envisions an activated Black community playing a leadership role in a broader struggle to create a more just society. "We have created this platform to articulate and support the ambitions and work of Black people. We also seek to intervene in the current political climate and assert a clear vision, particularly for those who claim to be our allies, of the world we want them to help us create." The platform consistently relates local concerns to broader processes, domestic African American issues to Black international struggles, and a program for Black liberation to one for human freedom more generally. The stated aim is "to move toward a world in which the full humanity and dignity of all people is recognized."[108]

In a similar spirit, but on a different scale, is the Atlantic-wide movement demanding reparations from Western governments for harms caused by the enslavement of Africans. Reparations activists seek recognition, accountability, and redistribution of resources. The latter were expropriated from enslaved people through centuries of unpaid labor. The value of this labor created the conditions for modern industrialization, the foundation of Western power and prosperity. The reparations movement also emphasizes the *aftermaths* of racial slavery and the legacies of Black social death. The deep social and psychic structures established by the Atlantic slave system have continued to authorize state violence, legal disenfranchisement, economic dispossession, and social stigmatism in the United States. These have consistently undermined Black material self-sufficiency and collective flourishing (e.g., depressed wages, expropriation of land, blocked home ownership, predatory lending, and mass incarceration). Uneven development that stretches back to the plantation system serving the global economy has had similar effects on Caribbean national states.[109]

But the reparations movement is not only concerned with economic redistribution. It emphasizes ongoing harm, intergenerational responsibility, and collective social repair. By doing so, the movement calls into question some of the basic assumptions of liberal democracy regarding injury, causality, responsibility, equity, and justice. A similar strategy animates the international movement to cancel the public debt of developing nations in the Global South. Prospects for popular democracy grounded in principles of socialist equity and collective self-management are foreclosed when a country must assume a crushing debt burden just to meet its population's basic human needs. This movement, which also employs the language of abolition and reparation, developed in parallel to the Third World Forum and alterglobalization movement. It did so in relation to a series of Global South debt crises and defaults as well as popular revolts against structural adjustment, austerity, and food insecurity. Through the 1990s, organizations including the Comité pour l'annulation de la dette du Tiers mondes (CADTM), Jubilee 2000, and Jubilee South created networks across Asia, Africa, Latin America, and Europe that made the case for the immediate, total, and unconditional cancellation of Third World public debts. They did so on the grounds that this debt was contracted under legally, politically, economically, and morally illegitimate terms.[110]

Activists challenge the legitimacy of sovereign debts contracted in support of dictatorial regimes during the Cold War period. Likewise, they challenge debts assumed in the neoliberal era when funds are loaned on the condition that debtor countries pursue antisocial Structural Adjustment policies or when creditors know that certain debts cannot possibly be repaid. These crushing financial obligations, often assumed by countries in order to meet their peoples' basic needs, compromise these states' sovereignty and fail to serve the interests of their populations who were not consulted about them. These countries were plunged into a debt trap that often compelled states to take out new loans to service the old. This public debt has become integral to a predatory global capitalism and new form of imperialism that systemically transfers the meager resources of poor countries to wealthy ones. The West, through institutions like the World Bank, International Monetary Foundation (IMF), and World Trade Organization (WTO), uses credit, debt, and trade as instruments of regulation that effectively subordinate the Global South. Critics point out that canceling these debts may ease mass social misery without threatening the global financial system (the sums are small in relation to the whole). Cancellation would also alert creditors that they will pay a financial price for extending illegitimate loans under impossible terms. From another angle, activists argue that after centuries of slavery, colonialism, and systemic pillage, it is the wealthy Western nations that owe an unpayable economic and moral debt to those of the Global South. The immediate and unconditional abolition of public debt would be a first step toward paying the reparations owed to them.

Some advocates of debt cancellation embrace a reformist position that promises temporary relief without challenging the existing capitalist system. But the CADTM International offers a holistic vision that challenges the very basis of neoliberal capitalism, uneven development, and contemporary imperialism. Pragmatically, the network's call to abolish the public debt of developing countries is tied to proposals for lending without usury and a redistribution of global wealth on more equitable terms. It proposes that future loans may only be contracted after democratic deliberation and then subject to popular oversight. It calls for a new global wealth tax to be levied on the wealthiest classes of all nations, a tax on all global currency transactions, the abolition of tax havens, and mandates that a minimum proportion of a nation's GDP must be spent on international development. This would enable poor nations to reclaim aspects of the commons that had been privatized and to pursue humane development policies oriented towards social justice, global equality, and environmental sustainability. On a different scale, the CADTM calls for abolishing the World Bank, IMF, and WTO; it demands that alternative global financial institutions be created under the rubric of regional economic and political zones that could pursue genuine development while mitigating the runaway production and consumption that is currently destroying the planet. These concrete demands are inseparable from a more capacious political vision.

The CADTM International's Political Charter announces that debt cancellation should be combined with "reparations and solidarity contributions" from the North in order "to work toward a world based on sovereignty, solidarity, and cooperation between peoples." Embracing an explicitly "internationalist approach," the network seeks "to build a broad-based movement" based on the belief "that the world's struggles for emancipation must converge" to "work toward equality, social justice, the conservation of nature, and peace" worldwide. Henceforth, it declares, "Legitimate public debt should fund a grand ecologist-feminist-socialist transition program."[111] The Charter recognizes that "both in the Northern and Southern hemispheres, debt is a mechanism used to transfer wealth created by workers and small producers to the benefit of capitalists" and "is used by lenders as an instrument of political and economic domination."[112] This position, combined with a critique of predatory ruling classes in Southern countries, thus opens onto a broader commitment to transversal anticapitalist solidarities worldwide.

The recent rise of private debt in the core capitalist states has also garnered much attention. Wolfgang Streeck traces the movement in Europe and the

United States since the late 1960s from the Keynesian "tax state," which was committed to providing all citizens with social welfare benefits, to the "debt state," which maintained these benefits in a period of declining growth and declining inflation through deficit spending, to the neoliberal "consolidation state," which has been defined by government austerity and an explosion of consumer debt. Through the latter, private citizens themselves were assigned responsibility for meeting rising housing, healthcare, and education costs in an era of wage stagnation, economic privatization, and financial deregulation. Streeck outlines a mutually reinforcing relationship between an austerity logic that values markets over people, the decrease in social investments, the declining power of labor, rising consumer debt, and the massive accumulation of capital in private hands.[113] Under such "fiscal consolidation" regimes, we witness "the drama of democratic states being turned into debt-collecting agencies on behalf of a global oligarchy of investors."[114] Such states

> institutionalize a political commitment and build a political capacity never to default on its debt, projecting an uncompromising determination to place its obligations to its creditors above all other obligations. It features a general configuration of political forces that makes spending increases difficult while making spending cuts, on everything except debt service, easy.[115]

Streeck regards the 2008 financial crisis and ensuing Great Recession as an overdetermined outcome of a process in which the power of capital worldwide triumphed over countervailing democratic forces.

We do not have to accept Streeck's claim that the 2008 crisis marked the eclipse of "democratic capitalism" (as if such a thing ever existed), to appreciate his attention to how finance capital (public and private debt, specifically) increasingly mediates the relation between state, society, and citizens. The crisis was precipitated by an overinflated housing market, propelled partly by predatory lending targeting Black communities in the United States. But it revealed the underlying contradictions of an economy increasingly dependent on speculative bubbles which also includes volatile markets in student, credit card, and automobile debt. These along with medical and probation debt have plunged millions of people into an inextricable trap that indentures their lives to debt servicing.

As the Great Recession devastated working people's life chances in both the West and the South, a series of Occupy, assembly, and antiausterity movements emerged worldwide. Reviving the legacy of the earlier alterglobalizaton revolts under new conditions, these movements have challenged the uncontested rule of capital at every scale. On a worldwide scale, capital has conscripted states to facilitate processes of accumulation by dispossessing the people and plundering the commons. Social wealth has been systemically transferred to ruling classes composing a new global oligarchy. Credit rating agencies have become more decisive than either sovereign states or existing international institutions in determining the life chances of much of the world's population. Even in the wealthiest countries, individual and collective futures are foreclosed by crushing debt obligations that endure across generations. Mass public outrage was stoked by the fact that after 2008, there was no accountability for the economic devastation caused by decades of parasitical speculation. Public funds were used to bail out banks whose often criminal executives were never prosecuted. Mortgage forgiveness was not extended to ordinary people whose houses were being repossessed in staggering numbers. The ensuing economic downturn was used to justify further austerity regarding jobs and government budgets for a range of social goods.

Occupy Wall Street (OWS) was a concrete utopian intervention that anticipated a world we wish to see. It dramatically enacted its social critique by re-claiming public space in ways that dramatized state violence. Peaceful gatherings were consistently targeted by militarized police forces. As importantly, Occupy initiatives practiced a prefigurative politics in which the means of struggle enacted its aims. Self-managing encampments were organized around principles of mutuality, reciprocity, and inclusion. Decisions were made through horizontal assemblies. Participants practiced, in order to cultivate and demonstrate the kind of political subjectivity that would correspond to a more democratic and just world. The OWS ethos and objective were crystallized in the rallying cry of "We Are the 99 Percent," through which the movement sought to trace transversal links among diverse groups who composed "the people" (or multitude) who could act as a self-determining subject of history to create a world organized around anti-capitalism and popular democracy.

However short-lived, OWS shaped public debate, mobilized a new generation of militants, and reminded an alienated populace to question that which we are told is impossible. It may take decades to fully appreciate that uprising's significance. It quickly fueled both a robust network of Mutual Aid organizations that mobilized in the wake of Hurricane Sandy and a burgeoning movement to cancel illegitimate private debts. Andrew Ross, a scholar directly involved in the latter, describes the contemporary U.S. as a "creditocracy," or society in which individuals must become indebted in order to meet "the basic requirements of life" such as housing, healthcare, and education.[116] He calls for "economic disobedience" (nonpayment) by ordinary people who have been thrust into unmanageable "debt traps" that undermine the very foundations of a democratic society.[117] Echoing the movement to cancel the public debt of developing countries, he writes, "Lending to borrowers who cannot repay is unscrupulous. . . . Extracting long-term profits from our short-term need to access subsistence resources or vital common goods . . . is usurious, antisocial conduct, to be condemned (or outlawed)."[118] More fundamentally, he invokes "the moral right to repudiate debt" as "the only way of rebuilding popular democracy."[119] For, "even if household debts were not intentionally imposed as political constraints, they unavoidably stifle our capacity to think freely, act conscientiously, and fulfill our democratic responsibilities."[120]

Mobilizing under the slogan "You Are Not a Loan," these antidebt movements are not only about securing relief for individuals.[121] The Debt Collective identifies itself as a "debtors' union fighting to cancel debts and defend millions of households" in order "to build a world where college is publicly funded, healthcare is universal, and housing guaranteed for all."[122] Strategically, they have organized a "debt strike" campaign through which masses of individuals refuse to pay their student loans in order to exert some leverage over the financial system. Strike Debt emphasizes the way debt both obstructs and enables the kind of solidarity politics that are imperative:

> Debt is a tie that binds the 99%. With stagnant wages, systemic un-
> employment, and public service cuts, we are forced to go into debt for
> the basic things in life—and thus surrender our futures to the banks.
> Debt is a major source of profit and power for Wall Street that works
> to keep us isolated, ashamed, and afraid . . . we are coming together
> to challenge this illegitimate system while imagining and creating al-
> ternatives. We want an economy in which our debts are to our friends,
> families, and communities—and not to the 1%.[123]

Like prison abolition, reparations for slavery, and public debt cancellation movements, these initiatives link a concrete demand to a holistic vision of a fundamentally different way of being (together). Like the CADTM, these movements reject liberal axioms about the moral obligation to repay one's debts regardless of their terms or the contexts in which they are assumed. They reject the logic of capital and rule of property upon which this antisocial and antidemocratic social order is founded. Such efforts will require and create a political subject that traverses conventional social divisions. An activated antidebt collective could link racialized communities (systematically targeted by predatory lenders and the prison industrial complex that are especially vulnerable to inextricable debt traps), the labor movement, precarious students, and a declining middle class afflicted by private debt in the North and those tyrannized by public debt across the Global South.

It is, of course, imperative to raise an aspect of "world" that I have not yet identified: the earth or planet as biosphere, the interdependent matrix of human (social) reproduction. In recent years, the breadth and intensity of climate change activism has accelerated in the UK, Europe, and North America. It has done so partly in relation to the mounting urgency of the unfolding global crisis as documented by the United Nation's Intergovernmental Panel on Climate Change (IPCC) in its 2018 Special Report on Global Warming.[124] Although it contained little new information, the report's dire analysis reverberated through the West as a last chance call to action. It confirmed the conviction among climate justice activists that the time for gradualism had passed. Groups like The Leap in Canada, the Sunrise movement in the United States, Extinction Rebellion in the United Kingdom, and DieM25 in Europe launched combinations of direct action and legislative campaigns calling for immediate, large-scale, and internationally coordinated action to halt the catastrophic effects of human-induced climate change on the earth and on the world's human population. Documents like the Leap Manifesto, the Green New Deal Resolution, the Three Demands Bill, and the European Green Deal, call variously for governments, guided by community mandates or citizens' assemblies, to act now to decarbonize our economies, societies, and ways of life.[125] These various initiatives offer an integrated analysis of the larger system of domination within which climate change is only one part. Each relates concrete policy proposals to a more expansive vision of the kind of world that such remediation efforts should contribute to building.

Radical climate justice activists insist that any program to "decarbonize, decommodify, decolonize, and democratize" global energy systems should be pursued through participatory mechanisms that empower ordinary people in local communities to make decisions about this transition.[126] These movements emphasize that such large-scale change must entail solidarity politics. Only a broad people's movement could possibly disrupt the organized power of capital, states, and commonsense ideology. It would require support from those workers who appear to have the most to lose in a transition to renewable energy systems and from those racialized, indigenous, and poor communities that are most devastated by climate change.

Although the climate crisis was primarily created by the world's wealthy consumers and nations, Naomi Klein underscores, "The impacts of those emissions are hurting the poorest first and worst, forcing growing numbers of people to move."[127] Any Green New Deal must therefore be oriented around broader demands for global justice, including "wealth redistribution, resource sharing, and reparations."[128] The alternative, Klein warns, will be a global "climate barbarism" with "the wealthy world . . . unleashing the toxic ideologies that rank the relative value of human lives in order to justify the monstrous discarding of huge swaths of humanity. And what starts as brutality at the border will most certainly infect societies as a whole."[129] She concludes that "a new form of democratic eco-socialism, with the humility to learn from Indigenous teachings about the duties to future generations and the interconnections of all life, appears to be humanity's best shot at collective survival."[130]

In short, the climate justice movement embraces solidarity politics because it recognizes that the forces currently destroying the earth cannot be separated from the imperatives of endless capital accumulation, the racialization of populations, imperial dispossession and geopolitical inequality, the reproduction of patriarchal arrangements, the de-democratization of societies, and the proliferation of rightless migrants and refugees. Climate change is entwined with a broad process of "world alienation" that circumscribes life chances and obstructs human flourishing for ever greater proportions of the world's population. Because these forces and their differential effects are global, any effective response to them must operate at every possible scale. Climate justice thus requires a new "internationalism of peoples" that seeks to construct a world in which all groups have the opportunity to live a sustainable good life on a shared planet. It will require fundamentally different ways of organizing economies, social relations, and political communities.

The IPCC report ties emission reduction efforts to sustainable development and poverty reduction efforts, especially in the Global South. Activists' proposals emphasize how climate change is entangled with intersecting forces of social domination and human devastation. In order to overcome these, they insist, the one-sided destructive relation between humans and nature must be abolished. In the world they wish to see, caring for the planet in sustainable ways is inseparable from creating social arrangements that provide adequate material necessities to all people, that do not create hierarchical divisions among groups, and that institutionalize democratic processes through which everyone may participate equally in the decisions about the kind of world they want to create and the kind of lives they want to have an opportunity to enjoy.

The authors of A Planet to Win declare, "There is enough on our Earth for people everywhere to have what they need to live well" which requires "freedom from want."[131] But "people are also entitled to freedom to want . . . to enjoy life, to be creative, to produce and delight in communal luxuries . . . to love those we love. . . . The freedom to live a good life means enjoying the wonders of knowledge, leisure, and adventure. . . . *The point of a radical Green New Deal is to build . . . a colorful democracy for all.*"[132] In similar terms, Klein argues that confronting climate change will require a "people's platform" that moves beyond "no" coalitions to create a broad "yes" coalition through which to "dream together about the world we actually want."[133] That world, as elaborated in the Leap Manifesto, will require "a shift from a system based on endless taking—from the earth and from one another—to a culture based on caretaking" and that "all of our relationships have to be grounded in those same principles of reciprocity and care."[134]

The orientation traced by these programmatic visions was powerfully enacted in the 2016 protests against the Dakota Access Pipeline in Standing Rock, North Dakota. A people's coalition, led by indigenous "water protectors," resisted the construction of oil infrastructure across the Sioux Reservation on the grounds that an oil spill there would endanger the Lakota community's water supply and sacred land. In one of the most remarkable recent experiments in solidarity politics, frontline activists established semi-permanent camps to halt pipeline construction and resist the forces of state violence then deployed against them. Indigenous and non-indigenous people came together as a multiracial collective that included people from across the socioeconomic spectrum with varying class and cultural backgrounds, skill sets, and political ideologies. They self-organized around indigenous leaders who reactivated a long tradition of resistance to colonial dispossession by the U.S. state.

As the indigenous scholar-activist Nick Estes writes, "The protesters called themselves Water Protectors because they weren't simply against a pipeline: they also stood for something greater: the continuation of life on a planet ravaged by capitalism. This reflected the Lakota and Dakota philosophy of Mitakuye Oyasin, meaning 'all my relation' or 'we are all related.'"[135] The resistance movement was at once opposed to natural destruction, neoliberal capitalism, settler colonialism, and an authoritarian state. Everyday life in the camps, whose population is estimated to have reached 15,000, modeled an alternative way of being based on non-commodified sociality, collective self-management, and cross-group solidarities. Such practices were invented by this conjunctural multitude in a specific situation. But they were also nourished by indigenous ways of life and a long Lakota tradition of anti-colonial and anti-capitalist resistance. Estes traces the latter back to nineteenth-century struggles against imperial dispossession to later militant land occupations in the 1970s. His claims, on this basis, that "the past is prophecy" and that "our history is the future" resonate with Glissant's "prophetic vision of the past."

This untimely orientation to political mobilization is also present in Green New Deal proposals that strategically conjure the legacy of the 1930s New Deal. The point is not that the racist Roosevelt program should be emulated. It is to remind us that massive government spending and societal mobilization for the public good in a time of crisis is both necessary and possible. To recall such earlier instances of the possible-impossible actually occurring reminds us that political choices do not have to align with market logics. Seemingly unimaginable reorientations may be realized relatively quickly. Diverse coalitions may be assembled around a new ideological consensus. Popular hegemonies may constrain capital and direct state action. When the existing pathways will certainly lead to mass suffering, radical intervention is the most rational and realistic alternative while inaction reveals itself as the naïvely idealistic position. Proposals for a Green New Deal regard the present as if from a distant future in order to identify what *will have been* missed opportunities and unrealized possibilities.[136]

These otherwise different movements illuminate, from the opposite direction, a political orientation that resonates with the theoretical visions I discussed above. They identify concrete issues that are entwined within much larger knots of social ills that obstruct individual and collective flourishing for masses of people. If the thread of prisons, policing, debt, or fossil fuel consumption were to be untangled from this knot, the whole social fabric may begin to unravel in ways that might allow openings for a world we wish to see. Said differently, these movements proceed from practical, often modest demands around specific matters that could only be properly realized under a radically different set of social arrangements. They anticipate a world in which the seemingly impossible would be an everyday affair. Such interventions identify possibilities immanent within a contradictory now. They are propelled by a circular relationship between action and vision, intervention and imagination. For these experimental undertakings, prefigurative means are integral to realizing emancipatory ends. Politics, ethics, and aesthetics are productively entwined. New social arrangements require and produce new historical subjects and political subjectivities. If such concrete utopian projects are oriented toward the world they wish to see, such a world would be both situated and planetary. These projects recognize that societal transformation will entail both solidarity politics within a social formation and something like an internationalism of peoples across social formations. We may understand them as pursuing a politics of *Tout-monde* such that situated places and a nonidentical world ground one another. This orientation to planetary politics rejects abstract universalism. It envisions new forms of differential unity, or concrete universalism, at every possible scale. Like the Black critical and heterodox Marxist traditions upon which they often draw, these movements point beyond the impasses of Left realism, presentism, and culturalism. Rooted in concrete historical experiences and singular lifeworlds, they also express an antiprovincial spirit that displaces conventional distinctions between *here* and *there, now* and *then, us* and *them.*

I have discussed multiple visions and movements to make clear that I am offering neither a dogmatic program of how struggles should proceed nor a fixed blueprint of the society that must be created. But in contrast to certain currents of recent critical theory, we should not allow the fact that the future is and must be uncertain to foreclose a politics of the world we wish to see. We might usefully recall Fernando Coronil's salutary insight that "the Left has no map, but it has a compass."[137] We should not allow any given set of conjunctural conditions, however grim, no matter how infinitesimal the prospects for structural transformation might be, to authorize a pessimist metaphysics or antipolitical fatalism that forecloses a politics of the possible-impossible. We should not allow the real risk of harm that is embedded in every attempt to translate, ally, and organize across differences to foreclose a planetary politics grounded in a new internationalism of peoples.

A *possible-impossible internationalism transforms the imperial war into a civil war. Uncanny and untimely optics which make the strange familiar and the familiar strange are indispensable for unthinking inherited assumptions about here, now, and us. Concrete utopianism regards the given world as it would appear from the standpoint of secular redemption (i.e., postcapitalist revolution). It anticipates—calls for and calls forth—a world we wish to see, so that every single one may wander without becoming lost. Wandering as the site of assembly!*

Acknowledgments

My deepest debt of gratitude is to Joan Wallach Scott, who encouraged me to stay focused on weaving these interventions together into a coherent book. She offered the invaluable gifts of her time, insight, and spirit by reading multiple drafts of the manuscript and providing detailed suggestions about strategies for revision. Special thanks are also due to Souleymane Bachir Diagne, one of the readers for the press, whose thoughtful comments also helped to guide my revisions.

My thinking about the concerns of this book has been nourished by years of intensive discussion with Anthony Alessandrini, Susan Buck-Morss, Ayça Çubukçu, Laurent Du Bois, Kaiama Glover, Joan Wallach Scott, Marina Sitrin, Massimiliano Tomba, and Jini Kim Watson. Temporality and solidarity were also constant reference points for years of discussion within the Committee for Globalization and Social Change, which I have been privileged to direct at the CUNY Graduate Center. I have benefited greatly from feedback on parts of this work and generally learned a great deal about these issues from the members of this group. In addition to some of those mentioned above, I would like to thank other participants in these discussions, including Nadia Abu El Haj, Siraj Ahmed, Fadi Bardawil, Herman Bennett, Claire Bishop, Grace Davie, Mara de Gennaro, Zahid Chaudhary, Colette Daiute, David Joselit, Mandana Limbert, Uday Singh Mehta, Jesse Schwartz, Julie Skurski, and Mischa Suter.

I would also like to thank a number of exceptional (former) graduate students at the GC who engaged with and offered feedback on aspects of this book, including Ana Flávia Bádue, Mark Drury, Scott Erich, Francisco Fortuno-Bernier, Jessie Fredlund, Thayer Hastings, Marty Kirschner, Romm

Lewkowicz, Linsey Ly, Sheehan Moore, Zeynep Oguz, Chinonye Alma Otu-onye, Debborah Philip, Nandini Ramachandran, Amir Reicher, Alexandra Schindler, China Sajadian, Amir Reicher, Cihan Tekay, and Alex Werner.

Over the years of its composition, I had valuable discussions with many generous interlocutors who stoked my imagination, offered insightful feedback, and/or offered me opportunities to present aspects of this work. They include: Sadia Abbas, Tanya Agathocleous, Valentina Antoniol, Emily Apter, Gavin Arnall, Caroline Arni, Étienne Balibar, Banu Bargu, Mauro Farnesi Camellone, Faisal Devji, Kate Derickson, Behrooz Ghamari Tabrizi, Vinay Gidwani, Alex Gil, Ruth Wilson Gilmore, Michel Giraud, Tao Leigh Goffe, Christian Lentz, Rachel Greenspan, Harry Harootunian, David Harvey, John Haskell, Dagmar Herzog, Deborah Jenson, Kelly Baker Josephs, R. A. Judy, Andreas Kalyvas, Ethan Kleinberg, Julie Livingston, Syliane Larcher, Jacques Lezra, Nancy Luxon, Vittorio Morfino, Robert Nichols, Adi Ophir, Charlie Piot, Kristin Ross, Naomi Schiller, David Gary Shaw, Miranda Spieler, and Ann Stoler. I am sure there are others whom I have forgotten to mention to whom I offer sincere apologies for the unwitting oversight.

I was privileged to have had the opportunity to present aspects of this work in a number of productive fora. These include: the Conference on Plural Temporalities and Anachronisms: The Marxist Tradition Against the Grain, Department of Political Science, University of Padua, Italy; Conference on Austerity, Authoritarianism, and Borders in the Age of COVID-19, CCRP Rutgers, Newark; Decolonization in the Global South Working Group, University of North Carolina, Chapel Hill and Duke University; Workshop on Sovereignty, Space, and Aesthetics: Greece and Europe in the World, hosted by Simon Fraser University and Rutgers University in Lesvos, Greece; The Caribbean Digitial V, The University of the West Indies, Saint Augustine, Trinidad and Tobago; conference on Forms of Pluralism and Democratic Constitutionalism, Sciences Politiques and Reid Hall, Paris, France; Seminar on the Theory and Practice of History, Wesleyan University Humanities Center; European Politics and History Workshop, Columbia University; Graduate School of History, University of Basel, Switzerland; Interdisciplinary Center for the Study of Global Change, University of Minnesota, Minneapolis; International and Comparative Law Center, Mississippi College School of Law; Political Concepts conferences at New York University, Brown University, and CUNY Graduate. I am grateful for these invitations, the hospitality of the organizers, and the engagement of participants, most of whose names, unfortunately, I did not know.

I owe special thanks to Jeff Maskovsky, who, as chair of the PhD Program in Anthropology at the Graduate Center, was able to offer me invaluable release time at crucial moments, Dan Perjovschi, the Romanian artist who generously made the mural on the wall of the meeting room of the Committee on Globalization and Social Change and granted permission for me to use it for the cover of this book, and Thomas Lay, my thoughtful, reliable, honorable, pragmatic, and supportive editor at Fordham University Press. I reserve the final word of gratitude for Isabel Wilder, whose open eyes, sharp mind, and full heart have nourished my thinking and writing from the start. We have spent untold hours discussing difference, alliance, movements, solidarity, change, imagination, and possible futures in these perilous times. Sharing the burden of her Gen Z cohort, she has a darker view than me of our—of their—prospects. I admire her immensely and constantly learn from her about being, thinking, relating, and creating.

Sections of this book were extracted from or published in earlier form as:

"Temporalizing the Postcolonial Present," Review Essay of David Scott, *Omens of Adversity: Tragedy, Time, Memory, Justice* in *Journal of Latin American and Caribbean Anthropology* 20, no. 1 (2015): 189–200.

"Anticipation," *Political Concepts: A Critical Lexicon* (2017), https://www.politicalconcepts.org.

"Making *Freedom Time*," *History of the Present* 7, no. 7 (Spring 2017): 122–37.

"If You Want to Build an Alternative to Trumpism, You Need to Read Black Freedom Fighter W. E. B. Du Bois," *Open Democracy: Free Thinking for the World*, May 2017.

"Decolonization and Postnational Democracy," in *Forms of Pluralism and Democratic Constitutionalism*, ed. Andrew Arato, Jean L. Cohen, and Astrid von Busekist (New York: Columbia University Press, 2018).

"Solidarity," in *Thinking with Balibar: A Lexicon of Conceptual Practice*, ed. Ann Laura Stoler, Stathis Gourgouris, and Jacques Lezra (New York: Fordham University Press, 2020).

Notes

Introduction: The Opposite of Pessimism Is Not Optimism

1. In previous work, I restricted my use of "internationalism" because of its statist implications, especially when employed in diplomatic history, political science, and International Relations scholarship by liberal policy makers and by orthodox Marxists. I preferred to recuperate a critical notion of cosmopolitanism. In this book, I use "internationalism" to convey translocal anticapitalist and anti-imperialist thinking and movements. The term is meant to recall the solidarity legacies established by the Marxist First International, revolutionary anticolonial mobilizations, and various Third World and Global South movements in the era of formal independence, rather than either the Soviet-led Comintern past or the liberal internationalist present.

2. Georg Lukács, "Class Consciousness," in *History and Class Consciousness: Studies in Marxist Dialectics* (Cambridge, MA: MIT Press, 1968), 81.

3. Lukács, "Preface to the 1967 Edition," in *History and Class Consciousness: Studies in Marxist Dialectics* (Cambridge, MA: MIT Press, 1968), xii.

4. Lukács, "Preface," xii.

5. Lukács, "Preface," xiv.

6. See Vanden and Becker, "Amauta: An Introduction to the Life and Works of José Carlos Mariátegui," in *José Carlos Mariátegui: An Anthology*, ed. Harry E. Vanden and Marc Becker (New York: Monthly Review Press, 2011).

7. Mariátegui, "Pessimism of the Reality, Optimism of the Ideal," in *José Carlos Mariátegui: An Anthology*, ed. Harry E. Vanden and Marc Becker (New York: Monthly Review Press, 2011), 395–96.

8. Mariátegui, "Pessimism of the Reality," 396.

9. Mariátegui, 395–96.

10. Mariátegui, "Imagination and Progress," in *José Carlos Mariátegui: An*

Anthology, ed. Harry E. Vanden and Marc Becker (New York: Monthly Review Press, 2011), 400; emphasis added.

11. Mariátegui, "Imagination and Progress," 400.

12. Mariátegui, 400–401; emphasis added.

13. Like his contemporary Antonio Gramsci, Mariátegui criticized economism and sought to integrate questions of ideology, culture, and art into his Marxist analyses. He was especially concerned with the distinctive character of South American social relations and how indigenous cultural forms and practices might create direct pathways to a socialist future. But he also engaged closely with European social theory, aesthetic theory, and cultural forms (high and low). His writings about the specific character of colonial capitalism in Peru challenged orthodox Marxism and abstract universal theories of capitalism. Yet his attention to the uneven, composite, and sedimented forms of production, power, and domination there indexed a systemic understanding of capitalism as a global formation that required an internationalist response. On Mariátegui's relation to a tradition of antistagist and nonteleological "non-Western" Marxism that analyzes capitalism as a worldwide system that continually presupposes and produces unevenness through formal subsumption, see Harry Harootunian, *Marx after Marx: History and Time in the Expansion of Capitalism* (New York: Columbia University Press, 2015).

14. During his time at the Friedrich Wilhelms University in Berlin (1892–1894), Du Bois, who was en route to a PhD in history at Harvard, studied political economy with Gustav Schmoller and Adolph Wagner, social reformers associated with the historical school of economics. Max Weber gave a series of lectures in one of his courses, and he attended talks by Heinrich von Treitschke, a conservative nationalist historian of Germany, and Wilhelm Dilthey. His immersion during this time in the history of political economy, historical sociology, and the history of peoples is evident in Du Bois's 1896 doctoral dissertation on "The Suppression of the African Slave Trade to the United States of America, 1638–1870." See Francis L. Broderick, "German Influence on the Scholarship of W. E. B. DuBois," *The Phylon Quarterly* 19, no. 4 (1958): 367–71; Kenneth D. Barkin, "Berlin Days," 1892–1894: W.E.B. Du Bois and German Political Economy," *Boundary* 2, vol. 27, no. 3 (Fall 2000). For an account that overemphasizes the influence of German idealism and romantic nationalism (Fichte, Herder, Hegel) on Du Bois's conception of "the folk," see Kwame Antony Appiah, *Lines of Descent: W. E. B. Du Bois and the Emergence of Identity* (Cambridge, MA: Harvard University Press, 2014). Appiah reaffirms the false dichotomy between nationalism and cosmopolitanism that Du Bois spent his life calling into question. For an account that minimizes any German influences on Du Bois's thought, see Aldon D. Morris, *The Scholar Denied: W. E. B. Du Bois and the Birth of Modern Sociology* (Oakland, CA: University of California Press, 2015).

15. On his interwar political reorientation, see Du Bois, "The Shadow of Years," in *Darkwater: Voices from Within the Veil* (1920) (New York: Oxford University Press, 2007), and Du Bois, *Dusk of Dawn: The Autobiography of a Race Concept* (1940).

16. Du Bois, "Credo," in *Darkwater: Voices from Within the Veil* (1920), 1.

17. Du Bois, "Hymn to the Peoples," in *Darkwater: Voices from Within the Veil* (1920), 134–35.

18. Du Bois, "Souls of White Folk," in *Darkwater: Voices from Within the Veil* (1920), xx.

19. Du Bois, "Souls of White Folk," xx.

20. See Gary Wilder, "Reading Du Bois's Revelation," in *The Postcolonial Contemporary: Political Imaginaries for the Global Present*, ed. Jini Kim Watson and Gary Wilder (New York: Fordham University Press, 2018).

21. Du Bois "Of Work and Wealth," in *Darkwater: Voices from Within the Veil* (1920), 47.

22. W. E. B. Du Bois, *Black Reconstruction in America* (New York: Simon and Schuster, 1999), 703. C. L. R. James makes a similar declaration: "Either the revolution succeeds in encompassing the whole of the world or the whole of the world collapses in counter-revolution and barbarism. The whole path of Western civilisation for two thousand years has reached an ultimate stage in Russia. There is no by-pass. There is no third alternative." C. L. R. James, "Dialectical Materialism and the Fate of Humanity," in *The C. L. R. James Reader*, ed. Anna Grimshaw (Oxford: Blackwell, 1992), 158.

23. Henri Lefebvre, *Introduction to Modernity: Twelve Preludes, September 1959–May 1961* (New York: Verso, 1995), 348, 358.

24. Karl Marx and Friedrich Engels, *The Communist Manifesto* (New York: International Publishers, 2014), 40.

25. Ernst Bloch, *The Principle of Hope*, vol. 1 (Cambridge, MA: MIT Press, 1986), 18, 197. See also Jose Muñoz, *Cruising Utopia: The Then and There of Queer Futurity* (New York: New York University Press, 2009), whose critique of antirelational queer theory and poststructuralist pessimism uses Bloch to reclaim utopian futurity. Although Muñoz reads Bloch's dialectical Marxism as a one-sided idealism, he offers an important corrective to dominant theoretical tendencies.

26. Bloch, *Principle of Hope*, 18.

27. Bloch, *Principle of Hope*, 146.

28. Bloch, *Principle of Hope*, 145.

29. Bloch, *Principle of Hope*, 146.

30. Bloch, *Principle of Hope*, 13.

31. Karl Marx, "The Civil War in France," in Karl Marx and V. I. Lenin, *The Civil War in France: The Paris Commune* (Moscow: International Publishers, 1993), 61.

32. I have been fruitfully discussing the question of "singularity and solidarity" with Anthony Alessandrini for many years. He employs the formulation in his important book, *Frantz Fanon and the Future of Cultural Politics: Finding Something Different* (Lanham, MD: Lexington Books, 2014).

33. Vladimir Ilyich Lenin, "Socialism and War: The Attitude of the R.S.D.L.P. toward the War" (July–August 1915), in *Collected Works*, vol. 21, August 1914–December 1915 (Moscow: Progress Publishers, 1964), 313. In the Preface to the second edition, Lenin notes that it was published in Russian, German, French, and

Norwegian and that it was secretly distributed through his network of revolutionary internationalists in anticipation of the historic Zimmerwald Conference which gathered international Socialists. Conflicts there between reformists and revolutionaries led to the collapse of the Second International. The editors of marxists.org note that G. Y. Zinoviev cowrote the original pamphlet but was not acknowledged in the Soviet English edition of the collected works (https://www.marxists.org/archive/lenin/works/1915/s-w/index.htm).

34. Lenin, "Socialism and War," 313.

1. The Possible-Impossible: Dialectical Optics and Uncanny Refractions (Here, Now, Us)

1. Karl Marx, *The Eighteenth Brumaire of Louis Bonaparte* (Moscow: International Publishers, 1994), 597.

2. Karl Marx, "The Civil War in France," in Karl Marx and V. I. Lenin, *The Civil War in France: The Paris Commune* (Moscow: International Publishers, 1993), 56.

3. Marx, *Civil War in France*, 61–62.

4. Marx, 61–62.

5. Marx, 56.

6. Marx, 54.

7. Marx, 60.

8. Marx, 57, 60.

9. Marx, 58.

10. It did so, in part, by reworking past forms such as medieval communes, federations of small states, and popular struggles against government centralization. See Massimiliano Tomba, *Insurgent Universality: An Alternative Legacy of Modernity* (New York: Oxford University Press, 2019), 71–119.

11. Marx, *Civil War in France*, 61.

12. Marx, 86–87. (Cf. Kant on how the French Revolution, even in failure, will permanently transform world history by introducing a new possibility into human affairs.)

13. Marx, *Civil War in France*, 62.

14. Marx, 48.

15. On the Commune as a "universal republic," see Kristin Ross, *Communal Luxury: The Political Imaginary of the Paris Commune* (New York: Verso, 2015).

16. Marx, *Civil War in France*, 80.

17. Marx, 80.

18. Marx, 81.

19. Marx, 82.

20. Marx, 75.

21. See Karl Marx and Friedrich Engels, *The Civil War in the United States*, 2nd ed., ed. Andrew Zimmerman; Marx, *Dispatches for the New York Tribune: Selected Journalism of Karl Marx* (New York: Penguin, 2009); and Kevin B. Anderson, *Marx*

at the Margins: On Nationalism, Ethnicity, and Non-Western Societies (Chicago: University of Chicago Press, 2010), 79–114.

22. W. E. B. Du Bois, *Black Reconstruction in America* (New York: Simon and Schuster, 1999), 55–83.

23. Du Bois, *Black Reconstruction*, 240.

24. Cf. Antonio Gramsci, "Some Aspects of the Southern Question," *Gramsci: Pre-Prison Writings* (Cambridge: Cambridge University Press, 1994).

25. Du Bois, *Black Reconstruction*, 634.

26. Du Bois, 346, 383.

27. On the "dialectics of seeing" as a guiding thread through Walter Benjamin's work, see Susan Buck-Morss, *The Dialectics of Seeing: Walter Benjamin and the Arcades Project* (Cambridge, MA: MIT Press, 1989). For one of the most fully realized attempts to employ the "dialectics of seeing" as method, see Susan Buck-Morss, *Dreamworld and Catastrophe: The Passing of Mass Utopia in East and West* (Cambridge, MA: MIT Press, 2000). On the centrality of nonrealist political imagination to the Black radical tradition, see Robin D. G. Kelley, *Freedom Dreams: The Black Radical Imagination* (Boston: Beacon Press, 2002).

28. Sigmund Freud, "The Uncanny," in *The Standard Edition of the Complete Psychological Works of Sigmund Freud, Volume XVII (1917–1919)*, trans. and ed. James Strachey (London: Hogarth Press, 1955), 237.

29. Freud, "Uncanny," 244, 250.

30. Freud, 220.

31. Freud, 241.

32. Freud, 241.

33. Freud, 241.

34. Walter Benjamin, *The Arcades Project* (Cambridge, MA: Harvard University Press, 1999), 463–64.

35. Walter Benjamin, "On the Image of Proust," in *Selected Writings*, vol. 2, 1927–1930 (Cambridge, MA: Harvard University Press, 1996), 240.

36. Benjamin, *Arcades*, 239.

37. Benjamin, "Image of Proust," 244.

38. Benjamin, 244.

39. Walter Benjamin, "Surrealism," in *Selected Writings*, vol. 2, 1927–1930 (Cambridge, MA: Harvard University Press, 1996), 208.

40. Benjamin, "Surrealism," 211.

41. Benjamin, 216.

42. Benjamin, 209.

43. Benjamin, 210.

44. Benjamin, 216.

45. Benjamin, 208.

46. Benjamin, 210, 215.

47. Benjamin, 216.

48. Benjamin, 216.

49. Benjamin, 217–18.

50. Surrealism thus differed fundamentally from the ironic, nihilistic, fatalistic, and complacent bourgeois radicalism, represented by the New Objectivity in Germany, whose "Left-wing melancholy" he would denounce two years later.

51. Benjamin, *Arcades*, 458.

52. Benjamin, 459.

53. Theodor W. Adorno, "Portrait of Walter Benjamin," in *Prisms* (Cambridge, MA: MIT Press, 1981), 240.

54. Adorno, "Portrait," 240.

55. Adorno, 240.

56. He had been invited to do so by Surrealist poet Pierre Mabille, then a cultural attaché with the French embassy, to spend several months in Haiti where he offered classes and gave public lectures.

57. Aimé Césaire, "Poetry and Knowledge," in *Lyric and Dramatic Poetry, 1946– 1982* (Charlottesville: University of Virginia Press, 1990), xlii–xliii.

58. Césaire, "Poetry and Knowledge," xlii.

59. Césaire, xxiii–xiv.

60. Césaire, xliv.

61. Césaire, xlix.

62. Césaire, li.

63. Césaire, lii.

64. Césaire, lii. Césaire's "dialectic of the image" and "instant of emergence" in which "everything becomes possible again" resonate with Benjamin's conceptions of "profane illumination" and awakening as a "dialectical point of rupture." Césaire's "poetic image" and Benjamin's "dialectical image" could be placed in fruitful dialogue.

65. Césaire, "Poetry and Knowledge," liv.

66. Césaire, l.

67. Cf. the very different redemptive divine violence in Walter Benjamin, "Critique of Violence," in *Reflections* (New York: Shocken, 1986).

68. Césaire, "Poetry and Knowledge," xlvii–xlviii.

69. Aimé Césaire, "Thoroughbreds," in *Aimé Césaire: The Collected Poetry*, trans. Clayton Eshelman and Annette Smith (Berkeley, CA: University of California Press, 1983), 101. This poem was originally published as "Fragments of a Poem" in *Tropiques* and later published in Césaire's collection *Les armes miraculeuses* (Paris: Gallimard, 1946).

70. Aimé Césaire, "Fragments d'un Poème," *Tropiques* 1 (April 1941), 9.

71. Césaire, interview with Nicole Zand, quoted in Georges Ngal, *Aimé Césaire: Un homme à la recherche d'une patrie* (Paris: Présence Africaine, 1994), 250.

72. I develop the idea of "radical literalism" as a strategy of poetic immanent critique, partly by building on Adorno's insight about the revolutionary efficacy of a "literalness" that "explodes [an object] by taking it more exactly at its word than it does itself" in Gary Wilder, *Freedom Time: Negritude, Decolonization, and the*

Future of the World (Durham, NC: Duke University Press, 2015), 7–8. Theodor W. Adorno, "Notes on Kafka," in *Prisms* (Cambridge, MA: MIT Press, 1983), 151.

73. Leiner, "Entretien avec Aimé Césaire," xiv–xv.

74. Theodor W. Adorno, *Negative Dialectics* (New York: Continuum, 1973), 28.

75. Adorno, *Negative Dialectics*, 52.

76. It is telling that the term emerged at a specific moment in the intersecting histories of science (concerned with optical truth, the regularities of heavenly motion, and natural laws of the material world), philosophy (concerned with epistemological truth, the regularities of society, and natural laws of justice), and art (concerned with perspectival truth, the regularities of bodily motion, and natural laws of light and pigment). Each field was founded upon a realist epistemology that put great stock in the link between optics and reality, vision, and truth. See Richard Rorty, *Philosophy and the Mirror of Nature* (Princeton, NJ: Princeton University Press, 1981); Jonathan Crary, *Techniques of the Observer: On Vision and Modernity in the Nineteenth Century* (Cambridge, MA: MIT Press, 1990); and Martin Jay, *Downcast Eyes: The Denigration of Vision in Twentieth-Century French Thought* (Berkeley, CA: University of California Press, 1993),

77. Voloshinov understands ideology as composed of signs, especially words that are at once elements of a given material reality and *refract* another reality. He also refers to the "refracting powers of the socioeconomic conditions" to underscore the "social existence refracted" in language. V. N. Voloshinov, *Marxism and the Philosophy of Language* (Cambridge, MA: Harvard University Press, 1986), 9, 158

78. Heidegger also recognizes the productive force of uncanniness. But rather than fuel a poetic politics of the possible-impossible, his uncanniness propels actors out of the inauthentic state of average everydayness into a resolute embrace of their singular Being-toward-death—an apolitical condition of authentic existence that separates the human being from society, locates them outside of history, and leaves existing arrangements undisturbed. Martin Heidegger, *Being and Time*, trans. John Macquarrie and Edward Robinson (New York: Harper Perennial, 2008).

2. Concrete Utopianism and Critical Internationalism: Refusing Left Realism

1. For the ways that neoliberal capitalism creates the illusion that there is no alternative to the given world, see Mark Fisher, *Capitalist Realism: Is There No Alternative?* (Winchester, UK: Zero Books, 2009).

2. Robert C. Hilderbrand, *Dumbarton Oaks: The Origins of the United Nations and the Search for Postwar Security* (Chapel Hill: University of North Carolina Press, 2001)

3. Article 2.7, Charter of the United Nations, 3.

4. William Roger Louis and Ronald Robinson, "The Imperialism of Decolonization," *Journal of Imperial and Commonwealth History* 22, no. 3 (1994): 462–511; William Roger Louis and Ronald Robinson, "Empire Preserv'd: How the

Americans Put Anti-Communism before Anti-Imperialism," in *Decolonization: Perspectives from Now and Then*, ed. Prasenjit Duara (London: Routledge, 2004).

5. Neil Smith, *American Empire: Roosevelt's Geographer and the Prelude to Globalization* (Berkeley: University of California Press, 2004).

6. For an overview, see Evan Luard, *A History of the United Nations*, vol. 1: *The Years of Western Domination, 1945–1955* (New York: Saint Martin's Press, 1982). On the imperial genealogy of the UN, see Mark Mazower, *No Enchanted Palace: The End of Empire and the Ideological Origins of the United Nations* (Princeton, NJ: Princeton University Press, 2009).

7. For the use of "nomos" as a way of referring to the global political order, see Carl Schmitt, *The Nomos of the Earth in the International Law of a Jus Publicum Europaeum* (Condor, NY: Telos Press, 2006).

8. For example, Talal Asad, "Thinking About Terrorism and Just War," *Cambridge Review of International Affairs*, 23:1 (2010): 3–24; Asad, "Reflections on Violence, Law, and Humanitarianism," *Critical Inquiry* 41, no. 2 (Winter 2015): 390–427; Ayça Çubukçu, "Thinking against Humanity," *London Review of International Law* 5, no. 2 (2017): 251–67; Richard Falk, *Humanitarian Intervention and Legitimacy Wars: Seeking Peace and Justice in the Twenty-First Century* (New York: Routledge, 2015); Richard Falk et al., "Humanitarian Intervention: A Forum," *Nation*, June 26, 2003; David Kennedy, *Of War and Law* (Princeton, NJ: Princeton University Press, 2006); Samuel Moyn, *The Last Utopia: Human Rights in History* (Cambridge, MA: The Belknap Press of Harvard University Press, 2010); Moyn, "Soft Sells: On Liberal Internationalism," in *Human Rights and the Uses of History* (New York: Verso, 2014).

9. For example, his conviction that greater commercial intercourse among distant and different peoples would promote planetary reconciliation and universalist politics rather than interstate conflict and global imperialism. Immanuel Kant, "Idea for a Universal History with a Cosmopolitan Purpose" and "Perpetual Peace: A Philosophical Sketch," in *Political Writings* (Cambridge: Cambridge University Press, 1970).

10. Hannah Arendt, *The Human Condition*, 2nd ed. (Chicago: University of Chicago Press, 1998).

11. Hannah Arendt, *The Origins of Totalitarianism* (New York: Harcourt Brace Jovanovich, 1979).

12. Hannah Arendt, *Eichmann in Jerusalem: A Report on the Banality of Evil* (New York: Penguin, 1977), 294.

13. Arendt, *Origins*, 298.

14. Hannah Arendt, "The Minority Question" and "The Political Organization of the Jewish People: Articles from *Auftau*, April 1944–April 1945," in *The Jewish Writings* (New York: Schocken, 2007), 125–34, 199–240.

15. For example: Albert Camus' demand that the planned United Nations be constituted as a genuine "international democracy" with a true "world parliament" able to enact binding legislation; W. E. B. Du Bois's insistence that the United Nations strip imperial powers of their colonies, declare itself unconditionally

opposed to colonialism, and include delegates from colonized territories; Gandhi's vision of a world federation of free, equal, and interdependent states through which the powerful nations would serve the weak, partly through resource redistribution, with the aim of creating "one world"; and Harold Laski's idea that a truly democratic world system could not be based on the principle of state sovereignty and required that capitalism be overcome. See Albert Camus, *Camus at "Combat": Writing 1944–1947* (Princeton, NJ: Princeton University Press, 2006), 172–73; W. E. B. Du Bois, *Color and Democracy: Colonies and Peace* (New York: Harcourt, Brace, 1945); Manu Bhagavan, *The Peacemakers: India and the Quest for One World* (New Delhi, India: HarperCollins, 2012); Harold Laski, "Toward a Universal Declaration of Human Rights," in *Human Rights: Comments and Interpretation: A Symposium Edited by UNESCO* (1949).

16. This fact alone should make us pause before any claim that anticolonial nationalism is intrinsically emancipatory and internationalism is inevitably imperial.

17. See Gary Wilder, *Freedom Time: Negritude, Decolonization, and the Future of the World* (Durham, NC: Duke University Press).

18. Partha Chatterjee, "Nationalism, Internationalism, and Cosmopolitanism: Some Observations from Modern Indian History," *Comparative Studies of South Asia, Africa, and the Middle East* 36, no. 2 (2016): 330.

19. Chatterjee, "Nationalism, Internationalism, and Cosmopolitanism," 332.

20. Chatterjee, 333.

21. For an account of nonliberal forms of Indian internationalism that belies the claims that twentieth century internationalisms either served the aim of national self-determination or were Eurocentric and elitist, see Manu Goswami, "Imaginary Futures and Colonial Internationalisms," *American Historical Review* 117, no. 5 (December 2012): 1461–85.

22. Chatterjee, 332.

23. Chatterjee, 332. The same anti-utopian realism (which conflates transformative political imagination with extravagant idealism) runs through much of Chatterjee's later work. See Chatterjee's *The Politics of the Governed: Reflections on Popular Politics in Most of the World* (New York: Columbia University Press, 2004); "Lineages of Political Society" and "Tagore's Non-Nation," in *Lineages of Political Society: Studies in Postcolonial Democracy* (New York: Columbia University Press, 2011); and *The Black Hole of Empire: History of a Global Practice of Power* (Princeton, NJ: Princeton University Press, 2012). I would argue that this orientation marks a sharp turn from his pioneering *Nationalist Thought and the Colonial World: A Derivative Discourse* (1986). The latter demonstrates how the (very structural logic of the) national state necessarily foreclosed the prospect for meaningful popular democracy in independent India.

24. Chatterjee, "Nationalism, Internationalism, and Cosmopolitanism," 330.

25. Chatterjee, 326.

26. Chatterjee, 332.

27. Chatterjee, 332.

28. Chatterjee, 333.

29. Chatterjee, 333.

30. Chatterjee, 333.

31. Chatterjee, 333.

32. A similar orientation informs the work of Samuel Moyn. He makes the important point that most colonized people after World War II were more concerned with securing substantive social rights through national states than abstract human rights. But rather than attend to the possibilities for "transnational politics" (whose absence he bemoans) by nonliberal forms of cosmopolitanism and internationalism, he simply declares that "the nation-state won as a political form and nationalism won as a political ideology," as if that settles the matter. Samuel Moyn, "The Universal Declaration of Human Rights of 1948 in the History of Cosmopolitanism," *Critical Inquiry* 40 (Summer 2014): 369. Here, as in Moyn's *Last Utopia*, a realist analytic leads him to ignore competing historical alternatives and posit a simple dichotomy between liberal internationalism, human rights, and empty cosmopolitanism on the one side, and the national welfarism of sovereign states on the other. He thereby implies that the historical triumph of the UN human rights order has exhausted the space of and ruled out the possibility for any other form of cosmopolitan internationalism. Moyn rightly challenges the depoliticizing character of human rights politics. But he does so on the grounds that they are utopian, not that they are liberal and imperial. Following this realist logic, in his book *Not Enough: Human Rights in an Unequal World* (Cambridge, MA: Harvard University Press, 2018), he treats the welfarism of the New International Economic Order as the best political alternative to human rights without recognizing that human rights and welfarism simply express, in another register, an unacceptable choice between national states and liberal internationalism. This is the perspective from which, like Chatterjee, he dismisses past attempts to enact nonnational political forms as fantastic and unrealistic, as losing out to or not being in sync with the new global order that became hegemonic — as if being aligned with the dominant direction of historical development is a political virtue. See Samuel Moyn, "Fantasies of Federalism," *Dissent* (Winter 2015).

33. Peter Linebaugh and Marcus Rediker, *The Many-Headed Hydra: Sailors, Slaves, Commoners, and the Hidden History of the Revolutionary Atlantic* (Boston: Beacon Press, 2000); Julius Scott, *Common Wind: Afro-American Currents in the Age of the Haitian Revolution* (New York: Verso, 2018); Paul Gilroy, *The Black Atlantic: Modernity and Double Consciousness* (New York: Verso, 1993); Neil Roberts, *Freedom as Marronage* (Chicago: University of Chicago Press, 2015); Laurent Dubois, *Avengers of the New World: The Story of the Haitian Revolution* (Cambridge, MA: The Belknap Press of Harvard University Press, 2004) and *Haiti: The Aftershocks of History* (New York: Picador, 2013); Jean Casimir, *La culture opprimé* (Lakay, 2001), Jean Casimir, *La culture opprimé* (Lakay, 2001); Ada Ferrer, *Freedom's Mirror: Cuba and Haiti in the Age of Revolution* (New York: Cambridge University Press, 2014); Guiseppe Mazzini, *A Cosmopolitanism of Nations: Giuseppe Mazzini's Writings*

on *Democracy, Nation Building, and International Relations*, ed. Stefano Recchia and Nadia Urbinati (Princeton, NJ: Princeton University Press, 2009); Benedict Anderson, *Under Three Flags: Anarchism and the Anticolonial Imagination* (New York: Verso, 2005); Rebecca E. Karl, *Staging the World: Chinese Nationalism at the Turn of the Twentieth Century* (Durham, NC: Duke University Press, 2002); reports of the International Socialist Bureau and International Socialist Congresses available at Lenin Marxists.org; Leon Trotsky, "The Program of the International Revolution or a Program of Socialism in One Country?," in *The Third International After Lenin* (New York: Pathfinder Press, 1970); Leon Trotsky, *The Permanent Revolution and Results and Prospects* (Seattle: Red Letter Press, 2010); Minkah Makalani, *In the Cause of Freedom: Radical Black Internationalism from Harlem to London, 1917–1939* (Chapel Hill: University of North Carolina Press, 2011), 71–102; Robin D. G. Kelley, *Freedom Dreams: The Black Radical Imagination* (Boston: Beacon Press, 2002), 13–59; Philippe Dewitte, *Les movements nègres en France, 1915–1939* (Paris: Harmattan, 1985); Brent Hayes Edwards, *The Practice of Diaspora: Literature, Translation, and the Rise of Black Internationalism* (Cambridge, MA: Harvard University Press, 2003); Gary Wilder, *The French Imperial Nation-State: Negritude and Colonial Humanism between the Two World Wars* (Chicago: University of Chicago Press, 2005), 149–200; Christian Hogsbjerg, *C. L. R. James in Imperial Britain* (Durham, NC: Duke University Press, 2014); Marc Matera, *Black London: The Imperial Metropolis and Decolonization in the Twentieth Century* (Berkeley: University of California Press, 2015); Robin D. G. Kelley, " 'This Ain't Ethiopia, But It'll Do': African Americans and the Spanish Civil War," *Race Rebels: Culture, Politics, and the Black Working Class* (New York: The Free Press, 1994) 123–60; "Final Communiqué of the Asian-African conference of Bandung (24 April 1955)," *Asia-Africa Speak from Bandung* (Djakarta: Ministry of Foreign Affairs, Republic of Indonesia, 1955); Anne Garland Mahler, *From the Tricontinental to the Global South: Race, Radicalism, and Transnational Solidarity* (Durham, NC: Duke University Press, 2018), https://www.thetricontinental.org. For an indispensable synoptic account of Third World internationalism, see Vijay Prashad, *The Darker Nations: A People's History of the Third World* (New York: New Press, 2007).

34. Samir Amin, *Re-Reading the Postwar Period: An Intellectual Itinerary* (New York: Monthly Review Press, 1994), 168.

35. For his autobiographical reflections, see Samir Amin, *A Life Looking Forward: Memoirs of an Independent Marxist* (London: Zed Books, 2006) and Amin, *Postwar Period*.

36. Amin, *Postwar Period*, 63, 64.

37. Amin, *Beyond US Hegemony?: Assessing the Prospects for a Multipolar World* (London: Zed Books, 2006), 90.

38. Amin, *Beyond US Hegemony?*, 91.

39. Amin regards the subsequent project for a New International Economic Order as a similar effort that "aimed at modifying the rules of the game to give capitalist development in the peripheries a second chance. As the strategy was in

contradiction with an autocentric strategy of delinking, it was bound to fail." Amin, *Postwar Period*, 165.

40. Amin, *Beyond US Hegemony?*, 91.

41. This conception should not be confused with the kind of epistemological boundary policing that, as I discuss in this chapter, Walter Mignolo characterizes as "decolonial delinking."

42. Samir Amin, *Delinking: Toward a Polycentric World* (London: Zed Books, 1990), 68, 74.

43. Amin, *Beyond US Hegemony?*, 84.

44. Amin, 150.

45. Amin, 1, 107, 156.

46. Amin, 6.

47. Samir Amin, *The World We Wish to See: Revolutionary Objectives in the Twenty-First Century* (New York: Monthly Review Press, 2008), 71.

48. Amin, *Beyond US Hegemony?*, 106.

49. Amin, *World We Wish to See*, 7.

50. Amin, *Beyond US Hegemony?*, 106.

51. Amin, 152.

52. Amin, 152.

53. Amin, *World We Wish to See*, 63.

54. Amin, *Beyond US Hegemony?*, 150, 154, 180.

55. Amin, 92.

56. By "triad" he means the U.S., Europe, and Japan. Amin, *World We Wish to See*, 45.

57. Amin, 45.

58. Amin, 63.

59. Amin, 63.

60. Amin, *Beyond US Hegemony?*, 155

61. Amin, 63.

62. On alterglobalization, see Tom Mertes, ed., *A Movement of Movements: Is Another World Really Possible?* (New York: Verso, 2004).

63. He refers to comprador labor unions, patriotic organizations, and religious sects in Northern centers as well as religious and ethnic fundamentalisms in the Global South. Amin, *Beyond US Hegemony?*, 162.

64. Amin, *World We Wish to See*, 39; emphasis added.

65. Amin, *Beyond US Hegemony?* 155.

66. Amin, *World We Wish to See*, 39; emphasis added.

67. Amin, *Beyond US Hegemony?*, 161

68. Amin, 161.

69. Amin, *World We Wish to See*, 40.

70. Amin, 77.

71. Amin, 79

72. Amin, 75.

73. Amin, 79.

74. Amin, *Beyond US Hegemony?* 157.

75. Amin, *Life Looking Forward*, 204.

76. Amin, 222.

77. Amin, 224.

78. Amin, 236–37.

79. Amin, 236–37.

80. Amin, 236–37.

81. Amin, 236–37.

82. Amin, 219, 240.

83. Amin, 246.

84. Amin, 241, 244.

85. An English translation of the Porto Alegre Manifesto can be found at https://www.opendemocracy.net/en/porto-alegre-manifesto-in-english/. Amin glosses the Bamako Appeal as a more modest iteration of his envisioned Fifth International. Dedicated to the fiftieth anniversary of the Bandung Conference, the Appeal calls for "a new popular and historical subject" that is "diverse and multipolar," committed to the "radical transformation of the capitalist system," to "harmony in societies by abolishing exploitation by class, gender, race, and caste," and to "a new balance of power between the South and the North." The Bamako Appeal is published as Appendix 2 in Amin, *World We Wish to See*. On the genesis of the Appeal in anticipation of the Polycentric World Social Forum meetings in Mali, Venezuela, and Pakistan, see John Catalinotto, "'Bamako Appeal' Promotes Struggle Against Market-Driven Society," *Workers World* (January 27, 2006); Marc Becker, "Report from the World Social Forum VI: Civil Society Meets Chavez's State," *Dollars and Sense* (March/April 2006): 7–8.

86. Amin, *Life Looking Forward*, 249.

87. Amin, 249.

88. In recent years, antirealist orientations have propelled some of the most insightful and subversive critiques of actually existing arrangements today. Here we might think of the commitment to enacting desired worlds and the festival-like atmosphere that suffuses disorderly General Assemblies and Occupy encampments; the absurdist campaigns launched by the anarchist collective Anonymous; the speculative fiction of radical thinkers like Samuel Delany and Octavia Butler; the fantastic—precisely because they are hyperbolically literal—accounts of everyday American racism in Paul Beatty's novel *The Sellout* and recent films such as *Get Out* and *Sorry to Bother You*.

89. Edgardo Lander, "The Venezuelan Oil Rentier Model and the Present Crisis the Country Faces" and Fernando Coronil, "Oilpacity: Secrets of History in the Coup against Hugo Chávez," in *The Fernando Coronil Reader: The Struggle for Life Is the Matter* (Durham, NC: Duke University Press, 2019).

3. Practicing Translation: Beyond Left Culturalism

1. Frank B. Wilderson III, *Red, White, and Black: Cinema and the Structure of U.S. Antagonisms* (Durham, NC: Duke University Press, 2010), 58.

2. Frank B. Wilderson III, "Afro-Pessimism and the End of Redemption," *The Occupied Times* (March 30, 2016), 5, https://theoccupiedtimes.org/?p=14236. For further elaboration of this position, see Wilderson "The Prison Slave as Hegemony's (Silent) Scandal," *Social Justice* 30, no. 3 (2003): 18–27.

3. Jared Sexton, "Afro-Pessimism: The Unclear Word," *Rhizomes* 29 (2106), http://www.rhizomes.net/issue29/sexton.html.

4. Sexton, "Afro-Pessimism."

5. Sexton, "Afro-Pessimism."

6. Rather than critique colonial universalism from the standpoint of local particularism, or colonial particularism from the standpoint of universal humanism, the very universal-particular binary needs to be historicized, criticized, and displaced. See Gary Wilder, *The French Imperial Nation-State: Negritude and Colonial Humanism Between the World Wars* (Chicago: University of Chicago Press, 2005).

7. Dipesh Chakrabarty, *Provincializing Europe: Postcolonial Thought and Historical Difference* (Princeton, NJ: Princeton University Press, 2000), 47–71.

8. This framing closely resembles the categorical distinction between system and lifeworld in Jürgen Habermas, *The Theory of Communicative Action*, vol. 2, *Lifeworld and System: A Critique of Functionalist Reason*, trans. Thomas McCarthy (Boston: Beacon Press, 1987).

9. On this basis, Chakrabarty treats liberalism and Marxism as two sides of the same Eurocentric coin. He mischaracterizes Marx's critique of how capitalism creates abstract equivalences across incommensurable differences (in order to reduce life to labor, and labor to value, which alienates humans from their land, their work, their social communities, and themselves) as Marx's normative vision of society.

10. Talal Asad, "The Limits of Religious Criticism in the Middle East: Notes on Islamic Public Argument," in *Genealogies of Religion: Discipline and Reasons of Power in Christianity and Islam* (Baltimore, MD: Johns Hopkins University Press, 1993) and *Formations of the Secular: Christianity, Islam, Modernity* (Stanford, CA: Stanford University Press, 1993). This insightful analysis begs questions about the ways that some traditions may be discursive but not embodied.

11. Anibal Quijano, "Coloniality of Power, Eurocentrism, and Latin America," *Nepantla: Views from South* 1.3 (2000): 533–80.

12. Walter D. Mignolo, *The Darker Side of Western Modernity: Global Futures, Decolonial Options* (Durham, NC: Duke University Press, 2011), xviii, 54, 74, 97.

13. He contends that decolonial thought is rooted in the Americas and seeks to transform social knowledge whereas postcolonial critique is rooted in the analysis of British colonialism in South Asia and seeks to shift academic knowledge.

14. Mignolo, *Darker Side*, 116.

15. Mignolo, 80.

16. Mignolo, 81.

17. Mingolo, 34, 54, 61, 70, 258.

18. Mignolo, 326.

19. Mignolo, 326.

20. Cf. Jini Kim Watson and Gary Wilder, "Introduction: Thinking the Postcolonial Contemporary," in *The Postcolonial Contempoary: Political Imaginaries for the Global Present* (New York: Forham University Press, 2018), 1–30.

21. See also W. E. B. Du Bois, *Black Reconstruction in America* (New York: Simon and Schuster, 1999); C. L. R. James, *The Black Jacobins: Toussaint L'Ouverture and the San Domingo Revolution*, 2nd ed., rev. (New York: Random House, 1963); Eric Williams, *Capitalism and Slavery* (Chapel Hill: University of North Carolina Press, 1994); Walter Rodney, *How Europe Underdeveloped Africa* (New York: Verso, 2018); Samir Amin, *Accumulation on a World Scale: A Critique of the Theory of Underdevelopment* (New York: Monthly Review Press, 1974); Cedric Robinson, *Black Marxism: The Making of a Black Radical Tradition*, 2nd ed. (Chapel Hill: University of North Carolina Press, 2000); Giovanni Arrighi, *The Long Twentieth Century: Money, Power, and the Origins of Our Times* (New York: Verso, 1994); Massimiliano Tomba, *Marx's Temporalities* (Leiden, Netherlands: Brill, 2012); Harry Harootunian, *Marx After Marx: History and Time in the Expansion of Capitalism* (New York: Columbia University Press, 2015).

22. Mignolo, *Darker Side*, xxvii; Talal Asad, "The Concept of Cultural Translation in British Social Anthropology," in *Writing Culture: The Poetics and Politics of Ethnography*, ed. James Clifford and George E. Marcus (Berkeley: University of California Press, 1986); Talal Asad, *Secular Translations: Nation-State, Modern Self, and Calculative Reason* (New York: Columbia University Press, 2018). When discussing intergenerational debates and revisions within the Islamic tradition Asad here employs a more nuanced understanding of translation as a practice of ongoing interpretation. Chakrabarty, *Provincializing Europe*, 71.

23. Barbara Cassin, ed., *Dictionary of Untranslatables: A Philosophical Lexicon*, trans. and ed. Emily Apter, Jacques Lezra, and Michael Wood (Princeton, NJ: Princeton University Press, 2004), xix.

24. Cassin, *Dictionary*, xix.

25. Cassin, xx

26. Cassin, xvi

27. Cassin, xvii

28. Cassin, xviii.

29. Cassin, xviii.

30. Cassin, xvii.

31. Cassin, xix.

32. Cassin, xvii.

33. See Jacques Derrida, "Des tours de Babel," *Psyche: Inventions of the Other*, vol. 1 (Stanford, CA: Stanford University Press, 2007).

34. Jacques Derrida, "Living On/Borderlines," *Deconstruction and Criticism*, ed. Harold Bloom et al. (New York: Routledge, 1979), 119.

35. He endorses Jakobson's typology of intralingual, interlingual, and intersemiotic translation. See Roman Jakobson, "On Linguistic Aspects of Translation," in *On Translation*, ed. Reuben A. Brower (Cambridge, MA: Harvard University Press, 1959).

36. Derrida, "Living On/Borderlines," 101; and Jacques Derrida, *Monolingualism of the Other; or, the Prosthesis of Origin* (Stanford, CA: Stanford University Press, 1998), 1.

37. Derrida, *Monolingualism*, 10.

38. Derrida, 49.

39. Cf. Adorno's "interpretive eye."

40. Derrida, *Monolingualism*, 47.

41. Derrida, 50–51.

42. Derrida, 51.

43. Derrida, "Living On/Borderlines," 102.

44. Walter Benjamin, "The Task of the Translator," in *Selected Writings, Vol. 1: 1913–1926* (Cambridge, MA: Harvard University Press, 1996), 257.

45. Benjamin, "Task of the Translator," 253, 256.

46. Benjamin, 260.

47. Benjamin, 257.

48. Benjamin, 261–62.

49. See also Walter Benjamin, "On Language as Such and the Language of Man," in *Selected Writings*, vol. 1, *1913–1926* (Cambridge, MA: Harvard University Press, 1996).

50. Derrida, *Monolingualism*, 24.

51. Souleymane Bachir Diagne, *The Ink of Scholars: Reflections on Philosophy in Africa* (CODESRIA, 2016), xx.

52. Diagne, *Ink of Scholars*, 16–17.

53. Diagne, 34.

54. Diagne contributed several entries to the American edition of Cassin's *Dictionary*.

55. Souleymane Bachir Diagne, "Philosopher en Afrique," *Critique* vol. 8–9, no. 771–72 (2011): 611–12.

56. Diagne, *Ink of Scholars*, 30.

57. Diagne, 64. Here, he is referring specifically to African socialism. He makes a similar point about the absence of an original or singular "Islam" (prior to any translation) in *Comment Philosopher en Islam?* (Paris: Éditions du Panama, 2008).

58. Diagne, *Ink of Scholars*, 24.

59. Diagne, 24.

60. Diagne, 17. He borrows this formulation from Antoine Berman, *The Experience of the Foreign: Culture and Translation in Romantic Germany* (Albany: State University of New York Press, 1992).

61. Diagne, *Ink of Scholars*, 51. Diagne makes this point in dialogue with Léopold

Sédar Senghor, who reminds readers that Birago Diop understood this Italian warning when he "translated" African folktales into written form. Rather than seek word-to-word equivalences, Senghor explains, Diop was a creative artist who rethought and reworked them.

62. In his own work, Diagne places African philosophy, literature, religion, and art, "in touch" with a wide range of Islamic and Western philosophers.

63. Édouard Glissant, *Poetics of Relation*, trans. Betsy Wing (Ann Arbor: University of Michigan Press, 1997), 103.

64. Glissant, *Poetics of Relation*, 103. In his 1956 resignation from the French Communist Party, Césaire famously refused the false alternative between a narrow particularism that would lead to walled-in segregation and dilution in an emaciated universalism. He envisioned an alternative "universal . . . enriched and deepened by all particulars, by the coexistence of all particulars." Aimé Césaire, *Lettre á Maurice Thorez* (Paris: Présence Africaine, 1956), 156.

65. Glissant, *Poetics of Relation*, 103, 105.

66. Glissant, 107. Note that Derrida first presented the paper that would become *Monolingualism of the Other* at a conference organized by Glissant. In it, he invokes Glissant's conception of Relation but does not take it up in ways that might have helped him to displace rather than reproduce the old antinomy between universality and particularity.

67. Glissant, *Poetics of Relation*, 107–8.

68. Glissant, 108. This dialectical understanding of place and world is further developed in Édouard Glissant, *Traité de Tout-Monde*, Poétique IV (Paris: Éditions Gallimard, 1997).

69. Glissant, *Poetics of Relation*, 109. Emphasis added.

70. Glissant, 192.

71. Glissant, 144.

72. Glissant, 144.

73. Glissant, 19.

74. Glissant, 144.

75. Glissant, 189.

76. Glissant, 189.

77. Glissant, 190. Cf. Emmanuel Levinas, *Totality and Infinity: An Essay on Exteriority*, trans. Alphonso Lingis (Pittsburgh, PA: Duquesne University Press, 1969).

78. Glissant, *Poetics of Relation*, 190.

79. Glissant, 190.

80. Glissant, 190, 191.

81. Glissant, 190.

82. Glissant, 190.

83. Glissant, 73.

84. Glissant, 65.

85. Glissant, 71.

86. Glissant, 74.

87. Glissant, 65.

88. Glissant, 190.

89. Glissant, 29.

90. Glissant, 33.

91. Glissant, 71.

92. Glissant, 155.

93. Glissant, 199.

94. Glissant, 293.

95. Glissant, 155.

96. I do not concur with the common interpretation that with *The Poetics of Relation*, the focus of Glissant's work shifts from politics to poetics, from concrete to abstract concerns, or from attention to Antillean specificity to generalizations about the world. I would argue that he seeks, in all his work, to explode these very oppositions. The register of his writings along with certain key terms may have shifted, but his underlying investments remained remarkably consistent. We might ask those who insist on a break between the early and late Glissant about their understanding of "politics" as self-evidently distinct from poetics and as only legible or legitimate when it takes the form of anticolonial nationalism. See the otherwise insightful analyses of Peter Hallward, *Absolutely Postcolonial: Writing Between the Singular and the Specific* (Manchester, UK: Manchester University Press, 2001), 66–142; Chris Bongie, "Édouard Glissant: Dealing in Globality," in *Postcolonial Thought in the French-Speaking World*, ed. Charles Forsdick and David Murphy (Liverpool: Liverpool University Press, 2009); Nick Nesbitt, *Caribbean Critique: Antillean Critical Theory from Toussaint to Glissant* (Liverpool, UK: Liverpool University Press, 2013), 133–56, 231–50.

97. Glissant, *Poetics of Relation*, 147.

98. Betsy Wing translates *donner-avec* as "giving-on-and-with" (Glissant, *Poetics of Relation*, 142).

99. Glissant, *Poetics of Relation*, 34, 155.

100. Glissant, 131.

101. Following Marx's Hegelian distinction between universal, particular, and singular, I use singularity to mean that which is irreducible and must be grasped on its own terms. The singular is not simply a part of a larger whole. The term "difference" usually functions to establish boundaries, whether in terms of the binary of same vs. different or between categories of phenomena. In contrast, singularity, as I employ and understand it, typically confounds categorization, classification, and tendencies to ontologize "difference" in determinate ways. My sense of singularities as being capable of entering into endless configurations with other singularities as source and force of transformative political potentiality, is informed by the way the concept is employed by Glissant, as discussed in this chapter, and in Michael Hardt and Antonio Negri in *Commonwealth* (Cambridge, MA: Belknap Press of Harvard University Press, 2011). See also Chapter 11 of this book.

102. Glissant, *Poetics of Relation*, 193.

103. Glissant, 155.

104. Glissant, 203. Emphasis added.

105. Boaventura de Sousa Santos, *Epistemologies of the South: Justice Against Epistemicide* (New York: Routledge, 2014).

106. Santos, *Epistemologies of the South*, 212.

107. Santos, 228.

108. Santos, 215, 216.

109. Santos, 112.

110. Santos, 219.

111. Santos, 232.

112. Santos, 213, 219.

113. Santos, 217, 218.

114. Santos, 214.

115. Santos, 214.

116. Santos, 213.

117. Santos, 222.

118. Santos, 222.

119. Santos, 233.

120. Santos, 233.

121. Signatories of the WSF's 2005 Porto Alegre Manifesto included those from Argentina, Belgium, Brazil, France, Italy, Mali, Mexico, Pakistan, Philippines, Portugal, Spain, United States, and Uruguay. See "Annexe III: Manifesto of Poro Alegre: Another World Is Possible: Twelve Proposals," in Boaventura de Sousa Santos, *The Rise of the Global Left: The World Social Forum and Beyond* (London: Zed Books, 2006).

122. "World Social Forum Charter of Principles" (April 2001), https://fsmm2018.org/world-social-forum-charter-principles/?lang=en.

123. "World Social Forum Charter of Principles."

124. Santos, *Rise of the Global Left*, 11, 12.

125. Santos, 129.

126. It was criticized by some Leftists as a gathering of representatives that were too focused on deliberation and should not have excluded revolutionary organizations involved in armed struggle.

127. Santos, *Rise of the Global Left*, 132.

128. Santos, 132.

129. Santos, 133.

130. Cf. Bakhtin on heteroglossia in M. M. Bakhtin, "Discourse in the Novel," *The Dialogical Imagination: Four Essays* (Austin: University of Texas Press, 1981).

131. On the latter, see Fadi Bardawil, *Revolution and Disenchantment: Arab Marxism and the Binds of Emancipation* (Durham, NC: Duke University Press, 2020). On what grounds could we say that these non-Western radicals were *not* members of the Marxist tradition?

132. Anderson, *Under Three Flags*, 5.

133. Ralph Ellison, "Hidden Name and Complex Fate," in *The Collected Essays of Ralph Ellison*, revised and updated (New York: Modern Library/Random House, 2004), 205.

134. C. L. R. James, "Preliminary Notes on the Negro Question (1939)" and "Notes Following the Discussion (1939)," in *C. L. R. James on the "Negro Question*," ed. Scott McLemee (Jackson: University of Mississippi Press, 1996).

135. C. L. R. James, "Education, Propaganda, Agitation: Post-War America and Bolshevism," in James, *Marxism for our Times*, ed. Martin Glaberman (Jackson: University Press of Mississippi, 199), 16.

136. James, "Education, Propaganda, Agitation," 16–17

137. Grace Lee Boggs, *Living for Change: An Autobiography* (Minneapolis: University of Minnesota Press, 1998), 60–61.

4. Of Pessimism and Presentism: Against Left Melancholy

1. Adorno, *Negative Dialectics*, 244.

2. Adorno, *Negative Dialectics*, 244, 245.

3. Cf. Joan Wallach Scott, *On the Judgment of History* (New York: Columbia University Press, 2020).

4. Fadi Bardawil, "The Solitary Analyst of Doxas: An Interview with Talal Asad," *Comparative Studies of South Asia, Africa and the Middle East* 36, no. 1 (2016): 156.

5. Bardawil, "Solitary Analyst," 164.

6. Bardawil, 164.

7. Bardawil, 170–71.

8. Bardawil, 171, 155–56.

9. Bardawil, 167.

10. Bardawil, 167.

11. Bardawil, 170.

12. Bardawil, 165.

13. Cf. Derrida on "waiting without horizon of expectation." Jacques Derrida, *Specters of Marx: The State of the Debt, the Work of Mourning, and the New International* (New York: Routledge, 1994), 211.

14. Lauren Berlant, *Cruel Optimism* (Durham, NC: Duke University Press, 2011), 199.

15. Berlant, *Cruel Optimism*, 4.

16. Berlant, 229–30.

17. Berlant, 224, 227.

18. Berlant, 229, 230, 231.

19. Berlant, 259.

20. Berlant, 259.

21. Berlant, 259.

22. Berlant, 260.

23. Berlant, 260.

24. Berlant, 260.

25. Berlant, 260.

26. Berlant, 261.

27. Berlant, 266.

28. Berlant, 266.

29. Berlant, 267.

30. Berlant, 262.

31. On the apocalyptic tendencies within recent theory that acts out aspects of the social reality it attempts to understand, see Dominick La Capra, *History in Transit: Experience, Identity, Critical Theory* (Ithaca, NY: Cornell University Press, 2004).

32. On prefigurative "horizontalist" politics that reject means-ends instrumentalism but insist on pursuing preferable forms of life, see Marina Sitrin, *Everyday Revolutions: Horizontalism and Autonomy in Argentina* (Zed Books, 2012); Marina Sitrin and Dario Azzellino, *They Can't Represent Us!: Reinventing Democracy from Greece to Occupy* (New York: Verso, 2014); and Carla Bergman, Nick Montgomery, eds., *Joyful Militancy: Building Thriving Resistance in Toxic Times* (AK Press, 2017).

33. Berlant, *Cruel Optimism*, 261.

34. David Scott, *Omens of Adversity: Tragedy, Time, Memory, Justice* (Durham, NC: Duke University Press, 2014), 2.

35. Scott, *Omens of Adversity*, 20.

36. Scott, 108, 109.

37. Scott, 96, 109.

38. Scott, 21.

39. Scott, 163–64.

40. Scott, 28.

41. Scott, 125.

42. Scott, 131.

43. Scott, 131.

44. Scott, 125.

45. Vijay Prashad's analysis of the 1970s debt crisis as marking the "assassination" of the Third World political project by undermining economic sovereignty suggests one way to account for what Scott asserts. Prashad, *The Darker Nations: A People's History of the Third World* (New York: New Press, 2007), 207–23.

46. Scott, *Omens of Adversity*, 28.

47. Scott, 5, 12.

48. Scott, 6, 12.

49. Scott, 6.

50. Scott, 15.

51. François Hartog, *Regimes of Historicity: Presentism and Experiences of Time* (New York: Columbia University Press, 2015), 195.

52. Reinhardt Koselleck, *Futures Past: On the Semantics of Historical Time* (New York: Columbia University Press, 2004).

53. Hartog, *Regimes of Historicity*, 9.

54. Hartog, 16.

55. Hartog, 203.

56. Hartog, 203.

57. Hartog, 203.

58. Hartog, 18.

59. Hartog, 17–18.

60. Hartog, 18.

61. Hartog, 191.

62. Hartog, 3.

63. Hartog, 146.

64. Hartog, 203, 196, 204.

65. Enzo Traverso, *Left-Wing Melancholia: Marxism, History, and Memory* (New York: Columbia University Press, 2016), 22, 38

66. Traverso, *Left-Wing Melancholia*, 51.

67. Traverso, 7, 57.

68. Traverso, 57.

69. Traverso, 22.

70. Traverso, 49.

71. Traverso, 2.

72. Traverso, 8.

73. Even a non-Marxist like Derrida recognized that 1989 created an unprecedented opening for renewing rather than renouncing, regretting, or mourning our relationship to Marxism. Jacques Derrida, *Specters of Marx: The State of the Debt, The Work of Mourning, and the New International* (New York: Routledge, 1994).

74. See Susan Buck-Morss, *Dreamworld and Catastrophe: The Passing of Mass Utopia in East and West* (Cambridge, MA: MIT Press, 2000). Obviously, the periodization employed by Hartog and Traverso is uncritically Eurocentric.

75. Traverso, *Left-Wing Melancholia*, 31, 25.

76. Traverso, 22–23.

77. Traverso, 45.

78. Traverso, 45.

79. Traverso, 45.

80. Traverso, 52.

81. Traverso, 20.

82. For s similar attempt to reclaim melancholy, through Benjamin, as grounds for political potentiality, see, David L. Eng and David Kazanjian, "Introduction: Mourning Remains," *Loss: The Politics of Mourning*, ed. Eng and Kazanjian (Berkeley: University of California Press, 2003).

83. Traverso, *Left-Wing Melancholia*, 48.

84. Wendy Brown, "Resisting Left Melancholy," *boundary 2*, Vol. 25, no. 3 (Fall 1999): 19.

85. Brown, "Resisting Left Melancholy," 19.

86. Brown, 19.

87. Brown, 26.

88. Brown, 26.

89. Brown, 26–27.

90. Frederic Jameson, "Future City," *New Left Review* 21 (May–June 2003): 76.

91. Stuart Hall, "The Great Moving Right Show," in *The Hard Road to Renewal: Thatcherism and the Crisis of the Left* (New York: Verso, 1988), 47.

92. Stuart Hall, "The Battle for Socialist Ideas in the 1980s," in *Hard Road to Renewal*, 184.

93. Stuart Hall (with Charles Critcher, Tony Jefferson, John Clarke, and Brian Roberts), "Living with the Crisis," in *Hard Road to Renewal*, 33, 35.

94. Walter Benjamin, "Left-Wing Melancholy," in *Selected Writings*, vol. 2, part 2, 1931–1934 (Cambridge, MA: Harvard University Press, 2005), 424.

95. Benjamin, "Left-Wing Melancholy," 423.

96. Benjamin, 423–24.

97. Benjamin, 426.

98. Benjamin, 424.

99. Benjamin, 424.

100. Benjamin, 424.

101. Benjamin, 424.

102. Benjamin, 424.

103. Benjamin, 424.

104. Benjamin, 424, 425, 426.

105. Benjamin, 425.

106. Benjamin, 425.

107. Benjamin, 425.

108. Benjamin, 426.

109. Benjamin, 425.

110. Benjamin, 425–26.

111. For further elaborations of this critique, see Benjamin, "Critique of the New Objectivity" (1931) and "The Author as Producer" (1934) in *Selected Writings*, vol. 2, 1927–1934 (Cambridge, MA: Harvard University Press, 1996).

112. Benjamin, "On the Concept of History," in *Selected Writings*, vol. 4, 1938–1940 (Cambridge, MA: Harvard University Press, 2006), 392.

113. Walter Benjamin, "Paralipomena to 'On the Concept of History,'" *Walter Benjamin: Selected Writings*, vol. 4, 1938–1940 (Cambridge, MA: The Belknap Press of Harvard University Press, 2006), 402.

114. Benjamin, *Arcades Project*, 475.

115. Benjamin, 473.

116. Benjamin, 388, 389.

117. Adorno, "Walter Benjamin," 240. In this way, he suggests, Benjamin peformed the "the paradox of the impossible possibility."

118. Benjamin, "Image of Proust," 239.

119. Benjamin, 239.

120. Brown, "Resisting Left Melancholy," 22.

121. Fernando Coronil, "The Future in Question: History and Utopia in Latin America (1989–2010)," in *Business as Usual: The Roots of the Global Financial Meltdown*, ed. Craig Calhoun and Georgi Derluguian (New York: New York University Press, 2011), 234.

122. Wendy Brown, *Undoing the Demos: Neoliberalism's Stealth Revolution* (New York: Zone Books, 2015), 219.

123. Brown, *Undoing the Demos*, 220.

124. Brown, 220.

125. Brown, 222.

5. Solidarity

1. Peter Linebaugh and Marcus Rediker, *The Many-Headed Hydra: Sailors, Slaves, Commoners, and the Hidden History of the Revolutionary Atlantic* (Boston: Beacon Press, 2000).

2. Thomas C. Holt, *The Problem of Freedom: Race, Labor, and Politics in Jamaica and Britain, 1832–1938* (Baltimore, MD: Johns Hopkins University Press, 1992). See also Jean Casimir, *La culture opprimée* (1982), and Laurent Dubois, *Haiti: The Aftershocks of History* (New York: Metropolitan Books, 2012).

3. E. P. Thompson, *The Making of the English Working Class* (New York: Vintage, 1966); William H. Sewell, Jr., *Work and Revolution in France: The Language of Labor from the Old Regime to 1848* (Cambridge: Cambridge University Press, 1980).

4. Pierre-Joseph Proudhon, *Solution of the Social Problem* (New York: Vanguard Publishers, 1927).

5. Proudhon, *Solution of the Social Problem*, 510.

6. Proudhon, 643.

7. Proudhon, 646.

8. Proudhon, 650.

9. Proudhon, 776

10. Proudhon, 452.

11. Karl Marx and Friedrich Engels, *The Communist Manifesto* (New York: International Publishers, 1948).

12. Marx and Engels, *Communist Manifesto*.

13. Marx and Engels.

14. Karl Marx, "Economic and Philosophical Manuscripts (1844)," in *Early Writings* (London: Penguin, 1992), 365.

15. Marx, "Philosophical Manuscripts" 365.

16. Marx, 350.

17. Karl Marx, "Theses on Feuerbach," in *The Marx-Engels Reader*, 2nd ed., ed. Robert C. Tucker (New York: W. W. Norton, 1978), 145.

18. Marx, "Philosophical Manuscripts," 350.

19. Marx, 352.

20. Karl Marx, "The German Ideology," in *The Marx-Engels Reader*, 2nd ed., ed. Robert C. Tucker (New York: W. W. Norton, 1978), 197.

21. Marx and Engels, *Communist Manifesto*.

22. Marx and Engels.

23. Karl Marx, *Grundrisse: Foundations of the Critique of Political Economy* (London: Penguin, 1993), 158.

24. Karl Marx, *Capital*, vol. 1, *A Critique of Political Economy* (London: Penguin, 1992), 171, 173. Marx famously uses the phrase "einen Verein freier Menschen."

25. Karl Marx, "First Draft of 'The Civil War in France,'" in *The First International and After: Political Writings*, vol. 3 (London: Penguin, 1992), 213.

26. Marx "Civil War in France," 250.

27. Marx, 250.

28. Karl Marx, "On the Jewish Question," in *Early Writings* (London: Penguin, 1992), 234.

29. Marx, "The Civil War in France," 216. "Captive Paris resumed by one bold spring the leadership of Europe . . . by giving body to the aspirations of the working class of all countries," 252.

30. Marx, "Civil War in France," 263.

31. Marx, 254.

32. Marx and Engels, *Communist Manifesto*, 44.

33. Friedrich Engels, "Preface," Marx and Engels, *Communust Manifesto*, 3.

34. Karl Marx, "Inaugural Address of the International Workingmen's Association," in *The First International and After: Political Writings*, vol. 3 (London: Penguin, 1992), 78.

35. Marx, "Inaugural Address," 81.

36. Marx, 81.

37. Marx, 82.

38. Marx, 83–84.

39. Marx, 84.

40. "Marx to Meyer and Vogt," April 9, 1870, in Marx, *The First International and After: Political Writings*, vol. 3 (London: Penguin, 1992), 169.

41. "Marx to Meyer and Vogt," 167.

42. "Marx to Meyer and Vogt," 169.

43. Marx, "Inaugural Address," 82–83.

44. Marx, "Inaugural Address," 84.

45. Marx, "Inaugural Address," 84.

46. W. E. B. Du Bois, *Black Reconstruction in America, 1860–1880* (New York: Free Press, 1997); Holt, *Problem of Freedom*; Samuel Clark, *Social Origins of the Irish Land War* (Princeton, NJ: Princeton University Press, 1979); Benedict Anderson, *Under Three Flags: Anarchism and the Anti-Colonial Imagination* (New York: Verso, 2007).

47. J. E. S. Hayward, "The Official Social Philosophy of the Third Republic:

Léon Bourgeois and Solidarism," *International Review of Social History* 6, no. 1 (1961): 19–48.

48. See Émile Durkheim, *The Division of Labor in Society*, trans. W. D. Halls (New York: Free Press, 1933).

49. For a critique of liberal notions of political solidarity that are unable to acknowledge the existence of a racial polity and associated forms of "racialized solidarity," see Juliet Hooker, *Race and the Politics of Solidarity* (Oxford: Oxford University Press, 2009).

50. The political logic of productivism, cooperation, and welfarism also allowed colonial states to instrumentalize "association" in order to preempt radical movements for either national liberation or democratic citizenship in Africa, Asia, and the Caribbean. Gary Wilder, *The French Imperial Nation-State: Negritude and Colonial Humanism between the Two World Wars* (Chicago: University of Chicago Press, 2005).

51. Marcel Mauss, *The Gift: The Form and Reason for Exchange in Archaic Societies* (New York: W. W. Norton, 1990).

52. Marx referred to "the cooperative movement" as a "victory of the political economy of labor over the political economy of property" and a "great social experiment" that "cannot be overrated" even as he warned that "however excellent in principle, and however useful in practice, cooperative labour, if kept within the narrow circle of the casual efforts of private workmen, will never be able to arrest the growth in geometric progression of monopoly, to free the masses, nor even to perceptibly lighten the burden of their miseries." Marx, "Inaugural Address, 79–80.

53. Wilder, *French Imperial Nation-State*; Marc Matera, *Black London: The Imperial Metropolis and Decolonization in the Twentieth Century* (Berkeley: University of California Press, 2015).

54. Antonio Gramsci, "Unions and Councils," *L'Ordine Nuovo* 11 (October 1919).

55. Antonio Gramsci, "Some Aspects of the Southern Question," in *Modern Prince and Other Writings* (New York: International Publishers, 1957).

56. Antonio Gramsci, *Selections from the Prison Notebooks* (New York: International Publishers, 1980).

57. W. E. B. Du Bois, *Dusk of Dawn*, in *W. E. B. Du Bois: Writings* (New York: Library of America, 1987), 712.

58. See Gary Wilder, "Reading Du Bois's Revelation: Radical Humanism and Black Atlantic Criticism," in *The Postcolonial Contemporary*, ed. Jini Kim Watson and Gary Wilder (forthcoming, Fordham University Press).

59. Manu Goswami, "Imaginary Futures and Colonial Internationalisms," *American Historical Review* 117, no. 5 (December 2012): 1461–85.

60. Kristin Ross, *Communal Luxury: The Political Imaginary of the Paris Commune* (New York: Verso, 2015).

61. Kristin Ross, *May '68 and Its Afterlives* (Chicago: University of Chicago Press, 2002); Jeremy Suri, *The Global Revolutions of 1968* (New York: W. W. Norton, 2007).

62. See Gareth Evans, "The Responsibility to Protect: Rethinking Humanitarian Intervention," *Proceedings of the Annual Meeting (American Society of International*

Law) vol. 98 (March 31–April 3, 2004): 78–89; Gareth Evans and Mohamed Sahnoun, "The Responsibility to Protect," *Foreign Affairs* 81, no. 6 (November–December 2002): 99–110; Michael Walzer, *Arguing about War* (New Haven: Yale University Press, 2004); Gary Bass, *Freedom's Battle: The Origins of Humanitarian Intervention* (New York: Alfred A. Knopf, 2008), Samuel Moyn, *The Last Utopia: Human Rights in History* (Cambridge, MA: Harvard University Press, 2010); Talal Asad, "Reflections on Violence, Law, and Humanitarianism," *Critical Inquiry* 41, no. 2 (2015): 390–427.

63. Reinhart Koselleck, "Introduction and Prefaces to the *Geschichtliche Grundbegriffe*," *Contributions to the History of Concepts* 6, no. 1 (Summer 2011): 8.

64. M. M. Bakhtin, "Discourse in the Novel," in *The Dialogic Imagination: Four Essays* (Austin: University of Texas Press, 1981), 284.

65. Étienne Balibar, "Concept," in *Thinking with Balibar: A Lexicon of Conceptual Practice*, ed. Ann Laura Stoler, Stathis Gourgouris, and Jacques Lezra (New York: Fordham University Press, 2020), xx. Certain concepts, Balibar explains, "are used not *despite* their conflictual nature, but precisely because of the *dissensus* they provoke and crystallize . . . such concepts are not made to reconcile viewpoints, but to divide them, and to foster controversies, if not antagonism" (xx).

66. Balibar, "Concept."

67. Emmanuel Levinas, *Totality and Infinity: An Essay on Exteriority* (Pittsburgh: Duquesne University Press, 1969) and *Otherwise Than Being, Or Beyond Essence* (Pittsburgh: Duquesne University Press, 1998); Jacques Derrida "Force of Law: 'Mystical Foundations of Authority,'" in *Deconstruction and the Possibility of Justice*, ed. Drucilla Cornel, Michel Rosenfeld, and David Gray Carlson (New York: Routledge Press, 1992), 3–67; Jacques Derrida, *Adieu to Emmanuel Levinas* (Stanford, CA: Stanford University Press, 1999); Ann Dufourmantelle and Jacques Derrida, *Of Hospitality* (Stanford, CA: Stanford University Press, 2000); Jacques Derrida, *On Cosmopolitanism and Forgiveness* (New York: Routledge, 2001); and Jacques Derrida, "Hostipitality," in *Acts of Religion*, ed. Gil Anidjar (New York: Routledge, 2002).

68. Immanuel Kant, "Idea for a Universal History with a Cosmopolitan Purpose," in *Political Writings* (Cambridge: Cambridge University Press, 1970), 50; Walter Benjamin, "On the Concept of History," in *Selected Writings*, vol. 4, 1938–1940 (Cambridge, MA: The Belknap Press of Harvard University Press, 2006), 389–400.

6. Anticipation

1. Theodor Adorno, *Minima Moralia: Reflections on a Damaged Life* (New York: Verso, 2006), 247. Emphasis added.

2. Reinhardt Koselleck, *Futures Past: On the Semantics of Historical Time* (New York: Columbia University Press, 2004), 37.

3. Walter Benjamin, "On the Concept of History," *Selected Writings*, vol. 4, 1938–1940 (Cambridge, MA: The Belknap Press of Harvard University Press, 2006), 393.

4. If evaluated from the standpoint of qualitative human flourishing or social

justice, purely quantitative evaluations of progress are ideological mystifications. But if figured in terms of greater control over nature, more food, people, goods, wealth, technology, and territory, larger cities, or faster change—modern history may indeed be understood in terms of "progress." With the advent of bureaucratic states, capitalist social relations, instrumental rationality, and scientistic worldviews, quantitative "progress" became a real source of alienation and unfreedom. In this sense, "progress" is a real abstraction, not just an ideological fiction

5. Koselleck, *Futures Past*.

6. Bourdieu reminds us that the very capacity to imagine, let alone plan for, the future is an index of social belonging and an instrument of social exclusion. Pierre Bourdieu, *Pascalian Meditations* (Stanford, CA: Stanford University Press, 2000), 225–26.

7. Lauren Berlant, *Cruel Optimism* (Durham, NC: Duke University Press, 2011); Lee Edelman, *No Future: Queer Theory and the Death Drive* (Durham, NC: Duke University Press, 2004).

8. Vincanne Adams, Michelle Murphy, and Adele E. Clarke, "Anticipation: Technoscience, Life, Affect, Temporality," *Subjectivity* 28 (2009): 246–65.

9. Berlant, *Cruel Optimism*, 2.

10. Edelman, *No Future*, 3–5. Edelman contends that every hope for a better social order only reinforces what he calls "reproductive futurism."

11. Lee Edelman, "The Future Is Kid Stuff: Queer Theory, Disidentification, and the Death Drive," *Narrative* 6, no. 1 (January 1998): 29.

12. Adams, Murphy, and Clarke, "Anticipation," 259–60.

13. Recall that the English word "progress" is derived from the Latin noun *progressus*, meaning "an advance," and the verb *progredi*, from *pro-* "forward" + *gradi* "to walk."

14. Gershom Scholem, "The Messianic Idea in Judaism," in *The Messianic Idea in Judaism and Other Essays on Jewish Spirituality* (New York: Schocken, 1971), 35.

15. Benjamin, "On the Concept of History," 397.

16. Benjamin, 396, 397.

17. Benjamin, 396, 397.

18. Benjamin, 390.

19. Benjamin, 392.

20. Benjamin, 392, 393.

21. Benjamin, 394

22. Benjamin, 394.

23. Adorno, "Progress," in *Critical Models: Interventions and Catchwords*, trans. Henry W. Pickford (New York: Columbia University Press, 2005), 147.

24. Adorno, "Progress," 144.

25. Adorno, 149.

26. Adorno, 147.

27. Adorno, 147.

28. Adorno, 154. In the spirit of immanent critique, Adorno is suggesting that real progress requires both a negation of bourgeois progress and an affirmation of the

promise, also contained within the bourgeois concept, to advance or create a better set of arrangements.

29. Adorno, 150. Emphasis added.

30. Adorno, 147.

31. Ernst Bloch and Theodor Adorno, "Something's Missing: A Discussion between Ernst Bloch and Theodor W. Adorno on the Contradictions of Utopian Longing," in Ernst Bloch, *The Utopian Function of Art and Literature: Selected Essays*, trans. Jack Zipes and Frank Mecklenberg (Cambridge, MA: MIT Press, 1988), 11.

32. Bloch and Adorno, "Something's Missing," 12.

33. Bloch and Adorno, 12.

34. Bloch and Adorno, 3–4.

35. Bloch and Adorno, 4, 13.

36. Bloch and Adorno, 12.

37. Bloch and Adorno, 12–13.

38. Bloch and Adorno, 13.

39. Bloch and Adorno, 16.

40. Henri Lefebvre, *Critique of Everyday Life*, vol. 1 (New York: Verso, 1991), 232.

41. Lefebvre, *Critique*, 230.

42. Lefebvre, 228, 247.

43. Lefebvre, 134.

44. Lefebvre, 134.

45. Lefebvre, 234.

46. Lefebvre, 232.

47. Lefebvre, 229

48. Lefebvre, 246

49. Lefebvre, 246.

50. Lefebvre, 248, 249.

51. Lefebvre, 250, 251.

52. Lefebvre, 252. Emphasis added.

53. Lefebvre, 251. Calling dialectically for "criticism of the trivial by the exceptional—*but at the same time* criticism of the exceptional by the trivial," he seeks to reintegrate the extraordinary into everyday life in order to reclaim everyday life and thereby remake society.

54. Henri Lefebvre, *Introduction to Modernity: Twelve Preludes, September 1959– May 1961* (London: Verso, 1995), 348, 358.

55. Lefebvre, *Critique*, 199.

56. Lefebvre, 136

57. Lefebvre, *Modernity*, 65–94.

58. Lefebvre, 356.

59. Lefebvre, 356.

60. Lefebvre, 360. "This "new utopianism . . . is testing itself; it is living itself; imagination is becoming a lived experience, something experimental" (357).

61. Lefebvre, 348.

62. Henri Lefebvre, "On the Theme of the New Life" and "Towards a New Romanticism?" in *Introduction to Modernity: Twelve Preludes, September 1959–May 1961* (London: Verso, 1995), 65–94, 239–388; and Lefebvre, *The Explosion: Marxism and the French Upheaval*, trans. Alfred Ehrenfeld (New York: Monthly Review Press, 1969).

63. He argued that May '68 challenged the false opposition between "sudden and gradual approaches, between rupture and constructive activity, between violent assault and activity within the institutions." Lefebvre, *Explosion*, 122, 126.

64. Lefebvre, 103.

65. Lefebvre, 118.

66. Lefebvre, 113.

67. Lefebvre, 123.

68. Lefebvre, 123.

69. Kristin Ross, *Communal Luxury: The Political Imaginary of the Paris Commune* (New York: Verso, 2015), 112.

70. Massimiliano Tomba, "1793: The Neglected Legacy of Insurgent Universality," *History of the Present* 5, no. 2 (Fall 2015): 122.

71. Tomba, "1793." Emphasis added. See also Lowe on the "the past conditional temporality of 'what could have been'"; Lisa Lowe, *The Intimacies of Four Continents* (Durham, NC: Duke University Press, 2015), 127; and Estes on "the past as prophecy"; Nick Estes, *Our History Is the Future: Standing Rock versus the Dakota Access Pipeline, and the Long Tradition of Indigenous Resistance* (New York: Verso, 2019), 44.

72. See for example, W. E. B. Du Bois, "Marxism and the Negro Problem," (1933), "Separation and Self-Respect," (1934), "Segregation," (1934), "A Nation Within a Nation," (1935), all in *W. E. B. Du Bois: A Reader*, ed. David Levering Lewis (New York: Henry Holt, 1995); Du Bois, "The Revelation of Saint Orgne the Damned," in *W. E. B. Du Bois: Writings* (New York: Library of America, 1986); Du Bois, *Dusk of Dawn: The Autobiography of a Race Concept*, in *Writings* (New York: Library of America, 1987), 760–77.

73. Du Bois on Black "second sight," in W. E. B. Du Bois, *Souls of Black Folk*, in *Writings*, 364.

74. Paul Gilroy, *The Black Atlantic: Modernity and Double Consciousness* (Cambridge, MA: Harvard University Press, 1993), 37.

75. Gilroy, *Black Atlantic*, 37.

76. Gilroy, 38. Emphasis added.

77. Gilroy, 37.

78. Gilroy, 37.

79. Gilroy, 38.

80. Gilroy, 39.

81. Gilroy, 39; emphasis added. Gilroy refers to Adorno, Benjamin, and Bloch throughout the book. He concludes with a comparison between modes of remembrance and strategies of critique developed by Jews and Blacks in the modern

West whereby collective suffering is figured as providing its victims with a privileged point of view and endowing them with a redemptive power for humanity as a whole (212–16).

82. Gilroy, *Black Atlantic*, 39; emphasis added.

83. Gilroy, 39. Although many currents of Marxism warrant this criticism, I would suggest that Marx's own thinking is consistent with Gilroy's vision.

84. Gilroy, 39.

85. Fred Moten, *In the Break: The Aesthetics of the Black Radical Tradition* (Minneapolis: University of Minnesota Press, 2003), 2.

86. Moten, *In the Break*, 93.

87. Moten, 93

88. Moten, 124.

89. Moten, 124–25.

90. Stefano Harney and Fred Moten, *The Undercommons: Fugitive Planning and Black Study* (New York: Minor Compositions, 2013), 130; emphasis added.

91. Moten, *In the Break*, 125; emphasis added.

92. Aimé Césaire, "The Thoroughbreds," in *The Collected Poetry of Aimé Césaire*, trans. Clayton Eshelman and Annette Smith (Berkeley: University of California Press, 1984), 101.

93. Benjamin, "On the Concept of History," 407.

7. Time as a Real Abstraction: Clock-Time, Nonsynchronism, Untimeliness

1. Hayden White, *Metahistory: The Historical Imagination in Nineteenth Century Europe* (Baltimore, MD: Johns Hopkins University Press, 1973), 30.

2. White, *Metahistory*, xxx, 2, 23–24, 30.

3. Reinhart Koselleck, "Perspective and Temporality: A Contribution to the Historiographic Exposure of the Historical World," in *Futures Past: On the Semantics of Historical Time* (New York: Columbia University Press, 2004), 150.

4. Reinhart Koselleck, "Historia Magistra Vitae: The Dissolution of the Topos into the Perspective of a Modernized Historical Process" and "*Neuzeit*: Remarks on the Semantics of Modern Concepts of Movement," in *Futures Past: On the Semantics of Historical Time* (New York: Columbia University Press, 2004), 37, 223–24.

5. On the relation between his approach to the history of time and his method of concept history, see Jan-Werner Müller, "On Conceptual History," in *Rethinking Modern European Intellectual History*, ed. Darrin M. McMahon and Samuel Moyn (New York: Oxford University Press, 2014).

6. Although Koselleck challenged Rankean empiricism, he was a conservative thinker whose critique was linked to an antipathy toward modernity and who shared early professional historians' fear of social upheaval. See Niklas Olsen, *History in the Plural: An Introduction to the Work of Reinhart Koselleck* (New York: Berghan, 2012).

7. On disciplinary history's capacity to domesticate critical openings, to recenter

that which had been decentered precisely through a superficial embrace of
the decentering operation, see Joan W. Scott, "History Writing as Critique," in
Manifestos for History, ed. Keith Jenkins, Sue Morgan, and Alun Munslow (New
York: Routledge, 2007), 19–38; and Gary Wilder, "From Optic to Topic: The
Foreclosure Effect of Historiographic Turns," *American Historical Review* 117, no. 3
(June 2012): 723–45.

8. Edmund Leach, "Two Essays Concerning the Symbolic Representation of
Time," in *Rethinking Anthropology* (London: Athlone Press, 1961); Pierre Bourdieu,
The Attitude of the Algerian Peasant Toward Time (The Hague, Netherlands:
Mouton, 1964); Maurice Bloch, "The Past and the Present in the Present," *Man* 12,
no.2 (1977): 278–92; Yosef Yerushalmi, *Zakhor: Jewish History and Jewish Memory*
(New York: Schocken, 1989). Alfred Gell, *The Anthropology of Time: Cultural
Constructions of Temporal Maps and Images* (Oxford: Berg, 1992); Nancy D.
Munn, "The Cultural Anthropology of Time: A Critical Essay," *Annual Review
of Anthropology* 21 (1992): 93–123; Dipesh Chakrabarty, *Provincializing Europe:
Postcolonial Thought and Historical Difference* (Princeton, NJ: Princeton University
Press, 2000).

9. Immanuel Kant, *Critique of Pure Reason*, trans. Paul Guyer and Allen W.
Wood (Cambridge: Cambridge University Press, 1998).

10. Kant, *Critique of Pure Reason*, 162–71.

11. Émile Durkheim, *The Elementary Forms of Religious Life* (New York: Free
Press, 1995), 11–13; George Woodcock, "The Tyranny of the Clock" (1944); Louis
Althusser, "The Object of Capital," in *Reading Capital*, ed. Althusser and Étienne
Balibar (New York: Verso, 2009), 101–31; Michel Foucault, *Discipline and Punish:
The Birth of the Prison* (New York: Vintage, 1977); Michel de Certeau, *The Practice
of Everyday Life* (Berkeley: University of California Press, 1984); Johannes Fabian,
Time and the Other: How Anthropology Makes Its Object (New York: Columbia
University Press, 1983); Lee Edelman, *No Future: Queer Theory and the Death Drive*
(Durham, NC: Duke University Press, 2004); Vanessa Ogle, "Whose Time Is It? The
Pluralization of Time and the Global Condition, 1870s–1940s," *American Historical
Review* 120, no. 5 (December 2013): 1376–1402; On Barak, "Outdating: The Time of
"Culture" in Colonial Egypt," *Grey Room* (May 2013).

12. David Couzens Hoy, *The Time of Our Lives: A Critical History of Temporality*
(Cambridge, MA: MIT Press, 2009). For a recent example of this approach, see
Espen Hammer, *Philosophy and Temporality from Kant to Critical Theory*
(Cambridge: Cambridge University Press, 2011).

13. Harvey explains how under capitalism, money, space, and time, which he
describes as interlinked sources of social power, are "abstractions" that became
"embedded in a social process that creates abstract forces that have concrete and
personal effects in daily life." David Harvey, "Money, Time, Space, and the City,"
in *The Urban Experience* (Baltimore, MD: Johns Hopkins University Press, 1989),
165. On labor and time as real abstractions under capitalism see Moishe Postone,
Time, Labor, and Social Domination: A Reinterpretation of Marx's Critical Theory

(Cambridge: Cambridge University Press, 1993), 123–225. On concrete abstractions, see Henri Lefebvre, *The Production of Space*, trans. Donald Nicholson-Smith (Oxford: Blackwell, 1992), 26–27; and Lukasz Stanek, *Henri Lefebvre on Space: Architecture, Urban Research, and the Production of Theory* (Minneapolis: University of Minnesota Press, 2011), 133–64.

14. Postone, *Time, Labor, and Social Domination*, 186–216.

15. Karl Marx, *Capital: A Critique of Political Economy*, vol. 1 (New York: Penguin, 1992).

16. Max Weber, *The Protestant Ethic and the Spirit of Capitalism* (New York: Routledge, 1992), 4.

17. Weber, *The Protestant Ethic*, 24.

18. Weber, 14–16.

19. See Clifford Sharp, *The Economics of Time* (Oxford: Martin Robertson, 1981), which questions the productivist logic of "saving time" with regard to economic utility, social welfare, and human happiness.

20. Alfred W. Crosby, *The Measure of Reality: Quantification in Western Europe, 1250–1600* (Cambridge: Cambridge University Press, 1997); Jacques Le Goff, "Merchant's Time and Church's Time in the Middle Ages" and "Labor Time in the 'Crisis' of the Fourteenth Century: From Medieval to Modern Time," in *Time, Work, and Culture in the Middle Ages*, trans. Arthur Goldhammer (Chicago: University of Chicago Press, 1980), 29–52; Daniel Rosenberg and Anthony Grafton, *Cartographies of Time: A History of the Timeline* (New York: Princeton Architectural Press, 2010); David S. Landes, *Revolution in Time: Clocks and the Making of the Modern World* (Cambridge, MA: The Belknap Press of Harvard University Press, 2000), 48–86; Eviatar Zerubavel, *Hidden Rhythms: Schedules and Calendars in Social Life* (Chicago: University of Chicago Press, 1981); E. P. Thompson "Time, Work Discipline, and Industrial Capitalism," *Past and Present*, no. 38 (December 1967): 56–97; Eviatar Zerubavel, "The Benedictine Ethic and the Modern Spirit of Scheduling: On Schedules and Social Life," *Sociological Inquiry* 50, no. 2 (April 1980): 157–69; Eviatar Zerubavel, "The Standardization of Time: A Sociohistorical Perspective," *American Journal of Sociology* 88, no. 1 (1982): 1–23; On Barak, *On Time: Technology and Temporality in Modern Egypt* (Berkeley: University of California Press, 2013); Ogle, "Whose Time Is It?"; Helge Jordheim, "Synchronizing the World: Synchronism as Historiographical Practice, Then and Now," *History of the Present* 7, no. 1 (Spring 2017): 59–95.

21. On the state's attempt to synchronize temporal heterogeneity under capitalism, see Massimiliano Tomba, "Historical Temporalities of Capital: An Anti-Historicist Perspective," *Historical Materialism* 17, no. 4 (2009): 44–65; and Tomba, *Marx's Temporalities* (Leiden, Netherlands: Brill, 2012), 149–86.

22. Karl Polanyi, *The Great Transformation: The Political and Economic Origins of our Times* (Boston: Beacon Press, 1971); Fernand Braudel, *Civilization and Capitalism, Fifteenth–Eighteenth Century*, vols. 1–3 (Berkeley: University of California Press, 1992); Charles Tilly, *Coercion, Capital, and European States, AD*

990–1992 (Oxford: Blackwell, 1992); Giovanni Arrighi, *The Long Twentieth Century: Money, Power, and the Origins of Our Times*, new and updated ed. (New York: Verso, 2010); Michael Mann, *The Sources of Social Power*, vol. 2, *The Rise of Classes and Nation-States, 1760–1914* (Cambridge: Cambridge University Press, 1993); Bob Jessop, *The State: Past, Present, and Future* (Cambridge: Polity Press, 2016).

23. See Benedict Anderson, *Imagined Communities: Reflections on the Origins and Spread of Nationalism*, new ed. (New York: Verso, 2006); Mona Ozouf, *Festivals and the French Revolution* (Cambridge, MA: Harvard University Press, 1991); and Nicos Poulantzas, *State, Power Socialism* (New York: Verso, 2014).

24. See, for example, Fernand Braudel, *Civlization and Capitalism, Fifteenth–Eighteenth Century*, vol. 3, *The Perspective of the World* (Berkeley: University of California Press, 1992).

25. Moishe Postone, *Time, Labor, and Social Domination: A Reinterpretation of Marx's Critical Theory* (Cambridge: Cambridge University Press, 1993), 186–225.

26. Harvey, "Money, Time, Space," 174, 173.

27. Norbert Elias, *Time: An Essay* (Oxford: Blackwell, 1992).

28. Karl Marx, *Capital: A Critique of Political Economy*, vols. 1–3 (New York: Penguin, 1992).

29. See David Harvey, *The Limits to Capital*, new and updated ed. (New York: Verso, 2006), 373–412.

30. David Harvey, The *Condition of Postmodernity: An Enquiry into the Origins of Cultural Change* (London: Blackwell, 1989), 260–307.

31. David Harvey, "The 'New' Imperialism: Accumulation by Disposession," *Socialist Register* 40 (2004): 63–87. These "spatiotemporal fixes" require readily available credit and large amounts of public and private debt. Harvey describes debt as a claim on already mortgaged future labor which will have to be redeemed at some point. Debt thus allows capitalism to reproduce itself, and to foreclose alternative futures, by encumbering indebted actors, accounting for their time and energy for years to come. David Harvey, "Anti-Value in Marx," Lecture, Development Studies Seminar Series, SOAS, University of London, November 17, 2016.

32. Postone, *Time, Labor, and Social Domination*, 298–306.

33. Reinhart Koselleck, "On the Need for Theory in the Discipline of History," in *The Practice of Conceptual History: Timing History, Spacing Concepts* (Stanford, CA: Stanford University Press, 2002), 6.

34. Karl Löwith, *Meaning in History: The Theological Implications of the Philosophy of History* (Chicago: University of Chicago Press, 1949).

35. George Stocking, *Victorian Anthropology* (New York: Free Press, 1991), 107, 69–77; Thomas Trautman, "The Revolution in Ethnological Time," *Man* 27, no. 2 (June, 1992): 379–97; Fabian, *Time and the Other*, 1–104 and 143–66; Michel Foucault, *The Order of Things: An Archaeology of the Human Sciences* (New York: Random House, 1970).

36. Koselleck, "Modernity and the Planes of Historicity" and "Historia Magistra Vitae: The Dissolution of the Topos into the Perspective of a Modernized Historical

Process," in *Futures Past: On the Semantics of Historical Time* (New York: Columbia University Press, 2004), 9–42.

37. Leopold von Ranke, "The Idea of Universal History," in *The Theory and Practice of History* (New York: Routledge, 2011), 8, 10. In contrast to von Ranke, Dilthey specifies historical thinking as distinct from both teleological philosophies of history and positivist natural sciences insofar as it focuses on the interpretation of integrated systems of meaning, value, and action. See Wilhelm Dilthey, *Selected Works*, vol. 1: *Introduction to the Human Sciences* (Princeton, NJ: Princeton University Press, 1989). In the early twentieth century, Croce criticizes Ranke's antiphilosophical and antipolitical positivist history that posits an objectivist indifference to the past that must be studied for its own sake. Benedetto Croce, *History as the Story of Liberty* (New York: W. W. Norton, 1941); and Croce, *History: Its Theory and Practice* (New York: Russell and Russell, 1960). Although Croce criticizes idealist philosophies of history, he insists that real historical understanding also requires philosophical thinking.

38. Ranke, "Idea of Universal History," 13.

39. Ranke, "On the Epochs of Modern History," in *Theory and Practice of History* (New York: Routledge, 2011), 22; Von Ranke, "Idea of Universal History," 22.

40. Ranke, "Idea of Universal History," 15. I would suggest that such understandings of sequence and causality enable what White called von Ranke's technique of "explanation by narration." White, *Metahistory*, 167. Cf. La Capra on how conventional history rewards the translation of archives into narrative. Dominick LaCapra, *History and Its Limits: Human, Animal, Violence* (Ithaca, NY: Cornell University Press, 2009), 36.

41. Ranke, "Epochs of Modern History, 22.

42. Ranke, "Idea of Universal History," 11.

43. Ranke, 11.

44. Walter Benjamin, "On the Concept of History," in *Selected Writings*, vol. 4, 1938–1940 (Cambridge, MA: The Belknap Press of Harvard University Press, 2003).

45. Conversely, nineteenth-century philosophy was increasingly refracted through history. On the shift from a classical concept of order to the nineteenth-century concept of History as the new ontological and epistemological foundation of the human sciences, see Foucault, *Order of Things*, 217–20 and 367–72.

46. Aristotle held that a successful tragedy, or story, should represent an action that is "complete in itself . . . a whole" with a clear beginning, middle, and end. It should be "of a certain definite magnitude," not too large or too small, and "comprehensible as a whole" which requires that it "present a certain order in its arrangements of parts" such that "the causes should be included in the incidents." "Poetics," in *The Basic Works of Aristotle*, ed. Richard McKeon (New York: The Modern Library, 2001), 1462–68. In these prescriptions, we can recognize assumptions about "context" as the self-contained unity and integrity of action, causality, setting, sequence, and spatial and temporal scale within a structured whole that continues to inform empiricist history and realist politics.

47. On the influence of this German model of historical scholarship for the professionalization of academic history in the United States, see Peter Novick, *That Noble Dream: The "Objectivity Question" and the American Historical Profession* (Cambridge: Cambridge University Press, 1988). For U.S. celebrations of Rankean empiricist history, see George Burton Adams, "History and the Philosophy of History," *American Historical Review* 14, no. 2 (January 1909): 221–36; and Edward G. Bourne, "Leopold von Ranke," *Annual Report of the American Historical Association* (1896) I, 67–81.

48. R. G. Collingwood, *The Idea of History* (Oxford: Oxford University Press, 1994), 363.

49. R. G. Collingwood, "Some Perplexities about Time with an Attempted Solution," *Proceedings of the Aristotelian Society* 26 (1925): 135–50.

50. Siegfried Kracauer, *History: The Last Things Before the Last* (Princeton, NJ: Markus Wiener Publishers, 1995), 142–54.

51. Kracauer, *History*, 155.

52. Kracauer, 135.

53. Kracauer, 158.

54. Kracauer, 158; emphasis added.

55. Kracauer, 155.

56. Kracauer, 155.

57. Jacques Rancière, "Le concept d'anachronisme et la vérité de l'historien," *L'Inactuel: psychanalyse et culture*, no. 6 (Fall 1996), 58.

58. Rancière, "Le concept d'anachronisme," 56.

59. Rancière, 56.

60. Rancière, 58.

61. Rancière, 58.

62. Rancière, 60.

63. Rancière, 62.

64. Jacques Rancière, *Names of History: On the Poetics of Knowledge* (Minneapolis: University of Minnesota Press, 1994). On Rancière's historical methodology, see Kristin Ross "Historicizing Untimeliness," in *Jacques Rancière: History, Politics, Aesthetics*, ed. Gabriel Rockhill and Philip Watts (Durham, NC: Duke University Press, 2009); and Mischa Suter, "A Thorn in the Side of Social History: Jacques Rancière and *Les Révoltes logiques*," *International Review of Social History* 57, no. 1 (2012): 61–85.

65. Rancière, "Le concept d'anachronisme," 66.

66. Rancière, 67.

67. Rancière, 66.

68. Rancière, 67–68.

69. Rancière, 68.

70. Rancière, 68, 66.

71. M. M. Bakhtin, "The *Bildungsroman* and Its Significance in the History of Realism (Toward a Historical Typology of the Novel)," in *Speech Genres and Other*

Late Essays (Austin: University of Texas Press, 1986), 28; and Reinhart Koselleck "'Space of Experience' and 'Horizon of Expectation': Two Historical Categories," in *Futures Past: On the Semantics of Historical Time* (New York: Columbia University Press, 2004), 269.

72. Koselleck, "Space of Experience," 260.

73. Reinhart Koselleck, "History, Histories, and Formal Time Structures" and "*Neuzeit*: Remarks on the Semantics of Modern Concepts of Movement," in *Futures Past: On the Semantics of Historical Time* (New York: Columbia University Press, 2004), 90–99 and 239–46. On the different ways Koselleck uses this term, see Wilder, *Freedom Time: Negritude, Decolonization, and the Future of the World* (Durham, NC: Duke University Press, 2015), 38–39. Note that the term in Koselleck that has been translated into English as "noncontemporaneity" (*Ungleichzeitigkeit*) is the same as used by Ernst Bloch, which is usually translated by Bloch scholars as "nonsynchronism." It also conveys nonsimultaneity. In English, of course, "contemporaneity" and "synchronism" have different, if related, connotations.

74. For example, Abraham Joshua Heschel, *The Sabbath: Its Meaning for Modern Man* (New York: Farrar, Straus and Giroux, 1951); and recent discussions of queer temporalities in Elizabeth Freeman, *Time Binds: Queer Temporalities, Queer Histories* (Durham, NC: Duke University Press, 2010); Jose Muñoz, *Cruising Utopia: The Then and There of Queer Futurity* (New York: New York University Press, 2009); Judith Halberstam, "Queer Temporalities and Postmodern Geographies," in *In a Queer Time and Place: Transgender Bodies, Subcultural Lives* (New York: New York University Press, 2005).

75. On immediate experience and the unity of life versus the reification of events and causality in history and by historians, see George Simmel, "The Problem of Historical Time," *Essays on Interpretation in Social Science* (Lanham, MD: Rowan and Littlefield, 1980).

76. Bergson elaborates this notion of time as a "pure duration" and "qualitative or heterogeneous multiplicity" in which all pasts persist by referring to "an indistinct and even undivided multiplicity, purely intensive or qualitative, which, while remaining what it is, will comprise an indefinitely increasing number of elements, as the new points of view for considering it appear in the world . . . a duration in which novelty is constantly springing forth and evolution is creative." Henri Bergson, *The Creative Mind: Introduction to Metaphysics* (New York: Philosophical Library, 1986), 15, 23.

77. Karl Marx, "Economic and Philosophical Manuscripts (1844), 324.

78. Marx, *Capital*, vol. 1, 289.

79. Marx, 289.

80. Marx, 128. "The worker himself constantly produces objective wealth, in the form of capital, as an alien power that dominates and exploits him; and the capitalist . . . produces the worker as a wage-laborer" (716).

81. Derrida suggests that Marx's concern with haunting specters and time that is out of joint somehow stands in contradiction to Marx's realist and rationalist

investments. He does not recognize that Marx identified subjective and objective forms of untimeliness as central features of capitalist society. The discovery of spectrality in Marx's writing is not in itself grounds for a critique of Marx. Jacques Derrida, *Specters of Marx: The State of the Debt, the Work of Mourning, and the New International* (New York: Routledge, 1994).

82. Karl Marx, *The Eighteenth Brumaire of Louis Napoleon* (New York: International Publishers, 1964), 15. See also Massimiliano Tomba, "Political Historiography. Re-Reading the *Eighteenth Brumaire*," in *Marx's Temporalities* (Leiden, Netherlands: Brill, 2012), 35–59; and Karajan Karatani, "On the Eighteenth Brumaire of Louis Bonaparte," in *History and Repetition* (New York: Columbia University Press, 2012).

83. Stephen Kern, *The Culture of Time and Space, 1880–1918* (Cambridge, MA: Harvard University Press, 1983), 82–88.

84. M. M. Bakhtin, "Forms of Time and Chronotope in the Novel," in *The Dialogic Imagination: Four Essays* (Austin: University of Texas Press, 1981), 206.

85. Bakhtin, "Forms of Time," 209.

86. Bakhtin, 211, 212.

87. Bakhtin, 213, 216.

88. Bakhtin, 216.

89. Bakhtin, 216.

90. M. M. Bakhtin, "*Bildungsroman*," 29.

91. Ernst Bloch, "Nonsynchronism and the Obligation to Its Dialectics," *New German Critique*, no. 11 (Spring 1977): 22–38.

92. Samir Amin, *Accumulation on a World Scale: A Critique of the Theory of Underdevelopment*, vol. 1 (New York: Monthly Review Press, 1974); Lefebvre, *Production of Space*, 62, 86–88, 122–23, 335–36, 342, 351, 403. See also Neil Smith, *Uneven Development: Nature, Capital, and the Production of Space* (Athens: University of Georgia Press, 1984); David Harvey, "Notes Towards a Theory of Uneven Geographic Development," *Spaces of Global Capitalism: A Theory of Uneven Geographical Development* (New York: Verso, 2006); Tomba, *Marx's Temporalities*, 159–86. Within the Subaltern Studies Project, Guha examines the contemporaneity of apparently "pre-political" peasant rebellions and modern colonial politics in India, and Dipesh Chakrabarty examines the presence of gods, spirits, and relations of direct domination in labor regimes and factory production in colonial Bengal. Ranajit Guha, *Elementary Aspects of Peasant Insurgency in Colonial India* (Durham, NC: Duke University Press, 1999); Dipesh Chakrabarty, *Rethinking Working-Class History, 1890–1940* (Princeton, NJ: Princeton University Press, 1989). See also Kalyan Sanyal, *Rethinking Capitalist Development: Primitive Accumulation, Governmentality, and Post-Colonial Capitalism* (Abingdon: Routledge, 2007).

93. Leon Trotsky, *History of the Russian Revolution*, trans. Max Eastman (Chicago: Haymarket, 2008), 4–11, 38; Antonio Gramsci, "Some Aspects of the Southern Question," in *Pre-Prison Writings* (Cambridge: Cambridge University Press, 1994); Ernst Bloch, *The Heritage of Our Times* (Cambridge: Polity Press, 1991);

Henri Lefebvre, *Critique of Everyday Life*, vol. 1: *Introduction* (New York: Verso, 2008). This tradition is analyzed in Harry Harootunian, *Marx after Marx: History and Time in the Expansion of Capitalism* (New York: Columbia University Press, 2015).

94. Harry Harootunian, "Remembering the Historical Present," *Critical Inquiry* 33, no. 3 (Spring 2007): 477. In subsequent work, Harootunian identifies this insight in Marx's writings about real and formal subsumption being ongoing features of even developed capitalism. He traces the elaboration of this idea in the work of peripheral and heterodox Marxists, not only Luxemburg, Trotsky, and Gramsci, but also José Carlos Mariátegui in Peru and Uno Kozo (and others) in Japan. Harootunian, *Marx after Marx*. On the co-existence of diverse temporal currents within a disjunctive present, see David Scott, "The Temporality of Generations: Dialogue, Tradition, Criticism," *New Literary History* 45, no. 2 (Spring 2014): 157–81.

95. Mikhail Bakhtin, "Discourse in the Novel," in *The Dialogic Imagination: Four Essays* (Austin: University of Texas Press, 1981), 284.

96. Bakhtin, "Discourse in the Novel," 291.

97. Bakhtin, 263. For example, I would suggest that Sigmund Freud, *Moses and Monotheism* (New York: Vintage, 1967); Yosef Hayim Yerushalmi, *Freud's Moses: Judaism Terminable and Interminable* (New Haven, CT: Yale University Press, 1991); and Jacques Derrida, *Archive Fever: A Freudian Impression* (Chicago: University of Chicago Press, 1995) compose a heteroglot unity whose components address questions related to history, memory, time, and truth. Similarly, we can treat Aimé Césaire's plays *The Tragedy of King Christophe* (1963) and *A Season in the Congo* (1966) as a heteroglot unity that encompassed the real-life tragedy of Patrice Lumumba along with the general drama of decolonization then unfolding. For an insightful analysis of the untimely character of C. L. R. James, *The Black Jacobins*, see David Scott, *Conscripts of Modernity: The Tragedy of Colonial Enlightenment* (Durham, NC: Duke University Press, 2004).

98. Koselleck, *Futures Past*, 4, 222–54, 271.

99. Reinhart Koselleck, "Introduction and Prefaces to the *Geschichtliche Grundbegriffe*," *Contributions to the History of Concepts* 6, no. 1 (Summer 2011): 8. Koselleck relates the development of modern time to the proliferation of temporal concepts and the temporalization of political concepts in public life.

100. "Effectively taking this into account," he insists, "should be the point of departure for a historical science." Rancière, "Le concept d'anachronisme," 68.

101. In *Marx after Marx*, Harootunian argues that entrenched assumptions about progressive time prevent even many Left and postcolonial historians from pursuing a Marxian approach to modernity's temporal unevenness.

102. Cf. LaCapra on history as a dialogue between past and present and historians' transferential relation to their object of study. Dominick LaCapra, *History and Criticism* (Ithaca, NY: Cornell University Press, 1985), 71–84, 94, 114.

103. Immanuel Kant, "Idea for a Universal History with a Cosmopolitan Purpose," in *Political Writings* (Cambridge: Cambridge University Press, 1970), 50.

104. Benjamin, "On the Concept of History," 390. "The past carries with it a

secret index by which it is referred to redemption. Doesn't a breath of the air that pervaded earlier days caress us as well? In the voices we hear, isn't there an echo of now silent ones? Don't the women we court have sisters they no longer recognize? If so then there is a secret agreement between past generations and our present one. Then our coming was expected on earth. Then like every generation that preceded us, we have been endowed with a *weak* messianic power, a power on which the past has a claim. Such a claim cannot be settled cheaply."

105. Note the difference between this charter to act politically in relation to a past generation that has a moral claim on us and Derrida's suggestion that Benjamin's "weak messianic power" is an invitation for a waiting without expectation. Derrida, *Specters of Marx*, 227–28.

106. Benjamin quotes Turgot: "politics always needs, so to speak, the present." Walter Benjamin, *The Arcades Project* (Cambridge, MA: Harvard University Press, 1999), 478.

107. Benjamin, "Paralipomena to 'On the Concept of History,'" in *Selected Writings*, vol. 4, 1938–1940 (Cambridge, MA: The Belknap Press of Harvard University Press, 2003), 407; emphasis added.

8. Dialectic of Past and Future

1. Michael Löwy, "Romanticism, Marxism, and Religion in the 'Principle of Hope' of Ernst Bloch," *Crisis and Critique* 2, no. 1 (February 2015): 352.

2. Michel Foucault, *Discipline and Punish: The Birth of the* Prison (New York: Vintage, 1977), 31.

3. Several of Foucault's early historical studies—*Madness and Civilization* (1961), *The Birth of the Clinic* (1963), *The Order of Things* (1966)—could be read as already implicitly genealogical despite the fact that he identified them with an archaeological approach.

4. Michel Foucault, "Nietzsche, Genealogy, History," in *Language, Counter-Memory, Practice: Selected Essays and Interviews* (Ithaca, NY: Cornell University Press, 1977), 156.

5. Foucault, "Nietzsche, Genealogy, History," 156.

6. Michel Foucault, "Questions on Geography," in *Power/Knowledge: Selected Interviews and Other Writings, 1972–1977* (New York: Pantheon, 1980), 64.

7. Michel Foucault, "What Our Present Is," in *The Politics of Truth* (Los Angeles: Semiotext(e), 1997), 137.

8. Foucault, "Nietzsche, Genealogy, History," 157.

9. Foucault, "What Our Present Is," 137.

10. Foucault, 138–39.

11. Michel Foucault, "What Is Revolution?," in *The Politics of Truth* (Los Angeles: Semiotext(e), 1997), 85.

12. Michel Foucault, "What Is Critique?," in *The Politics of Truth* (Los Angeles: Semiotext(e), 1997), 45.

13. Michel Foucault, "What Is Revolution?," 84.

14. Michel Foucault, 86.

15. Michel Foucault, "What Is Enlightenment?," in *The Politics of Truth* (Los Angeles: Semiotext(e), 1997), 114.

16. Michel Foucault, "What Is Enlightenment?," 118.

17. Michel Foucault, 116.

18. Foucault, "Nietzsche, Genealogy, History," 139.

19. Foucault, "What Is Enlightenment?," 109.

20. Foucault, "Nietzsche, Genealogy, History," xx.

21. Foucault, 160–61.

22. Foucault, 147.

23. Foucault, "What Is Critique?," 62–63, 64, 65.

24. Foucault, "Nietzsche, Genealogy, History," 146.

25. He reassures readers, and possibly himself, that Heidegger's analysis of Socrates "is not at all a matter of resorting to anachronism and of projecting the 18th century on the 5th" (Foucault, "What Is Critique?," 74).

26. Michel Foucault, *The Order of Things: An Archaeology of the Human Sciences* (New York: Vintage, 1970). Cf. Reinhart Koselleck, *Futures Past* on the temporalization of history.

27. "How can one capitalize the time of individuals, accumulate it in each of them, in their bodies, in their forces or in their abilities, in a way that is susceptible of use and control? How can one organize profitable durations?" (Foucault, *Discipline and Punish*, 157).

28. Friedrich Nietzsche, *On the Genealogy of Morals and Ecce Homo* (New York: Vintage Books, 1989), 20.

29. Nietzsche, *Genealogy of Morals*, 77.

30. Nietzsche, 78.

31. Friedrich Nietzsche, *The Birth of Tragedy* (New York: Doubleday/Anchor, 1956), 108.

32. Nietzsche, *Birth of Tragedy*, 137.

33. Nietzsche, 137.

34. Nietzsche, 139.

35. Nietzsche, 137.

36. Nietzsche, xx

37. Nietzsche, 138. Cf. Benjamin's lightning flashes of historical illumination in moments of danger.

38. Nietzsche, 121.

39. Nietzsche, 120–21.

40. Nietzsche, 122, 123.

41. Foucault, "Two Lectures," in *Power/Knowledge: Selected Interviews and Other Writings, 1972–1977* (New York: Pantheon, 1980), 80, 81.

42. Foucault, "Two Lectures," 85. Foucault regularly conflated Marxian theory with the orthodox Marxism of the Soviet state and the French Communist Party on

economic determinism, stagist laws of social development, and a teleological belief in historical progress.

43. Karl Marx, *Capital: A Critique of Political Economy*, vol. 1, trans. Ben Fowkes (New York: Vintage Books, 1977), 173.

44. Marx, *Capital*, 635

45. Karl Marx, "Economic and Philosophical Manuscripts (1844)," in *Early Writings* (New York: Penguin Books, 1992), 329.

46. Marx, "Economic and Philosophical Manuscripts," 329.

47. Marx, 329.

48. Marx, 348.

49. Marx, 347, 349.

50. Marx's understanding becomes clearer in his sixth thesis: "The human essence is not abstraction inherent in each single individual . . . it is the ensemble of the social relations" created through a "historical process" which cannot presuppose "an abstract—*isolated*—human individual." "Theses on Feuerbach," in *Marx-Engels Reader*, 145.

51. Marx, "Economic and Philosophical Manuscripts," 352.

52. Marx, *Capital*, 772.

53. Marx, 171, 172–73.

54. Marx, 173.

55. Marx, 517.

56. Marx, 532. "Owing to its conversion into an automaton, the instrument of labor confronts the worker during the labor process in the shape of capital, dead labor, which dominates and soaks up living labor-power" (548).

57. Marx, 548

58. Marx, 508.

59. Marx, 552.

60. Marx, 929.

61. Marx, 929.

62. Marx, 619.

63. Marx, 172.

64. Karl Marx, *Grundrisse: Foundations of a Critique of Political Economy* (London: Penguin, 1973), 488.

65. Marx, *Grundrisse*, 487–88.

66. Marx, 471.

67. Marx, *Capital*, 171.

68. Marx, 171–72.

69. Marx, 927.

70. Marx, 173.

71. Marx, 173.

72. Marx, 928.

73. Marx, 927.

74. Marx, 927.

75. Marx, 929.

76. Marx, 929.

77. Marx never argues that the postcapitalist "expropriation of the expropriators" is inevitable. It could only be realized concretely through the action of "the mass of the people." Marx, 930.

78. Karl Marx, *The Eighteenth Brumaire of Louis Napoleon* (International Publishers, 1964), 15.

79. Karl Marx, "For a Ruthless Criticism of Everything Existing," in *The Marx-Engels Reader*, 2nd ed., ed. Robert Tucker (New York: W. W. Norton, 1978), 14.

80. Marx, "Ruthless Criticism," 14; Marx, here, anticipates the Frankfurt School's later critique of instrumental reason.

81. Marx, 14.

82. Marx, "Economic and Philosophical Manuscripts," 348.

83. Marx, "Ruthless Criticism," 13.

84. Marx, 13.

85. Marx, 15.

86. Cf. Wilder, *Freedom Time: Negritude, Decolonization, and the Future of the World* (Durham, NC: Duke University Press, 2015); and Kleinberg on "past possibles," Ethan Kleinberg, *Haunting History: For a Deconstructive Approach to the Past* (Stanford, CA: Stanford University Press, 2017).

87. Tomba employs Ernst Bloch's term "multiversum" to describe how capitalism includes elements of past social formations and modes of production, each of which contains a different temporal velocity and developmental path. He contends that through the state, market compulsions, and the generalization of abstract time, modern capitalism works to synchronize these multiple temporalities among which he also includes the "countertemporalities" of workers' struggles. He also argues that capitalism produces such differentiations as a precondition for ongoing economic growth. Tomba thus demonstrates how, for Marx, primitive or "original accumulation cannot be confined to a precise historical moment at the beginning of the capitalist mode of production. Rather it is constantly reproduced by the capitalist mode of production itself." Massimiliano Tomba, "Layered Historiography," *Marx's Temporalities* (Leiden, Netherlands: Brill, 2013), 165. Harootunian develops the similar argument that Marx regarded formal subsumption as a systemic feature rather than a historical stage of capitalism. Harry Harootunian, *Marx after Marx: History and Time in the Expansion of Capitalism* (New York: Columbia University Press, 2017).

88. Marx, *Grundrisse*, 105.

89. Marx, 105; emphasis added.

90. Marx, 106.

91. Marx, 105–6. Likewise, he characterizes joint-stock companies as a late bourgeois iteration of early modern monopoly trading companies. Marx, *Capital*, xx.

92. Marx, "Preface to the First Edition," *Capital: A Critique of Political Economy*, vol. 1 (New York: Vintage Books, 1977), 91.

93. Marx, "Preface," 91.

94. Marx, "Critique of Hegel's Philosophy of Right: Introduction," in *Early Writings* (London: Penguin, 1992), 257.

95. Marx, "Hegel's Philosophy of Right," 245.

96. Marx, 249.

97. Marx, 249.

98. Marx, 249.

99. Karl Marx, 247.

100. Marx, 247.

101. Marx, 247.

102. Karl Marx, Letter to Vera Zasulich, March 8, 1881, https://www.marxists.org /archive/marx/works/1881/zasulich/reply.htm.

103. On Marx's growing interest in the Russian Commune as evidence that he moved away from a stagist theory of history, see also Kevin B. Anderson, *Marx at the Margins: On Nationalism, Ethincity, and Non-Western Societies* (Chicago: University of Chicago Press, 2016); Massimiliano Tomba, *Marx's Temporalities* (Chicago: Haymarket, 2014); Harootunian, *Marx after Marx*; and Kristin Ross, *Communal Luxury: The Political Imaginary of the Paris Commune* (New York: Verso, 2015).

104. Marx, Letter to Zasulich.

105. Marx, Letter to Zasulich; emphasis added.

106. Marx, *Grundrisse*, 110.

107. Marx, 110.

108. Marx, 111.

109. Marx, 111.

110. Marx, 111.

111. Marx, 111.

112. Cf. Aimé Césaire, "Poetry and Knowledge" (1944).

113. Marx, *Grundrisse*, 110.

114. Marx, 487–88.

115. Marx, 488.

116. Marx, 488.

117. Marx, 488.

118. Marx, 488.

119. Michael Löwy and Robert Sayre, *Romanticism against the Tide of Modernity* (Durham, NC: Duke University Press, 2001), 73–74.

120. Löwy and Sayre, *Romanticism*, 92.

121. Löwy and Sayre, 93.

122. Löwy and Sayre, 93.

123. Löwy and Sayre, 99.

124. Löwy and Sayre, 102.

125. Löwy and Sayre, 104.

126. Michael Löwy, "Naphta or Settembrini? Lukács and Romantic Anticapitalism," *New German Critique* 42 (Autumn 1987): 25.

127. Löwy, "Naphta or Settembrini?," 28.

128. Georg Lukács, "The Old Culture and the New Culture," in *Marxism and Human Liberation: Essays on History, Culture, and Revolution* (New York: Delta Publishing, 1973), 5.

129. Lukács, "Old Culture," 4

130. Lukács, 6–7.

131. Lukács, 6–7.

132. Lukács, 5.

133. This section was later published separately in English as Ernst Bloch, "Nonsynchronism and the Obligation to Its Dialectics," *New German Critique*, no. 11 (Spring 1977): 22–38.

134. Bloch, "Nonsynchronism," 31.

135. Bloch, 29.

136. Bloch, 29.

137. Bloch, 23.

138. Bloch, 31.

139. Bloch, 31.

140. Bloch, 30.

141. Bloch, 32.

142. Bloch, 32; emphasis added.

143. Bloch, 32.

144. Bloch, 30.

145. Bloch, 31.

146. Bloch, 34.

147. Bloch, 34.

148. Bloch, 32.

149. Bloch, 32; emphasis added.

150. Bloch, 32; emphasis added.

151. Cf. Césaire, "Poetry and Knowledge" (1944).

152. Bloch, "Nonsynchronism," 34.

153. Bloch, 36–37; emphasis added. Bloch later develops the idea of human history "moving not in unilinear development but entirely polyrhythmically and polyphonically" and as a "profusion, an interweaving of time and of epochs, and therefore a spaciousness in the flow of history" which he likens to a symphony. Bloch, *A Philosophy of the Future* (New York: Herder and Herder, 1970), 112, 123. On this basis, he refigures world history as "a *multiverse*" (123). Unfortunately, "Conventional history . . . does not recognize the *problem of* variable dimensions of time, let alone that a non-rigid concept of time itself might be called for" (128). Bloch therefore invokes "a 'multi-dimensionality' of the time-line" that can accommodate such "varied time structures" in which "different" and "often non-uniform types of progress (in economy, technology, art and so on) occur" (129, 130, 131).

154. Bloch, "Nonsynchronism," 33.

155. Bloch, 33.

156. Bloch, 34.

157. Bloch, 34.

158. Bloch, 34.

159. Bloch, 34.

160. Bloch, 33.

161. Bloch, 34.

162. Bloch, 34–35.

163. Bloch, 33.

164. Bloch, 36.

165. Bloch, 35, 36; emphasis added.

166. Bloch, 33.

167. Bloch, 36.

168. Bloch, 38.

169. Bloch, 38

170. "This totality must be *critical* so as not to load itself down with stale modes of being . . . for the sake of those very elements in the past which are not past and continue to be effective, for the sake of the *genuine nebulae* (which have yet to give birth to a star)." Bloch, "Nonsynchronism," 37. Bloch contrasted this new "critical totality" to the "idealist 'totality,' which is a mere totality of the [capitalist] system."

171. In later work, Bloch refers to the "still living, not yet discharged past" and praises Marxism for its capacity to recognize "the future in the past." He suggests that in Marx's thinking, "the rigid divisions between future and past . . . collapse" such that the "unbecome future becomes visible in the past, avenged and inherited, mediated and fulfilled." Ernst Bloch, *The Principle of Hope*, vol. 1 (Cambridge, MA: MIT Press, 1986), 8–9.

172. Walter Benjamin, "Surrealism," in *Selected Writings*, vol. 2, 1927–1930 (Cambridge, MA: The Belknap Press of Harvard University Press, 1996), 210.

173. Benjamin, "Surrealism," 210.

174. Benjamin, 215

175. Benjamin, 210; emphasis added.

176. He explains that whereas the seventeenth-century dramatists were slavishly loyal to church and state, their "present day heirs" are unconcerned with the state. And whereas the Baroque marked a "significant rebirth" of German literature, Expressionism "represents a decline" even though "it may be a decline of a fruitful and preparatory kind." Walter Benjamin, *The Origin of German Tragic Drama* (London: Verso, 2003), 56.

177. Benjamin, *German Tragic Drama*, 56.

178. Benjamin, 56.

179. On the qualitative density of (historical) time, see Bloch, *Philosophy of the Future*, 124–34.

180. Benjamin, "Concept of History," 395.

181. Benjamin, 391.

182. Benjamin, 392, 394.

183. Benjamin, 395.

184. Benjamin, "Paralipomena," 402.

185. Benjamin, "Surrealism," 214.

186. Löwy and Sayre trace this tradition of revolutionary romanticism in avant-garde movements stretching from Surrealism to the May '68 insurrection.

187. Henri Lefebvre, "Towards a New Romanticism?" in *Introduction to Modernity: Twelve Preludes, September 1959–May 1961* (New York: Verso, 1995), 356.

188. Lefebvre, "Towards a New Romanticism?," 301–2.

189. Lefebvre, 279.

190. Lefebvre, 263–64.

191. Lefebvre, 282.

192. Lefebvre, 315.

193. Lefebvre, 355.

194. Lefebvre, 312.

195. Lefebvre, 318.

196. Lefebvre, 273.

197. Lefebvre, 302.

198. Lefebvre, 302.

199. Lefebvre, 345, 346.

200. Lefebvre, 348.

201. Lefebvre, 356.

202. Lefebvre, 355.

203. Lefebvre, 355.

204. Tomba, *Marx's Temporalities*, 175. "Marx's problem was the co-presence and the friction between historical-political layers that could produce a path alternative to that of Western capitalist modernization" (173).

205. Massimiliano Tomba, *Insurgent Universality: An Alternative Legacy of Modernity* (New York: Oxford University Press, 2019).

206. Ross explains that she "altered the customary temporal and spatial limits of the Commune to include the way it spilled out into these adjacent scenes" in order to "trace, in the displacements, intersections, and writings of the survivors, a kind of afterlife that does not exactly *come after* but . . . is part and parcel of the event itself. Not the memory of the event or its legacy, although some of these are already in the making, but its *prolongation*, every bit as vital to the event's logic as the initial acts of insurrection in the streets of the city." Ross, *Communal Luxury*, 6.

207. Ross, *Communal Luxury*, 116.

208. Ross, 116.

209. Ross, 74.

210. Ross, 75.

211. C. L. R. James, *A History of Pan-African Revolt* (Oakland, CA: PM Press, 2012).

212. C. L. R. James, *Modern Politics* (Oakland, CA: PM Press, 2013).

213. C. L. R. James, *Mariners, Renegades, and Castaways: The Story of Herman Melville and the World We Live In* (Hanover: University Press of New England, 1978).

9. It's Still Happening Again: Ontology, Hauntology, and Ellison's Dialectics of Invisibility

1. Octavia Butler, *Kindred* (Boston: Beacon Press, 1979), 17.

2. *Kindred*, which stages the past in the present, differs from a multigenerational saga like Alex Haley's *Roots* (1977), which brings the obscured past into view.

3. Michelle Alexander, *The New Jim Crow: Mass Incarceration in the Age of Colorblindness* (New York: New Press, 2010).

4. See Michael Omi and Howard Winant, *Racial Formation in the United States from the 1960s to the 1980s* (New York: Routledge, 1986).

5. Christine Sharpe, *In the Wake: On Blackness and Being* (Durham, NC: Duke University Press, 2016).

6. "In the wake" is a dialogical rejoinder to Moten's discussion of how Black subjects may live and act subversively "in the break" pace Moten.

7. In contrast to Afro-Pessimists, Patterson explores the many contradictions created by slavery as a "parasitic" relation of domination that, in its modern New World form, was dialectically shadowed by the problem of freedom and the possibility of sublation. Orlando Patterson, *Slavery and Social Death: A Comparative Study* (Cambridge, MA: Harvard University Press, 1982),

8. Frank B. Wilderson III, "We're Trying to Destroy the World," Anti-Blackness and Police Violence after Ferguson: An Interview with Frank B. Wilderson III, 6, https://illwilleditions.noblogs.org/files/2015/09/Wilderson-We-Are-Trying-to-Destroy-the-World-READ.pdf.

9. Wilderson, "Destroy the World," 18, 12.

10. Wilderson, "Destroy the World," 22.

11. Wilderson, "Destroy the World," 22.

12. See Frank B. Wilderson III, "The Prison Slave as Hegemony's (Silent) Scandal," *Social Justice* 30, no. 3 (2003): 18–27.

13. Wilderson, "Destroy the World," 12.

14. Wilderson, "Destroy the World," 24.

15. Wilderson, "Destroy the World," 10.

16. Wilderson, "Destroy the World," 18.

17. Jacques Derrida, *Specters of Marx: The State of the Debt, the Work of Mourning and the New International* (New York: Routledge, 1994), 10.

18. Derrida, *Specters of Marx*, 11. "There has never been a scholar who really, and as scholar, deals with ghosts. A traditional scholar does not believe in ghosts—nor in all that could be called the virtual space of spectrality. There has never been a scholar who, as such, does not believe in the sharp distinction between the real and the unreal, the actual and the inactual, the living and the non-living, being

and non-being ('to be or not to be,' in the conventional reading), in the opposition between what is present and what is not." Derrida offers not only hauntology but deconstruction, generally, as the corrective.

19. Derrida, *Specters of Marx*, 1.

20. Stuart Hall, "Race, Articulation, and Societies Structured in Dominance," in *Sociological Theories: Race and Colonialism* (Paris: UNESCO, 1980), 322. Hall notes that while "economic analysis . . . may not supply sufficient conditions in itself for an explanation of the emergence and operation of racism . . . at least, it provides a better, sounder point of departure than those approaches which are obliged to desert the economic level, in order to explain the origin and appearance of racial structuring" (322).

21. Hall, "Race, Articulation," 322. See also Stuart Hall, "Gramsci's Relevance for the Study of Race and Ethnicity," *Journal of Communication Inquiry* 10, no. 5 (1986): 5–27; Stuart Hall, "Gramsci and Us," *Marxism Today* (June 1987): 16–21.

22. Hall, "Race, Articulation," 325.

23. Hall, 325. Against an orthodox Marxism that would read all social dynamics as expressing the primary economic contradiction between capital and labor, Hall writes: "such conjunctures are not so much 'determined' as overdetermined, i.e. they are the product of an articulation of contradictions, not directly reduced to one another" (326).

24. Hall, "Race, Articulation," 330, 338.

25. Hall, 336–37.

26. Hall, 336–37.

27. Hall, 337.

28. Hall, 337.

29. Hall's insistence on historical specificity is not a nominalist attempt to disavow structural analysis. He invites critics to navigate between "the Scylla of a reductionism which must deny almost everything in order to explain something, and the Charybdis of a pluralism which is so mesmerized by 'everything' that it cannot explain anything." Hall, 343.

30. See Chapter 7, note 92.

31. Cedric Robinson's *Black Marxism: The Making of the Black Radical Tradition*, 2nd ed. (University of North Carolina Press, 2000); Robin D. G. Kelley, "What Did Cedric Robinson Mean by Racial Capitalism," *Boston Review* (January 12, 2017); Ruth Wilson Gilmore, *Golden Gulag: Prisons, Surplus, Crisis, and Opposition in Globalizing California* (Berkeley: University of California Press, 2007).

32. Frantz Fanon, *Black Skin, White Masks* (New York: Grove Press, 2008). See Wynter, "Unsettling the Coloniality of Being/Power/Truth/Freedom: Toward the Human, After Man, Its Overrepresentation: An Argument," *CR: The New Centennial Review* 3, no. 3 (Fall 2003): 257–337. Robinson's *Black Marxism* may also be read as a culturalist attempt to ground racial capitalism in the deep structures of European civilization and consciousness.

33. Cf. Patterson's account of perpetual and inheritable "natal alienation" as a "constituent element of the slave relation" which rendered the enslaved a "socially dead person." *Slavery and Social Death*, 5.

34. Hortense Spillers, "Mama's Baby, Papa's Maybe: An American Grammar Book," *Diacritics* 17, no. 2 (Summer 1987): 67.

35. Spillers, "Mama's Baby," 68.

36. Spillers, 72.

37. Spillers, 67.

38. Spillers, 75.

39. Spillers, 68. Cf. Saidiya V. Hartman, *Scenes of Subjection: Terror, Slavery, and Self-Making in Nineteenth-Century America* (New York: Oxford University Press, 1997), which accounts for the continuation of U.S. anti-Black violence and dispossession after emancipation through a racist liberalism that emancipated enslaved Blacks as isolated individuals who were then held responsible for their own poverty which they were expected to overcome as self-possessed individuals. Rather than recognizing how the U.S. state and society had a moral and financial obligation to repair past harms by at least creating conditions for substantive freedom, this liberal logic held that newly freed Blacks actually owed a moral debt to former masters and white society for having emancipated them. On ways that the status and condition of Black enslavement, as a feature of racial capitalism, was reconstituted after emancipation through national, commercial, and personal debt, see Aaron Carico, *Black Market: The Slave's Value in National Culture after 1865* (Chapel Hill: University of North Carolina Press, 2020).

40. Spillers, "Mama's Baby," 68. She identifies this "Great Long National Shame" as running from the Slave Code, which decreed that "the condition of the slave mother is forever entailed on all her remotest posterity," through current state policies and public debates about what are perceived to be African American social pathologies (68, 79).

41. Spillers, "Mama's Baby," 72.

42. Spillers, 72.

43. Spillers, 77.

44. Spillers, 77.

45. Spillers, 80.

46. Spillers, 66.

47. Spillers notes that many Black male freedom fighters, including Frederick Douglass, accept this patriarchal understanding of "descent and identity through the female line" as "a fundamental degradation . . . comparable to a brute animality" (80). Of course, racist conditions had prevented masses of Black men across generations from functioning as heads of households.

48. Spillers, 80.

49. Spillers, 80.

50. Spillers, 80.

51. Spillers, 80.

52. Spillers, 80.

53. Cf. Patterson's discussion of the political function of eunuchs in Roman, Chinese, and Byzantian slave systems. As liminal outcasts who confounded gender norms, they served as stabilizing intermediaries who were also regarded as possessing a dangerous power. *Slavery and Social Death*, 322–31.

54. Avery Gordon, *Ghostly Matters: Haunting and the Sociological Imagination*, 2nd ed. (Minneapolis: University of Minnesota Press, 2008), xvi.

55. Gordon, *Ghostly Matters*, xvi; emphasis added.

56. Gordon, xvi. Cf. Hartmann on the "afterlife of slavery" whereby "its perils and dangers still threatened" because "slavery had established a measure of man and a ranking of life and worth that has yet to be undone." Saidiya Hartmann, *Lose Your Mother: A Journey along the Atlantic Slave Route* (New York: Farrar, Straus and Giroux, 2007).

57. Gordon, *Ghostly Matters*, xvi.

58. Gordon, xvi.

59. Gordon, 64.

60. Gordon, 63.

61. Gordon, 174.

62. Gordon, 27; emphasis added.

63. Gordon, 7. Cf. Ethan Kleinberg who argues that conventional historians can cite Derrida but are unable to actually write deconstructive histories that attend to the kind of unseen present absences that actually haunt both the historical record and the historian's present. Kleinberg, *Haunting History: For a Deconstructive Approach to the Past* (Stanford, CA: Stanford University Press, 2017).

64. Gordon, *Ghostly Matters*, 8.

65. Gordon, 26.

66. For another innovative attempt to elaborate a historical and political conception of haunting repetition in relation to anti-Black racism see Ian Baucom, *Specters of the Atlantic: Finance Capital, Slavery, and the Philosophy of History* (Durham: Duke University Press, 2005). Baucom places Derrida in dialogue with Marxist world-systems theory to understand how aspects of 17th-century materialism strangely repeated themselves in 19th-century commodity fetishism and how aspects of 18th-century speculation repeated themselves in late-20th-century finance capitalism. Building on the work of Benjamin, Giovanni Arrighi, Frederic Jameson, and Édouard Glissant, Baucom grounds these untimely repetitions—or "specters of the Atlantic"—in the cyclical movement between forms of global capitalism that privilege the commodity form and those that privilege the money form. Especially insightful is his comparison between the way Benjamin challenges linear history through a conception of lightning flashes of recognition and the way Glissant does so through a conception of history, rooted in the history of Atlantic slavery, as a process of sedimentation in which time does not pass but accumulates.

67. Ralph Ellison, *Invisible Man*, Second Vintage International Edition (New York: Random House, 1995), 5. Subsequent citations will be in-text.

68. We can read this as an example of what Moten means by acting creatively and subversively "in the break."

69. We may also think of the descending levels of Dante's inferno.

70. Benjamin, "Paralipomena," 405.

71. W. E. B. Du Bois, *The Souls of Black Folk*, in *W. E. B. Du Bois: Writings* (New York: Library of America, 1986), 364.

72. W. E. B. Du Bois, *Dusk of Dawn*, in *W. E. B. Du Bois: Writings* (New York: Library of America, 1986), 650.

73. Fanon, *Black Skin, White Masks*.

10. A Prophetic Vision of the Past: Glissant's Poetics of Nonhistory

1. Édouard Glissant, *Caribbean Discourse: Selected Essays*, trans. J. Michael Dash (Charlottesville: University of Virginia Press, 1989), 5.

2. Glissant, *Caribbean Discourse*, 2, 3. Glissant uses "painless oblivion" to convey the fact that the French Antilles had been spared the "spectacular . . . murders, shameless acts of genocide, [and] tactics of terror" that the West deployed elsewhere in the world "to crush the precious resistance" of "marginalized peoples" (2).

3. Glissant, 1–2; emphasis added.

4. Glissant, 4.

5. Glissant, 2.

6. Glissant, 4.

7. Glissant, 4.

8. Glissant, 4.

9. Glissant, 61.

10. Glissant, 61.

11. Glissant, 61–62.

12. Édouard Glissant, *Le Discours antillais* (Paris: Éditions Gallimard, 1997), 172. This and other passages I cite and translate from the French edition were unfortunately excised in Michael Dash's English translation.

13. Glissant, 63.

14. Glissant, 221.

15. Glissant, 172.

16. Glissant, 90.

17. Glissant, 90.

18. Glissant, 91. We can also regard this "phantom murderer" acting with impunity as representing the French state more generally.

19. Glissant, 91.

20. Glissant, 90.

21. Glissant, 90, 91.

22. Cf. Mbembe, on "the banality of power in the postcolony. Achille Mbembe, "The Aesthetics of Vulgarity," in *On the Postcolony* (Berkeley: University of California Press, 2001), 102

23. Glissant, *Discours antillais*, 173.
24. Glissant, *Caribbean Discourse*, 64.
25. Glissant, 65.
26. Glissant, 65, 66.
27. Glissant, 10.
28. Glissant, 10. He seems to be referring to the 1976 general strike in Martinique. Le Lorrain is a region in northern Martinique where there was a militant strike in 1974 for higher wages and the application of social laws that spread from banana plantations.
29. Glissant, 10.
30. Glissant, 10.
31. Glissant, 11.
32. Glissant, 11.
33. Glissant, 11.
34. Glissant, 154.
35. Glissant, 63.
36. Glissant, 64.
37. Glissant, 64.
38. Glissant, 64 (original is a quote).
39. Glissant, 64.
40. Glissant, 66.
41. Glissant, 161.
42. Glissant, 161–62.
43. Glissant, 8.
44. Glissant, 66.
45. Glissant, 66.
46. Glissant, 66–67.
47. Glissant, 67.
48. Glissant, *Discours antillais*, 221.
49. Glissant, *Caribbean Discourse*, 61.
50. Glissant, 61.
51. Glissant, *Discours antillais*, 221.
52. Cf. Du Bois on "second sight."
53. Glissant, *Caribbean Discourse*, 61.
54. Although the Atlantic abyss created the possibility for Antilleans to approach history otherwise, this was not an automatic outcome. Glissant contends that rather than open themselves to the "painful awareness" of a "lived history" characterized by "this time that was never ours," many Martinicans embraced an alienated "folkloric existence." *Caribbean Discourse*, 161.
55. Glissant, 162.
56. Glissant, 162.
57. Glissant, 162.
58. Glissant, 161.

59. Glissant, 163.

60. Glissant, 162. Cf. Bakhtin's heteroglossia.

61. Glissant, 162.

62. Glissant, 162.

63. Glissant, 165, 163.

64. Glissant, 166. Glissant contends that French is not a language of the people and Creole is not a national language.

65. Glissant, 165.

66. Glissant, 64.

67. Glissant, 65; emphasis added.

68. Glissant, 65.

69. Glissant, 65.

70. Glissant reminds us that European novels and historiography developed at the same time and both helped to enable imperial hierarchies (76).

71. Glissant, 77.

72. Glissant, 79.

73. Glissant, 80.

74. Glissant, 80.

75. Glissant, 83.

76. Glissant, 84.

77. Glissant, 84.

78. Glissant, 85.

79. Édouard Glissant, *The Fourth Century. Le Quatrième siècle*, trans. Betsy Wing (Lincoln: University of Nebraska Press, 2001).

80. Later in the novel, when incompetent and resentful government functionaries record the names of former slaves into the registers of free citizens after abolition in 1848, we learn about a surprising filiation: "When [the] impudence [of former slaves] became too obvious they amused themselves by turning the names around so that at least they would be further from their origins. Senglis, for example, resulted in Glissant." *Fourth Century*, 180.

81. Recall Ellison's injunction, through the Invisible Man, to *listen* to the past in order to *hear* around corners as well as Santos on contact zones and translation practices that humble and transform the translator.

82. Édouard Glissant, *Faulkner, Mississippi* (Chicago: University of Chicago Press, 2000), 38.

83. Glissant, *Faulkner, Mississippi*, 9.

84. Glissant, 138.

85. Glissant, 138.

86. Glissant, 139.

87. Glissant, 139.

88. Glissant, 142.

89. Glissant, 141.

90. Glissant, 140.

91. Glissant, 163.
92. Glissant, 143.
93. Glissant, 143.
94. Glissant, 176.
95. Glissant, 228.
96. Glissant, 228.
97. Glissant, 228.
98. Glissant, 152. Cf. Kracauer's "cataracts of time."
99. Glissant 30, 102.
100. Glissant, 207.
101. Glissant, 195.
102. Glissant, 195.
103. Glissant, 216.
104. Glissant, 222. Glissant invokes Aimé Césaire's attempt to figure "a new feeling of the world collectivity, where we neither lose nor dilute ourselves" (200).
105. Glissant, 223.
106. Glissant, 242–43.
107. Glissant, 132.
108. Glissant, 132, 241.
109. Glissant, 171.
110. Glissant, 226.
111. "It certainly was not up to Faulkner to do this work—but the work he did do would not have reached its fullness if it had not asked that one day others would take up this task from their own point of view." Glissant, 171. Recall C. L. R. James's similar engagement with Herman Melville and Aimé Césaire's engagement with Victor Schoelcher.
112. It does not matter whether Faulkner actually influenced Glissant's writing or Glissant transposed his own insights about antirealist epic writing in postabolition societies onto Faulkner.
113. Glissant, *Faulkner, Mississippi*, 231.
114. Running through Glissant's interlinked novels is the long-term entanglement of the Béluse, Longoué, Célat, and Targin families. Glissant uses Longoué's death to mark the end of this era in a way that resembles his claim that Faulkner uses the triumph of the Snopes family, which embodies America's vulgar materialism, opportunism, and instrumentalism, to figure the end of an era of tragic drama among epic lineages in his Mississippi county.
115. Glissant, *Fourth Century*, 279.
116. Glissant, 282.
117. Glissant, 278.
118. Glissant, 294.
119. Glissant, 281.
120. Glissant, 283.
121. Glissant, 285.

122. Glissant, 285.

123. Glissant, 285.

124. Glissant, 293.

125. Glissant, 285.

126. Glissant, 284.

127. Glissant, 272. Readers of Glissant's 1958 novel *La Lézarde* will know that when Mathieu fell in love with Mycéa, she had been living with her friend Desirée's family in the mountains. She shared their joyful vital country life, which was defined by peasant values and practices. Papa Longoué also lived there. In Glissant's experimental novel *La Case du commandeur* (1981) which traces the tragic lineage of the Celat family, we learn that Mycéa is both related to Papa Longoué and descended from another African maroon named Odono (after whom she named one of her two sons). Before Mathieu in *The Fourth Century*, she, too, had been visiting and consulting with Papa Longoué. Like the Celat women before her, she inherited a legacy of the alternative knowledge and vanishing form of life connected to ancestral Africa and autonomous maroons. Throughout this experimental novel, Mycéa attempts to remember and preserve these traces, to piece together fragmented narratives, and to defy the linear and sequential character of time itself. In *La Case du commandeur*, Mycéa scorns Mathieu's attachment to words, narrative, and rational truth. She embraces and pursues the poetic and nonchronological ways of knowing and relating embodied by Odono and Longoué as well as the maroons, healers, seers, rebels, and storytellers that descend from them.

128. Glissant, *Fourth Century*, 284.

129. Glissant, 286.

130. Glissant, 277–78.

131. Glissant, 278.

132. Despite sections of lyrical prose that have a dreamlike quality, *La Lézarde* is a less experimental novel than *The Fourth Century*. It focuses on the lead-up to and immediate aftermath of the 1945 elections when the people of the new Department of Martinique will select Deputies to represent them in the French National Assembly. The novel recounts how a group of young urban militants, including Mathieu and Mycéa, conspire to assassinate Garin, a corrupt and violent Martinican politician whom they fear might win the election and betray any possibility of an emancipatory future for postwar Martinique. They are skeptical about electoral politics as a medium for the real transformations they envision. But they fully support the candidate of the People's Party (presumably Aimé Césaire) as the first politician to ever really recognize the interests of ordinary Martinicans and promote a program for popular democracy. These conspirators realize that if Garin's murder appears to be politically motivated, the French state will interfere in these elections. For this reason, they recruit Thaël (aka Raphael Tagrin), a young peasant from the mountains, to kill Garin and make his death look like an accident. Thaël does so and the People's Party candidate is elected. But the novel is neither idealist nor optimistic. It relates how possibility and tragedy are fatally entangled with

one another. The Tagrins are descended from the Longoués and share their vital and enchanted orientation to the world. This is exactly what the educated urban activists need and desire in both the short term (to save the election) and the long term (to create a new postcolonial society). But Thaël is also forever transformed by his encounter with these town dwelling comrades who raise his consciousness about collective suffering and social struggle. The novel traces a series of attempts to create new syntheses between mountain and town, tradition and modernity, body and mind, enchantment and critique, peasant values and political vision. These are figured through Mathieu and Thaël's mutually transformative friendship. Thaël's tragic love for Valérie (one of the conspirators who decides to move in with Thaël and embrace a simple country life but is killed by his dogs on their first night together), and Mathieu's union with Mycéa. The latter unravels very quickly when, after having a child together Mathieu falls ill and decides to abandon this new family to pursue his studies in metropolitan France. We learn here that Mathieu was the town historian (hence his determination, in *The Fourth Century*, to interview Papa Longoué). Through the novel, book learning and rational knowledge are criticized, even as the power of naming and the command of language are praised as essential for politics and freedom. Mathieu's separation from Mycéa seems to enact the failure of an alternative way of being that would be both popular and political. Running through *La Lézarde* is the motif of "the flame," which signifies a transformative spark of collective consciousness and popular will. The prospect of a new synthesis is also signified by images of the meandering river (the Lézarde), which mediates between (the lifeworlds of) mountains, towns, and the sea. This river is both violent abyss and scene of open possibility. Thaël stalks Garin to the river along which they travel together. Garin does not know who Thaël is or what his intentions are. When they reach the sea, these new "friends" take a boat together which capsizes. Thaël allows the unsuspecting Garin to drown in what will be regarded as an accident. These blocked unions and failed syntheses presage the way Departmentalization will foreclose whatever political future, fueled by the flame of social equality and popular democracy, these activists had hoped to forge. We learn that Papa Longoué prophesizes doom, including Valérie's death, before dying on the actual day of the 1945 election. The point of view of the novel is both sober and utopian. We might call it a concrete utopian critique of political romanticism and youthful idealism. This critique continues through *La Case du commandeur*. Through wandering poetic prose and a fragmented narrative, this later novel relates how soon after Mycéa and Mathieu have a child, he leaves Martinique to pursue a career as a writer in France. Mycéa stays in Martinique where she lives on, bearing the weight of past generations of suffering Celat women as well as the general misery of Martinique in the era of rapid modernization, assimilation, and forgetting. Mycéa has two more children with an unnamed man who meet untimely deaths in their adolescence. Over the years Mycéa is less and less able to bear the alienation, disappointment, and dispossession of everyday life in postwar Martinique. Traumatized by personal loss and the disappearance of an enchanted world, she slowly goes numb, dissociates from self and community, and retreats into an untimely dream world of memory and maroons, ancestral suffering and African wisdom. She wanders the streets calling for Odono—the name of both her maroon ancestor and her dead son who had drowned—and accusing her neighbors of betraying the past and living a delusion. They cannot understand her ravings and accusations, decide that she is mad, and call the authorities who confine her to a mental hospital. Mycéa is eventually released from the hospital. She spends her time oscillating between learning to accommodate herself to ordinary life in alienated Martinique and retreating into an enchanted (if violent and terrifying) dreamworld where she relives supposedly past traumas. She is haunted by pasts present even as she also haunts her disenchanted contemporaries. In many ways, this novel is an even more successful expression than *The Fourth Century* of Glissant's hope to create a new epic of creolization and Relation. It does so by relating the collapse of his dream that such an epic could be realized concretely through the union of Mathieu and Mycéa on the eve of departmentalization. In *Mahogany*, which includes first-person narrations by Mycéa, Mathieu, and their daughter Ida, Mathieu breaks the narrative frame. He complains about the narrators of *La Lézarde* and *The Fourth Century*, thus speaking directly to Glissant the author, for having reduced him to a fictional character in their stories. Yet, throughout the novel, he, along with the many other narrators in the book, struggles with the impossibility of grasping the truth and giving an adequate account of what really happened to ordinary actors at critical moments of Martinican history. For a pioneering work that analyzes Glissant's writings across genres as an integral body of work, see J. Michael Dash, *Edouard Glissant* (Cambridge: Cambridge University Press, 1995).

133. Édouard Glissant, *Monsieur Toussaint: A Play* (2005), 15–16.

134. Glissant, *Monsieur Toussaint*, 16.

135. Glissant, 16.

136. Glissant, 16.

137. Glissant, 16.

138. Glissant, 16.

139. Glissant, 16.

140. Glissant, 38.

141. Glissant, 38.

142. C. L. R. James, *The Black Jacobins: Toussaint Louverture and the San Domingo Revolution*, 2nd ed. (New York: Random House, 1989) and Aimé Césaire, *Toussaint Louverture: La Révolution française et le probléme colonial* (Paris: Présence Africaine, 1981).

143. Glissant, *Monsieur Toussaint*, 98–99.

144. Glissant, 51.

145. Glissant, 47–48.

146. Glissant, 42.

147. Glissant, 64.

148. Glissant, 65.

149. Glissant, 50.

150. Glissant, 64.

151. Glissant, 70.

152. Glissant, 75.

153. Glissant, 75.

154. Glissant, 82.

155. Glissant, 51. Cf. Césaire, *Lettre*, cited above.

156. Cf. For a provocative argument that independent Haiti was a maroon society, see Neil Roberts, *Freedom as Marronage* (Chicago: University of Chicago Press, 2015), 89–112.

157. Glissant, *Monsieur Toussaint*, 96

158. Glissant, 96.

159. Glissant, 96.

160. Glissant, 77–78.

161. Glissant, 77.

162. Glissant, 23.

163. Glissant, 59.

164. Glissant, 24.

165. Glissant, 24.

166. Glissant, 114.

167. Glissant, 114.

168. Glissant, 114–15.

169. Glissant, 115.

170. Glissant, 115.

171. Glissant, 115.

172. Glissant, 116.

173. Glissant, 116.

174. Glissant, 117.

175. Glissant, 117.

176. Glissant, 118–19.

177. Glissant, 118.

178. Glissant, 119.

179. Glissant, 120.

180. Glissant, *Caribbean Discourse*, 236; emphasis added.

181. Glissant, 232–33.

182. Glissant, 221.

183. Glissant, 234.

184. Glissant, 249.

185. Cf. Leopold Senghor on "civilization of the universal."

186. Glissant, *Caribbean Discourse*, 249.

187. Glissant, 226. Cf. Césaire, *Lettre à Maurice Thorez*.

188. Glissant, 254.

189. Glissant, 254.

190. Glissant, 255.

191. Glissant, 4.

192. Glissant, 3.

11. The World We Wish to See

1. Theodor Adorno, *History and Freedom: Lectures 1964–1965* (Cambridge: Polity Press, 2006), 80.

2. Adorno, *History and Freedom*, 89.

3. Adorno, 93.

4. Adorno, 93.

5. Adorno, 93.

6. Adorno, 92.

7. Adorno, 67.

8. "Fourth Declaration of the Lacandon Jungle" (January 1, 1996), *Subcomandante Marcos, Ya Basta! Ten Years of the Zapatista Uprising* (Oakland, CA: AK Press, 2004), 669.

9. See, for example, Heidegger, *Being and Time*; Alfred Schutz, *On Phenomenology and Social Relations: Selected Writings* (Chicago: University of Chicago Press, 1970); Hans-Georg Gadamer, *Truth and Method* (Bloomsbury Publishing, 2004); and Jurgen Habermas, *The Theory of Communicative Action*, vol. 2: *Lifeworld and System: A Critique of Functionalist Reason* (Boston: Beacon Press, 1987).

10. See Hannah Arendt, *The Human Condition* (Chicago: University of Chicago Press, 1958) and *Origins of Totalitarianism* (New York: Harcourt Brace Jovanovich, 1979). This is the perspective through which we should understand Arendt's famous, and much criticized, reflection on "the right to have rights."

11. Arendt, *Human Condition*, 52.

12. "Under the conditions of a common world, reality is not guaranteed primarily by the 'common nature' of all men who constitute it, but rather by the fact that, differences of position and the resulting variety of perspectives notwithstanding, everybody is always concerned with the same object." Arendt, *Human Condition*, 57–58.

13. For Immanuel Wallerstein, a "world-system" refers to "a spatial/temporal zone which cuts across many political and cultural units, one that represents an integrated zone of activity and institutions which obey certain systematic rules." Immanuel Wallerstein, *World-System Analysis: An Introduction* (Durham, NC: Duke University Press, 2004), 16–17. He contends that each of these translocal formations is a world, but does not necessarily encompass the entire globe.

14. Édouard Glissant and Patrick Camoiseau, *Quand les murs tombent: L'identité nationale hors la loi?* (Paris: Éditions Galaade, 2007), 16–17.

15. Glissant and Camoiseau, *Quand les murs tombent*, 15–16.

16. Glissant, *Philosophie de la Relation*, 80.

17. Glissant, 13. Likewise, he invokes a "poem that is not universal but which *holds* [has value, relates to: valant] for each and all" (37).

18. Glissant, 105.

19. Glissant, 102.

20. Glissant, 89.

21. For states that only possess nominal state sovereignty, the first option would starve them of necessary capital and deprive them of a voice in geopolitical matters. Given the intensification of uneven development worldwide, the latter option would ensure their peripheral economic and semi-colonized political status.

22. Gary Wilder, *Freedom Time: Negritude, Decolonization, and the Future of the World* (Durham, NC: Duke University Press, 2014) and Wilder "Reading Du Bois's Revelation: Radical Humanism and Black Atlantic Criticism," in *The Postcolonial Contemporary*, ed. Watson and Wilder.

23. Wilder, "Reading Du Bois's Revelation."

24. On the centrality of political imagination to the Black radical tradition, see Robin D. G. Kelley, *Freedom Dreams: The Black Radical Imagination* (Boston: Beacon Press, 2002).

25. Paul Gilroy, *Postcolonial Melancholia* (New York: Columbia University Press, 2005), 63.

26. Gilroy, 64.

27. Gilroy, 30.

28. Gilroy, 67, 99.

29. Gilroy, 72.

30. Gilroy, 81, 68.

31. Achille Mbembe, "African Modes of Self-Writing," *Public Culture* 14, no. 1 (Winter 2002): 251–52.

32. Mbembe, "Afropolitanisme," *Africultures: Les mondes in relation* (25 Decembre 2005), [104].

33. Mbembe, "Afropolitanism," 105. See also Mbembe and Sarah Nuttall, "Writing the World from an African Metropolis," *Public Culture* 16, no. 3 (Fall 2004): 347–72, and Sarah Nuttall and Achille Mbembe, eds., *Johannesburg: The Elusive Metropolis* (Durham, NC: Duke University Press, 2008).

34. Mbembe, "Self-Writing," 259.

35. Mbembe, 257–58.

36. Achille Mbembe, *Critique of Black Reason*, trans. Laurent Dubois (Durham, NC: Duke University Press, 2017), 1. Achille Mbembe, *Necro-Politics* (Durham, NC: Duke University Press, 2019), 180.

37. Mbembe, *Necro-Politics*, 42–92.

38. Mbembe, *Black Reason*, 182.

39. Mbembe, *Necro-Politics*, 181, 176. Mbembe also elaborates notions of interdependence and reciprocity that traverse the invidious division between the

human and nonhuman. His notion of planetary politics encompasses the earth as natural formation. Cf. Judith Butler, *Precarious Life: The Powers of Mourning and Violence* (New York: Verso, 2004).

40. Mbembe, *Black Reason*, 179–80.

41. Mbembe, *Dark Night*, 229, and *Black Reason*, 18.

42. Mbembe, *Dark Night*, 229, 230.

43. Mbembe, 229.

44. Mbembe, *Necro-Politics*, 186–87.

45. Mbembe, 188.

46. Mbmembe, *Black Reason*, 92.

47. Cornel West, *Prophesy Deliverance!: An Afro-American Revolutionary Christianity*, anniversary edition with a new preface (Louisville, KY: Westminster John Knox Press, 2002).

48. West, *Prophesy Deliverance!*, 7.

49. West, 6.

50. Audre Lorde, "The Master's Tools Will Never Dismantle the Master's House," in *Sister Outsider* (Berkeley: Crossing Press, 2007), 112.

51. Audre Lorde, "Eye to Eye: Black Women, Hatred, and Anger," in *Sister Outsider: Essays and Speeches* (Berkeley: Crossing Press, 2007), 146.

52. Lorde, "Eye to Eye," 153.

53. Lorde, 175.

54. Lorde, 175.

55. Lorde, 151–52.

56. Lorde, "Master's Tools," 112, 111.

57. Lorde, "Eye to Eye," 152.

58. Audre Lorde, "The Uses of Anger: Women Responding to Racism," in *Sister Outsider*, 133.

59. Lorde, "Eye to Eye," 151–52. A similar ethos and politics runs through Saidiya Hartman, *Wayward Lives, Beautiful Experiments: Intimate Histories of Riotous Black Girls, Troublesome Women and Queer Radicals* (New York: W. W. Norton, 2019). Hartman, too, along with the women she studies, may be situated in the tradition described and embodied by Lorde.

60. Michael Hardt and Antonio Negri, *Commonwealth* (Cambridge, MA: The Belknap Press of Harvard University Press, 2009), 123.

61. Hardt and Negri, *Commonwealth*, 123.

62. Hardt and Negri, vii, 341, 342.

63. Hardt and Negri, 339.

64. Hardt and Negri, 339.

65. Hardt and Negri, 339.

66. Hardt and Negri, 373.

67. Hardt and Negri, 380–81.

68. Hardt and Negri, 380.

69. Hardt and Negri, 380.

70. Cf. Carla Bergman and Nick Montgomery, *Joyful Militancy Building Thriving Resistance in Toxic Times* (Oakland, CA: AK Press, 2017).

71. Étienne Balibar, *We the People of Europe? Reflections on Transnational Citizenship* (Princeton, NJ: Princeton University Press, 2004); Étienne Balibar, *Equaliberty: Political Essays* (Durham, NC: Duke University Press, 2014); Étienne Balibar, *Citizenship* (New York: Polity Press, 2015); Étienne Balibar, *Violence and Civility: On the Limits of Political Philosophy* (New York: Columbia University Press, 2015); Étienne Balibar, *Citizen Subject: Foundations for Political Anthropology* (New York: Fordham University Press, 2017); Miguel Abensour, *Democracy Against the State: Marx and the Machiavellian Movement* (Cambridge: Polity Press, 2011); Wendy Brown, *Undoing the Demos: Neoliberalism's Stealth Revolution* (New York: Zone Books, 2015); Sandro Mezzadra and Brett Neilson, *Border as Method, or The Multiplication of Labor* (Durham, NC: Duke University Press, 2013).

72. Slavoj Žižek and Costas Douzinas, eds., *The Idea of Communism* (New York: Verso, 2010); Alain Badiou, *The Communist Hypothesis* (New York: Verso, 2015); Jodi Dean, *The Communist Horizon* (New York: Verso, 2012); Vijay Prashad, *In the Ruins of the Present*, Tricontinental Working Document No. 1 (March 2018), https://thetricontinental.org/wp-content/uploads/2018/03/180918_Tricon_Working-Document-1_EN_Web.pdf.

73. David Harvey, Michael Hardt, Antonio Negri, "Commonwealth: An Exchange," *Artforum* 48, no. 3 (November 2009).

74. David Harvey, *Spaces of Hope* (Berkeley: University of California Press, 2000) and *Rebel Cities: From the Right to the City to the Urban Revolution* (New York: Verso, 2012).

75. David Harvey, *The Enigma of Capital and the Crises of Capitalism* (Oxford: Oxford University Press, 2010), 226.

76. Harvey, *Enigma of Capital*, 229.

77. Harvey, 247.

78. Harvey, 259, 260. Cf. Amin's vision of a new Fifth International.

79. Harvey, 227.

80. Harvey, 230–31. See also, David Harvey, "Epilogue: Ideas for Political Praxis," in *Seventeen Contradictions and the End of Capitalism* (Oxford: Oxford University Press, 2014), 294–97.

81. Harvey, *Enigma of Capital*, 227.

82. Harvey, 231.

83. Harvey, *Seventeen Contradictions*, 287.

84. Harvey, 263.

85. Angela Y. Davis, *Are Prisons Obsolete?* (New York: Open Media, 2003), 9–10.

86. See also Joy James, "Introduction: Democracy and Captivity," in *The New Abolitionists: (Neo)Slave Narratives and Contemporary Prison Writings*, ed. Joy James (Albany: State University of New York Press, 2005); Ruth Wilson Gilmore, *Golden Gulag: Prisons, Surplus, Crisis, and Opposition in Globalizing California* (Berkeley: University of California Press, 2007); Ruth Wilson Gilmore, "Ruth Wilson

Gilmore Makes the Case for Abolition," Podcast transcript, *The Intercept* (June 10, 2020), https://theintercept.com/2020/06/10/ruth-wilson-gilmore-makes-the-case-for -abolition/; Mariam Kaba, *We Do This 'Til We Free Us: Abolitionist Organizing and Transforming Justice* (Chicago: Haymarket Books, 2021); and Joshua Price, *Prison and Social Death* (New Brunswick, NJ: Rutgers University Press, 2015).

87. Davis, *Are Prisons Obsolete?* 112.

88. Davis, 108.

89. Davis, 103.

90. Davis, 100.

91. Davis, 18.

92. Davis, 112.

93. Davis, 114.

94. Davis, 107.

95. Davis, 107–8.

96. Angela Davis, *Abolition Democracy: Beyond Empire, Prisons, and Torture* (New York: Seven Stories Press, 2005), 97.

97. Davis, 97–98.

98. She is referring to struggles against slavery, lynching, and Jim Crow. Davis, *Are Prisons Obsolete?*, 25.

99. Du Bois, *Black Reconstruction*, 165.

100. Du Bois, 165.

101. Du Bois, 170–71.

102. Du Bois, 532.

103. Angela Davis discusses Du Bois's conception of abolition democracy in *Abolition Democracy*, 92–99.

104. *Critical Resistance*, http://criticalresistance.org; *Abolition Journal*, https:// abolitionjournal.org; Anti-Police Terror Project, https://www.antipoliceterrorproject .org/about-aptp.

105. See, for example, Alex S. Vitale, *The End of Policing* (New York: Verso, 2018) and Jordan Camp and Christina Heatherton, eds., *Policing the Planet Why the Policing Crisis Led to Black Lives Matter* (New York: Verso, 2016); Black Internationalist Unions, "A Call to Defund the Police and Mobilize Community Control over Attorneys General and Grand Juries," https://abolitionjournal.org /black-internationalist-unions/; Communities United For Police Reform, "The Path Forward: How to Defund the NYPD, Invest in Communities & Make New York Safer," June 16, 2020, https://www.changethenypd.org/sites/default/files/cpr_budget _justice_report_final_v3.pdf.

106. Keeanga-Yamahtta Taylor, *From #Black Lives Matter to Black Liberation* (Chicago: Haymarket Books, 2016); Alicia Garza, *The Purpose of Power: How We Come Together When We Fall Apart* (New York: Random House, 2020).

107. https://policy.m4bl.org.

108. We should understand the M4BL Platform in a longer tradition of concrete utopian programs elaborated from within the Black freedom struggle, including the

Black Panther Party's ten-point Platform and Program (1966) and The Combahee River Collective Statement (1977).

109. See Bernard Boxill, "Black Reparations," in *The Stanford Encyclopedia of Philosophy*, ed. Edward N. Zalta (Summer 2016), https://plato.stanford.edu/archives /sum2016/entries/black-reparations/.

CARICOM Reparations Commission, "Ten Point Reparation Plan," https:// caricomreparations.org/caricom/caricoms-10-point-reparation-plan/; Randall Robinson, *The Debt: What America Owes to Blacks* (New York: Penguin, 2000); Hilary McD Beckles, *Britain's Black Debt: Reparations for Caribbean Slavery and Native Genocide* (Jamaica: University Press of the West Indies, 2013); Ana Lucia Araujo, *Reparations for Slavery and the Slave Trade: A Transnational and Comparative History* (London: Bloomsbury Academic, 2017); Ta-Nahesi Coates, "The Case for Reparations," *The Atlantic* (June 2014); Martha Biondi, "The Rise of the Reparations Movement," *Radical History Review* 87 (Fall 2003): xx.

110. This summary, including that in the following two paragraphs, is drawn from Éric Toussaint and Damien Millet, *Debt, the IMF, and the World Bank: Sixty Questions, Sixty Answers* (New York: Monthly Review Press, 2010), 239–325. See also Eric Toussaint, *The Debt System: A History of Sovereign Debts and their Repudiation* (Chicago: Haymarket Books, 2019) and Jerome E. Roos, *Why Not Default: The Political Economy of Sovereign Debt* (Princeton, NJ: Princeton University Press, 2021).

111. "Political Charter of the CADTM International," February 28, 2020, https:// www.cadtm.org/Here-are-the-proposed-amendments-to-the-CADTM-Political -Charter-http-www-cadtm.

112. "Political Charter of the CADTM International."

113. Wolfgang Streeck, *Buying Time: The Delayed Crisis of Democratic Capitalism*, 2nd ed. (New York: Verso, 2017) and *How Will Capitalism End?* (New York: Verso, 2017).

114. Streeck, *How Will Capitalism End?*, 22.

115. Streeck, 123.

116. Andrew Ross, "In Defense of Economic Disobedience," in *Occasion*, vol. 7, November 6, 2014, 3. See also Andrew Ross, *Creditocracy and the Case for Debt Refusal* (New York: O/R Books, 2014).

117. Ross, "Economic Disobedience," 5.

118. Ross, "Economic Disobedience," 6.

119. Ross, "Economic Disobedience," 6.

120. Ross, "Economic Disobedience," 6.

121. *The Debt Resistor's Operations Manual: A Project of Strike Debt/Occupy Wall Street*, September 2012, https://strikedebt.org/drom/ and https://debtcollective.org. On the case against debt repayment under conditions of parasitic capitalism, see David Graeber, *Debt: The First 5000 Years* (New York: Melville House Publishing, 2011).

122. https://debtcollective.org.

123. https://strikedebt.org.

124. "IPCC, Global Warming of 1.5°C. An IPCC Special Report on the impacts

of global warming of 1.5°C above pre-industrial levels and related global greenhouse gas emission pathways, in the context of strengthening the global response to the threat of climate change, sustainable development, and efforts to eradicate poverty," Intergovernmental Panel on Climate Control, 2019, v.

125. https://leapmanifesto.org/en/the-leap-manifesto/; H. Res 109 Recognizing the duty of the Federal Government to create a Green New Deal, February 7, 2019, https://www.congress.gov/116/bills/hres109/BILLS-116hres109ih.pdf; https://extinctionrebellion.uk/the-truth/demands/; https://ec.europa.eu/info/strategy/priorities-2019-2024/european-green-deal_en.

126. Kate Aronoff, Alyssa Battistoni, Daniel Aldana Cohen, and Thea Riofrancos, *A Planet to Win: Why We Need a Green New Deal* (New York: Verso, 2019), 158, 39.

127. Naomi Klein, *On Fire: The (Burning) Case for a Green New Deal* (New York: Simon and Schuster, 2019), 45.

128. Klein, *On Fire*, 46.

129. Klein, 55.

130. Klein, 251. Aronoff et al. similarly argue because centrist positions and gradualism have only intensified the current climate crisis, we now face a stark choice between "eco-socialism" and the worldwide nightmare of "eco-apartheid." *A Planet to Win*, 183.

131. Aronoff et al., *A Planet to Win*, 190.

132. Aronoff et al., 190–91. Emphasis added.

133. Klein, *On Fire*, 175.

134. Naomi Klein, *No Is Not Enough: Resisting Trump's Shock Politics and Winning the World We Need* (Chicago: Haymarket Books, 2021), x.

135. Nick Estes, *Our History Is the Future: Standing Rock versus the Dakota Access Pipeline, and the Long Tradition of Indigenous Resistance* (New York: Verso, 2019), 44.

136. In this spirit, *A Planet to Win* begins and ends with a near-future vision of "carbon-free communal luxury" that could actually be unfolding in the mid-2020s." Aronoff et al., *A Planet to Win*, 172. In a similar vein, the animated video produced by the Sunrise movement and narrated by Alexandria Ocasio-Cortez "looks back" on 2020 from an imagined future as a turning point for entwined efforts to confront climate change and create a more just American economy through progressive government intervention. It "envisions the decade of the Green New Deal and the prosperity it will share." A Message from the Future, https://www.sunrisemovement.org/green-new-deal.

137. Coronil, "The Future in Question," 154.

Gary Wilder is a Professor of Anthropology, History, and French and Director of the Committee on Globalization and Social Change at the Graduate Center of the City University of New York. He is the author of *Freedom Time: Negritude, Decolonization, and the Future of the World* (Duke, 2015) and *The French Imperial Nation-State: Negritude and Colonial Humanism between the Two World Wars* (Chicago, 2005). He is co-editor of *The Postcolonial Contemporary: Political Imaginaries for the Global Present* (Fordham, 2018) and *The Fernando Coronil Reader: The Struggle for Life Is the Matter* (Duke, 2019).

Index